The Zodiac by Degrees

360 New Symbols

The Zodiac by Degrees

360 New Symbols

Martin Goldsmith

First published in 2004 by
Red Wheel/Weiser, LLC
York Beach, ME
With offices at:
368 Congress Street
Boston, MA 02210
www.redwheelweiser.com

Library of Congress Cataloging-in-Publication Data
Goldsmith, Martin.
The zodiac by degrees : 360 new symbols / Martin Goldsmith.
p. cm.
Includes bibliographical references.
ISBN 1-57863-304-4
1. Astrology. 2. Zodiac. I. Title.
BF1708.1.G62 2004
133.5'2—dc22

2003027101

Typeset in Aries Roman 10/14 by Garrett Brown
Printed in Canada
TCP
11 10 09 08 07 06 05 04
8 7 6 5 4 3 2 1

Contents

Foreword

Predicting next year's astrological enthusiasm is almost as difficult as predicting the direction of teenage fashion. For an "ancient art," astrology has always been astonishingly susceptible to trendiness. Like clothing from a few decades ago, certain Hellenistic analytic techniques were consigned to the Zodiacal Thrift Shop twelve hundred years ago. Now they're back. Harmonic charts came into the spotlight and went out again. Our venerable Ptolemaic aspects were julienned into increasingly nuanced bi-septiles, noviles, and quintiles that overlapped each other while contradicting each other in meaning. There's always been an asteroid du jour—and a House system du jour. Whatever happened to Primary Directions or prenatal eclipses?

The tide comes in; the tide goes out again.

For many years, I was pulled along by this or that trend. Now after about three decades of watching the parade, I've developed more caution. In my own practice, I rely primarily on the most elemental astrological tools—the signs, planets, houses, and the five major aspects. They seem really to do 90 percent of the practical work. While many of the "breakthrough" techniques actually seem to have merit, it's those core symbols that have withstood time's test. They are the common ground in the astrological community, the watering hole where we all come to drink. As for the rest, they've tended to recede into relatively small niches of passionate enthusiasts. I don't mean to dismiss them, only to catalog their location in the astrological ecosystem.

Every now and then, something new and lasting comes along. At first, it looks exactly like the rest of that year's nominees. But then the following year, it's still there. And the year after that, it's gathered more advocates and adherents. The recognition of the inescapable symbolic reality of the minor planet Chiron over the past three decades is a good example of that evolutionary, integrative process. And in the past century of astrological history, the best example is, I believe, the Sabian symbols, which Martin Goldsmith elucidates with unprecedented clarity and persuasiveness in the present volume.

I say "Sabian symbols" here, incorrectly, because that's the name by which I first came to know the symbolism of individual zodiacal degrees. Like many of my generation, I cut my teeth on Dane Rudhyar's epochal book, *The Astrology of Personality*, which contained a long section about the Sabians. There, Rudhyar referred me back to their source—the psychic Elsie Wheeler and the astrologer Marc Edmund Jones, working together in 1925 to come up with the 360 images that have now so imprinted themselves on the minds of four generations of astrologers.

One of the many illuminating delights of *The Zodiac by Degrees* is Goldsmith's placing of the Sabian symbols in their proper historical context. Creating symbols for each degree of the zodiac is a far older tradition than I personally had ever realized. As Goldsmith writes, "According to Hecataeus of Abdera, there was a circular ring of stone on the roof of the tomb, measuring 365 cubits in circumference, on which a different symbol was carved for each day of the year." With the loving attention to detail of a working scholar, Goldsmith goes on to describe many of the predecessors of the Sabian symbols. Then, blessedly escaping one of the standard pretenses of the scholarly, he avoids the temptation of sanctifying everything old and obscure, while declaring everything present and popular debased. He states flatly that "degree symbols had never achieved a lot of popularity among astrologers for the simple reason that they were not very accurate. The Sabians could be counted on to give insights into most of the degrees, and this led to their being studied much more closely than other systems."

Goldsmith goes further, however. While lauding the Sabians, he is not a blind advocate for them. In his work as a practicing astrologer, he came to realize that certain of the Sabian symbols did not seem to have the same reliability as others. The work of Elsie Wheeler and Marc Edmund Jones was brilliant, but flawed—while, by contrast, many of the older degree traditions were hopelessly flawed, but contained elements of brilliance. Where the Sabians failed, Goldsmith began to insert the more successful of the older images. Where nothing seemed to work, he boldly filled in the blanks by creating his own symbols, using the other systems as points of departure for his own creativity. The results are masterful. Here's one way to use them in your own life.

A constant challenge in practical astrology lies in the inherent uncertainty of people's times of birth. Even when a birth certificate loudly claims that someone came into this world at precisely 7:34 PM, you've got to wonder about the accuracy. For one thing, there's no universal agreement about what we mean by the "moment of birth," let alone the obvious issues about the precision of the clock on the wall, and so on. We can futz with transits and progressions over the Horizon and Mer-idian axes of the chart and thus "rectify" the time of birth—basically by adjusting the chart until "hits" on those angles correspond to the actual timing of events in a person's life. That's an essential astrological technique, and there's no substitute for it. But even with effective rectification, there's often a bit of uncertainty left over. For me, this problem presents one of the most useful practical applications of *The Zodiac by Degrees*: It can help lock in the exact degree of the Ascendant.

Here's how it worked for me. My birth certificate gives a birth time of 3:30 AM (January 6, 1949, Mt. Vernon, Westchester Co., NY, USA). I'd long suspected that time to be off by a bit, and through rectification techniques had determined the effective truth to be several minutes earlier. That meant I had 22, 23, or 24 degrees of Scorpio rising. I'd been waffling among those possibilities for a few years when the manuscript of *The Zodiac by Degrees* arrived. Being a cautious Capricorn, I started reading earlier degrees and moved forward systematically. As is often the case with astrological symbolism, I could find something to relate to in most of what I read. But I laughed out loud when I got to 23 Scorpio:

> A seated elf, one arm around a large book, looks quizzically at the viewer, then turns into a hare and hops through a stone wall.

Elves, books, and stones have always had a lot of personal meaning for me, as has the Welsh part of my genetic heritage that the image evokes. My wife, Jodie Forrest's, fantasy trilogy *The Rhymer and the Ravens*, is populated with elves, and the rock operas we've performed based on those volumes have been a huge part of my personal life. And nothing is easier for me than thinking of myself as an elf with a large book! Reading down through Goldsmith's interpretive hints, I read:

> . . . teachers and students of the metaphysical and theosophical structure of reality; getting others to transcend limited analytical frameworks; jarring people out of their complacency vs. glum resignation to human somnolence; elfin mischief . . .

It all locked in. Naturally, a 23 Scorpio Ascendant declares a 23 Taurus Descendant, along with an associated Midheaven/IC axis. I checked those degrees for corroboration. I'll spare you the personal confessionals here. Suffice it to say, the imagery locked in there too. The degree symbols had resolved my dilemma.

As I mentioned earlier, where none of the traditions seemed accurate, Goldsmith himself has created fresh imagery. Astrology must forever reinvent itself, but there are many pitfalls in the process. Even though I'd been impressed by his methodical approach in general, I was a little cautious at first about his work in that regard. Of all the steps he'd taken, this was where the greatest risks lay. Fortunately, my own chart again provided a good test. The Sabian symbol for my solar degree, taken from Rudhyar's *An Astrological Mandala*, is:

> School grounds filled with boys and girls in gymnasium suits. Keynote: The need for physical activity and play, especially in adolescence.

The symbol has some personal relevance for me, but it is almost entirely negative. Physically, I was a clumsy, weak kid. Gym was a bitter experience of humiliation and unending failure. I once sunk a big basket—at the wrong end of the court! Another time, a coach, observing me on a trampoline, likened me to "a spider with polio." The comment was, I suspect, quite accurate. My classmates certainly applauded it. I'm sure I would have developed a far better relationship with my own body had I just been left alone. Those wounding memories have carried forward into my sixth decade on the planet, so the symbol definitely speaks to me—but not helpfully or encouragingly. Turning to *The Zodiac by Degrees*, I read:

> Turbaned guru explains a path to higher awareness, while his assistant walks among his meditating disciples and prods them into the correct yogic posture.

I pray I always avoid identifying myself with the guru archetype! But otherwise, the symbol speaks eloquently of the actual orientation of my life and work—and also prods me gently into realizing that the practice of yoga might be a good way to get over the damage done to me by "school grounds filled with boys and girls in gymnasium suits"!

Books come and books go. An awful lot of innocent trees have been sacrificed on the altar of astrological publishing over the years. In many cases, we would have been better off leaving the poor birds, bugs, and squirrels to their happy homes. But the volume you are holding in your hands is that rarity: a truly monumental work that will stand the test of time and be remembered after its author and its present readers have gone into the cosmic recycling bin. I believe I am only the first in a long line of grateful astrologers when I offer Martin Goldsmith a heartfelt and sincere thank you.

Steven Forrest
Chapel Hill, NC

Acknowledgments

I would like to extend warm thanks to my brother Ken for his tireless efforts in collecting data, and for his careful elimination of factual errors from the manuscript. Karen Bolander-Claus helped me in too many ways to count. As an editor of the manuscript, she saved me from several grave errors in judgment that a more timid soul would have let slide. David Roell, of the Astrology Center of America, spent many hours on the phone clarifying various aspects of the publishing process. Finally, Tom Lambert guided me through a number of tricky software problems.

Introduction

The Importance of Degree Symbols

Astrology is complex by its very nature. The question may therefore arise as to whether there is any justification for complicating it further by giving symbols to each of the 360 degrees. For those who already use the Sabian symbols, the answer is obvious. The degrees give more specific information, and more interesting information, than any other element in the birth chart. To say that a person's Sun is in Aries associates him with a set of keywords traditional to the sign Aries: bold, honest, aggressive, etc. However, if you know that this person's Sun is on the 29th degree of Aries, symbolized in the Sabians by "A Heavenly Choir," you know that aggression is less important for him than attunement. The "celestial choir" degree has its aggressive side. People with the Sun on this degree often try to "orchestrate" events. However, once you know the Sabian symbol for 29 Aries, you are unlikely to attribute physical aggression to this person. The degree shows many other things as well—an interest in celestial phenomena, a talent for music. None of these things would be known to you if you were simply looking at "Sun in Aries."

The History of Degree Symbols

Astrologers have been trying to symbolize the degrees of the zodiac for thousands of years. We have reports of degree symbols from ancient Greece, where Metrodorus of Scepsis used them as a memory system.[1] Another set of symbols existed at the Ramesseum of Egyptian Thebes. According to Hecataeus of Abdera,[2] there was a circular ring of stone on the roof of the tomb, measuring 365 cubits in circumference, on which a different symbol was carved for each day of the year. Hecataeus' tale, which has come down to us only through the works of Diodorus Siculus, is historically questionable. Still, it shows that the idea of degree symbols was certainly around in Hecataeus' own time—that of Ptolemaic Egypt.

The astrologers of medieval and Renaissance Europe also used degree symbols. The most important set of symbols of this period was created by astronomer and astrologer Pietro d'Abano (1257-1315), a professor at the University of Padua. These symbols are still with us today.[3] D'Abano's symbols inspired a lineage of other symbol systems that might be called the Western line of degree symbols. These include the symbol systems of Johannes Angelus (16th century), and the more modern systems of Charubel, Carelli, Janduz, and Kozminsky.

The Sabian Symbols

The history of degree symbols took a remarkable turn in 1925 when a psychic named Elsie Wheeler, under the tutelage of the astrologer Marc Edmund Jones, channeled an entirely new set of symbols. The Sabian symbols had little in common with earlier systems. To begin with, they were much more modern than previous systems, for they included telephones, airplanes, and other accessories of modern life. In earlier systems, medieval imagery had predominated—even when they had been written in the 20th century. Notably absent from the Sabian symbols was the pessimistic fatalism of old-time astrology. Charubel, who lived in the late 19th century, had for the fifteenth degree of Aries "A black, or very dark, curtain, like a pall, which seems to defy my vision." By way of interpretation, he intoned that "it is to be hoped that such a one may die in infancy." The same degree in the Sabian symbols is "An Indian Weaving a Blanket."

In addition to their infinitely cheerier flavor, the Sabians are also much more accurate. Degree symbols had never achieved a lot of popularity among astrologers, for the simple reason that they didn't work very well. The Sabians could be counted on to give insights into most of the degrees, and this led to their being studied more closely than other systems. Two of the most important astrologers of the 20th century, Marc Edmund Jones and Dane Rudhyar, wrote entire books on the Sabian symbols,[4] and an increasing number of astrologers have come to use them as basic tools of chart interpretation. Because the Sabian symbols work so much better than other systems, they have essentially eclipsed the competition. This has been a mixed blessing, for it has afforded the Sabians a cult-like status, and has consequently discouraged further research into the degree symbols.

I myself was introduced to the Sabians in the early 1970s, just a few years after I began to study astrology. I was immediately impressed when I discovered that my Sun symbol was "A concert pianist." I have played piano seriously all my life and have even played with an orchestra. Many of my other symbols worked almost as well. The Sabians were by far the most exciting aspect of astrology that I had come across, and quickly became the first thing that I looked at in a chart. By the mid-seventies, I had joined up with other serious students of the Sabian symbols, notably Rick Klimczak, Lin Luttrell, Dale O'Brien, and Delores Allegra, all of whom lived around Washington D.C. This group met to discuss the symbols for a period of more than twenty years. Our ongoing interest was maintained by the *level* of analysis made possible by the Sabian symbols. Imagistic astrology allows you to penetrate to the level of soul and spirit. Symbols are like "windows to the soul," for, as religious thinkers have always known, symbols can put you in touch with the spiritual energies they represent. Keyword astrology, by contrast, has no real energy. When you read keywords, you begin and end by checking off points on a mental list—That's true; that's true; that's not true.

Symbols have the power to engage your intuitive faculties. They help you make a direct connection with a person's basic spiritual energies and penetrate the private language of their personal mythology. This understanding is essentially nonverbal; in fact, it is a kind of channeling of the energies themselves. At best, symbols help you connect directly to the level of cosmic energies, and to understand how these cosmic energies express themselves in human personalities. Degree symbols therefore add a gnostic[5] element to astrology, for they train the mind to "see" the energies of a higher plane. Since astrology operates on the level of planetary and zodiacal energies, the best astrologers work at this level. Their understanding is psychic and intuitive as well as intellectual, for the rational mind can take one only so far in understanding phenomena that are essentially energetic.

How This Book Evolved

In the late 1970s, I wrote a book of over a thousand manuscript pages on the Sabian symbols. It was never published. Like my fellow Sabian devotees, my approach was essentially intuitive. I interpreted the symbols much as you would interpret the imagery of a dream. I was certainly familiar with the Sabian interpretations of Jones and Rudhyar, but from the first, I felt that it was possible to arrive at a much deeper understanding of the symbols.

At this time I was not particularly interested in any of the other degree systems. I had looked briefly at the *Degrees of Life* and the systems of Charubel and Volasfera, but I found it hard to take Charubel seriously when his symbol for my Sun degree is "Two wolves devouring a carcass in the moonlight." The Sabians seemed both more positive and more accurate.

Over the next twenty years, my method of approaching the symbols changed slowly but radically. My brother Ken had collected solar charts for tens of thousands of people, and occasionally, when I did not know how to interpret a symbol, I gathered a large number of examples of people with planets on that degree and based my interpretation on an analysis of this sample. In the course of examining these degrees, it became obvious that some of them had at best a tangential relationship to the Sabian symbols. I therefore changed a few of the degree symbols so that they would make a better fit with the examples. However, I continued in my belief that the Sabian symbols as a whole were correct.

By the mid-eighties, I had been studying the Sabian symbols for about fifteen years, yet I was still uncertain about many of the degrees. The more research I did, the more I realized that I could not trust intuition alone to arrive at reliable interpretations. More importantly, I realized that the Sabian symbols themselves often had to be interpreted very freely if they were to fit the collected examples. In the end, I decided that I would never be confident of my interpretations until I had analyzed a large collection of examples for each degree.

Collecting the examples was a lot of work, but it was a fairly straightforward project, made immensely easier when Lois Rodden's *AstroDatabank* was published, with its 25,000+ full charts.[6] My brother's collection of charts is almost entirely lacking in birth times, so I could use it only for the outer planets, since the inner planets often change degrees in a single day. Rodden's charts, by contrast, have birth times, and a very large number of them are based on actual birth certificates.

By the end of the collection process I usually had around 170 examples per degree. I used the Sun, the Moon, the planets, the North and South Mean Nodes of the Moon, and Chiron. Only rarely did I use the Ascendant or Midheaven, since a few minutes registered incorrectly at the time of birth would give the wrong degree.

After I had collected the data, I began to analyze it. What is the first thing that stands out about the examples? What kind of people are they? The chief obstacle that I faced here was psychological projection. At this stage in my research, I had been using the Sabian symbols for many, many years. Years earlier, I had committed them to memory, and I was very attached to some of the more beautiful images. It was hard for me to see the degrees in any new way. Even when I had a large collection of examples in front of me, I tended to focus on the examples that worked with the Sabian symbols. Since I was trained in science, I at least understood the importance of looking at the data dispassionately. However, this was easier said than done, for without the impersonality of statistical methods, inaccurate preconceptions could easily prevail. I tried to get around this problem by going over the examples very carefully and by working through each degree repeatedly. The key lay in emptying my mind of all previous analyses and images before I considered the examples. I then simply looked for groups of people who had peculiar things in common. I started by identifying every common thread that I could find. Only after much thought and analysis did I begin to identify the central principle of each degree.

After going as far as I could from the sample, I went through ten different degree systems to see if they provided any new insights. I checked these systems against the examples themselves and against my previous analyses of the examples. In general, the Sabians tallied with the examples more often than any of the other symbol systems.

However, in isolated instances, a symbol from one of the other systems conformed to the data better than the Sabian symbol. (For a critical evaluation of these systems see Sources on page 367.)

By the end of this process, I had generated up to ten pages of notes for each symbol. I had already achieved a fairly good understanding of the dynamics of each degree. However, I still had to come up with a symbol. When the Sabian symbol fit the examples fairly well, I simply modified it in light of the examples. When the Sabian didn't fit the examples, I turned to the other symbol systems. Since I was looking at about ten other systems, I had a lot of images to choose from. Unfortunately, the fit between the examples and the degree symbols was often not particularly good in *any* of the systems. This made it necessary to create a new symbol. However, if even one aspect of a symbol seemed to work in any one of the systems, I found it much easier to come up with the rest of the image.

For example, the sixth degree of Scorpio is symbolized in the Sabians by "A Gold Rush." This symbol had never particularly impressed me, even before I had done any research. I knew a number of people with planets on this degree, and the image didn't seem to fit them. They were not, as one might have expected, greedy people who were always on the lookout for moneymaking opportunities. After I had collected around 170 examples, a new picture began to emerge. I noticed that a number of the people in the examples, including Sidney Toler (Charlie Chan), Jamie Lee Curtis, Don Johnson, J. Edgar Hoover, Robert Urich, Kim Basinger, and Ruth Snyder, who staged a fake burglary to murder her husband, were involved with guns and police investigations. The *Degrees of Life* has for this degree "Thou art a woman alone in thine house, defending thyself and thy possessions against thieves, in the absence of thine husband." This seemed to describe the examples a lot better than the Gold Rush. I therefore began with the image of thieves in the house, and then imagined some of the people in the examples in similar situations, until one of the images passing through my mind seemed to click.

For this particular degree, one of the symbol systems was already fairly accurate. With many others, I was more or less on my own. Creating new symbols has been the the most challenging aspect of this whole project.

With practice, I have gotten better at it, as images now suggest themselves fairly readily when I look at a collection of examples.

I am the first to admit that this method, which mixes empirical research, intuition, and a kind of channeling, is hardly scientific. In fact the second phase of my method is almost purely intuitive. In tuning in psychically, the researcher's psychological makeup comes into play, and this cannot help but act as a distorting filter. Furthermore, while *AstroDatabank*'s collection is very large, it is weighted towards movie stars, AIDS victims, and serial killers. In answering these objections, I can only offer the following advice: If you hold yourself to the ideal of rigorously dispassionate inquiry, you can get rid of some of these distortions. Because I know that the collections I use are biased toward actors and actresses, I try to see past this distortion. This is not entirely possible, but I can try. The subjective distortion in the "psychic" phase of the method is, however, impossible to get around. Nonetheless, I always come back to the examples. The new symbol has to fit the examples, because if the degree symbol doesn't fit the examples, how can one say that it "works" in an astrological sense?

An astrological symbol system is not a religious artifact to be used for spiritual contemplation. A symbol system has merit to the extent that it effectively describes the people who have planets on these degrees. And there is no easier way of arriving at a good symbol system than by studying example charts. Although this methodology is tedious and time-consuming, and even takes a fair amount of practice, it has great advantages. And it can be used to research almost every aspect of astrology.

Philosophical Considerations

While my approach to the symbols is empirical rather than philosophical, I could not help but wonder about the underlying nature of degree symbols. Philosophically, I have always assumed that the energies of the astrological signs, planets, and degrees have an objective reality outside of the consciousness of the perceiver. If this were not the case, then astrology would be purely imaginative, and it would be perfectly legitimate to invent an entirely new zodiac, or to introduce nonexistent planets.

It is my belief that there are more-or-less correct symbols for the degrees, though I am the first to admit that I have not always arrived at these symbols. After having studied all of the different systems in light of the examples, it is certainly clear that some symbols work and others don't. Occasionally, I found two different images that worked *because they described the same basic energies*. However, this was a rare occurrence. Generally speaking, I have leaned heavily on the Sabian symbols, not so much because they come from a superior channel, but because most of them make a good fit with the examples. It would be absurd to throw out the Sabians when so many of them work so well; but it is equally clear that they must be evaluated on a one-to-one basis.

I have seen some recently created symbol systems that do not rely on *any* earlier symbol systems; nor are they really based on research. They don't even claim to be channeled. In fact, it is hard to determine on what they are based, other than the poetic imagination of their creators. Such systems rest on the underlying philosophical assumption that *any* system is valid, and that astrology is essentially subjective. This position has become increasingly popular within the astrological community, and is usually framed in statements like "Every system is valid within itself." Perhaps one can make this statement about religions, but if there is any scientific reality behind astrology—and I believe there is—these statements merely excuse people from critically examining competing assertions. Such attitudes certainly do nothing to help astrology progress, since baseless ideas can never be weeded out if one refuses to condemn any idea as false.

In view of the fact that I see the symbols as objective realities beyond the personality of the observer, the question may then be asked: What *are* the degree symbols? Are they archetypes in the collective unconscious? Are they the divine Ideas of Plato and the neoplatonists? Philosophically, one should no doubt begin with neoplatonism. Astrology, like almost all of the other occult arts, tends to be grounded in neoplatonic philosophical assumptions. This is particularly true of symbolic astrology. The reality of the symbols is based on the reality of the archetypal ideas. This is one reason why channeled material is held in such high regard among astrologers; channelers purport to be in direct contact with the archetypal ideas and images in God's mind. Both of my books begin from channeled material. *Moon Phases* begins with Yeats' *A Vision*, and *The Zodiac by Degrees* begins with the Sabian symbols. Yet, I am also trying to perfect this channeled material by subjecting it to empirical research. My methodology is therefore mixed, even on a philosophical level, for one cannot say that the symbols I have created are "channeled" except inasmuch as they retain the images of the Sabian symbols or other channeled degree systems.

About the closest model that I have found for my philosophy is the Christian Neoplatonism of the Middle Ages. The Franciscan Order, and its great thinker Saint Bonaventure, inherited a Neoplatonic view of reality from Saint Augustine.[7] For the Franciscans, the names of God are real things—they are emanations of the Godhead. Beauty, Truth, Wisdom, Righteousness, and Courage are all actual emanations of the Godhead. Any earthly exemplar of beauty can only lead one to the higher beauty that is a name of God. This is the true residence of beauty.

Like most Franciscan philosophers, Bonaventure suggested that one could use sensory and natural knowledge as a ladder to this illuminative or revealed knowledge. One could study earthly exemplars and abstract these toward a general principle. If one were trying to arrive at an understanding of divine beauty, one could take the most beautiful people and things in the universe and contemplate what they have in common and draw conclusions based upon this research. These abstractions, based on empirical observations, are a kind of ladder to a direct understanding of divine beauty as a name of God. The abstraction can not get one all the way there, because the intellect can never reach God, who can only be experienced through a direct illumination of the intellect by the divine intelligence, in states of mystical communion. However, the empirical study of the virtues in earthly exemplars was seen as helpful in achieving the goal of God-realization. It took one as far as one could go before one needed to receive a direct revelation.

Medieval Augustinianism contains many elements that are completely obsolete. On the other hand, it has important features that can be applied to the study of astrological symbols. One collects a lot of examples and studies them to find their common themes. Then, after going as far as this empirical analysis can go, one "tunes in" on a purely intuitive or mystical level, and hopes to arrive at the right place. This is not an easy methodology, but from my own experience, it works.

Using the Symbols

The most important rule in using the symbols is that you must always round upward. For instance, if someone has Venus on 19°28' Aquarius, look in the book under "20 Aquarius." If someone has the Moon on 29°01' Aries, look up the symbol for "30 Aries." Every major symbol system rounds upward, including the Sabian. In fact, people familiar with the Sabian symbols often just say "15 Virgo" to signify the arc between 14°00' Virgo and 15°00' Virgo.

What about planets that are on the cusp between two degrees? A determination must be made, since in my experience people never manifest both degrees on either side of a cusp. My rule of thumb is that 19°58' is still the 20th degree, while 19°59' may be either the 20th or the 21st degree. 20°00' is generally the 21st degree, unless the planet is retrograde. Because the Sun and Moon occupy a fairly broad area of astronomical space, you must give them a bit more leeway, but this is still rarely more than two *minutes* on either side of the cusp. Deciding which symbol is correct isn't all that difficult, if you make this determination on the basis of the energy of the symbol rather than the descriptive phrases. You gain an understanding of the energy best by looking at the symbol in conjunction with the examples.

In reading the descriptive phrases for a degree in someone's chart, be clear that not everything is going to fit. I have tried to give a range of ways in which the degree commonly manifests. Some of these are negative; some are positive. Unless it is clear that the negative characterizations are an issue for a client, I see no point in putting them into a reading. I have written the symbols as interpretive aids; they should not be used in a reading without tailoring them to the individual. The symbols need to be integrated into the pattern of the whole chart, and astrologers should already have made such determinations before they even sit down with a client.

To this end, I have no problem with a person changing the sex of the main figure in a symbol. If you are reading for a woman, and her Sun degree is represented by a man, she may have an easier time relating to the degree if the main figure in the image is changed to a woman. The best thing you can do with the symbols is to discover how they fit into the personal psychology and personal mythology of the client. If you can put a spin on the degree that suddenly makes its relevance obvious, then don't hesitate to do so. Ask the client whether the symbol recalls an important event in her life, or even a powerful dream. This can be immensely revealing. If you can relate a degree to an event, you will have much more insight into the way the involved planet operates in a person's life. This more specific way of understanding the client's psychology will help you provide more relevant and insightful guidance.

The examples of famous people that are given with each degree afford another method of entering into the spirit of the degrees. The examples have been selected because they in some way epitomize the basic energy of the degree. They are less representative than they are instructive. They should, therefore, be examined fairly carefully in conjunction with the symbol. Ask yourself how each of these people manifests the energy of the degree. This can give you an understanding that goes beyond the descriptive phrases.

Among the examples, you will find a large number of actors, actresses, and other public figures. I include many public figures because readers may be familiar with their personalities, their energies, and even some details of their personal lives. Undoubtedly, the best examples in doing research are people one knows personally. However my friends, relatives, and clients would have been valueless as examples for a general readership.

You may also notice that I include actors who have starred in films that relate to the symbol in question. This may seem somewhat arbitrary, since actors and actresses play whatever role they have been hired to play. Yet it may not be so arbitrary. Directors choose actors because they fit the part, and actors become famous for roles that they can fully inhabit.

In judging whether a planet functions well or badly on a certain degree, you should begin by putting aside traditional assignments of rulerships, debilities, falls, and exaltations. The degree symbols give a more nuanced picture than any of these traditional categories. Consider, for instance, the 17th degree of Taurus, which pictures a sword fight. This is clearly a very Martian degree, despite the fact that Mars is traditionally "in detriment" in Taurus. Venus, which traditionally rules Taurus, would have some obvious problems on this degree. A person with that placement might be combative and devious, especially in matters of love. Formulas have the attraction of being easy to apply without a great deal of thought, but they shouldn't be used unless you are completely certain they work. Instead of looking to formulaic elements like rulerships, it is more important to ask, when examining a position, in what ways a planet is in harmony with the symbol, and in what ways it is in disharmony with the symbol. Venus will be strong on a degree like the "bride" in Virgo, but will be weak on a degree like Virgo's "pugilist." Yet even in each of these degrees, Venus will have its particular strengths and weaknesses.

The degree symbols work not only for the Sun, Moon, and planets, but also for any other celestial body or point in the horoscope. You can manifest a degree strongly even if you have Chiron there, or the South Node.

In using the Moon's nodes, however, be advised that it has been the experience of many Sabian practitioners that only the Mean Nodes of the Moon really work. The symbols for the True Nodes do not seem to have any significance.

The symbols for the house cusps are extremely useful in chart interpretation, but this is obviously a tricky business, since different house systems give different cuspal degrees. I use the Placidus house system because it seems to give the most meaningful degree symbols. Most of the other people in the Washington Sabian group also use Placidus house cusps. The only other house system that I have found interesting is Regiomontanus. But I leave this matter to your own experimentation.

The symbols for the house cusps, while rather uncertain, are extremely important if you can get them right, since they show the attitude a person will adopt toward the matters of the house in question. To some degree, the symbol on the cusp will indicate whether the affairs of that house will be "fortunate" or "unfortunate," since, if a person's attitude toward the affairs of a house is negative or inappropriate, this will necessarily cause a lot of problems. For instance, if the 4th house cusp—the house of the home—is on a very cozy degree, the native will probably feel that a pleasant home-life is within his grasp. However, if the degree is an uncomfortable or dangerous degree, there might be a fearful attitude towards affairs of the home. For instance, if the degree on the cusp of the 4th house is symbolized by a church under bombardment, there might be a tendency to expect and accept unstable living conditions.

Similarly, if the seventh house cusp has an attractive degree on it, the native will expect nice things in relationships. If the degree is scary, then the native will be afraid of relationships. Even if Venus is in the seventh house, there will still be a doorway through which the native will not willingly pass. Because some houses have more pleasant or exciting degrees on the cusp, the person will naturally tend to cultivate the affairs of these houses. The affairs of houses with unpleasant cusps will tend to be avoided, and may remain in a relatively immature state of development throughout life.

When you are not sure if the Ascendant or first house cusp in a horoscope is correct, degree symbols can provide an extremely useful way of "rectifying" or correcting the birth time. In erecting a horoscope, a birth certificate is always the best place to start. However, don't assume that the time on a birth certificate is always accurate. Be particularly suspicious of times like 10:00 PM or 3:30 AM, since they have probably been rounded off. When an odd number of minutes is given—as, for instance, 6:38 PM—you can proceed with more confidence.

If you have a birth certificate, begin by entertaining the idea that the Ascendant symbol for the given time is correct. If, however, this symbol doesn't seem to work, look at the degrees on either side of the calculated degree, while looking simultaneously to attendant changes in the Midheaven degree. When the time given is on the hour, entertain changes of up to fifteen minutes on either side. With a time like 3:30, give it eight minutes on either side.

How can you tell if a symbol works? Don't be misled by an apparent correlation between a person's character and the descriptive phrases in the symbol. Such correlations could be coming from somewhere else in the chart. Instead, you must determine whether the person expresses the *energy* of the symbol. The Ascendant degree should, in any case, be very pronounced. It should affect not only the kind of energy a person projects, but also their physical appearance. Ask yourself whether the person's projected image is reminiscent of any of the degree symbols in the immediate area. If you were to make an affectionate nickname for the degree symbol on the Ascendant, would that nickname be at all appropriate for the person in question? It should be.

As for the Midheaven, I don't think it is very accurate to think of this degree primarily in terms of career. The Midheaven, in my experience, has more to do with a kind of skill or personal magic that you perform for society. It is nice if this skill has a place in your job, but this is not always the case. Nonetheless, as a social skill, it should be fairly obvious, since it is how people identify you as an effective agent in society. Therefore, the symbol for the degree on the Midheaven should express this ability.

If You Don't Have Your Birth Chart

If you don't have a birth chart, there are several Web sites that will calculate your full chart for free. Robert Hand has a good one. You can find it at *www.alabe.com*. You can also see Liz Greene's Web site at *www.astro.com*. All you will need is your birth date, place of birth, and your birth time, preferably from a birth certificate. Even if your birth time is not particularly exact, the degree symbols will probably be correct for everything except the Ascendant and the house cusps.

1 Aries

Rebel commander leads a charge
down the gangplank of a huge warship.

Descriptive Phrases

Decisive action; confidence in the soundness of one's will and one's impulses; rejecting the present course of events and acting to secure a new and better future; following an inner vision toward a distant goal (one-track mind, refuse to be sidetracked; march inexorably along the path of success); military, political, or cultural leadership; setting a new agenda and enlisting an army of followers to put that agenda into effect; fighting to get one's way (quarrelsome, bossy); assessing one's forces and choosing one's battles accordingly; disciplining one's impulses vs. going off half-cocked (must struggle to control one's passions); beginning a new enterprise; catching one's stride; joyful exertion; impressing one's will on the world.

Examples

Stonewall Jackson (Pluto. Confederate general); Betty Ford (Chiron. First Lady, founded Betty Ford Clinic for alcohol and drug rehab); William Shatner (Sun. Actor—Captain Kirk on *Star Trek*); Janet Allen (Jupiter. Salvation Army Commissioner); Norman Breedlove (Mercury. Racer, jet-powered car); Clare Francis (Mercury. Competitive yachtswoman, author of *Night Sky*); Raisa Gorbachev (North Node. Stylish First Lady of the former U.S.S.R.); Jackie Cooper (South Node. Child actor—*Treasure Island*); Cesar Chavez (Uranus. Labor leader for Hispanic farmworkers); George C. Scott (Uranus. Actor—*Patton*); Battle of the Monitor and the Merrimac (Neptune. 3/9/1862); Eartha Kitt (Uranus, Jupiter. Outspoken singer, Catwoman on *Batman*); Wilson Ferreira (Chiron. Uruguayan opposition leader, forced into exile when he failed to unseat the dictator); Rosie Mittermaier (South Node. Ski racer); Viscount Edmund Allenby (Neptune. British general—took Jerusalem in 1917).

2 Aries

A comedian shares funny and insightful observations with his audience. Next to him is a table covered with props, among them several unlikely inventions.

Descriptive Phrases

The juggler-magician-trickster archetype; comedy's power to bring people's views of reality back in line with direct observation; fresh examination of people and the world; quick studies and provisional analyses; refining an analysis through research and testing; history, physics, mathematics, or sociology as ways of making sense of surface phenomena; rearranging data until it makes sense; juggling a number of factors; adapting to the changing pluses and minuses of one's situation; clever improvisation vs. inability to comprehend what is going on; observing human foibles (push people's buttons to see their reactions; get into trouble by exceeding society's limits); passionately sharing one's truths vs. bored search for superficial diversions; inventiveness.

Examples

Don Adams (Uranus. Comedian—*Get Smart*); Jay Leno (Jupiter. Talk-show host, comic); L. Frank Baum (Jupiter. Author of *Oz* books); Kim Commons (Moon. Teenage chess prodigy); Divine (Moon. Transvestite star of John Waters' movies); Arsenio Hall (Venus. Talk-show host, standup comic); Margot Seitelman (Uranus. Executive director of Mensa); Manfred Eigen (Uranus. Biophysical chemist studying high-speed reactions); Hyacinthe Vincent (Neptune. Research physician—created new vaccines); Susie Porter (Sun. Draftsman, Hebrew translator, editor of *Kosmos*); Shaquille O'Neal (Mercury. Basketball star, rap artist); Gerard Cordonnier (Mercury. Naval engineer, professor of geometrical analysis and shipbuilding theory); Maurice-René Frechet (Saturn. Mathematician, author—*Abstract Spaces*); Isadora Duncan (Saturn. Dancer); Hugh Downs (Mars. Emcee for *Concentration*).

3 Aries

The profile of a great patriot,
framed by the outline of his country.

Descriptive Phrases

The embodiment of national or cultural archetypes in one's personality; pride in one's heritage; recognizable national "types" who make a good first impression as travelers or diplomats; living up to inherited ideals vs. conventionality that embodies both the good and bad traits of one's culture (artistic exposés of the seedy realities of modern culture); political or cultural leadership; unshakeable faith that inspires the allegiance and service of others (noble, high-flown oratory); grasping the broad outlines of one's destiny; developing a personal mythology that integrates one's life into God's "Great Work" (prefer a compelling narrative to simple facts, need to embody their ideals in the details of everyday life); putting one's personal stamp on society.

Examples

Fidel Castro (Uranus, Jupiter. Cuban revolutionary leader, longtime president); Gina Lollobrigida (Jupiter. Italian sexpot actress, photographer); George Washington (Saturn. American revolutionary leader, first president—"Father of His Country"); Fess Parker (Jupiter, Uranus. Actor—Daniel Boone); Bette Davis (Saturn. Actress; ran USO club for servicemen during World War II); Akira Kurosawa (Sun. Japanese film director—*Seven Samurai*); Paul Hogan (Saturn. Aussie actor, screenwriter—*Crocodile Dundee*); Wernher von Braun (Sun. German missile scientist); Norman Lear (South Node. Television producer—*All in the Family* and *Mary Hartman, Mary Hartman*; leftist political activist); Judy Blume (Saturn. Realistic writer for children—*Are You There, God? It's Me, Margaret* and *Blubber*); Jacqueline Susann (Chiron. Trashy writer—*Valley of the Dolls*); Dane Rudhyar (Sun. Pioneering astrologer who resuscitated astrology in the U.S., avant-garde composer); Rosalynn Carter (Jupiter, Uranus. First Lady, author of *Helping Yourself Help Others*, founder of the Rosalynn Carter Institute).

4 Aries

In a school play, a little girl substitutes a cynical ditty for her regular lines. During the teacher's attempts to remove her, the whole set falls over.

Descriptive Phrases

Deciding how much of society's reality one is going to buy into (reject childish, cardboard reality frameworks); rebellion against appointed roles or belief-systems (bratty, but endearingly so); overturning old perspectives vs. enforcing the establishment line under the guise of objectivity; guiding children into socially appropriate behavior without damping their spirits; relentlessly voicing the truth as one sees it; impudent remarks from the "peanut gallery" vs. intellectual challenges to the established order; rote recitation vs. speaking from the heart; choosing one's words carefully vs. uncensored babbling; joyous self-dramatization (hams); overwhelming a situation through sheer force of personality; sabotaging the stupid or the fake.

Examples

Carl "Alfalfa" Switzer (Jupiter, Uranus. Child actor—*Little Rascals*); Lily Tomlin (Moon. Comedienne—little girl on a huge chair routine); Jason Alexander (South Node. Comic actor—*Seinfeld*); Vicki Lawrence (Mars. Comedienne—*Mama's Family*); John Chancellor (Uranus, Jupiter. Newscaster); Imogene Coca (Saturn. Comedienne); Noam Chomsky (Uranus, Stationary. Radical critic of the establishment media, academic linguistics); Patrick McGoohan (Uranus. Television actor—*The Prisoner*); Fred Rogers (Uranus. Children's show host—*Mr. Rogers' Neighborhood*); Thomas Kuhn (South Node. Author—*The Structure of Scientific Revolutions*, about paradigm shifts); Albert Einstein (Mercury. Revolutionary physicist—theory of relativity); Alan Alda (Moon. Actor—*M*A*S*H*, *Manhattan Murder Mystery*); Red Grooms (Saturn. Artist—dioramas of New York City life).

5 Aries

A teenager improvises a wild solo on his electric guitar. Realizing that he has lost his audience, he quickly returns to a more conventional style.[8]

Descriptive Phrases

Self-discovery through experimentation; discovering one's own limits and capacities; irrepressibility (childishly contrary, disobedient); having the courage to go out on a limb; following an idea wherever it may lead; following one's bliss; gleeful creativity; improvisation; the dilemma of the artist who wants to follow his inspiration wherever it leads, but must discipline himself to stay on the level of his audience; striking a balance between pleasing oneself and pleasing others (schlock art vs. rarified personalized art); living at full throttle vs. having to retire into nature to recharge one's batteries; highly individualistic perspectives; reports from the fringe on the state of the universe (crackpots); remaining focused and collected in the midst of the craziness of the human circus; sharing the unvarnished perspective of the outsider.

Examples

Scott Joplin (Jupiter. Ragtime composer); Paul Krassner (Mars. Iconoclast, editor of *The Realist*, suffered a nervous breakdown); Ilona Stoller (Jupiter. La Cicciolina—Italian porn star and politician); Albert Einstein (Saturn. Physicist who wrote a popularly accessible account of relativity); Aretha Franklin (Sun. Soul and gospel diva); Tennessee Williams (Sun. Playwright—*Cat on a Hot Tin Roof*); Jules Feiffer (Uranus. Loopy political cartoonist); Margaret Merrick (Uranus. "Whiz kid" on radio quiz shows); Steve Norman (Sun. Lead singer of Spandau Ballet); Aldous Huxley (North Node. British writer on consciousness and mysticism, experimented with LSD); Jules Piccard (South Node. Balloonist); Tom Stoppard (Saturn. Wildly innovative playwright); Carole King (South Node. Songwriter, singer); Tom Lehrer (Uranus. Satirical songwriter).

6 Aries

A honeybee wrestles a large piece of debris from the hive, while other bees work on the walls of their palatial new abode.

Descriptive Phrases

Sense of social duty; forcing society to come to grips with its problems; testy calls to action; stirring things up; collective action against powerful opponents (labor unions, political committees); rebuilding society according to a rational plan (Utopian planners who envision a God-centered society); attaining a position of greater social leverage (engineers, administrators, bossy folks who understand the division of labor); influencing the group mind; getting across one's vision of the future to everyone one meets; focusing on a problem amid total confusion vs. scattering one's energies among many different jobs; perseverance and incremental progress; self-indulgence vs. self-discipline; impish razzing of silly conventions vs. angry denunciations.

Examples

Isambard Brunel (Mars. Engineer of the Great Western Railroad); John Calvin (Uranus. Protestant theologian, leader of the theocratically organized city of Geneva); Rosa Parks (North Node. Began major civil-rights protest by refusing to give up bus seat); Vicki Lawrence (Sun. Comedienne—*Mama's Family*); Henrik Ibsen (Pluto. Playwright—*A Doll's House*); Robert Woodward (Sun. Journalist—Watergate investigation); Erica Jong (Sun. Feminist writer—*Fear of Flying*); Spanky McFarland (Uranus. Ringleader of the *Little Rascals*); Anita Bryant (Sun. Singer, anti-gay propagandist); Bill Cosby (Saturn, Stationary. Comedian); David Koresh (South Node. Cult leader of Branch Dravidians); Sally Field (Moon, Mercury. Actress—*The Flying Nun, Norma Rae*); Stevie Wonder (North Node. Soul singer); Yasir Arafat (Uranus. Palestinian leader); Elie Wiesel (Uranus. Historian of the Holocaust).

7 Aries

The king's fool, in cap and bells, sits under a flowering tree. When the king and the archbishop pass him, lost in conversation, the fool surprises them by yelling out an angry but penetrating criticism of their views.

Descriptive Phrases

Refusing to be boxed in by social expectations or assigned roles (create their own role in life); Auntie-Mame-like disregard for social conventions (mischievous, contrary); voicing uncensored opinions; pulling the rug out from under people's feet; waking people up to what is in front of their eyes, especially studiously ignored issues like sex, death, and power (see a surreal nightmare of unconscious living all around them, socially claustrophobic, must periodically withdraw into the peaceful beauty of nature); uniting inner thoughts and desires with personal actions vs. feeling split into a spiritual and a worldly self; existential mindfulness vs. losing oneself in fantasies that aren't rooted in reality; the childlike wisdom of the natural man.

Examples

Dr. Ruth Westheimer (Uranus. Outlandish sex educator); Frank Zappa (South Node. Rock singer, trenchant social critic); Betty Friedan (Uranus. Feminist, founder of NOW); Giulietta Masina (Mars. Actress—*Juliet of the Spirits*); Danny Kaye (North Node. Actor, pianist—*The Court Jester, The Inspector General*); Lina Wertmuller (Uranus. Filmmaker—*Swept Away*); Max Weber (Neptune. Sociologist and historian—*The Protestant Ethic and the Spirit of Capitalism*); Jack Kevorkian (Uranus. Right to die advocate, assisted suicide); Arlo Guthrie (Moon. Folk singer—"Alice's Restaurant"); Bill Moyers (Moon. Cultural gadfly); Sri Chinmoy (North Node. Spiritual guru); Alfred Kinsey (North Node. Sexual researcher—*The Kinsey Report*); Dick York (Uranus. Actor—*Bewitched*); Chris Farley (Venus. Fat comedian); Carol Channing (Chiron. Ditzy Broadway star).

8 Aries

Eyes fixed intently on the horizon, a Samurai chief on horseback leads a ragtag band of warriors through enemy territory.

Descriptive Phrases

Steely resolve; steadfastness of purpose; tactical maneuvers that don't deviate from ultimate goals (pseudo-compromises, don't really give an inch); mental maneuverability vs. fear-based prejudice; struggling for ascendancy; emerging as a power; setting out bravely to meet one's destiny (tests of courage, mastering one's fears); inspiring others through one's faith in the attainability of one's goals; gaining a following by setting an example of commitment, self-sacrifice, and self-discipline (undisciplined, need to face down the demands of their own desires); chains of command; giving or taking orders (mavericks who reject all external authority); righteousness; taking full responsibility for one's effects on others; decisive leadership (ruthlessness).

Examples

Che Guevara (Uranus. Marxist revolutionary); Susan Atkinson (Moon. Adventurer, drowned while sailing in a typhoon); Neil Kinnock (Sun. Labor Party opposition leader to Thatcher); Rudyard Kipling (Neptune. Poet, writer—*Captains Courageous, The Jungle Book*); Lily Tomlin (Jupiter. Comedienne, political activist); Hillaire Belloc (Chiron. Anti-Protestant Catholic propagandist); Matt Damon (Chiron. Actor, screenwriter—*Good Will Hunting*); Mia Farrow (Venus. Actress—*Rosemary's Baby*, adopted a troop of children); Dianne Wiest (Sun. Broadway actress, Woody Allen movies—*Bullets over Broadway*); Betty Friedan (Chiron. Feminist leader, NOW founder); KKK founded (Neptune, Stationary. 12/24/1865); Richard Nixon (North Node. U. S. president who opened up relations with China); Lord Baden-Powell (North Node. Founder of the Boy Scouts); Abraham Lincoln (Venus. U. S. president, led the country through the Civil War).

9 Aries

A seer gazes into a glowing crystal ball.

Descriptive Phrases

Looking for inner illumination or guidance (gnostic or alternative religion); getting a glimpse of higher truths in the cloudy realm of psychic intuition (represent tenuous intuitions as certainties); testing one's hypotheses vs. insulating oneself in a flattering bubble; detached control of the imagination; working out problems in advance through inner visualizations (envisioning machines or molecules, occult symbols, visionary art, or sexual fantasies); following the inner light wherever it leads vs. losing the path in strange byways (may end up in an illusory hell-world rather than in the light of truth); creating a stir with an arty, magical persona; clarifying one's inner model of the world vs. conjuring up flashy but empty effects; portentous revelations.

Examples

Judy Chicago (Jupiter. Artist, vagina-like forms); Doctor John (South Node. Voodoo-influenced blues pianist); Bill Gates (Moon. Computer engineer, Microsoft CEO, philanthropist); Elizabeth Clare Prophet (Mercury. Gnostic Christian with prophetic pretensions); Rosalyn Bruyère (Venus. Healer, occultist); Gustave Doré (Pluto. Engraver, illustrated Dante's *Divine Comedy*); Arne Lein (Ascendant. Psychic, healer, author of *What's Your Card?*); Jeffrey Dahmer (Mars. Crazed serial killer, cannibal); Nikola Tesla (Jupiter. Inventor of alternating current, etc.); Charles Steinmetz (Neptune. Electrical engineer and inventor); Andy Warhol (North Node. Silkscreen and lithography artist, hosted a decadent but influential art salon); Hunter Thompson (Jupiter. Gonzo journalist—*Fear and Loathing in Las Vegas*); Ursula LeGuin (Uranus. Sci-fi and fantasy author—*The Earth-Sea Trilogy*); Bruno Bettelheim (South Node. Psychiatrist—*The Uses of Enchantment*).

10 Aries

Before going out to meet the cameras, an adolescent star strikes a pose in front of a round convex mirror.

Descriptive Phrases

Physical appearance as a reflection of inner character; tending to one's public image without ever deviating from one's true self (childishly self-centered, take-it-or-leave-it attitude, narcissistic); physical beauty based on just proportions vs. exaggerated features that are nonetheless expressive of one's inner self (the mirror as the lens of the eye, which is either perfectly formed or distorted); having faith that one sees things clearly; seeing through false appearances, especially on a political level vs. self-serving distortions (artistic license—distortion as a way of showing new truths); strong drive for worldly success (highly competitive, run roughshod over opponents); exploring a new facet of one's personality; energetic self-expression.

Examples

Warren Beatty (Sun. Actor, political themes—*Bulworth, Reds*); Audrey Hepburn (Uranus. Long-necked actress—*Sabrina*); Russ Meyer (South Node. Soft-core filmmaker devoted to women with giant breasts); Vincent Van Gogh (Sun. Colorful artist famous for his distorted landscapes); Leonardo da Vinci (Mercury. Painter—realistic self-portraits, inventor, used mirror writing); Carol Burnett (Mercury. Comedienne known for her mugging and social satire); Steve Allen (Chiron. TV comedian, activist against TV violence, mystery writer, pianist-composer); Lyndon Johnson (Saturn. U. S. president); David Frost (Mercury. Host of *That Was the Week That Was*, an important source of political satire); Eric Clapton (Sun. Rock guitarist); Gloria Steinem (Mars. Feminist leader); Naomi Campbell (Chiron. Black supermodel); Burt Bacharach (Uranus. Songwriter); Liza Minelli (Mercury. Singer); Betty White (Chiron. Actress—*The Mary Tyler Moore Show, Golden Girls*); Tab Hunter (North Node. One-time teen idol).

11 Aries

An emperor stands before his people, a sword at his side and a scepter in his hand.

Descriptive Phrases

Nobility of spirit; dignity; uprightness; holding oneself to high standards; exemplifying one's ideals in one's words, deeds, and bearing; idealistic political or moral leadership (championing the rights of the underdog); loyalty to the light force as the basis of good government; seeing beyond immediate conditions to a better future; shaping national culture through long-range planning; patriotism; rough-and-tumble gregariousness; social gallantry vs. expecting special treatment (self-important, hold court); recognizing the best in others and inspiring them to reach their full stature (foster unhealthy dependencies—presumptuously parental); frankly sharing one's beliefs and one's viewpoint vs. demanding loyalty or insisting on having the upper hand.

Examples

Otto von Bismarck (Sun. Statesman, unified Germany); Eugene McCarthy (Jupiter. Presidential candidate who campaigned against the war in Vietnam); Will Rogers (Saturn. All-American storyteller); Laura Ingalls Wilder (Neptune. Author—*Little House on the Prairie*); Yogi Bhajan (Uranus. Authoritarian spiritual leader, kundalini yoga); Beverly Sills (Uranus. Opera star, popularizer of high culture); William Butler Yeats (Neptune. Poet, promoted Irish culture); Henry VIII (Moon. English king who broke with the Catholic Church and promoted English culture); Nikolaus Gross (Moon. German trade union secretary, actively resisted the Nazis); Amy Vanderbilt (Saturn, Stationary. Etiquette guru); Helen Gurley Brown (Chiron. Editor of *Cosmopolitan*); Carry Nation (Uranus. Radical temperance leader); Cesar Chavez (Sun. United Farm Workers organizer, Chicano spokesperson); Sun Yat-sen (Neptune. Chinese revolutionary who overthrew Manchu dynasty); Oliver Cromwell (Mars. Puritan revolutionary who overthrew Charles II of England).

12 Aries

Sitting on the porch of a cabin hard by the forest, a settler strums a guitar and sings, his children at his feet.[9]

Descriptive Phrases

Following the unmarked trail of natural instinct rather than society's paths (wanderers, lose their way in life); mavericks who live on the fringe (uncivilized, wild, come into conflict with the law); attunement to the friendly and hostile moods of nature; promoting the values of the simple, rustic life; teaching the spiritual values of an older tradition to the younger generation ("Let the circle be unbroken"); imprinting of one's vision upon the young; maintaining the purity of one's childhood vision of life (naïve, expect life to conform to their dreams); recognizing the presence of spiritual archetypes within nature; telling gripping stories that join the natural and archetypal realms; letting the spirit soar through music; sharing joys that one has found along the way.

Examples

Gary Snyder (Mars. Poet, naturalist); Dale Evans (North Node. Cowgirl); Clyde Barrow (Saturn. Outlaw—*Bonnie and Clyde*); Tom Fogerty (Mars. Singer, songwriter—Creedence Clearwater Revival); Art Garfunkel (Mars. Folk singer—Simon and Garfunkel); Anne McCaffrey (Sun. Science fiction writer—*The Lady in the Tower*); Cassandra Peterson (Jupiter. Horror show host—Elvira); Nicholas Cage (Jupiter. Actor—*Raising Arizona*); Alec Guinness (Sun. Actor—*The Lavender Hill Mob, Star Wars*); Jane Powell (Sun. Hollywood musicals—*Seven Brides for Seven Brothers*); Johann Sebastian Bach (Sun. Baroque composer); Carl Jung (North Node. Archetypal psychology); Daniel Pinkwater (Mars. Author of children's books—*Alan Mendelsohn, Boy from Mars*); Hans Christian Andersen (Sun. Fairy tale writer and compiler).

13 Aries

Commandos in an armored car speed through an artillery barrage. A grenade lands in the car, but is ejected just before it explodes.

Descriptive Phrases

Being out in the open about one's goals and values, and suffering attacks on that account; defiant honesty and integrity (feel like misfits who have no place in society and must fight for their personal truth at every turn, see society as an irrational dystopia); surviving threats through sheer willpower vs. being shattered by society; identifying and attacking social problems at a core level; blowing away lies and social hypocrisy; assembling a motley crew of confederates for a counter-attack; making adjustments when things don't go as planned; taking responsibility for one's effects as an individual vs. lashing out in blind anger; life as an ongoing series of comic challenges and disasters (freewheeling surrealism).

Examples

Malcolm McDowell (Mars. Actor—*A Clockwork Orange*); Camille Paglia (Sun. Iconoclastic social critic); Pete Townsend (Mars. Lead guitarist of The Who, famous for teen anthem, "My Generation"); Isabel Peron (Uranus. Singer, took over Argentina after the death of her husband); Julius Lester (Saturn. Black writer—*Look Out Whitey! Black Power's Gon' Get Your Mama*); Sissy Spacek (North Node. Actress—*Carrie, Badlands*); Max Ernst (Sun. Surrealist painter); Mark Twain (Pluto. Author—*Letters from the Earth, Huck Finn*); Tina Turner (Mars. Rhythm and blues singer, acted in *Mad Max Beyond Thunderdome*); Pat Buchanan (Saturn. Populist demagogue); James Dean (Uranus. Rebellious teen icon, killed in a high-speed car crash); Michelangelo Antonioni (North Node. Film director—*Blow-Up*); Norman Spinrad (South Node. Science-fiction writer—*The Iron Dream, Agent of Chaos*); Kurt Russell (Mars. Actor—*Stargate*, in which he must defuse a bomb).

14 Aries

The temple of wisdom, whose four entrances are bordered by columns in the shape of intertwined serpents. Inside, a man and a woman face each other and exchange gifts of knowledge.

Descriptive Phrases

Kundalini as the evolutionary force within the historical process; immersion in the senses vs. yearning to achieve a new level of consciousness; the wisdom of desire, knowing what one lacks sexually, intellectually, or spiritually; quickly sizing up a person and what they have to offer; connecting with people who have a quality that one lacks (difficulties of approach, sexual politics); unification of opposites (the intertwining of sperm-and-egg DNA after sexual union); joining intuitive and rational, or Eastern and Western forms of knowledge; achieving a new synthesis; seeing potential in people and situations, and providing the piece of the puzzle that will energize and transform them; invigorating society by promoting cutting-edge culture.

Examples

Chogyam Trungpa (Saturn. Tibetan guru in the West—founded Naropa Institute in Boulder, CO); Paul Foster Case (South Node. Author on the tarot, founded Builders of the Adytum); Jean-Baptiste Colbert (Jupiter. Chief cabinet minister of Louise XIII, founded the French Academy of Sciences); Johnny Depp (Chiron. Actor—*The Ninth Gate*); Luc Besson (South Node. Filmmaker—*The Fifth Element*); Germaine Greer (Saturn. Feminist writer—*The Female Eunuch*); Margaret Sanger (Saturn. Nurse, birth-control advocate); George Blake (Chiron. Double-agent); Christianne Vasse (Chiron. Research into ESP); Anne Perry (Saturn. Writer of detective fiction); Anjelica Huston (Jupiter. Actress—*The Royal Tenenbaums*); Fritjof Capra (Saturn. Author of The Tao of Physics—A union of Eastern and Western knowledge); Jerry Garcia (Moon. Rock singer—The Grateful Dead).

15 Aries

In a spaceship orbiting the sun, the captain argues with his copilot over whether to change course. Covertly glancing at his copilot's radar screen, he sees the blip of an enemy vessel.

Descriptive Phrases

Weaving visible and invisible factors into a comprehensive picture before deciding how to proceed; reorienting oneself in a situation that's in spin (caution vs. taking calculated risks); developing a powerful analysis through behind-the-scenes fact-gathering, and then coming out into the open and fighting for one's beliefs; waging war against liars and traitors; keeping one's overall mission in mind; staying the course vs. temporary maneuvers to avoid unnecessary conflict; self-reliance; keeping one's own counsel vs. being a team player (alternately deaf to warnings and prey to treachery, must learn whom they can trust); scientific or technical expertise; interests in astronomy, cosmology, or aviation; students and guardians of the cosmic order; brave adventurers.

Examples

William Shatner and Leonard Nimoy (Uranus. Actors—*Star Trek*); Richard Hatch (Mars. Actor—*Battlestar Galactica*); Sheila Scott (Chiron. First British pilot to fly solo around the world); René Descartes (Uranus. Early scientific theorist who saw the universe as vortices of particles); Theodor Landscheidt (Venus. German attorney and Supreme Court justice, amateur astronomer—established galactic center); Kepler's revelation that the universe was a set of boxed solids (Uranus. 7/9/1595); Wilhelm Roentgen (Jupiter. Physicist—discovered X-rays); Sean Connery (Uranus. Actor—James Bond); Whoopi Goldberg (North Node. Actress—*Star Trek: Nemesis, Captain Planet and the Planeteers*); Steve McQueen (Venus. Actor—*Papillon*); Daniel Ellsberg (North Node. Released the Pentagon Papers); Jeanette Rankin (Jupiter. Feminist leader); Daniel Cohn-Bendit (Sun. Radical activist—1968 French student strike).

16 Aries

In the ruddy light of the setting sun, harvesters put down their scythes and sheaves and strike up a song.[10]

Descriptive Phrases

Being alive to the moment; grateful appreciation for life's abundant gifts; snatching opportunities for fun; openness to the unfolding poetry of life; drinking in the refreshing beauty of nature vs. missing life's deeper significance in everyday routines; attunement to cycles of nature and human life; seeing the glimmers of new possibilities on the horizon vs. wrapping up an old phase of experience (have trouble letting go of the past); the Death card (cutting something down); finding a job one enjoys and working hard at it; singing and dancing (even while one works); working harmoniously with others; coaxing people to participate fully in life; sweeping others along in one's exuberant energy; sharing sage advice on life's ups and downs; *bonhommie.*

Examples

Paul Simon (Mars. Folk singer—Simon and Garfunkel); Gale Storm (Sun. Actress—*My Little Margie*); Robert Louis Stevenson (Saturn. Writer—*Treasure Island*); Shirley MacLaine (Mercury. Actress, spiritual seeker); Baba Ram Dass (Uranus. Guru); William Shatner (North Node. Actor—*Star Trek*); Willie Nelson (Mercury. Country-folk singer); Diana Ross (Mercury. Lead singer of The Supremes); Chris Elliot (Mars. Comic actor); Richard Speck (Mars. Mass murderer—playing Death); Arnold Palmer (Moon. Golfer—swinging a club like a scythe); Mao Tse Tung (North Node. Communist leader, wielding the hammer and sickle); Annette Funicello (Moon. Mouseketeer and actress in beach-party movies); Emiliano Zapata (Saturn. Mexican peasant leader, revolutionary); Huey Long (Moon. Populist demagogue); Alexander Dubcek (South Node. Presided over the liberalization of Czechoslovakia before the Russian invasion); Richard Lester (Uranus. Filmmaker—*Help*).

17 Aries

The porch of a country home. An old couple sits in stony silence, while their daughter, suitcase in hand, walks out the door to live with her musician-boyfriend.

Descriptive Phrases

Pausing to think things through before setting out on a new course in life vs. acting out of boredom, passion, or anger (rash, impulsive actions abort one's efforts and bring one back to square one; repeated errors, especially in romance); learning to establish communication between the "parental voice" and "adolescent voice" within one's mind; conflicts between the primly traditional and the excitingly modern (reject old patterns of life); sexual adventurousness and high romantic expectations (short-lived affairs); mellowing with age; giving others slack because one has been there; renewing ties by letting go of anger or suspicion; taking what one wants from life without waiting for permission vs. giving people what they want without compromising one's values; prudence.

Examples

Merle Haggard (Sun. "Outlaw" country-western singer); Maria Callas (Chiron. Operatic diva, tempestuous love affairs); Tom Ewell (Saturn, Actor—*The Seven Year Itch*, about marital infidelity); Mary Astor (Mercury. Actress, many marriages, alcoholic); Gordon Jackson (Chiron. Played the highly correct head butler in *Upstairs, Downstairs*); Lauren Chapin (Mars. Actress—played daughter in *Father Knows Best*, got into drugs and prostitution before finding Jesus); Gay Talese (Uranus. Sociologist, student of American culture—*Thy Neighbor's Wife*); Ted Kennedy (Uranus. Politician known for moral rectitude in the Senate and serious moral lapses in his personal life); David Frost (Sun. Dry political comedy—*That Was the Week That Was*); Judy Garland (Chiron. Singer, actress, "There's no place like home"); Martha Stewart (Mars. Fulfills the fantasy of being a rich homemaker); Charlotte Brontë (Mercury. Author—*Jane Eyre*).

18 Aries

After resolving an argument, a couple stands hand-in-hand, and looks into each other's eyes.

Descriptive Phrases

Egalitarian ideals that make it difficult to accept abuse or domination either in private life or in the political arena (rebels); mutual respect as the basis of good relationships; working out emotional tensions (may have to negotiate basic issues before arriving at a comfortable, stable union); establishing a natural rhythm in marriage (flirtatious banter vs. sparring); robust physical self-expression (sports, sex); looking for an emotional or sexual partner (honesty vs. physical bullying or cynical attempts to score); embracing life with an open heart; sharing nature's broad tolerance for all life-forms (long-suffering); achieving reconciliation between the races or sexes by fighting for social justice; getting problems out in the open.

Examples

James Garner (Sun. Actor—*The Rockford Files*); Liz Taylor (Uranus, Venus. Film star—*Who's Afraid of Virginia Woolf?*, *Cleopatra*, AIDS activist); Elliott Gould (Saturn. Film star—*Bob & Carol & Ted & Alice*); Jesse Jackson (Mars. Black political activist, reverend); Shelley Winters (Chiron. Actress—*The Poseidon Adventure*); Rod Laver (Saturn. Tennis star); Alan Dershowitz (Saturn. Lawyer, free-speech advocate, defended porn star Harry Reems); Bruce Springsteen (North Node. Rock singer); Fanny Brice (Jupiter. Comedienne); Babe Zaharias (North Node. Early female golfer); Robert Carradine (Venus. Actor—*Revenge of the Nerds*); Isabel Peron (North Node. Showgirl, president of Argentina); Jerry Rubin (Saturn. Yippie radical at the 1968 Democratic Convention); Queen Victoria of England (Mars. Utterly devoted to her husband Albert).

19 Aries

A man rides a magic carpet over an ugly, smoky, coal town.

Descriptive Phrases

Poised detachment from immediate circumstances; watching the script or story of one's life unfold, as in the abstract patterns of an oriental carpet (surprising twists and turns in the overall trajectory of life); passive and amused self-observation vs. being in the driver's seat; observing current or past events and outlining their basic patterns (journalism, history); telling fanciful, escapist stories vs. using literature to reveal timeless patterns of existence; the power of beauty and art to lift one above life's tragedies; bringing others a brief glimpse of life's magic (sensual interludes, swooping down into the realm of the luxuriantly sensual); discovering a path through present-day evils to a more pleasant and civilized way of living.

Examples

Winsor McCay (Neptune. Cartoonist—*Little Nemo in Slumberland*); Anne Rice (Mars. Writer—*The Vampire Lestat*); Charles Fourier (Sun. Creator of a fictional erotic Utopia, inspiration for several intentional communities); Seymour Hersh (Sun. Investigative reporter—My Lai massacre, domestic wiretapping); Betty Ford (Sun. First Lady—founded alcoholism clinic); Anaïs Nin (South Node. Erotic diarist); René Descartes (Pluto. Scientific philosopher—"I think therefore I am," envisioned a universe of particles in vortices); Ludwig Prantl (Chiron. Father of Aerodynamics); Émile Zola (Pluto. Author of sordidly realistic adventure stories, got involved in politics when he defended Dreyfus, accidentally died from coal fumes); Jean Houston (Venus. Writer—*Varieties of Psychedelic Experience*); Nicholas Campion (Mars. Astrologer, author—*The Great Year*); Richard Gere (North Node. Buddhist actor—*Pretty Woman*); Douglas Adams (Jupiter. Author—*A Hitchhiker's Guide to the Galaxy*); Jane Jacobs (Jupiter. Progressive urban planner).

20 Aries

A Victorian playwright walks arm-in-arm with his mistress in a public park. He is wearing a sleek black morning coat, while she wears a frilly white dress.

Descriptive Phrases

Developing an intimate relationship with one's Muse, that is, with one's instinctive, intuitive, sexual side; giving one's desires and impulses wide rein (self-indulgent voluptuaries); creative union of the cultural elite and the demimonde (jazz, poetry, dance, and other "Bohemian" arts); brazenly overstepping the bounds of bourgeois morality; using notoriety to one's advantage; causing a stir, but remaining unflappable amid the public's ruffled feathers[11]; making people face up to hidden truths or underlying realities; frank confidences; telling it like it is; exposing the truth vs. being exposed; having the courage to act upon one's beliefs; going after one's true desires (attraction of opposites—Leda and the swan); chutzpah.

Examples

Emma Goldman (Neptune. Anarchist, practiced free love); Hugh Hefner (Sun. Founder of Playboy Enterprises, political educator); Traci Lords (Saturn. Underage porn star, actress in John Waters' *Hairspray*); George Bernard Shaw (North Node. Playwright—*Man and Superman*); Mary Shelley (Jupiter. Author—*Frankenstein*); Charles Baudelaire (Sun. Dissolute poet—*Flowers of Evil*, sadistic relationships with prostitutes); Paul Krassner (Sun. Editor of the radical magazine *The Realist*); Michelle Pfeiffer (Mercury. Actress—*The Witches of Eastwick*, Catwoman in *Batman*); Henry Kissinger (Chiron. Evil genius behind the Vietnam War); Vladimir Ilyich Lenin (Neptune. Communist theorist, revolutionary); Andy Warhol (Uranus. Artist, cultivated an important artistic demimonde); Guillaume Apollinaire (Jupiter. Proto-surrealist poet, author of humorous pornography); Studs Terkel (North Node. Commentator on American life—*Working*).

21 Aries

Cutting-edge thinker outlines his views from the podium, calmly ignoring the jeers from the audience.

Descriptive Phrases

Innate confidence in one's intellectual and spiritual powers; courageously following through on one's projects and plans; self-education (prodigies with unusual powers of concentration); raptly listening to the voice of one's inner "genius" and tuning out the opinions of the mob (arrogance, insouciance); determination to penetrate some difficult problem; isolated reflection on the guiding principles of the universe (spiritual or physical science); securing a social position from which to promote one's views; defending one's beliefs against all comers (hardheaded—should choose their battles wisely or their enemies may defeat them); tests of moral fortitude; forerunners and prophets—"He goes furthest who goes alone."

Examples

Galileo Galilei (Moon. Groundbreaking astronomer who came into conflict with the Inquisition over heliocentrism); Zenobe Gramme (Uranus. Invented a generator for alternating current); Elizabeth Clare Prophet (Saturn. Gnostic Christian cult leader); Girolamo Savonarola (Mars. Religious prophet, eventually burned at the stake); Elaine Pagels (Uranus. Historian of gnosticism and Christianity—*A History of Satan*); Pete Townsend (Venus. Lead guitarist for The Who); Richard Trumka (North Node. Labor leader); Ruth Slenczynska (Chiron. Piano prodigy); Jamie Lee Curtis (South Node. Actress in the *Halloween* series); Anton La Vey (Sun. Satanist); Werner von Braun (Mercury. Headed first Nazi and then U. S. missile program); Ed Koch (Chiron. Mayor of New York, judge); Marlene Dietrich (Jupiter. Expatriot German actress—*The Blue Angel*); Émile Zola (Mars. Writer—*Nana*, publicly defended Dreyfus in *J'Accuse*).

22 Aries

Standing before the huge gateway of a lost African city, the commander of an expedition exhorts his men to bravery.

Descriptive Phrases

Adventurousness; life as an exciting drama with one grand scene opening after another; conquering one's fears before entering upon some new realm of experience (deny their real aspirations for fear they will not measure up); alertness to danger in a new or primitive environment; grasping the big picture; clarifying for others the basic framework of the situation; power of command—stirring oratory vs. ideological rants; striding forward into one's projected reality vs. bumping into situations that don't conform to expectations; testing limits vs. shutting the door on unwanted experiences (retreat into the imagination); vivid and expansive visual imagination (novelists, filmmakers); hunger for exciting new experiences; travel.

Examples

D. W. Griffith (North Node. Filmmaker—*Intolerance*, in which the heroine tries to protect the giant gate of Babylon); New York opening of *King Kong* (Uranus. 3/2/1933, recall the giant gate to King Kong's lair); Joan Grant (Sun. Metaphysical novelist—*Winged Pharaoh*); H. Rider Haggard (North Node. Novelist—*She, King Solomon's Mines*); Albert Schweitzer (North Node. Missionary, doctor in Africa); Pearl Buck (Jupiter. Novelist—*The Good Earth, Dragon Seed*); Drew Barrymore (Uranus. Actress, producer—*Charlie's Angels*); Alex Haley (South Node. Author—*Roots*); Diana Rigg (Moon. Actress—*The Avengers*); Huey Long (North Node. Populist demagogue); Italian nationalist troops enter Rome through a huge Roman gate (Neptune. 9/20/1870); Maxfield Parrish (Neptune, Stationary. Illustrator); Sir Thomas More (Jupiter. Martyred for opposing Henry VIII's divorce, author of *Utopia*); Michael Caine (Uranus. Actor—*The Man Who Would Be King*).

23 Aries

At a high-society gathering, a fresh-faced newcomer discusses current affairs with an old lady wearing a veil.

Descriptive Phrases

Penetrating beyond outer appearances to the gifts of spirit that each person has to offer (intently absorbing the wisdom of the very old and the very young); insatiable desire to know; developing a cutting-edge spiritual and cultural analysis, yet speaking to one's audience's level (affected naiveté); guarding one's innocence and naturalness in the face of growing experience (jaded); confronting half-truths with finely woven explanations (sticklers for accuracy, prim, correct); making inferences, testing hypotheses; refining one's viewpoints and manners so one can enter an intellectual elite (hide infirmities behind a veil of reticence); easy and skillful sociability vs. difficulty in finding a spiritual helpmeet; generous sharing of informed advice.

Examples

Juliette Binoche (Jupiter. Actress—*Chocolat,* in which a newcomer injects new life into a stuffy French town); Dorothy Parker (North Node. Writer, member of the Algonquin Society); Céline (Venus. Embittered author—*Death on the Installment Plan*); Joan Blondell (Saturn. Hollywood star—"good-time-girl" roles); David Letterman (Sun. Talk-show host with cultural pretensions); Eunice Kennedy (South Node. Founder of the Special Olympics); L. Frank Baum (North Node. Writer of the *Oz* series); Andreas Vesalius (Uranus. Pioneer anatomist); Jim Varney (North Node. "Hayseed" comic actor—*Ernest Goes to Camp*); Michael Rennie (Saturn. Actor—*The Day the Earth Stood Still*); Audrey Hepburn (Venus. Actress—*My Fair Lady, Roman Holiday*; world hunger activist); R. H. Tawney (Saturn. Historian); Thomas Jefferson (Sun. Founding father, president, author of the Declaration of Independence).

24 Aries

A beautiful woman in a gauzy dress whirls ecstatically in a fresh spring breeze.[12]

Descriptive Phrases

Throwing off one's inhibitions; seeking a joyous and unfettered existence; living within a whirl of intoxicating possibilities; breathing fresh life into a situation; rebelling against social repression and confining analyses (stuck in the mind, have difficulty entering into the spontaneity of erotic life); the centrality of sexual desire in human psychology and behavior; the blossoming of personal talents, including sexuality, at their proper time; romantic experimentation; physical beauty and sexual magnetism (exhibitionism); the goddess Venus as the naked formless spirit behind all nature's forms; artistic experimentation in the realm of form; uncovering the underlying significance of a situation; getting lost in a dream vs. seeing what goes on in front of one's eyes.

Examples

Andie McDowell (Mercury. Actress—*sex, lies and videotape*); Emma Thompson (Sun. Actress—*Sense and Sensibility*); Marcello Mastroianni (Chiron. Romantic lead in Fellini films—*8 ½*); Janis Joplin (Ascendant. Hippie blues singer); Judy Collins (Saturn. Folk singer, political activist); Peter O'Toole (Uranus. Actor—*Lawrence of Arabia, The Ruling Class*); Harold Pinter (North Node. Absurdist playwright); Loretta Lynn (Sun. Country singer); Ruth St. Denis (Mars. Dancer, choreographer—*The Veil of Isis*); Fernand Léger (Saturn. Futurist artist); Hans Arp (Moon. Dadaist sculptor); Fabio (Venus. Romance novel model); Alix Schulman (Uranus. Writer—*Diary of an Ex-Prom Queen*); Kevin Sorbo (South Node. Actor—*Tarzan*); Steve Reeves (Chiron. Sword and sandal muscleman); Jayne Mansfield (Uranus. Blonde bombshell); Maria von Trapp (Jupiter. Singer upon whom *The Sound of Music* was based).

25 Aries

Five red roses and an ornate valentine have been placed outside a woman's door.

Descriptive Phrases

Old-fashioned gallantry; exuberantly creative expressions of affection vs. frivolous symbolic gestures aimed at breaking down emotional barriers; serious courtship vs. casual flirtation; impulse and desire blossoming into romantic adventure vs. fear that one is being led down the primrose path (withdraw into thorny emotional defensiveness, have difficulty accepting other people's affection); learning to decipher a lover's words and actions; getting to know one's own heart through a series of relationships (promiscuous); having to choose between many attractive possibilities vs. throwing oneself into one's latest infatuation; plunging into sensual experience (gluttonous indulgence in routine pleasures); gamboling like nymphs and satyrs; romantic idealism.

Examples

Alan Bates (Uranus. Actor—*Far from the Madding Crowd, Women in Love*); Julie Christie (Sun. Actress—*Far from the Madding Crowd, Tonite, Let's All Make Love in London*); Charles Fourier (Mercury. Philosopher whose Utopian society was based on a program of chivalrous sexual escapades); Frédéric Chopin (Jupiter. Floridly romantic classical composer); William Powell (Jupiter. Actor—*Thin Man* series with Myrna Loy); Gloria Swanson (Mercury. Actress—*Sunset Boulevard*); Phyllis Schlafly (Chiron. Anti-feminist activist); Fred Astaire (Mercury. Dancer, singer, actor); Jack Nicholson (Venus. Actor—*As Good as It Gets*); Willie Nelson (Uranus. Country singer); Lawrence Durrell (North Node. Writer—*The Alexandria Quartet*); Mae West (Jupiter. Sex-crazed comedienne); *The Scarlet Letter* is published (Uranus. 3/16/1850); Carolyn Jones (Uranus. Morticia on television's *Addams Family*).

26 Aries

After receiving an award for his contributions, an artist delivers an emotional acceptance speech.

Descriptive Phrases

Rising to the top on the basis of one's talent and accomplishments; winning wide recognition for significant and well-loved cultural contributions in either elite or mass culture; creating a hit that becomes one's signature (one-hit wonders vs. steady achievers); giving the public what it needs vs. giving it what it wants (schlockmeisters); prolific artistic production; seeing one's ideals through to their consummation; energetically throwing oneself into one's work; controlled passion (creative frenzy); intellectual sincerity—belief that one's work is truly important (egomaniacs—peremptory, dictatorial); touching the creative fire in God's mind vs. paralyzing intoxication with personal potentials; exuberant self-expression.

Examples

Sergei Rachmaninoff (Neptune. Classical composer); Adolf Hitler (Mercury. Evil genius, dictator); Madonna (South Node. Pop singer, dancer); Vincent Van Gogh (Mercury. Post-impressionist painter); Elizabeth Montgomery (Sun. TV star—*Bewitched*); Bertrand Russell (Neptune. Mathematician, political activist); Tristan Tzara (Mercury. Dadaist artist, ideologist); Bob Fosse (Moon. Choreographer, director—*Cabaret*); Jerry Lewis (Chiron. Comedian); Betty Grable (Jupiter, Stationary. Actress, famous pinup girl); Albert Schweitzer (Moon. Humanitarian doctor, organist); Yury Gagarin (Neptune. First man in space); Del Shannon (South Node. One-hit wonder—"Runaway"); Jackie Kennedy (Moon. Adored First Lady); Burt Bacharach (Jupiter. Talented composer of pop ballads—"What the World Needs Now"); Pablo Casals (Chiron. Cellist); Ingrid Bergman (Moon. Actress—*Casablanca, Suspicion*); Tina Turner (Saturn. Rock singer).

27 Aries

A private investigator sits in front of a piece of paper and plots out possible methods to outwit a criminal.

Descriptive Phrases

Overcoming obstacles to a mission by pausing and analyzing the difficulties; shrewdness and cunning in facing dangers and snares (unscrupulous maneuverers); trying to foresee problems, but initiating a course of action even before a matter has become clear (reformulating plans as the situation progresses by factoring in new data); working through problems in one's mind; considering possible solutions until one clicks (psychic premonitions based on inner visions); drawing upon subconscious or occult symbolism for use in one's daily life; translating images from one's dreams or imagination into practical plans of action; soliciting help from others, especially in deciphering a cryptic problem, vs. arrogant isolation that invites attacks; game plans.

Examples

Angela Lansbury (Uranus. Actress—*Murder, She Wrote*); Sean Connery (North Node. Actor—best known as secret agent James Bond); Lloyd Bridges (Moon. Actor—*Sea Hunt*); Peter Graves (Chiron. Actor—*Stalag 17*); Warner Oland (Saturn. Actor—Charlie Chan movies); Sigmund Freud (Venus. Wrote on dream analysis); Amy Lowell (Neptune. Poet); Jane Goodall (Uranus. Lived with chimpanzees and deciphered their world); Daniel Berrigan (South Node. Antiwar activist; tried for a purported attempt to kidnap Henry Kissinger); Alice Bailey (Saturn. Occultist); Dick Gregory (Ascendant. Black political activist); Gore Vidal (Chiron. Writer who reconstructed the political machinations surrounding Lincoln and Burr); Francis Crick (Jupiter. Molecular biologist—deciphered DNA); F.M. Cornford (Neptune. Commentator on Plato's *Dialogues*); Barbara Watterson (Saturn. Egyptologist); Ernesto Montgomery (Chiron. Psychic who worked for British Intelligence).

28 Aries

Amid laughs of recognition, a comedian delivers a fast-paced monologue satirizing human foibles.

Descriptive Phrases

Trying to influence the beliefs of the public through humor or serious discussion; securing a public platform so one can reach more people; topical humor that demonstrates the absurdity of common ways of thinking and acting; revealing something amazing vs. debunking the false or the insincere (don't miss a trick, sly, clever); psychological acuity; figuring out people's agendas (dodging people's games); thinking on one's feet; mental and physical acrobatics (manic energy, out of control); sinewy independence of thought vs. looking for a partner who's fun to bounce around with (dynamic duos); creating a showy, dramatic, and likeable personality (lightweights, emotionally dependent on the approval of the public); deepening or sharpening public discussion; asking fresh questions; liberating iconoclasm.

Examples

Jerry Seinfeld (Mercury. Comedian—*Seinfeld*); Vicki Lawrence (North Node. TV comedienne—*Mama's Family*); Dick Smothers (South Node. *Laugh-In* comic with brother Tom); Geraldo Rivera (Mars. Talk-show host, alternately serious and sensationalistic); Bob Denver (Uranus. Maynard G. Krebs on *Dobie Gillis*, also Gilligan on *Gilligan's Island*); Shirley MacLaine (Uranus. Actress—promoter of the spiritual); Harry Houdini (Neptune. Stage magician, debunker); The Great Kreskin (Uranus. Stage magician, debunker); Hugh Hefner (Chiron. *Playboy* magnate, promoted free speech, civil rights, and sexual tolerance); Augustus Owsley III (Uranus. Key distributor of LSD in the 1960s); Grace Slick (Saturn. Lead singer of The Jefferson Airplane); Arthur Conan Doyle (Venus. Writer—Sherlock Holmes stories, spiritual interests); Charlie Chaplin (Sun. Comedian, political radical); Ann Richards (Uranus. Feisty ex-governor of Texas).

29 Aries

Visiting conductor raises his baton and vibrates it rapidly, whereupon the violins enter on a tremolo.

Descriptive Phrases

Being so attuned to the truth of a situation that one knows exactly what is needed (quick to take over from incompetents or hypocrites); attacking discordant or hateful elements in society (testy, accusatory); identifying the pivotal power-point in a chaotic situation; orchestrating an event vs. allowing for spontaneity; seeing one's destiny in the larger pattern of events; seizing one's opportunity; breaking through to a higher level of success; hitting a chord with the public; stirring things up culturally (gadflies); integrity—courageously living out one's philosophy even when one is out of synch with society; awareness of all the forces impinging on the moment (the music of the spheres); participating in the higher harmony of God's mind (sage skeptics).

Examples

Winston Churchill (Neptune. British prime minister, moral leader during World War II); Marilyn Monroe (Venus. Movie star); Carl Sagan (Uranus. Public scientist, astronomer); Madalyn Murry O'Hair (Mars. Atheist who got prayer thrown out of public schools); Dane Rudhyar (Venus. Astrologer, avant-garde musician); H. L. Mencken (Saturn. Acerbic journalist, essayist); Nino Rota (North Node. Composer for Fellini films); Leopold Stokowski (Sun. Conductor; featured in Disney's *Fantasia*); Gore Vidal (Moon. Political gadfly, novelist); Gustave von Holst (North Node. Composer—"The Planets"); Grace Slick (South Node. Singer—Jefferson Airplane); Dr. Jack Kevorkian (Jupiter. Aggressive advocate of the right to die); Martin Luther (North Node. Theologian, led the Protestant revolt against the Catholic Church); Petula Clark (Uranus. Pop singer—"Downtown"); Albert Schweitzer (Neptune. Mission doctor in Africa, theologian, organist); D. W. Griffith (Neptune. Filmmaker—*Intolerance*).

30 Aries

A duckling breaks away from the brood and sets out across the lake.

Descriptive Phrases

Trying something new (showing off); taking an innocent, instinctive approach to life (expect life to conform to inner scenarios; fail repeatedly before trying more realistic approaches); accurately assessing one's abilities vs. having to fall back on other people's help (stubborn pride); taking bold steps vs. taking baby steps or backpedaling; steadily pursuing one's goals vs. belief that the dream of life always returns to square one; holding to childhood's faith and peace of mind vs. unwillingness to grow up or to take moral responsibility for one's actions; wanting to be "one of the crowd" vs. goading the mainstream to expand its breadth of understanding; finding one's social niche vs. getting trapped within an adorable social persona.

Examples

Dwayne Hickman (Uranus. Actor—*Dobey Gillis*); Josephine Baker (Midheaven. Singer, exotic dancer, adopted a brood of children); Kevin Corcoran (Mars. Disney child star—Moochy); Ross Perot (North Node. Businessman, presidential aspirant); Drew Carey (South Node. TV sitcom star); Pat Boone (Venus, Uranus. Boyish Christian singer); Peyo (Mars. Cartoonist—*The Smurfs*); Chay Blyth (Jupiter. Crossed the Atlantic in a rowboat with a pal); Celine Dion (Sun. Pop singer—"My Heart Will Go On"); Ryan O'Neal (Sun. Actor—*What's Up Doc?*, *Love Story*); Jayne Mansfield (Sun. Blonde bombshell); Jean Genet (Saturn. Homosexual writer, habitual criminal with an innocent self-image); Robert Zemeckis (Mercury. Director—*Forrest Gump* and *Back to the Future*); the Dionne Quintuplets (Uranus); Michael Dunn (Uranus. Dwarf actor); Danny Kaye (Saturn. Comic actor).

1 Taurus

High above an industrial mill town, a beautiful woman bathes in a fresh mountain stream.

Descriptive Phrases

Easy flow of vital energies; having strong, natural, and undiluted responses to the environment; trusting one's instinctive responses—embracing what is beautiful and rejecting what is repulsive (sensualism); being immersed in one's subjective, emotional world vs. keeping one's head above water; confident observations and opinions; giving a running commentary on life; exercising naked honesty in relationships (outraged by deceit; may make angry scenes); knowing when to come up against a rocky obstacle and when to go around it; arriving at one's ideals by ridding society and one's relationships of impurities, corruption, and lies; fighting the corruption and dishonesty of society, and its destructive effects on nature; truth as beauty and beauty as truth.

Examples

Sophia Loren (Uranus. Actress—*Two Women*); Brigitte Bardot (Uranus. Sexy actress, environmentalist); Jack London (Neptune. Writer—*The Call of the Wild*); Christopher Isherwood (Jupiter. Gay writer—*A Meeting by the River*); Anita Bryant (Saturn. Singer, anti-gay activist); Olivia de Havilland (Jupiter. Actress—*The Snake Pit*, took on the studios); Roy Rogers (Moon. Cowboy actor, worked on behalf of abused children); Hunter Thompson (Saturn. Gonzo journalist); Ayatollah Khomeini (Mars. Iranian leader—Muslim purist who wanted to rid Iran of Western influences); Mahalia Jackson (North Node. Folk and gospel singer); Leonard Cohen (Uranus. Folk singer—"Suzanne"); Prince Charles (Moon. British royal, environmental concerns); Adolf Hitler (Sun. German dictator obsessed with the purity of the German race); Miles Davis (Chiron. Jazz trumpeter); Andy Griffith (Chiron. Actor—*The Andy Griffith Show*); Vance Packard (Moon. Writer—*The Hidden Persuaders*); John Muir (Sun. Naturalist, conservationist, behind the founding of Yosemite Park); Delio Cantimori (Jupiter. Historian of heresy).

2 Taurus

A satyr capering in the midst of an electrical storm.

Descriptive Phrases

Stirring things up; generating some electricity; charging up a boring or lifeless scene (separating the living from the dead by seeing who responds to a vital new element); getting a rise out of people (sexual arousal—commotion caused by aggressive sexual moves); sexual adventures (lecherous, slyly irresponsible approach); impish mischief; shenanigans; seizing the potential of the moment (guerilla theater); emotional "venting" that clears the air of tension (temper tantrums); seizing natural forces and putting them to use (sexual or political power trips); turning things upside down; general excitability and desire for action (experience inertia and depression, rely on alcohol or drugs for excitement); preferring a stormy life to a boring one; vitalization.

Examples

Burt Reynolds (Uranus. Actor—*Smokey and the Bandit*); Carol Burnett (Uranus. Comedienne); Marty Feldman (Uranus. Comic—*Young Frankenstein*); Charlotte Brontë (Sun. Writer—*Jane Eyre*); Elizabeth Ashley (Saturn. Temperamental actress); Ed Sanders (Saturn. Obscene satirist—The Fugs); Maurice Sendak (Jupiter. Children's books—*Where the Wild Things Are*); Tokyo Rose (Jupiter. Japanese radio propagandist, World War II); Judith Malina (Venus. Dramatist—*Living Theater*); Anton Lavey (Mercury. Satanist); Joe Dallessandro (North Node. Warhol star—*Flesh, Andy Warhol's Frankenstein*); Donna Summer (North Node. Disco queen); Michael J. Fox (Moon. Actor—*Back to the Future* films); Ruth Brown (Chiron. Black rhythm-and-blues singer—*Hairspray*); Gerard Depardieu (North Node. Sexually charismatic actor—*Green Card*); Joe Cocker (Moon. Rock singer noted for his spastic dancing); Little Richard (Uranus. Flamboyant, high-energy rock star); Diane di Prima (Uranus. Beatnik poet).

3 Taurus

A multi-storied colonial mansion at the edge of a jungle. On the ground level, the native population goes about their business, while on the upper terrace a group of intellectuals discusses the reorganization of society.

Descriptive Phrases

The coexistence of various levels of culture within any one person—civilized and savage; rising or falling in life according to whether one cultivates one's higher or lower nature (danger of degeneration into savagery); protecting society against barbarism through cultural norms and taboos vs. restructuring society to harmonize with nature and with the natural within man; discriminating between life's higher and lower pleasures; exercising self-discipline vs. going to seed (resent being walled in by social rules, but won't let themselves break out; may develop a secret life; need to periodically escape into nature); gaining access to the decision makers or the intelligentsia; influential social critiques vs. ungrounded Utopianism or mere subversion.

Examples

King Chulalonghorn (Pluto. Royal heir of Thailand and son of the King upon whom *The King and I* was based); Jean Auel (Uranus. Writer—*Clan of the Cave Bear*); Edgar Rice Burroughs (Neptune. Writer—*Tarzan*); William Golding (North Node. Writer—*Lord of the Flies*); Woody Allen (Uranus. Filmmaker—*Sleeper, Bananas, Crimes and Misdemeanors*); Tennessee Williams (Venus. Playwright—*Cat on a Hot Tin Roof, A Streetcar Named Desire*); Jack Nicholson (Sun. Actor—*Chinatown, As Good as It Gets, Wolf*); Margot Seitelman (Chiron. Mensa director); Barbara Jordan (Uranus. Black Democratic congresswoman, professor of political ethics); Murray Bookchin (South Node. Eco-anarchist theorist); Gary Snyder (North Node. Poet, ecologist); Marion Barry (Uranus. Ex-mayor of Washington D. C., cocaine problems); Malcolm X (Mercury. Political revolutionary); Jerry Brown (Venus. Mayor of Oakland).

4 Taurus

A man looks for treasure in the rubble of a ruined castle. Immediately behind him, unnoticed, is a shining pot of gold at the end of a rainbow.

Descriptive Phrases

Faith that the spiritual world will provide the experiences one needs for growth vs. looking for happiness in all the wrong places; calm inner assurance that allows one to hold a steady course in life vs. greed for symbolic confirmations at every turn; "luck" as the reward for the good karma of previous lives (feel spiritually lost in their own era); collecting things of permanent value in one's journey through life; assessing how much of one's projected reality is based in hard fact; having a real treasure vs. talking about an imagined one; alerting people to the treasures of the invisible world (distinguishing trickery or blarney from the real item, digging for proof, research); envy for what one lacks vs. gratitude for one's gifts; generous sharing of knowledge.

Examples

Shirley Temple (Sun. Child star—*The Bluebird*); Jack Albertson (Saturn. Actor—*The Flim-Flam Man*); Reverend Ike (Uranus. Scammy preacher—"pray for money"); Girolamo Cardano (Jupiter. Mathematician, gambler, wrote on probability theory); Natalie Davis (Jupiter. Historian—*The Return of Martin Guerre*); Patrick McGoohan (Chiron. Actor—*The Prisoner*); Robert Zemeckis (Jupiter. Film director—*Back to the Future, Forrest Gump*); Shirley MacLaine (Sun. Hollywood actress and spiritual seeker—*Out on a Limb*); Barbara Streisand (Sun. Singer, actress—*Funny Girl*); Euell Gibbons (North Node. Herbalist—*Stalking the Wild Asparagus*); Geena Davis (Moon. Actress—*Beetlejuice, Earth Girls Are Easy*); Carl Jung (Neptune. Depth psychologist); Edgar Cayce (Neptune. Psychic—The Sleeping Prophet); Arthur Evans (Saturn. Archaeologist—excavation of ancient Minoa).

5 Taurus

Having breached the wall of a forbidden city, an explorer in outlandish military attire relays his findings via walkie-talkie.

Descriptive Phrases

Looking at society with the freshness of a child or a foreigner; insightful cultural commentary; refusing to be culturally assimilated or corrupted; respecting vs. ignoring social expectations and boundaries; bringing attention to outmoded cultural attitudes by thwarting them (create *causes célèbres,* sometimes by getting thrown in jail); forcing society to re-examine its behavior and laws in light of its ideals (Utopianism); embracing one's nation's basic values, yet following a personal ethical and moral code; smuggling vital new cultural elements into some cultural backwater (subversion); pulling off a cultural coup vs. getting shot down by the locals; cultural clashes; foreign travel; intrepid, high-flying adventurers (delinquents).

Examples

Ken Kesey (Uranus, Stationary. Writer—*One Flew over the Cuckoo's Nest,* LSD kamikaze); Robert Morse (Mercury. Actor—*The Loved One, How to Succeed in Business without Really Trying*); Lucille Ball (North Node. Comedienne—broke up a spy ring, but was herself accused of being a Communist); Hunter Thompson (South Node. Writer—*Fear and Loathing in Las Vegas*); Cantinflas (North Node. Comic actor—*Around the World in Eighty Days*); George C. Scott (Chiron. Actor—*Patton, Dr. Strangelove*); Henri Pétain (Sun and Pluto. World War I hero, then Nazi collaborator); Sue Grafton (Sun, Saturn. Writer of detective stories); Ruth St. Denis (Neptune. Modern dancer with Oriental influences); L. Levy-Bruhl (Pluto. Anthropologist); John Astin (North Node. Actor—*The Addams Family*); Jerry Brown (Mercury. Mayor of Oakland); Daniel Ellsberg (Mercury. Released the Pentagon Papers); F. Scott Fitzgerald (Moon, Writer, icon of the Jazz Age).

6 Taurus

A cat is being petted by its owner. Tiring of this, it jumps down from her lap and begins to play with a piece of string.

Descriptive Phrases

Amusing oneself; delighting in the foibles of human behavior (comic antics); eliciting affection by giving affection (susceptible, big-hearted, lovers of beauty); pleasing others by pleasing oneself; romantic dalliance (vain, narcissistically self-involved); seeing through social games; untangling emotional complications between people; coy aloofness vs. knowing on which side one's bread is buttered; seeing after one's primary relationships; playful openness to all of life's possibilities; giving a whirl to every possible solution to a problem (going out on a limb with a new solution and pursuing it persistently vs. painting oneself into a corner); curiosity, intellectual exploration (scientific analysis and invention); testing new ideas to see if they will bear up on a practical level; strikingly independent viewpoints.

Examples

Carol Burnett (Sun. Comedienne); Al Pacino (Sun. Actor—*The Godfather*); Rudolf Serkin (Venus. Nimble-fingered classical pianist); Dorothy Provine (Uranus. Actress—*It's a Mad, Mad, Mad, Mad World*); Eva Marie Saint (Jupiter. Actress—*North by Northwest*); Tennessee Williams (Saturn. Playwright—*Cat on a Hot Tin Roof*); George Bernard Shaw (Pluto. Playwright—*Man and Superman*); Mr. T (Jupiter. Bodybuilder, actor); Frank Zappa (Jupiter. Bedraggled rock star, composer); Steffi Graf (Saturn. Tennis star); Kyle Rote (Jupiter. Football star); Ginger Rogers (North Node. Actress in romantic comedies with Fred Astaire); Pat Oliphant (Uranus. Impudent political cartoonist); Shirley Temple (Chiron. Child actress); A. A. Milne (Saturn. Writer—*Winnie the Pooh*); Mata Hari (Neptune. Courtesan, spy).

7 Taurus

Standing by an ancient well, a Middle Eastern woman ladles out water for a thirsty wayfarer.

Descriptive Phrases

Generous dispensation of spiritual and emotional sustenance; giving an accurate reflection to anyone who asks for it (bluntly honest); gauging what others need to hear (good listeners); ladling out truth in the right doses (character flaws may make one a "leaking vessel" who can't effectively serve others; self-forgiveness for past failures; self-purification); patient forbearance with less-evolved people (exasperation, may blow up in the face of willful ignorance); protecting a tranquil place within, where one can draw upon wellsprings of natural wisdom; isolated self-reflection that keeps one in touch with the deeper realities of life (love of tranquil country life); coming up with something truly relevant vs. coming up empty-handed.

Examples

Mother Teresa (Saturn. Modern-day saint, worked with the dying in India); David Carradine (Uranus. Actor—*Kung Fu*); Rachel Carson (Venus. Environmentalist—*Silent Spring*); Coretta King (Sun. Widow of Martin Luther King, activist); Robert Bly (Mars. Poet—men's movement); Teddy Roosevelt (Pluto. U. S. president, conservationist); Scott Nearing (South Node. Environmentalist); Selma Lagerlof (Pluto. Storyteller, writer); Joyce Brothers (Jupiter. Pop psychologist); Gian Carlo Menotti (North Node. Composer—*Amahl and the Night Visitors*); Dick Cavett (Uranus. Talk-show host); Rosalynn Carter (Chiron. Wife of President Carter and a partner in his decision-making, Habitat for Humanity activist); Anton Chekhov (Pluto. Playwright—*The Cherry Orchard, The Sea Gull*); Tom Snyder (Uranus. Talk-show host); Anne Frank (Venus. Diarist).

8 Taurus

Lecturing on the city of the future, a scientist holds a drawing compass over a perspective drawing of a monorail.

Descriptive Phrases

Forerunners; knowing the means to get from point A to point B, either for oneself or for humanity; articulating social problems and solutions; knowing what missing component must be acquired to reach some goal (put off dealing with the very problems that are hanging them up); keeping a chain of reasoning before the mind's eye; pushing people along a mental trajectory; interjecting missing facts that push people toward correct conclusions; confident exposition (salesmanship); planning a campaign in detailed stages; maintaining one's goals in an unsupportive environment vs. jumping ahead of oneself or being sidetracked (feel left behind); inventions; physical sciences; realistic blueprints for the future; articulated visions of things to come.

Examples

Alfred North Whitehead (Pluto. Philosopher of science who wrote *Science in the Modern World*, a critique of Newton); Arthur Conan Doyle (Pluto. Writer—Sherlock Holmes stories); Albert Einstein (Neptune. Scientific genius—theory of relativity); Dr. Bart Bok (Sun. Astronomer, popularizer); Keir Dullea (Uranus. Actor—*2001: A Space Odyssey*); Frank Herbert (South Node. Sci-fi writer—*Dune*); Transatlantic cable finished (Pluto. 8/5/1858); Isambard Brunel (Mercury. Engineer of the Great Western Railway); Mario Andretti (Mars. Auto racer); Queen Elizabeth I of England (Moon); Emmeline Pankhurst (Pluto. Suffragette); John Dewey (Pluto. Progressive educational theorist); Harper Lee (Sun. Author—*To Kill a Mockingbird*); M. C. Escher (Mars. Artist—structural puzzles).

9 Taurus

A homeless shelter on Christmas day. Volunteers pass out presents while a folk musician sings a song about social justice.

Descriptive Phrases

Telling it like it is; sincere emotional communication vs. turning a deaf ear to other people's suffering, needs, and desires; gift-wrapping one's message in an attractive artistic package vs. blunt assertions of fact; telling people what they need to hear about their own situation whether they want to hear it or not (realize that people cannot fill a need until they acknowledge it); distinguishing between what people want and what they need in order to grow; emotional and spiritual nurturing of the young; teaching children lessons about human values vs. loosening up and playing with them on their own level; celebrating life's rituals in a thoughtful, relevant way; dependably dramatizing one's ideals in everyday life; sharing the gifts of the spirit; music and imaginative literature.

Examples

Phil Ochs (Saturn. Folk singer); Judy Collins (South Node. Folk singer—"Marat Sade"); Barbara Streisand (Mercury. Singer, actress—*Funny Girl*); Tom Snyder (Venus. Plainspoken TV anchorman, interviewer); Max Robinson (South Node. Newscaster who went public with having AIDS); Carole King (Jupiter, Saturn. Singer, songwriter); Juliette Low (Pluto. Founder of the Girl Scouts); Terry Gilliam (Jupiter. Monty Python comic, directed *Time Bandits, Brazil*); Jim Henson (Uranus. Puppeteer—*The Muppets*); Franz Kafka (South Node. Morbidly imaginative writer); Frank Zappa (Saturn. Rock singer); Isadora Duncan (Neptune. Dancer with a reckless lifestyle); Dionne Warwick (Saturn. Singer, telephone-psychic entrepreneur); Spanky McFarland (Jupiter. Child actor—*Our Gang*).

10 Taurus

A Red Cross nurse calls for help on the battlefield, a bleeding child at her feet.

Descriptive Phrases

Moral courage in dealing with tough problems; heroism; disciplining oneself to diligently perform one's moral duty; enlistment in a cause vs. extricating oneself from a destructive behavior or course of action (pacifism); sensitivity to human suffering; dealing with human cruelty (emotional retaliation, sadistic impulses); healing the emotional wounds of childhood; victimization vs. acting out, like a playground bully who is being beaten up at home (mired in victim/inflictor psychology, always planning a new move in some ongoing power struggle); cutting to the heart of a situation through empathetic understanding; reading people's hearts; oratorical power; having the heart to care.

Examples

Clara Barton founds the Red Cross (Jupiter. 5/21/1881); Cesar Chavez (Sun. Labor organizer); the original Lassie (Saturn. Canine hero); Joseph Heller (Sun. Writer—*Catch 22*); Robert Altman (Mars. Film director—*M*A*S*H, Short Cuts*); Lina Wertmuller (Jupiter. Film director—*Swept Away, Seven Beauties*); Laurie Metcalf (Moon. Actress—played Roseanne's sister); Ian Brady (Uranus. Sadistic murderer of children); Hans Christian Andersen (Moon. Fairy-tale collector, writer—*The Ugly Duckling*); Willie Nelson (Sun. Country-rock singer, farm-aid activist); Frances Farmer (Moon. Leftist actress—institutionalized and given shock treatments); Jack Nicholson (Uranus. Actor who specializes in nasty or sadistic roles); Mary Tyler Moore (Uranus. Actress—*The Mary Tyler Moore Show*, where she is alternatively assertive and bullied).

11 Taurus

A Dutch woman pulls weeds and plants seeds, while her daughter employs a shiny tin watering can to water the flowers.

Descriptive Phrases

The mirror of the heart, which reflects things as they could be if they were properly cared for; recognizing good and bad seeds in people's character; promoting inborn talents in others (mentorship); offering gentle guidance to youth (bad relations with parents or children); speaking to the heart; incisive, commonsense explanations (socially awkward, shy); having a pleasant, attractive facade; displaying good breeding vs. allowing one's worst traits to take over one's life, like some rampant weed (must examine their own motives as closely as they do other people's); nurturing the world as one would a garden; promoting good tendencies in society, and rooting out destructive social usages; planting an idea that catches on in a big way; growing into the future.

Examples

Judy Collins (Sun. Folk singer, activist); Dick Clark (North Node. *American Bandstand* host, promoted rock-and-roll musicians, cleaned up rock's image, helped desegregate television); Benjamin Spock (Sun. Baby-book author, political activist); Audrey Hepburn (Chiron. Actress—*My Fair Lady*, worked on problems of world hunger for the United Nations); Joe Sorrentino (Uranus. Judge, juvenile rights advocate); David Baltimore (Uranus. Nobel biochemist who worked with RNA); Cesar Chavez (Venus. Strike leader for grape and lettuce harvesters); Sam Peckinpah (Mars. Director—*Invasion of the Body Snatchers*); Judy Blume (Uranus. Author of socially realistic children's books); Dick York (Jupiter. The first Darren on *Bewitched*); first showing of Disney's *Snow White* (Uranus. 12/27/1937); Ringo Starr (Jupiter. Drummer for The Beatles—"Octopus's Garden"); Gertrude Stein (North Node. Writer, ran an intellectual salon).

12 Taurus

At a drawing table, an army general sketches out a further refinement of an upcoming military campaign, pausing to get feedback from his adjutant.

Descriptive Phrases

Setting concrete goals and going after them; visionaries who discern future potentials that are in harmony with the trajectory of history; catching the outlines of the future; detailed visualization of one's objectives and course of action; cautious calculation vs. hastily seizing an opportunity (ruthless opportunism—grabbing whatever comes one's way); deciding what is worth fighting for; mustering support for an ambitious project or cause; inspired leadership (military or cultural); having an impact on others; cutting a bold figure; attention to aesthetic detail (precision without fussiness); designing and implementing plans for a livable future; kibbitzing in other people's projects vs. knowing what one wants for oneself.

Examples

Napoleon (Uranus. Conqueror); George Lucas (Venus. Director—*Star Wars*); Bella Abzug (South Node. Politician and activist in radical causes); Robert Enrico (Mercury. Directs training films for the French armed forces); Walt Disney (South Node. Cartoonist, creator of Disneyland theme park); José Marti (Saturn. Revolutionary leader); Ulysses S. Grant (Jupiter. Defeated the Confederacy); Ed Asner (North Node. Boss on *The Mary Tyler Moore Show*, activist); Barbara Feldon (Saturn. Second banana on *Get Smart*—always getting Max out of trouble); Jane Jacobs (Sun. City planner with communitarian values); Henri Matisse (Jupiter. Highly linear artist); Kathy Bates (North Node. Actress—*Dolores Claiborne*); J. Robert Oppenheimer (Mars. Head of the Manhattan Project to create the atomic bomb); Harold Washington (Venus. Mayor of Chicago); Bob Crane (Mars. Actor—*Hogan's Heroes*); David Hockney (Uranus. Cartoonish modern painter).

13 Taurus

A porter studies a pile of luggage and then deftly hoists the bags to his shoulders.

Descriptive Phrases

Assessment—seeing the basic problem underlying seemingly unrelated problems; getting a good handle on a situation; makeshift but serviceable solutions; calmly reassessing one's balance of priorities and readjusting one's use of time and energy accordingly (juggling acts); serving society by taking on its weightier problems, but only on one's own terms (bail out when personal freedom is threatened, ramblers, working-class heroes); keeping one's head and shoulders above one's worldly problems; cheerfully accepting one's lot in life (worriers); escaping a rut vs. being mired in problems; robust and competent handling of everyday problems vs. obstinately sticking with a method that isn't working; putting in the requisite effort; taking the bull by the horns; resourcefulness.

Examples

Henry Ford (Pluto. Capitalist empire-builder); Ursula LeGuin (North Node. Sci-fi writer—*Earth-Sea Trilogy, The Dispossessed*); Bruno Ganz (Saturn. Actor—*Wings of Desire*); Slavery abolished in the U. S. (Pluto. 12/18/1865); Anne Frank (Chiron. Diarist in hiding from the Nazis); Manuel Garcia (Pluto. Bullfighter); Ludwig von Beethoven (Uranus. Classical composer); Ann B. Davis (Sun. Actress—peppy domestic in *The Brady Bunch* and *The Bob Newhart Show*); Fran Drescher (South Node. Peppy domestic in *The Nanny*); Pete Seeger (Sun. Folk singer, political activist—"If I Had a Hammer"); Willie Nelson (Venus. Country-rock singer); Isak Dinesen (Mercury. Author—*Out of Africa*); Pelé (Jupiter, Saturn. Soccer superstar, incredibly deft ball-handler); George Washington Carver (Pluto. Black agriculturalist and inventor).

14 Taurus

Crayfish are groping toward land, while high above the shore a modern city rises upon the ruins of an ancient civilization[13].

Descriptive Phrases

The slow, natural evolution of consciousness or social structures; the instinctive urge to press forward despite internal and external resistance; small steps forward that eventually result in tidal shifts; learning from the mistakes of the past; crawling out of the muck of ignorance and prejudice and rebuilding society along more humanitarian lines; shedding outlived social structures vs. getting stuck in a shell; crawling out from under an oppressive situation once one has seen the light of day (tentative fumbling while one is still "in the dark"); forming an underground brotherhood or sisterhood that shares breakthroughs in consciousness and tries to guide human evolution; refusing to be bullied or pushed back once one has seen where one is going; the Moon card of the tarot.

Examples

Karl Marx (Sun. Social and political theorist, revolutionary); Germaine Greer (Uranus. Feminist theorist); Helen Keller (Neptune. Blind and deaf, socialist); William Butler Yeats (Pluto, Venus. Poet, Rosicrucian occultist, Irish nationalist); Alice Bailey (Neptune. Theosophist, fought for Indian independence and birth control); Thomas Huxley (Sun. Evolutionist—"survival of the fittest"); Teilhard de Chardin (Neptune. Evolutionary mystic, geologist); Lester Thurow (Uranus. Farseeing economist); Franklin Roosevelt (Neptune, Stationary. Farseeing president, put the eye on the pyramid on the dollar bill); Barbara Tuchman (Saturn. Historian—*A Distant Mirror, The March of Folly*); Virginia Woolf (Neptune, Stationary. Writer—*Orlando*); John Lennon (Saturn, Jupiter. Beatle); ASPCA established (Pluto. 4/10/1866).

15 Taurus

The figure of a magician in a top hat, as seen in a dream. He opens a black bag and plays some strange music on an Indian flute, whereupon a snake rises from the bag.

Descriptive Phrases

Drawing artistic inspiration from the deeper levels of the subconscious; materializing a dream; creating magical works of art that explore archetypes in the group unconscious; seizing people's imaginations and taking them for a magic carpet ride; resourcefulness—finding the right solution in one's bag of tricks; finding something new and mysterious and playing with it to discover its potentials; displaying an unusual talent or potency (animal magnetism); working with sexual energies (aggressive come-ons); connecting up with the primitive, nonverbal layers of the human psyche; shamanism—following up on signs or omens found in nature or in dreams; using divination or observed synchronicities to align oneself with powerful natural forces.

Examples

Orson Welles (Sun. Film-noir director, actor, magician); Pearl Buck (North Node. Writer—*The Good Earth*); H. G. Wells (Pluto. Philosopher, writer—*The Time Machine*); Carla Bley (Uranus. Crazed jazz keyboard artist); Ray Manzarek (Uranus. Keyboard player for The Doors); Carlos Castaneda (Moon. Occultist—*The Adventures of Don Juan*); Barbara Steele (Uranus. Queen of horror—*Black Sunday*); Jon Voight (Uranus. Actor—*Deliverance*); Debbie Harry (Mars. Rock singer—Blondie); Antonio Gaudi (Saturn. Architect who used wild natural forms); Alexei Panshin (Saturn. Science fiction writer—*Earth Magic*); Raquel Welch (Saturn. Sexual icon—*The Magic Christian*); Michael Palin (Sun. Comic—*Monty Python*); Ronald Reagan (North Node. President with a bag of tricks); A. E. Waite (Jupiter. Occultist who designed the Waite tarot deck); Franz Cumont (Pluto. Author of *Astrology and Religion among the Greeks and Romans*); Joan Prado (Mars. Psychic composer).

16 Taurus

Dashing old artist tries to impart his vision of life to an audience of young painters.

Descriptive Phrases

Slowly materializing a romantic vision of oneself, and sharing it with the world; ministering to the aesthetic and emotional needs of humanity (the arts); cultivating a broad audience through charm and accessibility (sweethearts—attract a lot of love); patiently working through conflicts of desire and passion to achieve psychological integration and emotional health (tormented by discrepancies between outer persona and untamed emotions); determined effort to overcome personal obstacles vs. getting stuck (modesty vs. self-doubt); attaining self-knowledge through a lifetime of reflection vs. falling into a rut; giving support to other people's dreams (buy into superficial images of beauty or coolness); bold and uncompromising integrity of vision.

Examples

Pablo Picasso (Neptune. Cubist artist); Käthe Kollwitz (Pluto. Artist—themes of suffering humanity); Scott Joplin (Pluto. Ragtime pianist, composer); Oscar Wilde (Uranus. Poet, playwright—*The Importance of Being Earnest*); Marie Dressler (Jupiter. Silent films—*Tillie's Punctured Romance*); Carl Jung (Moon. Archetypal psychologist); Rudolf Valentino (Sun. Romantic actor in silents—*The Sheik*); Basil Rathbone (North Node. Actor—*Sherlock Holmes, Robin Hood*); Ali McGraw (Uranus. Activist, actress—*Love Story, Goodbye, Columbus*); Carole King (Mars. Songwriter—"Tapestry"); Claude Bragdon (Pluto. Architectural theorist—*The Beautiful Necessity*); Marie Curie (Pluto. Scientist, codiscovered radium); Stuart Brand (South Node. Editor of *The Whole Earth Catalog*); Konstantin Tsiolkovsky (Jupiter. Rocketry pioneer, first to predict space travel).

17 Taurus

Sword-wielding crusaders battle the Saracens to secure a bridge into enemy territory.

Descriptive Phrases

The crusading spirit; fighting for the truth in every situation; sharp political, social, or spiritual analysis; seeing the crux of a debate; winning an argument through superior logic vs. bullying people with bluster or force (fight dirty); developing confidence in one's own viewpoint (ideologues who demonize their opponents, inner struggles to put the passions at the service of the spiritual will); arming others with the "sword of truth"; cutting the Gordian knot—slicing through big, messy problems with simple but radical solutions (will move mountains to clear a path to the future); decisive leadership of large political or business enterprises; establishing a free flow of goods or ideas (transportation issues); fighting to secure the future.

Examples

Franklin Roosevelt (Jupiter. U. S. president who mobilized the country during the Depression and during World War II); Adolf Hitler (Venus, Mars. Fought for world domination under the German sword); George Eastman (Uranus. Established Eastman Kodak); Oliver Stone (Moon. Film director—*Platoon, JFK*); Elizabeth Clare Prophet (Uranus. Gnostic Christian leader with apocalyptic, racist ideas); Suez Canal opens (Pluto. 11/17/1869); Transcontinental railroad finished (Pluto. 5/10/1869); David Frost (Uranus. TV commentator—*That Was the Week That Was*); Roseanne Barr (Jupiter. Argumentative comedienne—*Roseanne*); Emperor Charles V (Saturn. Last Holy Roman Emperor who believed he would fulfill the prophecies of freeing the Holy Lands); St. Francesca Cabrini (Saturn. Nun who set up many Christian hospitals and orphanages); Sir Alexander Fleming (Neptune. Discovered penicillin); Stonewall Jackson (Saturn. Confederate general); Rosa Luxembourg (Pluto. German communist revolutionary leader).

18 Taurus

Populist leader hangs the party banner from the window of his new headquarters, and then makes a stirring speech to the crowd below.

Descriptive Phrases

Acting as a spokesperson for some popular cause; resonating to the will of the people, and giving voice to their hopes; leadership; openly challenging the powers that be; showing one's true colors (revolutionaries); setting up a business or enterprise to suit oneself; organizational and business skills; conscientiousness; calm dependability that wins over others; oratorical skill; grassroots organizing; forging alliances (bullheaded ideologues who see only one side); single-minded dedication to the realization of one's ideals (bulldoze opponents); breathing new life into the situation; throwing out outworn traditions and throwing open the door to new possibilities; keeping up with modern sensibilities (trendy); fighting for freedom and independence.

Examples

Gandhi (Pluto. Leader in fight for Indian independence); Lenin (Pluto. Revolutionary communist leader); Gary Snyder (Sun. Poet, environmentalist); Emma Goldman (Pluto. Anarchist); Philip La Follette (Sun. Politician—Progressive Party); Charles Fourier (Uranus. Utopian thinker); Cosimo de Medici (Pluto. Benevolent despot—patron of Ficino's Neoplatonic Academy); Edmund Dulac (Neptune. Children's book illustrator); Chuck Berry (Mars. Early and highly influential rock musician); Frank Lloyd Wright (Pluto. Architect, founder of the Prairie School); Bramwell Booth (Uranus. Founded Volunteers of America); Werner von Braun (Saturn. Sold U. S. the space program); Brigham Young approves polygamy (Saturn. 8/29/1852); Marilyn Ferguson (Mars. Writer—*The Aquarian Conspiracy*); Jerry Rubin (Uranus. Yippie leader in the 1960s).

19 Taurus

A beautiful queen stands on a flowery hillside and gazes out upon billowing clouds. Her lover kisses her bare shoulder from behind, but she does not turn.

Descriptive Phrases

Susceptibility to natural or physical beauty; attunement to the most beautiful possibilities of nature (the Empress Card); materializing one's ideals; shaping one's experience according to one's wishes, especially on a romantic level (daydreamers who build cloud castles); romantic idealism (unrealistic standards, may be taken unawares by other people's coarse motives); guarding one's spiritual dignity and autonomy vs. being tricked into bad deals; showing discrimination in love vs. plucking the daisies in the Elysian fields; courtship; amorousness; Venus and Mars (expect to be treated as gods); living life as a romantic adventure; openness to life's luxuriant possibilities; graciously sharing a rich fullness of life experience.

Examples

Paul McCartney (Venus. King of romantic ballads—The Beatles, Wings); Glenda Jackson (Sun. Actress—*Women in Love*); Albert Finney (Sun. Actor—*Tom Jones*); Donovan (Sun. Folk-rock singer, "Jennifer Juniper"); Anna Magnani (Moon. "Earth-mother" actress—*The Miracle, Open City*); John F. Kennedy (Mars. Womanizing president); James Galway (Uranus. Classical flutist); Alice Roosevelt Longworth (Neptune. Wit, *bon vivant*); Colette (Pluto. Author of racy romantic novels); Cicely Tyson (Uranus. Actress—*The Autobiography of Miss Jane Pittman, Sounder*); Charles Fourier (Uranus. Hedonistic Utopian thinker); Thomas Hart Benton (Venus. Painter of dreamy American landscapes—"Persephone"); Maxfield Parrish (Pluto. Artist and illustrator, specializing in beautiful women in natural landscapes); Billy Joel (Sun. Singer); Joe Namath (Moon. Football superstar, *bon vivant*); Demi Moore (Moon. Actress—*Striptease*).

20 Taurus

Flying amid wisps of clouds, the pilot of a reconnaissance glider surveys a line of tramping soldiers and radios their commander that they need to change their course.

Descriptive Phrases

Getting an overview of one's situation; seeing the larger sweep of events; redirecting energies into a more productive path; acting upon vital new possibilities in the wind vs. trudging along some unproductive or dangerous path out of sheer inertia; plotting one's next move vs. being caught off-guard and having to think on one's feet (mad scrambles); knowing when to gather one's forces and attack and when to sidestep an obstacle and let a crisis blow over (cultural crusaders who glide along the positive cultural currents of their times); keeping sight of distant goals; watching the horizon for upcoming events vs. accepting life's essential unpredictability (fatalistic, feel that the course of events is beyond their control); farsightedness.

Examples

Bob Dylan (Saturn. Folk-rock singer-songwriter—"All along the Watchtower," "Blowing in the Wind"); Peter Bergman (Uranus. Comic—The Firesign Theater); Ellen Goodman (Jupiter. *Boston Globe* political columnist); John Maynard Keynes (Neptune. Economist); Ariel Durant (Saturn. Historian—*The Story of Civilization*); Johan Huizinga (Pluto. Historian—*The Autumn of the Middle Ages*); Alcide de Gaspari (Venus. Italian leader who prevented the communists from taking over in post-World War II Italy); Orville Wright (Pluto. Airplane inventor); Phil and Steve Mahre (Sun. Olympic skiers); Tina Turner (Uranus. Rock star, actress—*Mad Max Beyond Thunderdome*); Cantinflas (Saturn. Actor—*Around the World in Eighty Days*); Robert Taylor (Saturn. Actor, Navy pilot); Hugh Dowding (Venus. Head of British air-raid defense during the Battle of Britain); Minnie Theobald (Pluto. Mystic—*The Three Levels of Consciousness*).

21 Taurus

A finger points to an uncannily relevant passage in a book of ancient wisdom.

Descriptive Phrases

Pointing out relevant truths; summing up the situation in succinct terms; gathering enough facts and observations to arrive at a definitive conclusion (summary pronouncements); forcing people to look at some overlooked truth; explicating the deeper meaning of events; finding truths within fiction vs. exploding false stories that society tells itself, especially about other races; examining inherited cultural myths (contempt for common opinion, finger-pointing criticism); putting one's finger on underlying causes and hidden motivations (wary of being conned, but may be conartists themselves); uncanny discernment (psychic powers); translating a truth from another language (or dimension) to more familiar terms; penetrating analysis of underlying realities.

Examples

Bob Dylan (Saturn. Aphoristic folk singer); Grace Slick (Uranus. Lead singer—Jefferson Airplane); Harry Truman (Neptune. U. S. president, noted for blunt honesty); Margaret Sanger (Neptune. Early advocate of birth control); Sigmund Freud (Uranus. Founder of psychoanalysis); Jeddu Krishnamurti (Sun. Indian spiritual teacher); Paul Goodman (Saturn. Radical educational theorist—*Growing Up Absurd*); Louise Lasser (Uranus. Lead actress in muckraking TV series *Mary Hartman, Mary Hartman*); Guglielmo Marconi (Pluto, Venus. Inventor of wireless telegraphy); André Gregory (Sun. Actor, intellectual—*My Dinner with André*); Paul Solomon (Uranus. Psychic, commune leader); Franz Kafka (Neptune. Writer—*The Trial*); Barbara Watterson (Uranus. Egyptologist); Hubert Urban (Mercury. Neurologist, parapsychological researcher); Sinclair Lewis (Neptune. Novelist, social critic—*Babbitt*); Katharine Hepburn (Jupiter. Frank and insightful actress).

22 Taurus

Returning to the hive from the flowery fields of heaven, a honeybee uses its antennae to excitedly communicate its discovery to several other bees.[14]

Descriptive Phrases

Bridging two worlds; determination to impart an important message from a higher vibrational plane (obnoxiously insistent, have a bee in their bonnets, spew out undigested and often incoherent impressions and ideas); providing spiritual nourishment to a public that is starving for spiritual purpose; getting people on one's wavelength; raising people's vibrational levels (stir up a bee's nest of confusion, troublemakers, pranksters); having one's "antennae" out for the images of the group-mind (psychism); attacking social myths by weaving counter-mythologies or fantasies from lucidly recalled mental impressions (tall tales); gaining a transcendent if alien perspective on a difficult worldly situation; inspired rants vs. information dumps; fast-talking monologues vs. psychic communication.

Examples

Lily Tomlin (Uranus. Comic—*The Search for Signs of Intelligent Life in the Universe*); Paul Krassner (Chiron. Editor of *The Realist*, prankster); Sandra Bernhard (Venus. Standup comic, actress—*King of Comedy*); Spalding Gray (Saturn. Mile-a-minute monologuist); Elliot Gould (South Node. Actor—*Getting Straight, M*A*S*H*); Curt Ducasse (Chiron. Brown philosophy professor, research in parapsychology and ESP); Helen Nearing (Moon. Author—*Develop Your Psychic Skills*); Hunter Thompson (Uranus. Writer—*Fear and Loathing: On the Campaign Trail, '72*); A. E. Van Vogt (Saturn. Sci-fi writer—*Slan*, about telepathic human mutants); Federico Fellini (South Node. Surrealistic filmmaker—*8 ½*); John McLaughlin (Saturn. Jazz musician); Katharine Hepburn (Sun. Actress—*Bringing Up Baby*); Bob Dylan (Moon. Folk-rock singer—"Subterranean Homesick Blues").

23 Taurus

A jeweler casts a critical eye on a jewel that he has just cut, then tosses it carelessly into an informal display of varicolored gems.

Descriptive Phrases

Seeing life from an odd but curiously insightful angle; distinguishing real from false; directing public attention from the glittering and sham to what has eternal value (scatter pearls of insight indiscriminately, hoping some will find an appreciative audience); letting the lovelight of the heart provide the unifying focus of the personality vs. losing sight of life's meaning and letting oneself fall apart; social activism based on a sense of life's preciousness; alerting others to destructive social values (sarcasm); merchandising one's talents without forgetting which parts of oneself are nonnegotiable; craftsmanship; being a perfectionist vs. humbly remembering one's own flaws; being critical vs. seeing the divine light in others (spiritual teachers who are treasured for their caring wisdom); planting seeds of love; the Pleiades.

Examples

Joan Baez (Uranus. Folk and protest singer—"Diamonds and Rust"); Neil Diamond (Uranus. Pop singer); Spike Lee (South Node. Filmmaker—*Do the Right Thing*); Frank Zappa (Uranus. Trenchantly sarcastic rock singer); Petra Kelly (North Node. Human rights and Green Party activist); Mao Tse Tung (Jupiter. Once-idolized Chinese leader); Eleanor Roosevelt (Neptune. First Lady, activist); Carole King (Uranus. Singer-songwriter—"Tapestry"); Barbara Feldon (Uranus. Actress—*Get Smart*); Jack Benny (Jupiter. Beloved comedian); Norman Rockwell (Jupiter. Whimsical illustrator with positive social messages); Max Planck (Jupiter. Physicist who developed the quantum theory); D. S. Windell (Neptune. Swindler, embezzler); Hazrat Inayat Khan (Saturn. Musician, Sufi teacher).

24 Taurus

At the entrance of a cavern, an Indian brave sits proudly on his horse, scalp locks at his belt.

Descriptive Phrases

Developing physical and psychosexual confidence (push people around physically or sexually); keeping score (notches on one's gun or one's bedpost); getting important experiences under one's belt (retreat into a "heroic" fantasy life); physical life as the lens through which all the images of the psyche must either find expression or be cast into the subconscious (perverse championing of shadowy potencies); fighting to gain authority within one's own "tribe" (feel unappreciated); keeping up one's courage in the face of defeats; bravely championing one's own talents in the public sphere vs. hapless impotence in responding to personal challenges; physical training; learning to rely on the body's rhythms and instinctive wisdom; mastering one's fears.

Examples

Bruce Lee (Uranus. Martial arts); Natalia Makarova (Uranus. Classical ballet dancer); Mother Teresa (North Node. Worked with the poor and dying in India); Harry Tracy (Pluto. Murderer, burglar, rustler); Studs Terkel (Saturn. Author—*Hard Times: An Oral History of the Great Depression*); Max von Sydow (North Node. Actor—*The Seventh Seal*); Nikos Kazantzakis (Neptune. Author—*Christ Recrucified, Zorba the Greek*); Ann Margaret (Jupiter. Actress—Kitten with a Whip); Debbie Harry (Venus. Rock singer); James Mason (Sun. Actor—*20,000 Leagues Under the Sea*); Pablo Picasso (Jupiter. Abstract artist); H. Rider Haggard (Uranus. Writer—*She, King Solomon's Mines*); Carl Jung (Pluto. Archetypal psychologist); J.R.R. Tolkien (North Node. Author—*Lord of the Rings*); John F. Kennedy (Jupiter. Womanizing president); Jerry Rubin (South Node. Sixties radical); Gary Cooper (South Node. Dignified actor—*High Noon*).

25 Taurus

An artist's model poses with her arms upraised and her body twisted, while a satyr-like sculptor chisels her image from a column of black marble.

Descriptive Phrases

Sublimating raw sexual energy into solid artistic achievements; developing a disciplined relationship with one's Muse, or having Muse-like relationships with the opposite sex; putting lovers on a pedestal vs. dragging them into wild, unbridled sex (leering lustfulness—passions can get out of control); appreciation of natural beauty; staying attractive and in shape (narcissism); bringing one's deeper qualities to the surface to be admired by the world; making oneself into a work of art; discovering and exulting in one's extravagant personal style; physical and sexual vitality; sharing one's *joie de vivre* through art; solitary toil followed by public unveilings; close students of nature; dark, dizzying whirlwinds of creative activity.

Examples

Henry Miller (North Node. Novelist—*Tropic of Cancer, Black Spring*); Erica Jong (Saturn. Writer—*Fear of Flying, Fanny*); Tina Turner (Saturn. Rock-and-roll star with tempestuous love life); George Bernard Shaw (Uranus. Playwright—*Pygmalion*, upon which the movie *My Fair Lady* was based); Swami Muktananda (Sun. Kundalini yoga guru); Bela Lugosi (Saturn. Actor—*Dracula*); Lisa Bonet (Moon. Actress—*Angel Heart*); Philip Roth (Chiron. Writer—*Portnoy's Complaint*); Leonardo da Vinci (Sun. Renaissance artist, inventor); Albert Einstein (Pluto. Atomic physicist, philosopher); Twyla Tharp (Saturn. Modern dance); Edward Hopper (Saturn. Realist artist); Mata Hari (Pluto. Courtesan, dancer, and spy); Norman Lindsay (Pluto. Erotic artist who was the subject of the film *Sirens*); Robert von Gulik (North Node. Expert on Oriental erotic art, writer of racy detective stories set in ancient China).

26 Taurus

A man in an exaggerated Mexican get-up serenades his girlfriend from below her window.

Descriptive Phrases

Romantic idealization; courtly adoration of the beloved; sincerity of feeling vs. throwing around outworn emotional forms; baroque formality vs. unadorned expression of sentiment; creating and inhabiting a romantic or comic persona; making oneself a work of art (cartoon-like self-caricature, use costumes and eccentric behavior to create a recognizable personality); sublimating passion into highly original artistic work; visualizing some as-yet-unmaterialized ideal (fantasy, science fiction); giving form to a new vision or vibration; uniting with others in some lofty vision of the future; visionary leadership vs. deluding people with pie-in-the-sky promises; sincerity of belief and feeling vs. entertaining frivolity.

Examples

Johnny Depp (Mercury. Actor—*Don Juan de Marco, Edward Scissorhands*); Al Jolson (Neptune. Blackface crooner—"Mammy"); Beverly Sills (Jupiter. Operatic soprano); Carrie Fisher (Moon. Actress—Princess Leia in *Star Wars*); John Lennon (Uranus. Singer-songwriter specializing in love ballads); Olivia Newton-John (North Node. Singer—*Grease, Xanadu*); Geena Davis (South Node. Actress—*Earth Girls Are Easy*); Marshall Applewhite (Sun. Cult leader, mass suicide); Dean Martin (Jupiter, Mars. Romantic crooner, fantasy adventure movies); Harpo Marx (Jupiter. Harpist, comic—The Marx Brothers); Carl Barks (South Node. Cartoonist—*Donald Duck*); Bugs Bunny first appears (Uranus. 7/27/1940); Billie Burke (Neptune. Glinda in *The Wizard of Oz*); Harlan Ellison (Mars. Sci-fi writer); D. H. Lawrence (Neptune. Writer—*Lady Chatterley's Lover*); Daniel Pinkwater (Saturn. Writer of funny children's fantasies—*Fat Men from Space, The Snark-Out Boys and the Avocado of Death*).

27 Taurus

Smiling guardedly, a withered squaw sells a piece of turquoise jewelry to a fat tourist.

Descriptive Phrases

Looking oppression in the eye; penetrating analysis of power relationships; fighting for human dignity and social justice; touchstones; recognizing friends and enemies by whether they receive an offered truth; leveling with people (warning rattles vs. venomous tongue-lashings); political radicalism (intolerant ideologues); spying out significant details that give away a misrepresentation; puncturing complicated pseudo-explanations; bemused view of human stupidity (loopy humor, surrealism); demanding social acknowledgment (feel marginalized, present their views like performers in a surreal sideshow); clear, unemotional perspective on life (don't acknowledge their own feelings); rejecting the tyranny of common assumptions; eloquent protest.

Examples

Buffy St. Marie (Uranus. Folk singer, Native American activist); Georgia O'Keeffe (Neptune. Artist, Southwestern subjects); Leon Trotsky (Pluto. Communist revolutionary); Muhammad Ali (Uranus. Boxer, opponent of the Vietnam War); Huey Newton (Uranus. Black Panther leader); Dennis Hopper (Sun. Actor who plays crazed fanatics); Ayatollah Khomeini (Sun. Fanatical Iranian revolutionary leader); Dietrich Bonhoeffer (Jupiter. German pastor who led Christian opposition to Nazi anti-Semitism, was hanged); Jules Feiffer (North Node. Loopy leftist political cartoonist); Michael Palin (Moon. Comic—*Monty Python*); Bob Dylan (Uranus. Folk singer who is both surrealistic and hyperrealistic); Jane Curtin (North Node. Testy newswoman and conehead on *Saturday Night Live,*); Doris Lessing (South Node. Feminist author—*Prisons We Choose to Live Inside, The Golden Notebook*); John Irving (Uranus. Author—*The World According to Garp*); Dr. Albert Hoffman (Jupiter. Discovered LSD).

28 Taurus

An older woman, ready for romance,
inspects herself appraisingly in the mirror.

Descriptive Phrases

Mature understanding of what can and can't be changed; earthy savvy; determination to prevail over obstacles or physical handicaps; keeping as fit and attractive as possible; realistic approach to love; going after what one wants (romantic escapades—reining in vs. indulging a wild streak); mature appraisal of one's situation based on a rich fund of experience vs. falling into the same dumb mistakes; leaving defeat behind and making a new start (ignore mocking voices, both internal and external); refusing to be pushed around (pushy); political awareness grounded in personal experience; fighting for human rights, including women's rights; spiritual and physical fatigue vs. rising to the occasion; spunk.

Examples

Katharine Hepburn (Moon. Actress—*On Golden Pond, African Queen*); Rosalind Russell (North Node. Actress—*Auntie Mame*); Joe Namath (Mercury. Quarterback, *bon vivant*, crippled knees); Rosa Parks (Saturn. Began Black bus boycott in the South); Franklin Roosevelt (Pluto. President, New Deal programs, adulterer, wheelchair-bound but incredibly active); Clara Blandick (Pluto. Aunty Em in *The Wizard of Oz*); Elizabeth Kenny (Neptune. Nurse who developed a muscle therapy for polio); Reverend Jesse Jackson (Saturn. Black political leader); Richard Nixon (Saturn. President, "He's back"); Helen Keller (Pluto. Overcame multiple handicaps); Aretha Franklin (Uranus. The queen of soul music); Paul Simon (Saturn. Folk singer); Stephen King (North Node. Writer—*Dolores Claiborne, The Shawshank Redemption*); Peter Coyote (Saturn. Actor, writer—*Sleeping Where I Fall*).

29 Taurus

Moses argues with the Pharaoh about the enslavement of the Jews. The Pharaoh threatens to kill him for his insolence, but Moses proceeds with his argument, undeterred.

Descriptive Phrases

Moral courage; moral or political leadership; showdowns; confronting or blocking some evil despite personal risk; trying to get through people's insensitivity and make them see the light (Messianic intensity); engaging others in honest dialogue (may rely on force if argument doesn't work, need to exercise the heart as well as the mind in coming to terms with others); hammering out an argument or a position; driving home a point (poor listeners—have to have the final word); passionate oratory in service of the common man (should deal with common problems in common language and avoid philosophical abstruseness); living out the consequences of one's argument by adapting one's lifestyle to one's philosophy; being crucified by the truth; sense of inescapable spiritual duty.

Examples

Ho Chi Minh (Sun. Vietnamese revolutionary leader); Lorraine Hansberry (Sun. Black playwright—*A Raisin in the Sun*); Galileo Galilei (Mars. Stood up for the Copernican theory over the Church's threats of torture); Linda McCartney (Saturn. Photographer, animal rights activist); Pete Townsend (Sun. Lead guitarist of The Who—*Tommy*); Malcolm X (Sun. Black Muslim leader); Czar Alexander II (Mercury. Freed the Russian serfs); Bertrand Russell (Sun. Mathematician, atheist philosopher); Antonia Fraser (Uranus. Historical writer—*Mary, Queen of Scots*); Paul Ricoeur (Saturn. Philosopher—*Freedom and Nature*); Barbara Streisand (Saturn and Uranus. Actress—*Prince of Tides, Yentl*); Ernest Renan (Jupiter. Historian—*The Life of Jesus*); Pier Paolo Pasolini (Moon. Filmmaker—*The Gospel According to St. Matthew*).

30 Taurus

A peacock spreads its feathers on the grounds of an old mansion.

Descriptive Phrases

Showy displays of knowledge or talents; stylistic flair; class acts; daring extension of traditional artistic forms (tail end of a tradition, splashy effects, mannered excess); appreciation of beauty (need to attend to personal grooming, manners, and poise, even if they consider such things superficial); peacocks as guard-animals—gaining admittance to circles that define cultural values vs. scandalous displays that close society's doors; deciding whether to play insider games or outsider games; penetrating social criticism concerning the use of society's money and resources; serving as an influential arbiter of cultural values vs. undercutting one's position with vain and peevish moral posturing; packaging content in harmonious social forms.

Examples

Igor Stravinsky (Pluto. Composer—*The Firebird Suite*); Richard Wagner (Venus. Decadent classical composer); Bette Davis (Venus. Great melodramatic actress—*Jezebel, Dead Ringer*); Sir Lawrence Olivier (Sun. Shakespearean actor, ham); Bela Lugosi (Pluto. As Count Dracula, he spread his cape like a peacock); Martha Stewart (Uranus. Offers high-class luxuries on a budget); Cher (Sun. Peacock-like clothing, starred in *Mask*, which deals with the social acceptance of a deformed child); George Wallace (South Node. Tried to keep Blacks from gaining full access to Southern society); George Bush, Sr. (Mercury. Peevish ruling-class president); Elsa Maxwell (Pluto. Society columnist); Dalton Trumbo (Jupiter. Blacklisted leftist scriptwriter); Ralph Nader (Chiron. Consumer advocate); Frida Kahlo (Moon. Painter).

1 Gemini

Standing in front of a mirror, a famous artist paints a semirealistic self-portrait, pausing to explain its most salient features to his curious house guests.[15]

Descriptive Phrases

Sharing a personal vision of life (self-promotion); ushering people into another world or another way of seeing things; uniting people around a common vision (believe that they see things more clearly than others); the mind as a magic mirror that reflects images of the outer world and of the imagination, though in a distorted, individualistic way (uncomprehending readings of reality; getting lost in superficials vs. alerting the public to hidden, underlying patterns); the personality as a work of art that effectively channels archetypes of the group-mind, and thus has a fascinating or electrifying effect on the public (class acts vs. self-obsessed egomaniacs); trying to leave one's mark on society; translating mental images into words, actions, art, or architecture.

Examples

Mary Cassatt (Sun. Impressionist artist); Henri Rousseau (Sun. Primitive painter); Linda McCartney (Uranus. Photographer of rock stars, animal-rights activist); Adolf Hitler (Neptune. Charismatic dictator, ex-artist); Isak Dinesen (Pluto. Writer—*Out of Africa*); Lois Rodden (Sun. Astrological researcher); Herbert von Karajan (Venus. Conductor); Janis Joplin (Uranus. Rock star); Vance Packard (Sun. Wrote *The Hidden Persuaders*, on the negative effects of advertising); Stephen Jay Gould (Uranus. Evolutionary scientist, propagandist); Woody Guthrie (Saturn. Leftist folk singer); Richard Wagner (Sun. Operatic composer); Brooklyn Bridge opens (Saturn. 5/24/1883); Mies van der Rohe (Neptune. Founder of the "International School" that formed the prototype of modern architecture); Mr. T (Sun. Black actor with an exaggerated persona); Henry VIII (Venus. King who brought the Renaissance to England).

2 Gemini

Spellbound, a child looks on as Santa dexterously giftwraps a children's book and some gold-foiled chocolates, and ties them up in bows.

Descriptive Phrases

Maintaining the openness and wonder of childhood throughout one's life; seizing opportunities to delight and entertain others (fun and games vs. secret indulgences); setting up a delicious mood; casting a spell (magical presence); studying the laws of influence; using an understanding of human psychology to convince people of just about anything; charming the pants off people (storytellers—harmless fictions vs. self-serving misrepresentations); bringing together various facts and observations into a coherent story (confabulation, unlikely explanations); tying it all together; harmonizing disparate elements; clever solutions; learning a skill by sitting at the feet of a master; showering children with affection; giving gifts that nourish the spirit.

Examples

Paul McCartney (Uranus. The Beatles—*Magical Mystery Tour, Sergeant Pepper's Lonely Heart's Club Band*); Gracie Allen (Jupiter. Comedienne—Burns and Allen); Tony Sarg (South Node. Puppeteer); Groucho Marx (Moon. Comedian—*The Big Store*); Art Linkletter (Saturn. TV personality—*People are Funny*); Shirley MacLaine (Chiron. Actress, writer—*Out on a Limb*); Antoine de St. Exupéry (Mars. Aviator, author of *The Little Prince*); Ishmael Reed (South Node. Novelist—*Mumbo Jumbo*); Eleanor Roosevelt (Pluto. First Lady); Edward Everett Horton (Pluto. Actor—prissy butler roles, *Fractured Fairy Tales*); Sir John Orr (Moon. Nutritionist who won the Nobel Peace Prize, wrote *Food and the People*); Coco Chanel (Pluto. Fashion designer); Mike Nesmith (Uranus. Rock star—The Monkees, patron of the Santa Fe Institute); Franz Mesmer (Sun. Pioneer in hypnosis—animal magnetism).

3 Gemini

His castle under attack by former members of the government, a monarch confers with a military advisor on different strategies of defense.[16]

Descriptive Phrases

Social reform vs. revolution; working inside or outside the system to promote justice and social order (change their tactics to fit changing political situations; may be very ruthless); conditional loyalty and civility based on an assumed social contract; the instability of societies built on rank and privilege vs. the stability of meritocracies; showing one's usefulness to the state and rising in rank vs. mavericks who are laws unto themselves but remain loyal to their social ideals; errant knights vs. outlaws; sense of inner nobility that may or may not be recognized by society (unstable personal fortunes); retaining one's civilized ways even if the social order breaks down; independence of judgment; boldly proclaiming one's position on pressing issues.

Examples

Maggie Kuhn (Jupiter. Activist—Grey Panthers); Mario Savio (Uranus. Leader of Berkeley Free Speech movement); Eunice Kennedy (Venus. Founder of Special Olympics); Bill Moyers (Mars. Journalist); Daniel Berrigan (Mars. Antiwar priest, arrested many times); Queen Victoria (Sun. Imperialist regent); Charles IX (Venus. French king, dominated by wife, ordered St. Bartholomew's Day massacre of Protestants); Martin Scorsese (Uranus. Director—*Taxi Driver*); Alan Brooke (Chiron. General—chief military advisor to Churchill); Linton Wells (Mars. Undersecretary of Defense, war operations analyst); Jan Smuts (Sun. Boer War guerilla, Allied tactician in World War I, promoted the United Nations); Myrna Loy (Jupiter. Actress—*The Thin Man*, U.N. activist); Diego Rivera (Pluto. Socialist artist—murals); Emmeline Pankhurst (Uranus. Suffragette who escalated the tactics of the movement to include chaining oneself to the Parliament building).

4 Gemini

At an opulent Roman feast, guests offer a toast to the gods. Invisible to the crowd, Bacchus, wearing a wreath of holly and cherries, pours gifts of the spirit from a cornucopia.

Descriptive Phrases

Honoring and celebrating the divine as it manifests in everyday things; rituals that work because the right spirit has gone into them vs. going through the motions or relying on empty spiritual trappings; invoking the invisible realm in order to be nourished in spirit as well as body; exquisite pleasures offered to the senses, to others, and to the gods (overindulgent partying); the joy of giving as the real reward of getting; old-world hospitality; studying the laws by which the spiritual realm manifests on the physical plane (astrology); penetrating to the spiritual meaning of events; perceiving spiritual essences in outer forms (clairvoyance); walking a magical path seen only by oneself; gaiety; effervescence; unbounded generosity of spirit.

Examples

Julia Child (Saturn. Gourmet cook, *bon vivant*); Countess Dorothy di Frasso (Pluto. The ultimate hostess of the Roaring Twenties); William Butler Yeats (Mercury. Poet, occultist, had run-ins with the fairy host); Arthur Conan Doyle (Uranus. Writer—Sherlock Holmes stories, believed in fairies); Jamie Farr (Venus. Transvestite "bacchant" in *M*A*S*H*); Eduardo Molinaro (Mercury. Director—*La Cage aux Folles*); Doug Henning (North Node. Stage magician); Dudley Moore (Venus. Actor, director—*Arthur*); Beverly Sills (Sun. Opera star); Richard Ideman (Moon. Astrologer); Nikita Khruschchev (Jupiter. Russian leader); Rick Klimczak (Moon. Astrologer); Annette Funicello (Uranus. Mouse-keteer); Jean Cocteau (Neptune. Writer and film director—*Beauty and the Beast*); Jerry Garcia (Uranus, Leader of The Grateful Dead); Billie Burke (Pluto. Showgirl, actress—Glinda in *The Wizard of Oz*).

5 Gemini

An outrageously dressed artist bursts into a quiet museum and shocks the patrons by nailing up a painting and a printed manifesto.

Descriptive Phrases

Publicity; passionate desire to get one's message across; putting one's message in a catchy, original form (slipping important messages into humor, crazy wisdom); catalyzing social change by bringing fringe ideas to the attention of the public; throwing a complacent public off-balance through extremist tactics (attention-seekers, may cultivate notoriety if fame is not forthcoming, publicity stunts); presenting reality in a startling new light (visual arts); faith in direct perception; living with few assumptions (constantly amazed by life's surprises); jauntily dancing within a situation in spin; keeping one's edge vs. relying on proven formulas; staying true to one's viewpoint vs. selling out; developing a trademark style; self-advertising.

Examples

Hans Arp (Pluto. Dadaist sculptor); Mies van der Rohe (Pluto. Influential architect—International Style); Marcel Duchamp (Jupiter. Ultramodern artist—"Nude Descending a Staircase"); Charlie Chaplin (Pluto. Comedian, leftist); Madeline Kahn (Uranus. Comedienne in Mel Brooks' movies); George Kuchar (Uranus. Underground filmmaker—*Hold Me While I'm Naked, Thundercrack!*); Angela Davis (Uranus. Communist professor); George Lincoln Rockwell (Jupiter. Leader of the American Nazi Party); John Cage (Saturn. Avant-garde composer); Jean Paul Marat (Sun. French revolutionary); Vincent Price (Sun. Actor—campy horror movies); Jane Fonda (South Node. Antiwar activist, actress—*The China Syndrome*); Prince (Mercury. Smutty rock star); Chico Marx (Neptune. Comedian—the Marx Brothers); Max Ernst (Neptune. Surrealist painter); Adolf Hitler (Pluto. Dictator, consummate propagandist); Paul Krassner (Venus. Editor of the radical journal *The Realist*).

6 Gemini

Highly choreographed rock group performs on a rotating stage. One of the band members sees a girl wandering through the crowd in a dazed state and jumps down to offer help.

Descriptive Phrases

Facing a dehumanized scene with warmth and intelligence; reaching out and emotionally touching someone in the midst of the mechanical chaos of modern life; extremes of emotional engagement and emotional disengagement (emotionally mechanical, sexually sadistic); gaining popularity by developing a warm personality and an impressive "act"; perfecting an artistic form through repetition and drill; artistic or sexual prowess built on technical mastery vs. going through "the same old grind" (alienated—robot-like detachment, sense of meaninglessness); aggressively introducing a more humane frame of values to an alienated or barbaric environment; pouring oneself into one's work (self-exploitation); opening up vs. shutting down.

Examples

Janis Joplin (Saturn. Self-destructive blues singer); Paul McCartney and George Harrison (Saturn and Saturn. The Beatles—often drowned out by screaming fans); Bill Griffith (Uranus, Mars. Absurdist cartoonist—*Zippy the Pinhead*); Fritz Lang (Neptune. Filmmaker—*M*, *Metropolis*); Karel Capek (Pluto. Wrote about a robot takeover of society in *R.U.R.*); Katherine Ross (Saturn. Actress—*The Stepford Wives*); Eugene O'Neill (Pluto. Playwright—*The Emperor Jones*, *The Hairy Ape*); Malcolm X (Venus. Black Muslim radical—major restructuring of values); John Wayne Gacy (Mars. Gay serial killer, sadist); Roseanne Barr (Moon. Comedienne who tried to connect family values on television to real values); Diana Ross (Uranus. Singer—The Supremes); Stevie Nicks (Sun. Rock singer—Fleetwood Mac); Lina Wertmuller (North Node. Filmmaker—*Swept Away*, *Seven Beauties*).

7 Gemini

An old man leans against a spreading tree by a well and smokes his pipe. Approached by a boy about a problem, he spins out a story that relates to the boy's situation.

Descriptive Phrases

Natural wisdom that is available to everyone who pauses to tap into it; stilling the mind in order to connect with one's inner wellsprings; getting at the essence of a problem by reflecting on symbols and images as they arise from the subconscious (morbid fantasies); the reflection of the archetypal world in the real world; tapping into the memory of nature (clairvoyance—seeing into the essence of things); reflecting on the unchanging aspects of human nature (see people as part of nature, with much in common with the animal kingdom); embedding wisdom in children's books; dispensing helpful information or diverting others with charming fictions (storytellers); finding refreshment in the restful beauty of nature; quiet charm and rustic humor.

Examples

J.R.R. Tolkien (Neptune. Fantasy author—*Lord of the Rings*); A.A. Milne (South Node. Author—*House at Pooh Corner*); Art Garfunkel (Moon. Folk singer—Simon and Garfunkel); Agatha Christie (Neptune, Stationary. Mystery writer—Miss Marple stories); H.P. Lovecraft (Neptune. Horror writer); Dwight D. Eisenhower (Neptune. U. S. president—presided over the quiet fifties); Victoria Sackville-West (Neptune. Rich Edwardian poet, developed the Sissinghurst gardens); Morning Glory Zerr (Sun. Pagan priestess); Jean Cocteau (Pluto. Symbolist filmmaker); Dietrich Fischer-Dieskau (Sun. Tenor—specialist in lieder); Marilyn Monroe (Mercury. Comic actress); Anne Landers (Venus. Advice columnist); William Shakespeare (Neptune. Playwright); James Barrie (Uranus. Writer—*Peter Pan*); Buffalo Bob Smith (Jupiter. *Howdy Doody* host).

8 Gemini

Human rights officials burst into the business office of an immigrant sweatshop and confront the manager.

Descriptive Phrases

Fighting for human freedom; confronting an enemy on his own turf (combative—see life as a battle between good and evil, obsessed with dark forces); penetrating observations of the negative underpinnings of society; odd reflections on life, as if in a funhouse mirror (fantasy fiction); keeping one's head in an alien situation (skeptical detachment); fighting for one's own perspective vs. being a slave to the values and analyses of the ruling class (alienated, sense of impotence); autocratic attempt to enforce one's own analytical framework vs. recognizing other points of view and negotiating a workable compromise; self-extrication—re-examining a tactic that isn't getting anywhere; internal conflicts between the selfish and altruistic sides of the personality.

Examples

John F. Kennedy (Sun. President, whose term was noted for civil-rights legislation and the Cuban missile crisis); Henry Kissinger (Mercury. Power broker during the Vietnam War); J.R.R. Tolkien (Pluto. Fantasy writer—*The Lord of the Rings*); Billy Jean King (Uranus. Tennis star); Ernie Pyle (South Node. War journalist); Loretta Swit (South Node. Actress—*M*A*S*H*); Indira Gandhi (Jupiter. Indian prime minister); Bob Woodward (Saturn. Reporter, cracked Watergate case); U. S. Marines put down Boxer Rebellion (South Node. 8/14/1900); Herman Melville (Mars. Writer—*Moby Dick*); Roger Taney (Uranus. Supreme Court justice, presided over the *Dred Scott* case); Agatha Christie (Pluto. Writer—mystery novels); Irwyn Greif (Sun. Psychic—spots cancer from photographs); Joni Mitchell (Uranus. Folk singer); Alfred Dreyfus (Uranus. French officer unjustly imprisoned for espionage).

9 Gemini

Medieval archer with a pointed beard and a feathered hat, shooting at a target.

Descriptive Phrases

Clarifying moral issues by bringing them into sharp focus; deciding which side one is on; drawing up battle lines (propagandists who oversimplify the issues); identifying the crux of a problem; hitting the mark; pointed observations; keenly trained perceptions; alertness to danger signals in the environment (distrustful, emotionally suspicious); seeing through complicated schemes to a person's underlying motives; Zen-like unity of mind and body vs. being high-strung and mentally unbalanced; training in martial arts or modern dance; submitting to military discipline vs. playing a lone hand; translating one's spiritual or moral understanding into a course of action vs. precipitate, hair-trigger reactions; outwitting or outmaneuvering one's enemy.

Examples

Albrecht Dürer (Sun. Renaissance engraver); Clint Eastwood (Sun. Macho actor—*Dirty Harry*); Farrah Fawcett (North Node. Actress—*Charlie's Angels*); Rommel (Pluto, Neptune. Nazi military commander); U. S. Declaration of Independence (Uranus. 7/4/1776); Confederate States of America formed (Uranus. 2/9/1861); Martha Graham (Jupiter. Modern dance giant); Rosey Reed (Venus. Equestrian demonstrator); Rudolf Steiner (Uranus. Spiritual guru—eurhythmy); Christine Jorgenson (Sun. Transsexual); Basil Rathbone (Pluto. Actor who played Sherlock Holmes and the Sheriff of Nottingham); Robert de Niro (Uranus. Macho actor—*Taxi Driver*); Alan Brooke (Mars. Military advisor to Churchill); Gloria Allred (Jupiter. Lawyer, NOW activist); Lech Walesa (Uranus. Polish labor leader, first democratically elected leader of the new regime); Margaret Rutherford (Neptune. Actress—Miss Marple); J. William Fulbright (Moon. Government watchdog).

10 Gemini

At an air show, a stunt pilot executes a tricky nose dive.

Descriptive Phrases

Plunging wholeheartedly into life; courageously venturing into uncharted territory (shoot for the stars); radical or extremist postures, especially on the level of personality or art; musical ecstasy as a bridge to the celestial or invisible world; getting into a musical or artistic groove and going wherever it leads; going after high times (drug abuse); surrendering to the magical potentials of the moment; psychedelic or mosaic-like rush of events; embarking on a project at full throttle; self-possession in fast-moving situations (lose control); impressive confidence and lack of hesitation based on technical mastery; meteoric success vs. crashing and burning (usually bounce back after failure); living in the fast lane; going for broke.

Examples

Harold Lloyd (Pluto. Comedian who did his own cliff-hanging stunts); Tama Janowitz (Venus. Writer—*Slaves of New York*); Joe Namath (Sun. Football star, personality); Dr. Ruth Westheimer (North Node. Outrageous television sex therapist); Jimi Hendrix (Saturn. Psychedelic guitarist who used buzz-bomb effects); Walt Whitman (Sun. Poet— "Song of Myself"); Leontyne Price (Moon. First Black operatic superstar); Rainer Fassbinder (Sun. Outrageous film director); Bolshevik revolution (Jupiter. 11/7/1917); Space shuttle blows up (Chiron. 1/28/1986); First atom bomb test (Venus. 7/16/1945); Julian Beck (Sun. Dramatist—"Living Theater"); Tristan Tzara (Moon. Dadaist artist); Mae West (Pluto. Singer, actress); Tazio Nuvolari (Pluto. Race car driver); John Dillinger (Mercury. Desperado, bandit); Rudolf Hess (Pluto. Nazi Party leader who made a daredevil flight to England to seek peace); Piers Anthony (Chiron. Prolific sci-fi writer); Harpo Marx (Pluto. Comedian—The Marx Brothers).

11 Gemini

*Stepping through the forked trunks of two aspens,
a woman emerges from the woods. On seeing her,
a neighbor leans out of her window and waves.*

Descriptive Phrases

Friendliness; neighborliness; seeing beyond divisions of form to the underlying unity of things; sense of implicit connectedness; being true to one's spiritual roots; humorous familiarity with nature and people; charming naturalness of manner; folksiness vs. sophistication; urbane wittiness vs. country humor; calm and clearheaded view of one's situation and its possibilities; openness to life; innocence of heart that survives negative experiences and springs anew from the ideal plane; healing through forgiveness; passing on information vs. nasty gossip (overly trusting—must learn to see beyond the surface to underlying motives); egalitarian puncturing of pretenses; commonsensical wisdom vs. mystical insights that elude common language (Kether-Malkuth connection).

Examples

Andy Griffith (Sun. Actor—sheriff of Mayberry); John Denver (Ascendant. Folk-rock singer—"Country Roads," "Looking for Space"); Marianne Faithfull (North Node. Folk singer); Al Capp (North Node. Cartoonist—*L'il Abner*); Dorothy Parker (Pluto. Humorist, journalist); Donovan Leitch (Ascendant. Folk-rock star); Robbie Robertson (Uranus. Musician—The Band); Marilyn Monroe (Sun. Comic actress, sex symbol); Norman Rockwell (Neptune. Popular illustrator of rural Americana); Mary Cassatt (Mercury. Realistic oil paintings of women and children); Burt Reynolds (Chiron. Comic actor—*Smokey and the Bandit*); Raphael of Urbino (Mars. Pioneered landscape painting in the Renaissance); Gary Snyder (Venus. Poet, environmentalist); William Carlos Williams (Saturn. Country doctor and avant-garde poet); Pat Boone (Sun. Singer); Grant Wood (North Node. Artist—"American Gothic"); Spencer Williams (Pluto. Andy Brown on *Amos and Andy*).

12 Gemini

A Black slave girl looks directly into her master's eyes and demands her rights.

Descriptive Phrases

Rebellion against arbitrary authority; refusing to be put into someone else's box; promoting the culture of one's own people by giving it a more self-conscious edge vs. playing into racial or cultural stereotypes; escaping the psychology of the oppressed vs. falling into abusive relationships again and again; transformations that accompany a more self-conscious cultural identity; resisting cultural imperialism by attacking the values of the dominant culture and by waging an ongoing propaganda campaign for one's own point of view; honest communication (taunting, impudent, full of jive); honest expression of one's needs (sexually up-front; feel that the physical level of reality is more real than the mental level); fighting for civil rights by fighting for oneself.

Examples

Muhammad Ali (Jupiter. Boxing champ—"The Greatest"); Shirley Temple (North Node. Child actress, later an ambassador to Ghana); Emmeline Pankhurst (Jupiter. English feminist leader, chained herself to the Parliament building); Aretha Franklin (Mars. Queen of soul music—"Respect"); Allen Ginsberg (Sun. Gay beat poet—"Howl"); Erica Jong (Mars. Feminist author—*Fear of Flying*); Buffy St. Marie (Jupiter. Native American protest singer); Cagliostro (Sun. Alchemist, forger, soothsayer, and scoundrel); Mao Tse Tung (Neptune. Communist revolutionary, dictator); Ayatollah Khomeini (South Node. Revolutionary Islamic leader in Iran); Ralph Ellison (Saturn. Black author—*Invisible Man*); Fanny Lou Hamer (Jupiter. Endured jailings and beatings to gain voting rights for Blacks in Mississippi); Huey Newton (Jupiter. Black Panther leader); Wilhelm Reich (Pluto. Sexual researcher who attempted to link sexual liberation to Marxism—"orgone energy").

13 Gemini

A pianist performs an original composition in the salon of a bordello while one of the girls does a dance.

Descriptive Phrases

The universal need to express oneself, no matter what one's talents (self-exposing exhibitionists); creating wildly original art that celebrates both beauty and ugliness, the ridiculous and the sublime; integrating discordant notes into the song of life; resonating to a full range of human emotion and behavior; rising high or sinking low according to what one nourishes in oneself (serious slummers, but must not fall into the bad habits of their associates); creating a happening scene; getting down to the nitty-gritty vs. hanging around with lowlifes (defend the dignity and worth of all people); enthusiastically and eloquently sharing one's observations of life; developing artistic proficiency so one can shine in public; joyous self-expression vs. creative inhibition or performance anxiety.

Examples

Josephine Baker (Sun. Black cabaret dancer, famous for her banana dress and her nude poses); Henri Toulouse-Lautrec (Mars. High-class poster-art of Bohemian Paris); Madeline Kahn (Saturn. Comedienne, singer—*Blazing Saddles*); Tennessee Williams (Saturn. Playwright—sordid soap operas with class); Bob Dylan (Venus. Folk-rock pioneer, poet); Martha Graham (Neptune. Innovative modern dancer); Georg Grosz (Neptune. Trenchantly political painter who also did watercolors documenting his experiences in brothels); Bertold Brecht (Pluto. Playwright—*The Threepenny Opera*); First performance of *Ubu Roi* (Pluto. 12/9/1896); Keith Emerson (Moon, Uranus. Rock singer, keyboard artist—has a piano that rotates upside-down as he plays); Carla Bley (Mars. Crazed keyboard artist); Kinky Friedman (Uranus. Shamelessly self-revealing mystery writer); Marquis de Sade (Sun. Writer of lurid accounts of perverse sexual adventure); Stacy Keach (Sun. Successful leading man, despite harelip—*Mike Hammer*); Dashiell Hammett (Neptune. Detective writer—*The Maltese Falcon*).

14 Gemini

In the wee hours, a man looks from his window to see two beams of light flickering a message across the city. Minutes later, he is on the street with a flashlight, in pursuit of a mysterious lady.

Descriptive Phrases

Following up on intuitions or psychic flashes; tracking down some plot or nefarious influence (getting to the bottom of something vs. relying on inference); developing a reliable information network vs. tapping into untrustworthy sources (tend to confirm their own biases and get trapped in a narrow reality construct); heroically battling evil, yet recognizing evil's seductive power; waking up a sleeping public to some hidden danger; projecting a fascinating self-image; developing one's unique magic (charisma); following up on an uncanny talent or vision; being onto something (know less than they claim); passionate pursuit of social ideals in the face of opposition vs. entanglements with shady characters for base motives.

Examples

Woody Allen (Chiron. Director—*Manhattan Murder Mystery, Alice*); Pola Negri (Neptune. Silent movie vamp); Edward Peters (Mercury. Historian of the witch hunts); Michael Douglas (Uranus. Director, actor—*Fatal Attraction*); J. Edgar Hoover (Neptune. FBI director obsessed with communism); Karen Silkwood (Uranus. Probably murdered while tracking down a company's radioactive contamination of the environment); Dennis Gabor (Sun. Scientist—holography); Hubert Urban (Sun. Professor of neuropsychiatry who studied ESP before and after electroshock); Colin Wilson (Venus. Author of *The Occult,* interest in ESP); Yogi Bhajan (Jupiter. Kundalini yoga guru); Queen Elizabeth I (Mars. Queen who had to keep track of constant plots against her own life, and against England); James Stewart (Mercury. Actor—*Rear Window, The Man Who Knew Too Much*).

15 Gemini

Two children play circus, creating a tent from a sheet and animals from a variety of household objects.

Descriptive Phrases

Using the imagination to creatively restructure the elements of one's life-experience into a meaningful whole; resisting the imposed realities of the adult world and putting things together for oneself; life's tendency to conform to one's own way of conceiving it (live in a fantasy-world, and then stumble unexpectedly upon the dark realities of the adult world); constant renegotiation of what is real and what is not; teamwork; developing a creative partnership with someone who will help one realize one's fantasies; love affairs built on common dreams (*folies à deux*) vs. feeling one's partner trips one up or ties one down; successfully manifesting one's artistic visions by devising and following a practical method vs. scattering one's energy in a million unrealized projects.

Examples

Hayley Mills (Uranus. Actress—*Pollyanna, The Parent Trap*); Albert Brooks (Mars. Filmmaker—*Defending Your Life, Lost in America*); Robert Ringling (Pluto. Ringling Brothers Circus); Fred Astaire and Ginger Rogers (Pluto and Ascendant, respectively. Hollywood dance duo); Giacomo Puccini (Jupiter. Operatic composer—*Madame Butterfly*); René Magritte (Pluto. Surrealist painter); Louis Aragon (Pluto. Surrealist poet); John Waters (Uranus. Made surrealistic underground films with his friend Divine); Diane Keaton (Uranus. Actress in Woody Allen movies—*Annie Hall*, directed *Unstrung Heroes*); Ursula LeGuin (Moon. Sci-fi, fantasy writer—*Earth-Sea Trilogy*); Brett Butler (Moon. Comedienne—*Grace Under Fire*); Spencer Tracy (South Node, Pluto. Actor—*Adam's Rib*); Martha Stewart (Jupiter. Presents a cornucopia of do-it-yourself home projects); Luis Buñuel (Pluto. Surrealist film director—*Un Chien Andalou*).

16 Gemini

Alternately humorous and passionate,
a soapbox speaker harangues a crowd.

Descriptive Phrases

Bracing freshness of viewpoint; verbalizing a problem and offering inventive solutions; pointing out overlooked factors that crack open the conventional worldview (indignant when people refuse to see the obvious); provoking strong, honest reactions from others; stirring things up; street theater; Dadaism; disrupting the normal order (anarchistic); bawdy or topical humor—seeing the funny, surrealistic side of modern life (zany characters); deep sense of emotional pathos hidden beneath a stream of chatter; being on the fringe because one is put there vs. valuing ideas because they are on the fringe (crackpot theories); trusting one's first thoughts vs. failing to develop or test one's ideas; guerillas in the culture wars.

Examples

Sandra Bernhard (Sun. Confrontational lesbian comic); Randy Newman (Mars. Comic singer—"Short People"); Howard Cosell (Moon. Acerbic sportscaster); Erica Jong (Jupiter. Writer—*Fear of Flying*); Oliver Stone (North Node. Filmmaker—*JFK*, *Platoon*); Federal troops expel hobo army from Washington D.C. (Neptune. 8/11/1894); Ralph Ginzburg (Jupiter. Editor of *Screw* magazine); Ethel Merman (Pluto. Loud-voiced comedienne, Broadway singer—"Anything Goes"); Frances Yates (Pluto. Historian of the Western occult tradition); Alexander Calder (Pluto. Artist—mobiles); Tristan Tzara (Neptune. Dadaist writer); Alexandra Kollontai (North Node. Bolshevik agitator, proponent of Free Love); Bette Midler (Uranus. Singer, comedienne, actress—*Ruthless People*); Immanuel Velikovsky (Neptune. Fringe science—*Worlds in Collision*); Arthur Rimbaud (Saturn. Poet—"A Season in Hell"); Petrarch (South Node. Early Renaissance poet and writer, famous for his rants against the Church); Ken Osmond (Saturn. Actor—Eddie Haskell on *Leave It to Beaver*); Groucho Marx (Pluto. Anarchic comedian).

17 Gemini

Measuring his son's height against a wall, a proud father admonishes the boy to stand up straight. The scene dissolves to a future date, when the child—now much older—is being measured once again.

Descriptive Phrases

Attending to the development of innate faculties; having enough trust in oneself to follow one's star; living out a clearly visualized personal myth with dramatic flair (may overdevelop their unique genius and become unbalanced and eccentric); gaining perspective on one's early conditioning; compensating for developmental deformities by referring back to a seed-vision of one's highest potentials; living up to early promise (prodigies); measuring up vs. making big mistakes and disappointing family and friends (very aware of being judged by others); looking down benevolently on others vs. harsh criticisms and demands that provoke rebellion; steady progress vs. making hay while the sun shines; bringing one's potentials into full flower.

Examples

Benjamin Spock (Venus. Influential expert on child-rearing); Suzanne Farrell (Mars, Uranus. Accepted into the New York City Ballet at age 15); Patty McCormack (Uranus. Child actress—*The Bad Seed*); Peter Serkin (Mars. Pianist mentored by father, Rudolf Serkin); Beverly Nichols (Pluto. Wrote of child abuse in *Father Figure*); Bette Davis (Moon. Actress—*Now, Voyager*); Adelle Davis (Moon. Nutritionist); Cher (Uranus. Pop singer who branched out into a serious acting career); Justin Greene (Uranus. Underground cartoonist who wrote of his triumph over childhood psychosis); Anne Frank (Mercury. Diarist); Johannes Kepler (Moon. Astronomer whose flaky early theories matured into an accurate planetary theory); Neil Young (Uranus. Pioneering rock star, has children with cerebral palsy); John F. Kennedy (Venus. U. S. president whose career was orchestrated by his father).

18 Gemini

In a crowded midwestern diner, two Chinese-Americans watch a television newscast, then argue about it in Chinese.

Descriptive Phrases

Disputing social norms that do not serve the needs of one's subgroup; paying attention to official opinions and social expectations, but tuning them out if they cramp one's style (provoke a response with *outré* behavior); trying to create unity of opinion, at least within one's own subgroup vs. alienating would-be allies by patronizing or bullying them; one-sided conversations and summary pronouncements vs. listening carefully to others to understand their emotional and intellectual assumptions; being well-informed about current events and their portrayal in the media, but getting the lowdown by keeping an ear to the ground (gossips, ferret out secrets); outsiders who introduce new values to the dominant culture.

Examples

John Lithgow (Uranus. Actor—plays an alien in *Third Planet from the Sun*); Margaret Mead (Pluto. Anthropologist who studied sexual norms in Samoa); Swami Vivekananda (Uranus. Brought Vedanta yoga to the West); Vaclav Havel (Moon. Dissident Czech playwright, later the first president of liberated Czechoslovakia); Josephine Baker (Jupiter. Black American entertainer who lived most of her life in Paris); Hillaire Belloc (Jupiter. Catholic propagandist who attacked secularism and Protestantism); Roscoe Drummond (Pluto. Newscaster who had a personal pipeline to Eisenhower and other presidents); Connie Chung (North Node. Newscaster); Jason Alexander (Moon. Actor—purveyor of New York Jewish culture, in *Seinfeld*); Alan King (North Node. *Alan King's Final Warning* was one of the few pieces of political comedy to break the wall of silence in the Reagan era); Joan Rivers (Sun. Gossipy comedienne); Paul Harvey (South Node. Controversial talk-radio host).

19 Gemini

A man reads a children's book about a lost city with the aid of magnifying glass.

Descriptive Phrases

Interpenetration of the mythic or archetypal realm and objective reality; books as doorways to the inner realm vs. living out a myth or story in real life; clarifying the outlines of one's life-story; re-examining events of one's past and discovering overlooked facts that change the whole picture; being drawn into an exciting adventure through a series of discoveries; tracing out hunches (blow findings out of proportion); bringing light to dark places; heroic confrontations with evil forces vs. perilous flight from enemies; clarifying moral issues through symbolic allegories (oversimplifying the issues vs. getting lost in a forest of details); creating a persuasive fiction vs. debunking destructive myths; focused examination; trusting one's inner lights.

Examples

Judy Garland (Sun. Singer, actress—*The Wizard of Oz*); Elton John (Uranus. Singer—"Goodbye Yellow Brick Road"); Agatha Christie (North Node. Mystery writer); Elaine Pagels (Moon. Researches early Christianity—*Adam, Eve, and the Serpent* and *The Origin of Satan*); Arthur Conan Doyle (Mars. Writer—Sherlock Holmes stories, believed in fairies); Johnny Depp (Sun. Actor—*The Ninth Gate, Don Juan de Marco*); Gilda Radner (Uranus. Comedienne); Camille Paglia (Uranus. Cultural critic); Donald Johanson (Saturn. Anthropologist who discovered the prehistoric skull of "Lucy"); Paul McCartney (Mercury. Singer-songwriter for The Beatles—"Magical Mystery Tour"); Alfred Kinsey (Jupiter. Kinsey report on sexual practices); Harrison Ford (Venus. Actor—*Indiana Jones and the Temple of Doom, Star Wars*); J. B. Rhine (Neptune. ESP researcher); Paolo Soleri (Mars, Utopian architect—blueprints for the future); Pierre Benoit (Venus. Writer—*The Queen of Atlantis*).

20 Gemini

A worker fills compartments in an automated, self-service cafeteria with a variety of sandwiches, and wonders whether his superior new sandwich will find favor with the public.

Descriptive Phrases

Assessing the tastes of the public, including their artistic and intellectual tastes; sticking with the tried and true vs. seeing how far one can go; giving people what they want vs. gaining a public platform to broadcast an important and original message; modifying and perfecting a successful method; developing technical expertise through repetition (overspecialization); cranking out a product to meet a deadline; getting stuck in a rut vs. branching out into a new field; freshness vs. staleness; rapid and routine analysis by which the ego processes incoming data into an internal representation of reality vs. shoving reality uncritically into ready-made categories; having an accurate measure of a situation vs. half-baked analyses; developing one's skills to better serve the public.

Examples

Ray Kroc (Pluto. Founder of MacDonald's fast food restaurants); Sue Grafton (Venus. Prolific writer of detective stories—*B is for Burglar*); Arthur Murray (Mars. Dance classes); Ed Sullivan (Pluto. Variety show host who introduced Elvis and The Beatles to American audiences); Bill Griffith (Saturn. Cartoonist—*Zippy the Pinhead*); Salvador Dali (Pluto. Surrealist artist who sold lots of tossed-off work later in life); Chevy Chase (Mars. Predictable comedian); Sylvester Stallone (North Node. Director, actor—*Rocky* and *Rambo* series); Jacques Cousteau (Sun. Oceanographer, environmental activist); Daniel Pinkwater (Jupiter. Children's author—*Fat Men from Space*); Ann Jillian (Moon. Actress—*Gypsy*, spokeswoman for breast examinations); Geraldo Rivera (Saturn. Tabloid talk-show host who switched to a more serious format); Dr. Lendon Smith (Mars. Nutritionist).

21 Gemini

A man in a labor demonstration, realizing that fights are breaking out at the front of the march, steps out of the ranks and considers what to do next.

Descriptive Phrases

Deciding for oneself what direction to take in life, without forgetting one's duty to the collective; joining a movement vs. marching into the future to the beat of one's own drum; knowing how far one should go in one's actions and behavior vs. taking an impulse to its extreme; indifference to the judgment of the crowd that allows one to lead the crowd; providing a focal point for the gathering of collective energies; going one's own way vs. working within a group; being a spectator vs. being an active participant; energizing the public; picking up on a vital new sensibility that is in the wind and bringing it to the public; taking an idea or a personality trait as far as it can go; individuation vs. leadership based on a cult of personality; boldly independent intellectual or political stances.

Examples

Cass Elliot (Jupiter. Singer for The Mamas and the Papas—"Dancing in the Streets"); Mairead Corrigan (Saturn. Irish housewife turned peace activist); Cesar Chavez (Mars. Boycott organizer and union leader—United Farm Workers); Emancipation Proclamation (Uranus. 9/22/1862); Stephen Jay Gould (Jupiter. Harvard evolutionary theorist, popularizer); Frances Yates (South Node. Historian of the hermetic tradition in the West, intellectual maverick); Alan Watts (North Node. Popularizer of Zen Buddhism); Louis B. Leakey (Pluto. Anthropologist who challenged the accepted view of man's origin); Gilda Radner (North Node. *Saturday Night Live* comedienne); Bonnie Raitt (Moon. Bluesy singer, political activist); Clyde Barrow (North Node. Outlaw); Mike Barnicle (Mars. Prize-winning journalist who admitted making up some of his stories); Angela Davis (Saturn. Black communist activist, professor).

22 Gemini

A joyous barn dance. After a spin around the floor, a young couple walks out under the stars, where they speak to each other of their hopes and dreams.

Descriptive Phrases

Dancing within the magic of the moment; participating fully in life vs. being a wallflower; exploring a new step in the dance of life; staying young by pursuing new interests vs. returning to simple and familiar pleasures; bringing foreign perspectives back to one's native community (world-weary critics vs. naive bumpkins); finding a temporary dancing partner vs. finding one's spiritual twin; sharing confidences; artless sincerity vs. guarding one's heart (shy, virginal—emotional or sexual blocks); getting other people on one's wavelength or dancing to one's tune; getting social energies moving (capricious—live within a whirl of mental and physical activity); marching bravely into life to the tune of one's ideals vs. corny, untested beliefs.

Examples

Richard Thomas (Sun. John-Boy on *The Waltons*); Jim Nabors (Sun. Actor—*Gomer Pyle*, gospel singer); Ann Landers (South Node. Advice columnist); Joni Mitchell (Mars. Folk and jazz singer); Penny Marshall (Mars. Actress—*Laverne and Shirley*, director—*Big*); Linda McCartney (Jupiter. Photographer, animal-rights activist); Bill Clinton (Uranus. Saxophone-playing president); John Clifford (Sun, Uranus. Ballet dancer, choreographer); Chubby Checker (Jupiter. Pop-rock singer—"The Twist"); Susan Sarandon (Uranus. Actress—*The Rocky Horror Picture Show, "Let's Do the Time Warp Again"*; social activist); Georges Lemaitre (Venus. Professor of astronomy who wrote on the expansion of the universe); Gerard Croiset (North Node. Psychic—one of several with this degree); Lionel Trilling (Pluto. Political commentator); Jerry Rubin (Midheaven. Prominent sixties radical, wrote *Do It*); John Denver (Saturn. Corny folk singer); Kathie Lee Gifford (Jupiter. Too-good-to-be-true talk-show host).

23 Gemini

A flapper in a crowded speakeasy convinces the owner to seat her in the balcony above the stage, along with the society set.[17]

Descriptive Phrases

Gaining admittance to an in-crowd vs. feeling like an outsider; jockeying for social position; egalitarianism vs. being on the lookout for personal advantage; sharp observation of the social structure and its biases (loud protests against unmerited privilege, attempts to level the class structure); honest argumentation; expounding one's views in a clear and convincing way; arriving at a higher level of truth by putting one's heads together vs. refusing to budge from a position one knows to be true (believe that the truth will eventually win out); championing one's position in open public dialogue; being in-the-know (intelligent social commentary vs. petty gossip); loyalty to friends and family; fraternization; effervescent sociability.

Examples

Bette Davis (Pluto. Actress—*Jezebel*); Billy Wilder (Pluto. Director—*Some Like it Hot*, which begins with a raid at a speakeasy); Dianne Wiest (Uranus. Actress—*Bullets over Broadway*); Al Capone (Neptune. Gangster); Agnes Moorehead (Pluto. Character actress—Endora on *Bewitched*); Duke Ellington (Neptune. Jazz-band leader); Reggie Jackson (North Node. Baseball great); Oscar Levant (Pluto. Pianist, comic); Clara Bow (Venus. Silent film star, sexually promiscuous and a wild partier, ruined by blackmail); William Butler Yeats (Sun. Poet, occultist; set up a secret society); Che Guevara (Sun. Revolutionary); Lech Walesa (Mars, Stationary. Polish labor leader, kept Solidarity alive for years as an underground organization); 1000 die in Civil War draft riots (Uranus. 7/13/1863); Robert Preston (Jupiter. Actor—*The Music Man, Victor, Victoria*); Tom Hulce (Jupiter. Actor—*Amadeus*); Maggie Kuhn (Pluto. Founder of the Grey Panthers—rights for the aged).

24 Gemini

An artist is painting a strangely compelling alien landscape, pausing occasionally to speak about her work to an interested bystander.

Descriptive Phrases

Inner focusing—seeing pictures form before the mind's eye; imaginative arts; withdrawing from the world to cultivate a better relationship with one's muse (channel visions from another plane); confidence in one's visions, analyses, and perceptions, but insecurity about one's own appearance (want others to come to them and to accept them, warts and all); shaking up other people's worldviews; winning people over to one's point of view or one's vision; the open-endedness of reality; the thin line between art and life; reality as determined by what one identifies as essential, significant, or beautiful (subjective projection); inhabiting one's own myth; visionaries and dreamers, with personalities implying whole worlds; developing artistic facility and smoothness of execution.

Examples

Hermann Rorschach (Saturn. Developed Rorschach test); Frida Kahlo (Pluto. Symbolic realist painter); Lorraine Hansberry (Venus. Black playwright—*A Raisin in the Sun*); Sylvester Stallone (Mercury. Actor—*Rocky*, *Rambo*, an accomplished painter); Herbert Marcuse (Neptune. Radical political theorist—*One-Dimensional Man*); Gerard Croiset (Pluto. Psychic, police work); Simone de Beauvoir (Pluto. Feminist writer—*The Second Sex*); Denis de Rougemont (Pluto. Philosopher of history—*Love in the Western World*); William Empson (Pluto. Poet—*Seven Types of Ambiguity*); Philo T. Farnsworth (Pluto. Pioneered the development of television); David Benge (Chiron. Occultist—*Inner Guide Meditations*); Karl Munch (Uranus. Abstract expressionist artist); Peter Falk (North Node. Actor—*Columbo*, accomplished artist); Robert Heinlein (Pluto. Sci-fi writer—*Stranger in a Strange Land*); Alfred Eisenstadt (Neptune. Photojournalist).

25 Gemini

Setting out on a family vacation, a man in a Hawaiian shirt drives past a turn (ignoring the advice of his wife and kids) and travels straight along the palm-lined shore.[18]

Descriptive Phrases

Keeping one's sights on tangible life-goals, yet having fun along the way (uncompromising nature leads to serious breaks with others); sticking to one's plan vs. scrambling to deal with unforeseen circumstances (bumbling into a series of comic mishaps); making every day count in reaching one's life goals (micro-manage their lives; inflexibly set upon a single outcome); revealing the essential features of a situation by peeling away the hokum; playing it as one sees it; abiding by the simple law of cause and effect; coordinating divergent goals or desires into a single plan of action; taking care of oneself and one's family (exercise, financial planning); exaggerating the essential features of one's personality; cutting a recognizable figure (silly get-ups); finishing up daily business so one can relax and enjoy life.

Examples

Albert Brooks (Uranus. Filmmaker—*Lost in America*); William Steig (Pluto. Children's book author—*Dr. DeSoto*); Josephine Baker (Mars. Cabaret dancer); Arnold Schwarzenegger (Uranus. Bodybuilder, politician, actor—*Twins, True Lies, Scavenger Hunt*); Spencer Tracy (Neptune. Actor—*It's a Mad, Mad, Mad, Mad World*, with its denouement at two crossed palm trees); Joyce Carol Oates (Sun. Novelist—*Lives of the Twins*); Groucho Marx (Neptune. Leader of the Marx Brothers—*Coconuts*); Henry VIII (Jupiter. King of England—took over the Church so he could divorce); Clint Eastwood (Jupiter. Cowboy actor—*Dirty Harry*); Eleanor Roosevelt (Saturn. First Lady, social activist); Richard Simmons (Venus. Exercise guru—"lose weight while having fun"); Melvin Belli (Pluto. Showboating lawyer).

26 Gemini

In the depths of the forest, an exiled king looks through ice-covered branches to the far reaches of the night sky.

Descriptive Phrases

Isolated reflection on one's place in the cosmos; sensing the divine intelligence underlying natural structures (Tolkienesque, Druidic); nature as an eternal kingdom whose transient external forms are built up on eternal archetypes; perceiving the archetypal level of personality (astrology); giving testimony to neglected truths (reflect sadly on man's separation from his own higher nature, craggy prophets in the wilderness); developing an interlocking, structural analysis of reality; seeking worldly authority in order to impose a more natural and enlightened order (partisan battles led by Utopian ideologues); teaching important truths through symbolic or paradigmatic stories; magical lines of force found in fairy tales; the crown chakra.

Examples

Roger Waters (Uranus. Rock musician—Pink Floyd, "Dark Side of the Moon"); Alice Bailey (Sun. Occultist); Joni Mitchell (Saturn. Folk singer); Van Morrison (Mars. Folk-rock musician); Cher (Venus. Actress—*Moonstruck*); Dalai Lama (Mercury. Exiled Tibetan leader, spiritual teacher); Ho Chi Minh (North Node. North Vietnamese revolutionary leader); R. Crumb (Saturn. Underground cartoonist—*Mr. Natural*); Martin Goldsmith (Uranus. Astrologer); Jean de Brunhoff (Neptune. Babar stories); Lorne Greene (Saturn. Actor—*Bonanza, Battlestar Galactica*); Barry Goldwater (North Node. Right-wing presidential contender); Idries Shah (Sun. Writer on Sufism); George Lucas (Saturn. Filmmaker, director—*Star Wars*); Holling C. Holling (Mars. Children's book writer, illustrator—*Minn of the Mississippi*); Liza Minelli (North Node. Singer); Kevin Kline (Uranus. Actor—*Dave*).

27 Gemini

Cinderella turns the corner of a mountain path and catches sight of the shining spires of the prince's castle.

Descriptive Phrases

Following one's star vs. losing one's ideals in a thicket of everyday concerns; imitating the image of one's idealized self until it becomes a reality; perfect agreement between looks and personality (deceptively transparent, lead a secret life, surprised by life's twists); materializing an eternal archetype in the group mind; drawing admiration from others for one's looks or wit; entering rich, sophisticated circles (social climbers who are overly concerned with fitting in, posers); keen observation of social custom; separating the real from the phony; attaining the consciousness of the immortal celestial self (remote viewing; strange, well-articulated visions); shining one's light from afar.

Examples

Myrna Loy (Venus. Actress—*The Thin Man* series); Paul McCartney (Sun. The Beatles; basically moved from the slums to a castle); Katharine Hepburn (Pluto. Actress—*The Philadelphia Story*); Dean Martin (Sun. Crooner, actor); Penny Marshall (Saturn, Stationary. Actress—*Laverne and Shirley*, director—*Big*); Ronald Reagan (Pluto. Actor, president); Olivia Newton John (Uranus. Singer, movie star—*Saturday Night Fever, Xanadu*); Alfred Hitchcock (Neptune, South Node. Director—murder mysteries); M. C. Escher (Sun. Artist, optical illusions); Lawrence Durrell (Pluto. Writer—*Alexandria Quartet*); Michael Rennie (Pluto. Actor—*The Day the Earth Stood Still*, in which he is brought back from the dead); Thomas Merton (Saturn. Christian mystic who traveled to Tibet—*The Seven-Storey Mountain*); Jorge Luis Borges (Neptune. Surrealistic writer); D. T. Suzuki (Jupiter, Stationary. Buddhist scholar, Zen master); Ruby Keeler (Pluto. Thirties glamor star); Clark Gable (Neptune. Glamorous actor—*Gone with the Wind*).

28 Gemini

Offered a cabinet post by a questionable leader, a man attempts to negotiate terms before withdrawing to consider the offer.[19]

Descriptive Phrases

Knowing when to invest energy, emotion, or money in something and when to shrug it off; thinking things through to their probable outcomes; extricating oneself from no-win situations vs. trying hard to remedy a bad situation; trying to gain a voice in political and social policy making without compromising one's principles vs. making a career within an irredeemably corrupt system; making practical, justifiable compromises vs. making a clean break with the past; impassioned attempt to communicate one's needs and wishes (dejected belief that one's overtures will not be reciprocated); carrying the weight of the world on one's shoulders vs. humorous or Zen-like detachment from the world-illusion; weighing the trade-offs of worldly success.

Examples

Barbara Tuchman (Pluto. Historian—*The March of Folly*, which treats stupid social policies in history); Henry Kissinger (Mars. Architect of various ruthless political policies); Sylvia Porter (Sun. Writer on investment strategies); Robert Muldoon (Moon. Chairman of the World Monetary Fund); Francesco Petrarca (Venus. Poet whose decisive rejection of medieval culture initiated the Italian Renaissance); Dane Rudhyar (Jupiter. His decisive break from old-line astrology began the recent astrological renaissance); Archibald Cox (Pluto. Watergate prosecutor who quit when the truthfulness of the hearings was seriously compromised); Virginia Woolf (Mars. Writer—*Orlando*); Alan Watts (Saturn. Popularizer of Zen); Studs Terkel (Pluto. Sociological writer, researcher—*Working*); Mother Teresa (Pluto. Worked for the poor and dying in Calcutta, yet championed Catholic strictures against birth-control); Doris Day (Moon. Singer, comic actress); Clifford Odets (Jupiter. Blacklisted writer—*None but the Lonely Heart*).

29 Gemini

A mockingbird sings from the top of a flowering tree, while its mate worries a stick into their nest.

Descriptive Phrases

Singing a happy song; joyful appreciation of life; tuning in to a higher vibratory level; living in the moment and for the moment, an innocent child of nature; simple and direct approach to one's situation; letting problems take care of themselves vs. needlessly complicating matters with unconscious nervous behavior (worrying, meddling, nagging); playfully affectionate behavior (marital problems due to romantic adventurousness); entertaining oneself by improvising playful riffs on one's daily routine; making it up as one goes along; sharing snippets of truth through art or entertainment (skits, sketches, songs, stories); trying out new ideas by seeing if other people resonate to them; awakening others to life's bright possibilities; quickening.

Examples

Ella Fitzgerald (Saturn. Jazz singer—scat); Cole Porter (Venus. Songwriter); Dolly Parton (North Node. Country singer); Arne Sultan (Venus. Comedy writer—*Get Smart, Barney Miller*); Euell Gibbons (Pluto. Expert on finding food in the wild); Ladybird Johnson (Pluto. First Lady who spearheaded a very successful effort to "beautify America"); Anne Landers (Jupiter. Advice columnist); Rosa Parks (Pluto. Started Alabama bus boycott); Jimmy Stewart (Mars. Actor—*It's a Wonderful Life*); L. Frank Baum (Saturn. Author of Oz stories); A. A. Milne (Mars. Author—*Winnie the Pooh*); Richard Bach (Mars. Author—*Jonathan Livingston Seagull*, pilot); Dana Carvey (Mercury, Stationary. Comedian, expert at mimicry); Spike Jones (Pluto. Crazed band leader); Ansel Adams (Neptune. Nature photographer); Rona Barrett (South Node. Gossip columnist).

30 Gemini

Beauty contestants in bathing suits stand before the judges in a circular hall of mirrors. In the background, unseen, a maid is sweeping the floor.

Descriptive Phrases

Social masks that both reveal and conceal who one really is; integrating the public and private self vs. leading a double life; being fooled by appearances or first readings of events vs. seeing through false fronts (deception); cluing people in; sharing penetrating observations; rejecting a consensual reality built on flattering reflections vs. belief that reality is built on nothing more than social agreement; artful imitation of some accepted norm of beauty or respectability; radiant self-confidence based on the esteem of others vs. suffering invisibility when one doesn't rate on a scale of accepted social values; being wise to one's own games vs. closing an eye to dishonesty; distraction by superficials vs. threading one's way through illusions.

Examples

Shirley Temple (Moon. Cutesy child actress); Ringo Starr (Venus. Drummer for The Beatles); Arlene Francis (Pluto. Panelist—*What's My Line*); Dale Evans (Pluto. Cowgirl actress, child abuse activist); Joe Namath (Ascendant. Football star, shady business dealings); J. Edgar Hoover (Jupiter. FBI director with a secret life); Tennessee Williams (Neptune. Playwright—*Suddenly Last Summer*); Ralph Ellison (Pluto. Author—*Invisible Man*); Jean Paul Sartre (Sun. Existentialist philosopher—*Nausea*); Raoul Wallenberg (Pluto. Secretly protected many Jews from the Nazis); Herbert Philbrick (Saturn. Agent and counteragent); Art Linkletter (Pluto. TV personality—*People Are Funny*); Orson Welles (Saturn. Famous for *War of the Worlds* hoax and the hall-of-mirrors scene in *The Lady from Shanghai*); Marlene Dietrich (Neptune. Actress—*The Blue Angel*).

1 Cancer

A sailor hauls down the old flag and hoists up a new one.

Descriptive Phrases

Shifting allegiances; breaking off old relationships and forming new ones (emotionally torn—have a hard time letting go of unhealthy ties); openly declaring changes in one's feelings vs. undercover maneuvers; openness to romantic adventure; susceptibility—swaying and being swayed (dramatic mood swings vs. staying on an even keel); taking up a course in life that has real heart (anchored in their fantasies and desires rather than reality; fail to see obstacles to the realization of their dreams); joining a group united by common ideals; championing a noble cause; redefining one's identity according to one's associations; heading up a group—a family, a company, or even a nation; patriotism; loyalty vs. disloyalty.

Examples

Karen Carpenter (Uranus. Depressive, anorexic singer—"Rainy Days and Mondays"); Mary Martin (Saturn. Actress, singer—*Peter Pan*); Kris Kristofferson (Sun. Songwriter, actor—*The Man who Fell from Grace with the Sea*); Ross Perot (Jupiter. First candidate of the new Reform Party); Giuseppe Mazzini (Sun. Italian revolutionary, tried to unify Italy around humanist ideals); Moshe Dayan (Pluto. Israeli politician, bailed out of extreme right-wing coalition); John Dean (Moon. Turned state's evidence against Nixon gang in the Watergate affair); Coretta King (North Node. Stuck by Martin Luther King despite his affairs, because of strong shared ideals); Lusitania torpedoed by German U-Boat (Pluto. 5/7/1915); Margaret Mead (Neptune. Anthropologist—cross-cultural comparisons); Stephen Bechtel (Mars. CEO of Bechtel Corporation); Mary McCarthy (Sun. Writer—*The Group*); James Kunen (Uranus. Student radical—*The Strawberry Statement*); Meryl Streep (Sun. Actress—*Sophie's Choice, Out of Africa*); Herbert Philbrick (Pluto. FBI mole in the Communist Party, U.S.A.).

2 Cancer

A stage magician in a white tuxedo takes off on a magic carpet, to the amazement of the audience.

Descriptive Phrases

Confronting a mystery; suspended judgment; puzzling out an intricate problem; following a line of evidence to get behind false appearances ("Pay no attention to the man behind the curtain"); explaining puzzling phenomena through science, occult powers, psychology, or hidden strings; constant revision of beliefs in light of new evidence; being open to all the possibilities (flights of fantasy, ungrounded); seeing the magic behind the structure of life and the universe; being transported into a fantastic world by the power of love (*folies à deux*); playfulness; real-life hat tricks—creatively combining the elements or people in a situation into a beautiful and surprising new whole; finding a way to be supported by the public (fall out of favor).

Examples

Paul McCartney (Jupiter. Rock idol—"Magical Mystery Tour"); Jackie Gleason (Pluto. Comedian—*The Honeymooners*, Reginald Van Gleason); Mary Martin (Pluto. Actress—*Peter Pan*, it's done with strings); Bela Lugosi (Jupiter. Began monster-movie craze); Allen Funt (Saturn. Prankster host of *Candid Camera*); Marshall Nirenberg (North Node. Figured out the genetic code); Goldie Hawn (North Node. Perpetual ingénue, dances in midair in *Everyone Tells Me I Love You*); Fred McMurray (North Node. Actor—*The Absent-minded Professor*); Georges Simenon (Neptune. Writer—detective novels); José Feliciano (Mars. Blind guitarist, singer); Edmund Dulac (Jupiter. Children's book illustrator); Fred Hoyle (Sun, Pluto. Sci-fi writer who wrote about a sentient nebula in *The Black Cloud*, believed that viral epidemics originate in outer space; the degree does have some connection with outer space); First sighting of UFOs (Sun. June 24, 1947).

3 Cancer

Head forward and hair blowing back in a snowy wind, a beautiful woman rides a reindeer toward distant lands, orienting herself by the light of a single star.

Descriptive Phrases

Spiritual courage in facing life's deeper questions; venturing into the unknown; penetrating a mystery; traveling great distances both physically and mentally; blazing a new path; unstinting efforts to advance human knowledge; seeing past a series of obstacles to the realization of one's goal (one-pointed fixation on solving a single problem); moving incessantly from the known to the unknown, and thus ever increasing one's knowledge; puncturing false assumptions (critical, sarcastic); exploring new directions of inquiry opened up by new understandings (stuck in old formulas); research, especially scientific research; "cold" logic and abstract or mathematical thought; penetrating understanding ("superior," aloof); noble but lonely quest for truth.

Examples

Daniel Boorstin (Saturn. Popular historian—*The Discoverers*); Thor Heyerdahl (Saturn, Pluto. Sailed Kon-Tiki to prove his theories); United States of America (Venus. 7/4/1776); Margaret Hamilton (Neptune. Actress—Wicked Witch on her broom); Richard Bach (Sun. Writer—*Jonathan Livingston Seagull*, had a long out-of-body experience); Olivia de Havilland (Pluto. Actress—*The Snake Pit, Gone with the Wind*); Carson McCullers (Pluto. Writer—*The Heart is a Lonely Hunter*, champion of the underdog); Nat Hentoff (Venus. Leftist political columnist); Eric Hoffer (Neptune. Writer—*The True Believer*); Helen Keller (Venus. Deaf-mute, socialist); Jonas Salk (Saturn. Created first polio vaccine); Francis Crick (Pluto. Codiscovered the structure of DNA); Isaac Newton (Moon. Tireless researcher, unified physics and astronomy); Dorothy Sayers (Mercury. Writer, critic, translator).

4 Cancer

Fascinated by a cartoon mouse on television,
a cat takes a swat at it; then, having recognized
that it isn't real, turns away in contempt.

Descriptive Phrases

Playful interface between fantasy and reality; probing to see how far one's projected desires and fears extend into real life (bizarre flights of fantasy); providing the public with imaginative fare that whets a real appetite (popular culture that explores curious images or archetypes); getting vicarious enjoyment from media vs. wanting more than mere imagery; suspending disbelief vs. calling someone's bluff; probing others to arrive at a new level of emotional understanding vs. refusing to let others pin one down; honing one's mental claws through playful sparring (push people's buttons, cruel); tapping one's primitive instincts in games of love or war; outmaneuvering one's opponents; being agreeable vs. having to show one's claws to keep from being put upon.

Examples

Dr. Seuss (Neptune. Author of children's books—*The Cat in the Hat, Oobleck*); Antonio Gaudi (Sun, Architect of strange, organic forms); Sissy Spacek (Uranus. Actress—*Carrie*); Colin Wilson (Sun. Writer—*The Occult, Mind Parasites*); Rob Reiner (Saturn, Stationary direct. Director—*This Is Spinal Tap*); June Lockhart (Sun. Actress—*Lost in Space*); Cary Grant (Neptune. Debonair actor); Ian Fleming (Mars. Writer—James Bond stories); Raymond Burr (Pluto. Actor—*Perry Mason*); Leni Riefenstahl (Neptune. Nazi filmmaker—*Triumph of the Will*); Philo T. Farnsworth (Jupiter. Inventor of television); Elisabeth Kübler-Ross (Moon. Writer—*On Death and Dying*); Lili St. Cyr (Pluto. Striptease artist); Piers Anthony (Moon. Sci-fi writer—*The Macroscope*); Anjelica Huston (Mars. Actress—*The Witches*); Bob Crane (Mercury. Actor—*Hogan's Heroes*); John Lithgow (North Node. Actor—*The Adventures of Buckaroo Banzai*); Hugh Lofting (Saturn. Writer—*Doctor Doolittle*).

5 Cancer

Radio blaring, teenagers in a souped-up convertible race a train to the crossroads. The owner of the local bar looks on in disgust, hands on his hips.

Descriptive Phrases

Mature vs. immature judgment; knowing when to speak and act, and when not to; calculating outcomes before speaking or acting vs. recklessly jumping into something (want to know what they can get away with); thinking on one's feet; instant analysis and rapid decision-making that makes all the difference when a situation is in spin; assessing the separate elements of a situation as they come together (or blow apart); creating a happening scene; bringing excitement and energy to a scene that's going nowhere (party-makers vs. party-crashers); throwing cultural bombshells to destabilize a moribund scene; disrupting people's expectations and mental ruts (pranks vs. antisocial violence); knowing when to bail out of a bad situation vs. attempting to change a situation that has too much of its own inertia or momentum; rebelliousness.

Examples

Fats Waller (Neptune. Stride pianist, incorrigible high-liver); Bonnie Raitt (Uranus. Blues musician); Bruce Springsteen (Uranus. Musician); Willy Mosconi (Sun. Billiards champ—break shot); Floyd Taylor (Mars. Was shot down three times as a pilot in World War II, now designs space capsule seats); Kitty Hawk flight (Neptune. 12/17/1903); Draft lottery instituted in the U. S. (Pluto. 7/20/1917); Tom Selleck (Saturn. Actor—*Magnum P.I.*); Farrah Fawcett (Moon. Actress—*Charlie's Angels*); Dustin Hoffman (Venus. Actor—*The Graduate*); Mayfair Boy (Pluto. Robbed Cartier's of London as a lark); Madalyn Murry O'Hair (Pluto. Got prayer kicked out of public schools); Jerry Rubin (Chiron. Helped disrupt the 1968 Democratic Convention); Lawrence Ferlinghetti (Pluto. Helped found the San Francisco poetry scene).

6 Cancer

A woman places stuffed animals and educational toys in her baby's crib, while her husband builds a high fence around the house.

Descriptive Phrases

Finding a social niche that provides support for oneself and one's family; establishing a "nest"[20] and stocking it with everything one needs; looking after people's emotional and intellectual needs; protecting the interests of one's family and country (defensive nationalism); consolidating one's position in some problematical but secure situation (want to feel competent and secure at one level before venturing to the next); establishing mastery over some province of life (narrow, controlling); making good on early promise vs. getting bogged down and failing to carry through; working out the ramifications of one's beliefs (fussing over details); setting up an information network vs. working new data into a pre-existent analytical framework (promoting teamwork).

Examples

United States of America (Jupiter. 7/4/1776); Indira Gandhi (Pluto. Ruthless Indian politician); Anwar Sadat (Pluto. Patriarchal politician of Egypt); Buckminster Fuller (Mercury, Stationary. Invented the geodesic dome); Aleksandr Solzhenitsyn (Pluto. Soviet dissident, writer—*The Gulag Archipelago*); Richard Hofstadter (Mars. Historian—*The Paranoid Style in American Politics*); Jessica Mitford (Pluto. Writer—*The American Way of Death*); Morris Berman (Saturn. Writer—*The Reenchantment of the World*); Paris Commune founded (North Node. 3/29/1871); Ayn Rand (Neptune. Writer—*The Fountainhead*); Bob Keeshan (Sun. Children's show host—*Captain Kangaroo*); Anne Landers (Pluto. Advice columnist); Pearl Buck (Sun. Author—*The Good Earth*, story of the rise and fall of a great household); Paolo Soleri (Pluto. City planner, whose Utopian community failed due to its bad location—no water); Duncan Philipps (Sun. Art collector—the Philipps Gallery of Washington D.C.).

7 Cancer

In a moonlit forest, a captured man is forced to dance for the king of the leprechauns.

Descriptive Phrases

Resistance of the natural self to society's repressive expectations; untamed children of nature (satyr-like sexual kinkiness, unbridled fantasy life); awakening of creative natural energies under cover of darkness; looking for an opening to express one's sexual or magical energies; hanging on to one's personal myths; breaking the mental chains of imposed culture; stump speeches for freedom (brow-beating rants); subversive challenges to consensual reality; making people come to grips with one's own reality; turning the tables; provocative social commentary; penetrating observation of human behavior; testing psychological insights by pushing people's buttons (cruel bullying); irrepressible individuality; droll and mischievous humor.

Examples

Mel Brooks (Sun. Comedian—*Blazing Saddles*); Gilda Radner (Sun. Comedienne—Rosanne Rosanna-Dana); Helen Keller (Sun. Blind and deaf, socialist stump speaker); Maurice Béjart (North Node. Ballet dancer); Augusto Sandino (Jupiter. Central American revolutionary); Jay Kinney (Uranus. Modern writer in the gnostic-Subgenius mythos); Billy Graham (Pluto. Influential evangelist); Nikos Kazantzakis (Saturn. Writer—*Zorba the Greek, The Last Temptation of Christ*—gnostic fantasy concerning the crucifixion); William S. Burroughs (Mars. Writer—*Naked Lunch*—homosexual heroin fantasies); Nancy Sinatra (Mercury. Singer—"These Boots Are Made for Walking"); Pietro Aretino (Jupiter. Licentious Renaissance poet); Oscar Levant (Jupiter. Pianist, bad-tempered wit); Albert Ellis (Mars. Sexual psychologist); Adolf Hitler (Chiron. German dictator); Van Morrison (North Node. Rock singer); Gale Storm (Pluto. Elfin actress); Sun Myung Moon (Pluto. Cult leader); Alex Haley (Neptune. Writer—*Roots*).

8 Cancer

Animals dressed as human courtiers are performing a satirical comedy of manners.

Descriptive Phrases

Irreverent parody of the human animal and his bestial institutions; confronting society with its unconscious assumptions, as if in a mirror; epitomizing human behavior and human character in art or drama (see life as a moral fable); showing up phoniness and pretense; exposing the artificiality of conventional sex-roles; fear and erotic desire as the real motivations behind most behavior; life as a chase (social games, vying for prestige); knowing how to compete in the cultural marketplace; wittiness vs. slander; amorous indiscretion (need to rein in their impulses and occasionally bite their tongues); brave individualism vs. hiding behind a social role; serious social criticism vs. crabby contrariness; savvy and penetrating soliloquies.

Examples

George Orwell (Neptune. Writer—*Animal Farm, The Lion and the Unicorn: Socialism and the English Genius*); William Shakespeare (Mars. Playwright); George Bernard Shaw (Saturn. Playwright); Oriana Fallaci (Sun. Interviewer); Doris Lessing (Pluto. Feminist writer—*The Golden Notebook*); Robert Bly (North Node. Poet, men's movement); Sandra Bernhard (Mars. Outrageous lesbian stand-up comic); Oscar Wilde sentenced to Reading Gaol for sodomy (Jupiter. 5/25/1895); Justin Green (North Node. Cartoonist—*Binky Brown Meets the Virgin Mary*); Karen Horney (Saturn. Psychologist); Honoré de Balzac (Mars. Satirist of French society); Bill Moyers (Mercury. Journalist); Spalding Gray (Mercury. Monologuist); D. H. Lawrence (Saturn. Novels exposing human desires); Jean-Paul Sartre (Neptune. Existentialist philosopher—*No Exit*); Gary Goldschneider (Chiron. Coauthor of *The Secret Language of Birthdays*); Tony Auth (Mars. Political cartoonist); Mary Calderone (Venus. Early champion of birth control).

9 Cancer

From the marble rim of a pool, a naked little girl is trying to catch a goldfish.

Descriptive Phrases

Curiosity and open-mindedness about life's mysteries (walling off unacceptable beliefs); trying to get a handle on a problem by experimenting with various approaches; tentative grasp of life's elusive paradoxes; slippery truths of philosophy and religion ("fish stories," fantasy and sci-fi); glimpsing hints of a mystery (blurt out any odd idea that pops up from their subconscious); fishing for the truth and finding one piece of it (the elephant's trunk); selling people on one's beliefs; catching someone's interest and reeling them in; seductiveness (conquering shyness and inhibition); innocent, experiential approach to sex vs. trollish leering; the subjectivity and fluidity of reality (silly speculations vs. establishing the bounds of good sense); playful experimentation.

Examples

Gracie Allen (Neptune. Mind-twisting comedienne—Burns and Allen); Ernie Kovacs (Jupiter. Zany comedian—Percy Dovetonsils); Roger Waters (Saturn. Rock musician—Pink Floyd); Robert Millikan (Uranus. Physicist who studied the wave/particle dichotomy of the electron); Karen Black (Sun. Actress—*Nashville, Plan Ten from Outer Space*); Helen Gurley Brown (Pluto. Editor of *Cosmopolitan*); Zelda Fitzgerald (Venus. Flapper—symbol of the jazz age); Jean Cocteau (Mars. Symbolist filmmaker—*Beauty and the Beast, L'Age d'Or*); Timothy Leary (Pluto. LSD guru, flaky philosopher); H. G. Wells (Uranus. Novelist, philosopher—*The Time Machine*); Arthur Schopenhauer (Mars. Philosopher influenced by Eastern thought—*The World as Will and Idea,*); Cardinal Giuseppe Siri (Neptune. Hardline reactionary Catholic); David Susskind (Pluto. Political commentator); Clyde Tombaugh (Neptune. Astronomer who discovered Pluto by comparing photos and finding a star that "moved").

10 Cancer

After a waltz beneath the stars, a man takes out an impressive diamond ring and proposes to his sweetheart. While she examines the ring, she is inwardly considering her boyfriend's virtues and liabilities.[21]

Descriptive Phrases

Sharing rapturous moments of purest beauty vs. seeing through myths and glamor to practical realities (open to flattery and the lure of the high life); looking at all the facets of a problem; working through doubts to a state of moral certainty; sure sense of self-worth; perfecting the highest image of the soul; knowing one's own strengths and weaknesses and judging others by the same high standards (imperious, drag other people's faults into the light); demanding to be taken on one's own terms (want to be courted, even by the public); balancing various roles, especially career and family; hard-heartedness vs. tender-heartedness (scandalized by injustice and moral ugliness); giving shape and focus to shared romantic or political ideals.

Examples

Grace Kelly (Mars, Stationary retrograde. Actress, Princess of Monaco); William Powell (Venus. Actor—*The Thin Man*); Myrna Loy (Neptune. Actress—*The Thin Man,* worked for U.N.); Cher (Ascendant. Actress—*Moonstruck*); Jackie Gleason (Saturn. Comic—Reginald van Gleason); Zsa Zsa Gabor (Pluto. Multiple marriages for money); Eugene McCarthy (Saturn. Antiwar candidate for president); Norman Mailer (Pluto. Writer—*Ancient Evenings, Armies of the Night*); Debbie Harry (Sun, North Node. Lead singer—Blondie); U. N. charter signed (North Node. 6/26/1945); Thomas Jefferson (Neptune. Author of the Declaration of Independence); Josephine Baker (Neptune. Cabaret star, adopted children of all races); A. H. Maslow (North Node. Psychology of self-realization).

11 Cancer

A mother moderates a difficult discussion at the dinner table.

Descriptive Phrases

Engaging others emotionally and intellectually; having a heart-to-heart talk vs. sidestepping a difficult issue until the time is right; straining to find the right words or the right expression; being cautious of one's effects on others vs. irresponsible and childish outbursts; discretion vs. indiscretion; factoring in the characters of the people one is talking to; seeing beyond social masks and listening with the heart (sensitive, tenderhearted); treating people with respect and care vs. being overly blunt; upping the emotional ante vs. using humor to lighten things up; getting a good dialogue going between the rational and the emotional mind (surprising revelations); tailoring one's public image vs. coming off as a clown; public forums; setting the tone of public debate.

Examples

Norman Lear (Pluto. Television producer—*All in the Family and Mary Hartman, Mary Hartman*); Robert Young (Neptune. Actor—*Father Knows Best*); Barbara Billingsley (Pluto. Mother on *Leave It to Beaver*); Geraldo Rivera (Sun. Talk-show host); Hal Linden (Jupiter. Actor—*Barney Miller*); Redd Foxx (Pluto. Comic—*Sanford and Son*); Rupert Murdoch (Jupiter. Tabloid king); Toni Morrison (Jupiter. Black writer—*Beloved, The Bluest Eye*); Jesse Helms (Pluto. Reactionary senator, cultural censor); Dorothy Kilgallen (Sun. Quiz shows); Judy Garland (Ascendant. Actress); Martha Mitchell (Jupiter. Loudmouthed Watergate coverup victim); Paul Harvey (Jupiter. Controversial radio show host); Woodrow Wilson (Saturn. U. S. president and key organizer of the League of Nations—to prevent future wars); Charles Schulz (Pluto. Creator of *Peanuts* cartoon-strip); Kevin Corcoran (Saturn. Disney child-actor—Moochie); Doris Day (Venus. Singer, Actress); Amy Tan (Uranus. Author—*The Joy Luck Club*).

12 Cancer

A Chinese child looks up at his mother, who is reading aloud from a holy book. For a few moments, she seems illumined by a halo of light, and he hears words that transcend the text she is reading.

Descriptive Phrases

Bringing an important message to humanity; preaching empathy and toleration; having faith in one's spiritual intuition and one's insight into the world-situation vs. expecting recognition before one has clearly manifested one's message in speech or writing (speculative glimmerings); clearly envisioning the higher potentials of the race vs. being exasperated by humanity's spiritual blindness (may have to write for future generations, since they are often ahead of their times); tender-hearted compassion vs. hiding one's heart behind a shell of cynicism (may use black humor to plug people in); getting people to come to grips with an issue vs. self-defeating insistence on a very specific reading of the situation; planting seeds of higher consciousness; nurturing the inner light.

Examples

Alice Bailey (Mercury. Spiritual teacher, champion of Indian independence and birth control); Pete Townsend (North Node. Lead guitarist for The Who); Rachel Carson (Jupiter, Neptune. Pioneering ecologist—*Silent Spring*); Kurt Vonnegut (Pluto. Science fiction writer—*The Sirens of Titan, Welcome to the Monkey House*); Robert Altman (Pluto. Film director—*The Player, Nashville*); Ann Landers (Sun. Advice columnist); Pete Seeger (Jupiter. Folk singer and left-wing patriot); Jeddu Krishnamurti (Mars. Spiritual teacher, groomed as a child to be the new messiah); Leonard Nimoy (Jupiter. Actor, director—*Star Trek*); Daniel Ellsberg (Jupiter. Stole and published the Pentagon Papers); Jerry Garcia (Jupiter, Venus. Lead singer of The Grateful Dead); Giuseppe Garibaldi (Sun. Italian patriot and revolutionary); Immanuel Velikovsky (Jupiter. Scientist—*When Worlds Collide*).

13 Cancer

Approaching a stranded steamer, a tugboat captain sounds his horn and holds up his hand in a gesture of good will.

Descriptive Phrases

Friendliness; openhanded helpfulness; confidence in one's ability to deal with any obstacle that comes up (carefully assessing a situation before acting vs. trying to plow through a problem by sheer willpower); holding one's course vs. being on the lookout for excitement and adventure (mavericks, gamblers); strong desire to connect; quick friendships and alliances made on the road; open society of the good at heart; loosening things up emotionally by demonstrating one's good will (ulterior motives, scam artists, glad-handers); gathering confederates to help in some big task; looking for the right mate and a stable, anchored relationship (tests of loyalty); extending one's grasp of life by extending the range of one's experience (travel); sturdy individuality; impelling personal magnetism.

Examples

United States of America (Sun. 7/4/1776); Errol Flynn (Venus. Dashing actor, yachtsman); Drew Barrymore (Saturn. Actress—*Charlie's Angels*); Ernest Hemingway (Venus. Writer—*The Old Man and the Sea*); Ann B. Davis (Pluto. Actress—Schultzy on *Bob Cummings*, *Brady Bunch*); Jimmy Stewart (Neptune. Actor—*Mr. Smith Goes to Washington*, *It's a Wonderful Life*); Tony Curtis (Pluto. Actor—*Some Like It Hot*, *Trapeze*); Gertrude Lawrence (Sun. Actress—*The King and I*); June Allyson (Pluto. Actress); Ramsey Clark (Pluto. Ex-attorney general, famous for his goodwill mission to North Vietnam); Michael Milken (Sun. Junk-bond speculator); Neal Cassady (Pluto. Car-stealing, joy-riding beatnik); Phineas Barnum (Sun. Barnum and Bailey Circus); Stephen Foster (Sun. Sentimental songwriter); Paul Newman (Pluto. Actor, openhanded philanthropist).

14 Cancer

Alone under the stars, a man of the world contemplates the course of his life.

Descriptive Phrases

Reappraising long-range goals in light of one's higher sense of self; seeking a religious framework of meaning for one's life rather than a relative or social framework; "dark nights of the soul" when one questions the course of one's life; wanting to be remembered for something significant vs. not taking oneself all that seriously (self-parody); living by one's own lights; psychological autonomy; guarding one's individual freedom; fighting for the freedom and dignity of the individual against social oppression (biblical heroics); moral or intellectual leadership of social movements (don't want to lose their freedom by getting too involved, criticize from the sidelines); bearing witness; spiritual crisis followed by renewed seriousness of purpose.

Examples

Gian Carlo Menotti (Sun. Composer—*Amahl and the Night Visitors*); Carl Jung (Mercury. Psychologist—*Answer to Job*); Max von Sydow (Mars. Actor in Bergman movies); Charlton Heston (Pluto. Played Moses in *The Ten Commandments*, head of the National Rifle Association); Gina Lollobrigida (Venus. Played the priestess in biblical epics, became a professional photographer after her film career ended); Ernest Hemingway (Venus. Writer—*The Old Man and the Sea, The Sun also Rises*); Aleksandr Solzhenitsyn (Jupiter. Writer—*The Gulag Archipelago*); Olivia de Havilland (Venus. Actress—*The Snake Pit, Robin Hood*); Kurt Cobain (Moon. Lead singer of Nirvana, committed suicide); Frida Kahlo (Sun. Painter, wife of Diego Rivera, lived in constant pain); Dalai Lama (Sun. Leader in exile of Tibet, spiritual teacher); Sidney Poitier (Pluto. Actor—*Lilies of the Field*); Isadora Duncan (Mars. Dancer); Lady Isabelle Gregory (North Node. Leader of the Irish Renaissance, cofounded the Abbey Theatre with Yeats).

15 Cancer

A fat, smiling chef lifts the cover of a silver platter and presents a suckling pig to a group of appreciative diners.

Descriptive Phrases

Feeding one's appetites; luxuriating in the pleasures of the senses (gluttony, sexual excess); taking what one wants from life (selfish, amoral); differentiating what one needs from what one wants; finding a middle ground between asceticism and overindulgence ("pigging out" in one area of life to compensate for poverty in another); understanding one's own and other people's appetites; transforming the images of one's dreams and desires into an artistic creation that the public can enjoy (expose their inner desires, or suffer exposure); catering to the needs of the public; ministering to those who have been shortchanged by society or by nature; popularity (win friends through their emotional generosity, hospitality, and fun-loving, larger-than-life personality).

Examples

Henry VIII (Sun. Took over the English church in order to divorce and remarry, many wives, luxurious tastes); Mae West (Venus. Comic actress, married to a bodybuilder, she tried to set a record for days of nonstop sex); Jonathan Winters (Pluto. Comedian—*The Loved One*); Robert Morley (Venus. Actor—*Who Is Killing the Great Chefs of Europe?*, *Oscar Wilde*); Sebastian Cabot (Sun. Actor); Edith Head (Neptune. Created the most luxurious costumes for Hollywood stars while she herself wore plain unisex clothing); Claudette Colbert (Neptune. Actress—*Cleopatra*); Cherry Boone O'Neill (Sun. Anorexic—*Starving for Attention*); Cab Calloway (North Node. Band leader—*Reefer Man*); Ringo Starr (Sun. Drummer for The Beatles, actor—*The Magic Christian*); Tennessee Williams (Mars. Playwright—*A Streetcar Named Desire* and other potboilers); Sammy Davis, Jr. (Pluto. Nightclub singer with seamy secret life); Melina Mercouri (Pluto. Actress—*Never on Sunday*, Greek political activist).

16 Cancer

A jester in cap and bells recites an obscene limerick. Offended, the king sends him off to the dungeon.

Descriptive Phrases

Truth-telling cultural agitators; breaking down cultural barriers (risqué, cutting-edge culture); rebelling against a repressive power structure with topical humor vs. trying to maintain the status quo (perpetual struggle between uptight assholes and free spirits); finding a balance between social stability and individual freedom; issues of containment—clamping down vs. loosening up; adapting organizational structures to demands for reform vs. stonewalling that could incite open rebellion; finding a practical compromise vs. holding to an ideology; the necessity of breaking out of old (Cancerian) shells when one is evolving to a more conscious level of social organization; poking holes in the official story vs. gleefully blowing off steam; uncensored remarks.

Examples

Robin Williams (Uranus. Comic—*Good Morning Vietnam, Dead Poets Society*); Eric Idle (Jupiter. Monty Python comedian); Shirley Temple (Pluto. Mischievous child star); Bill Haley (Pluto. Early rock-and-roll star); Lenny Bruce (Pluto. Foul-mouthed comic harassed by the law); Spiro Agnew (Jupiter. Blunt vice president); Jeane Kirkpatrick (Pluto. loud-mouthed harridan in the U.N.); Robert MacNamara (Saturn. Vietnam War advisor, president of World Bank); Ivan Illich (Pluto. Anarchist critic of American education); Larry O'Brien (Sun. Democratic Party national committee leader); Robert Woodward (Jupiter. Broke open the Watergate case; Watergate is a big, tiered building); Sylvia Porter (Mercury. Economist); John Chancellor (Pluto. Reads the official story on the news); Lester Maddox (Saturn. Ardent segregationist who became governor of Georgia); Eartha Kitt (Pluto. Entertainer who was blacklisted for mouthing off to President Johnson about the war in Vietnam); Marty Feldman (Sun. Comedian—Igor in *Young Frankenstein*).

17 Cancer

Young insurgents gather around the portrait of a nationalist martyr that has been nailed to a huge tree stump. Suckers growing from the stump have framed the picture in a leafy bower.

Descriptive Phrases

Taking responsibility for the evolution of one's culture toward its ideals; passionate demand that society conform to ideals of humanity and justice; willingness to suffer and even to die for one's beliefs; deathlessness of the life-force, which passes from one life form to another; infusing others with one's spirit, ideals, and courage; abiding influence of those who have dedicated their lives to their ideals; gathering patrons and supporters; taking up the slack when one loses a leader; doing what needs to be done (withdraw into hermitlike solitude); adventurousness; exploring unknown territory; representing national ideals abroad; reformers and pioneers who are pushing some vital cultural or political agenda; keeping the faith.

Examples

William Proxmire (Saturn. Politician, reformer); Milan Kundera (Pluto. Czech writer—life during the invasion); Jim Jones (Jupiter. Utopian minister gone wrong, mass suicide in the Guyana jungle); Maria Montessori (North Node. Innovative educator); Bob Marley (North Node. Jamaican reggae singer); Fess Parker (Pluto. Actor—Davy Crockett); Odetta (Jupiter. Folk singer); Claude Levi-Strauss (Neptune. Anthropologist); Che Guevara (Pluto. Guerilla, revolutionary); Kathé Kollwitz (Sun. Artist—the sufferings of war); Claus von Stauffenberg (North Node. Tried to kill Hitler); Liza Minelli (Mars. Singer); Alec Guiness (Mars. British actor—*Star Wars*, and many comic and military roles); Emma Goldmann (Neptune. Anarchist leader); Akira Kurosawa (Neptune. Japanese filmmaker—*Throne of Blood*); Yasir Arafat (Pluto. Palestinian leader).

18 Cancer

Mother Goose holds a birthday party for one of her children, who sits next to her at the head of the table, wearing thick, heavy-rimmed glasses.

Descriptive Phrases

Odd ducks; shy awkwardness vs. being at home with oneself, and bopping cheerfully through life (charmingly eccentric); strange, myopic vision of the world, which focuses on the most personal and psychologically relevant aspects of experience (live in a dream world); colorful and fantastic reworkings of one's experience in the imagination; cockeyed look at human behavior; focusing on life's shadow-side or psychological underpinnings (morbid obsession with madness and monstrosity); sensitivity to others' feelings (can be easily manipulated by their parents); finding a safe haven, and only venturing forth when one is ready (momma's boys, arrested development); helpful nurturing vs. being unwilling to grant independence to one's creations; unusual cultural offerings.

Examples

Cloris Leachman (Pluto. Actress—*Young Frankenstein*); Fred Gwynne (Sun. Actor—*Car 54, Where Are You,* Herman Munster); Carl Jung (Venus. Alchemical psychology); Günter Grass (Pluto. Author—*The Tin Drum, Dog Years*); Nicola Tesla (Sun. Inventor with incredible powers of visualization); Sally Struthers (Mercury. Actress—*Feed the Children*); Don Martin (Jupiter. *Mad* magazine cartoonist); Edith Head (North Node. Hollywood costumer); Philip K. Dick (Pluto. Sci-fi writer—*Ubik, Man in the High Castle*); Joy Adamson (Neptune. Writer—*Born Free,* raised a lion cub and then released it); Jean de la Fontaine (Sun. Writer of fables); George Kuchar (Jupiter. Underground filmmaker—*The Mammal Palace, Thundercrack!*); Paul Simon (Moon. Musician with a sociological bent); Malcolm Lowry (Neptune. Writer—*Under the Volcano*).

19 Cancer

A prince marries a beautiful showgirl in the great hall of his family castle. After the ceremony, the couple is mobbed by a throng of well-wishers.

Descriptive Phrases

Romantic love that bridges two worlds (odd couples); acting as a representative of one's culture; displaying confidence and poise in awkward social situations; loosening up a stuffy scene; expanding the bounds of acceptable taste (use shock value to open people up to new sensibilities); disseminating new ideas through popular culture; achieving popularity even while one breaks the mold; knowing what people are saying behind one's back, but winning them over with charm and savoir-faire; cultivating one's individual beauty and taste (unusual or striking beauty); shaping one's public image (striking glamorous poses); appreciating the richness and beauty of life (childlike wonder vs. false naiveté); "fairy-tale" romances based on mutual adoration.

Examples

Marilyn Monroe (North Node. Actress—*The Prince and the Showgirl,* married Arthur Miller and Joe DiMaggio); Grace Kelly (Pluto. Actress who married a prince); Emperor Mutsohito (Moon. Admitted foreigners to Japan); Yul Brynner (Sun. Actor—*The King and I, The Magic Christian*); Lily Tomlin (Ascendant. Comedienne with a longtime female partner and creative collaborator); Antonia Fraser (Venus. Popular historian—*Mary, Queen of Scots,* married into immense wealth); Arnold Schwarzenegger (Mercury. Bodybuilder, film star, politician, married Maria Shriver of the Kennedy clan); John Waters (Saturn. Scandalous film director—*Polyester*); Rupert Murdoch (Pluto. Tabloid magnate); John Lennon (Chiron. Beatles songwriter, controversial marriage to Yoko Ono); Annie Besant (Jupiter. Early birth-control advocate, Theosophist); Jack Anderson (Ascendant. Newspaper columnist); Leonard Nimoy (Pluto. Paired with William Shatner on *Star Trek*); Jackie Kennedy (Pluto. First Lady, storybook marriage).

20 Cancer

The main gate of a castle, guarded by a bloodhound and a man in armor. Seeking to gain admittance, an outsider plies the guard with flattery, whereupon the dog begins to growl.

Descriptive Phrases

Protecting home or country from destabilizing elements (conservatism vs. radicalism); Saturn as gatekeeper; having a good nose for people's hidden intentions (psychic); getting around people who stand in one's way; using good manners and disarming charm vs. dropping all pretense and expressing oneself in a rude and direct manner (won't back off, sabotage their own efforts by harassing people); being smooth vs. being slippery; anticipating routine bureaucratic responses and "oiling the hinges"; going through established channels vs. using extralegal means; gaining privileged information and using it to advantage (spying); questioning others to determine if they can be trusted; being above-board vs. slipping something by the censors.

Examples

Anthony Blunt (North Node. British art historian, spy for Russia); Ursula LeGuin (Pluto. Writer—*The Dispossessed*); G. Gordon Liddy (Jupiter. Watergate plumber who kept mum and went to jail); Patty Hearst (Uranus. Kidnapped and involved in a bank robbery, rescued and "deprogrammed"); Arnold Schwarzenegger (Ascendant. Actor—*The Terminator*, gained entrance into high society by marrying Maria Shriver); Dick Clark (Pluto. Helped legitimize rock and roll); Joseph McCarthy (Neptune. Tried to keep communists out of government); Judy Garland (Venus. Actress—barred at the gates of the Wizard); Van Cliburn (Sun. Classical pianist, heads an important annual competition); Anne Marie Rasmussen (Venus. Norwegian maid who married into the Rockefeller family); Mia Farrow (Saturn. In *Radio Days*, she breaks into society by improving her accent and diction).

21 Cancer

A volunteer nurse attends a mortally wounded young soldier. Smiling down at him, she wipes off his brow and hums a little song.

Descriptive Phrases

Rising to the occasion; moving into the breach; adopting whatever role is most needed, or is appropriate to one's situation or stage of life (feminine mysteries, women as presiders over the mysteries of birth and death; women as both Virgin and Kali); showing one's love for humanity through commitment, exertion, and sacrifice; seeing oneself as the hero or heroine of a spiritual drama; living up to other people's expectations and projections (live for others rather than themselves); providing a positive role model; protecting or reassuring others; instilling hope and courage; big-heartedness (pained by the suffering of humanity); taking a stand for one's beliefs (argumentative); showing fortitude in situations that test one's moral or physical courage; fighting the good fight.

Examples

Father Flanagan (Sun. Founded Boy's Town); William Mayo (Venus. Founder of the Mayo Clinic, surgeon); Mother Teresa (Neptune. Established a hostel for the dying in India); Anne Landers (Mercury. Advice columnist); Sister Elizabeth Kenny (Saturn. Nurse—polio research); Jim Nabors (Pluto. Gospel singer, actor—*The Jim Nabors Show*); John Cleese (Chiron. Comic specializing in pompous roles); Harrison Ford (Sun. Actor—*Indiana Jones*); Ted Kennedy (Pluto. Liberal leader in the U. S. Senate); Elizabeth Taylor (Pluto. Actress—*Cleopatra*, AIDS activist); Ingmar Bergman (Sun. Film director—*Fanny and Alexander, The Seventh Seal*); James Barrie (Jupiter. Writer—*Peter Pan*); Odetta (Pluto. Folk singer); Leslie Caron (Pluto. Actress—*Gigi*); Candice Bergen (Saturn. Actress—*Murphy Brown*); Rosalind Russell (Mars. Actress—*Auntie Mame*); Grace Slick (Chiron. Rock star); Frank McCourt (Pluto. Author—*Angela's Ashes*).

22 Cancer

On the beach, under the stars, a beautiful woman watches expectantly as a sailboat approaches.

Descriptive Phrases

The power of imagination and inherited mythologies to shape reality, whether in romance or in politics; imposing one's own vision on things (magic); adding touches of color and romance to one's world; cultivating an amusing and creative scene with one's friends and intimates; having the mental poise to see past one's own expectations and other people's beliefs to what is really there vs. being sucked into one's own or other people's games; poised judgment of the good or bad possibilities of emerging situations; judging the drift of circumstances and acting accordingly vs. passively waiting for one's ship to come in; the reality of deeply felt emotions even when they find no counterpart in external reality; unswerving loyalty to emotional ideals.

Examples

A.E. Van Vogt (Neptune. Sci-fi writer—*Slan*); Ingrid Bergman (Mars. Actress—*Suspicion*); Antoine de St.Exupéry (Venus. Pilot, writer—*The Little Prince*); Winsor McCay (Uranus. Cartoonist—*Little Nemo*); Eve Arden (Neptune. Actress—*Our Miss Brooks*); John Lithgow (Mars. Actor—*The Adventures of Buckaroo Banzai, Third Rock from the Sun*); Frantz Fanon (Moon. Writer on colonialism); Gandhi (Uranus. Spiritual leader of the Indian independence movement); Woody Guthrie (Sun. Leftist folk singer); Umberto Eco (Pluto. Semiologist, author—*The Name of the Rose*); Elaine Pagels (Pluto. Revisionist historian—*The Gnostic Gospels*); E. O. Reischauer (Neptune. U.S. ambassador to Japan); Ingmar Bergman (Sun. Filmmaker—*Fanny and Alexander*); Henri Alain-Fournier (Saturn. Wrote *The Wanderer*, a quintessential novel of adolescent longing); Gus Grissom (North Node. Astronaut); Robert Graves (Jupiter. Author—*The White Goddess*); Gian Carlo Menotti (Neptune. Composer—*Amahl and the Night Visitors*).

23 Cancer

Under the vine-covered pergola of an outdoor cafe, a group of intellectuals is holding a lively discussion. A woman who had previously been silent forcefully outlines her position.

Descriptive Phrases

Free exchange of ideas and feelings vs. dominating or being dominated by a group (corral others into agreement); developing a wide network of informants; having an ear for the views of the group, while maintaining a fiercely independent perspective (outsiders who figure things out for themselves); collecting facts and experiences that fit one's aesthetic (the Moon as a net); personal experience as the foundation for any grounded philosophical system; balancing Sun and Moon, concrete perception and interpretation; balancing male and female components of the psyche; dominance and submission in intellectual or sexual relationships; critical discussions of the general situation; pulling together important factors so one can decide on a wise course of action vs. ineffectually open-ended blather.

Examples

Albert Camus (Mars. Existentialist philosopher—*The Stranger*); André Gregory (Pluto. *My Dinner With André*, existentialist cultural critic); Diane Keaton (Saturn. Actress, director—*Unstrung Heroes*); Robert Anton Wilson (Pluto. Writer—*The Illuminatus Trilogy*); Rainer Fassbinder (Saturn. Decadent filmmaker); Rudolf Arnheim (Sun. Philosopher—*Visual Thinking*); Ginger Rogers (Sun. Dance partner of Fred Astaire); Marquis de Sade (Saturn. Sexually depraved writer); Emmeline Pankhurst (Sun. Women's rights pioneer); Walt Kelley (Venus. Cartoonist—*Pogo*); Versailles Treaty (Jupiter. 6/28/1919); Barbara Walters (Pluto. Interviewer); Mary McCarthy (Neptune. Writer—*The Group*); Dwayne Hickman (Pluto. Actor—*Dobey Gillis*); Barbara Stanwyck (Sun, Jupiter. Mannish actress).

24 Cancer

Two men and a woman—the survivors of a shipwreck—are building a fort on the promontory of their new island home, one man directing the others.

Descriptive Phrases

Dealing with chaotic situations in a levelheaded way; sizing up a situation that's in flux and taking command (swimming against the tide vs. waiting for one's chance); envisioning the best outcome for a situation vs. wasting one's time in unrealistic dreams; the power of a visualized ideal to structure one's activities and relationships (swept up in romantic adventures); adapting to disruptive new elements (relationship complications); deftly playing the hand one has been dealt; directing others toward some collective goal (didactic, meddlesome, tell others how to live); making one's home more comfortable and secure vs. having to start all over again; riding the ebbs and flows of worldly fortune; working to better one's conditions vs. idle dreaming.

Examples

Jim Backus (Neptune. Actor—*Gilligan's Island*); William Golding (Neptune. Author—*Lord of the Flies*); Robert Heinlein (North Node. Sci-fi writer—*Stranger in a Strange Land*); Clark Gable (Moon. Hollywood romantic lead—*Mutiny on the Bounty*); Bryan Ferry (Saturn. Romantic rock singer—*Siren*); Kate Chase (Mars. Ambitious socialite who promoted the careers of her father and husband during the Lincoln administration and was eventually ruined); Gloria Swanson (Mars. Plays a has-been actress living out a fantasy in *Sunset Boulevard*); Marla Gibbs (Saturn. Actress—the bossy maid on *The Jeffersons*); Larry Fine Howard (Neptune. Comedian—*The Three Stooges*); Farley Granger (Mercury. Actor—*Strangers on a Train*); Dudley Moore (Pluto. Actor, director—*Bedazzled*); Jean Marsh (Mercury. Actress—*Upstairs, Downstairs*); Susan Atkinson (Jupiter. Writer—*It's All Her Fault* and *It's All His Fault*).

25 Cancer

Upon hearing his cue, an actor throws his jacket across his shoulder and makes his entrance.

Descriptive Phrases

Heeding one's calling; having a sense of personal destiny; confident pursuit of personal goals (wrapped up in their own plans); living out a self-created role; taking delight in one's act; theatrical grandstanding; brashness; panache; developing a bold, colorful personality vs. self-caricature; maximizing one's strong points and playing down one's weak points (tough-minded self-confidence impervious to criticism); conscientious preparation for one's larger role on the world stage (isolated practice vs. obtaining coaches, agents, and a "supporting cast"); playing one's hand skillfully (roguish schemes, covering up one's misdeeds); waiting for the right time to make a bid for recognition (giving one's talent time to unfold); daring to live life as a grand adventure.

Examples

Phyllis Diller (Sun. Comedienne); Hunter Thompson (Sun. Gonzo writer, drug abuser); Stephen King (Mars. Horror writer); Bette Midler (Saturn. Comic singer, actress); Neal Cassady (North Node. Car-stealing beatnik); Peter O'Toole (Pluto. Actor—*The Ruling Class*); Divine (Saturn. Fat transvestite actor in John Waters' films); William Kunstler (Jupiter. Grandstanding lawyer for controversial clients); Jerry Rubin (Mars. Chicago Seven defendant, author of *Do It*); Annette Funicello (Jupiter. Actress—*Beach Blanket Bingo*, Mouseketeer); Richard Nixon (Neptune. U.S. president); Julia Child (Neptune. Television chef); Lord Byron (Moon. Romantic poet, relentless self-promoter); Jimi Hendrix (Jupiter. Flamboyant acid-rock guitarist); Lil Son Jackson (Saturn. Blues musician); Christo (Pluto. Flamboyant artist—draped buildings); Dalai Lama (Pluto. Tibetan spiritual and political leader).

26 Cancer

Cocktails and conversation at a diplomatic soirée in the library of an old mansion.

Descriptive Phrases

Cultivating a polished, dignified social persona (put forth an attractive, sociable front, but are actually very private and secretive); witty, cultivated drawing-room conversation; social sophistication; penetrating observations based on a wealth of knowledge, culture, and worldly experience; gathering information and evidence (as in *Clue*); winkling out secrets; building an analytical model that adequately houses all the facts (poorly supported theories); emergence of a new level of understanding once one has digested all the facts; publicly representing the viewpoints of some constituency (pushing an "official story" vs. providing the real lowdown); gaining admittance and influence within privileged circles; class acts vs. elitism.

Examples

Basil Rathbone (Venus. Actor—Sherlock Holmes); Sophia Loren (Pluto. Actress); Eric Sevareid (Neptune. Newscaster); Ellen Goodman (Chiron. Political columnist); Tennessee Williams (Neptune. His plays usually involve the exposure of ugly secrets); Erle Stanley Gardner (Saturn. Author—Perry Mason mysteries); Shere Hite (Jupiter. The *Hite Report* on sexuality); Alec Guiness (Neptune. Actor); Martha Stewart (Mercury. Home and garden specialist, hostess); Pat Oliphant (Pluto. Political cartoonist); Jan Myrdal (Sun. Political writer—*Report from a Chinese Village*); L. Patrick Gray III (Sun. Ex-head of the F.B.I.); Kate Millett (Pluto. Feminist writer); Audrey Hepburn (Mars. Actress—*Roman Holiday, My Fair Lady*); Dumbarton Oaks Conference (North Node. 8/21/1944); Stewart Alsop (Neptune. Columnist); Howard K. Smith (Neptune. Columnist); Alfred Harbage (Sun. Literary critic).

27 Cancer

Barbarians on horseback swoop down on a wilderness fort, a violent lightning storm following close behind them.

Descriptive Phrases

Individuals who are untamed "forces of nature" (barbarian, uncouth); mobilizing one's energy, especially in a fight; overwhelming one's foes with a higher order of force (violent frenzy; descent into barbarism, as during war); surrendering to primal instincts in a fight, while keeping one's mental and physical poise (martial arts); obeying natural laws vs. being destroyed by nature; precariousness of civilization in the face of unleashed human passions (dammed-up collective emotions that finally break free); taking on an evil culture (intolerant); pressing a point in public dialogue; shocking the public into recognizing some imminent danger; getting a charge from dangerous adventures (lose out by going too far); fearless sexual or physical confrontation; naked force.

Examples

Arnold Schwarzenegger (Venus. Actor—*Conan the Barbarian*, politician); Ulysses S. Grant (Moon. Union general); Norman Mailer (Moon. Writer—*Armies of the Night*); Jack Nicholson (Pluto. Actor—*Easy Rider, The Shining*); Diana Rigg (Sun. Actress—*The Avengers*); Xaviera Hollander (Jupiter. Prostitute, sexual advice columnist); Rachel Carson (North Node. Environmentalist who wrote *Silent Spring*); Morris Berman (North Node. Ecological writer—*The Reenchantment of the World, Coming to Our Senses*); Debbie Harry (Mercury. Lead singer for Blondie); Rubin "Hurricane" Carter (Pluto. Boxer, falsely convicted of murder); Phil Donahue (Pluto. Controversial talk-show host); John Calvin (Sun. Extremist Protestant leader); Charlie Manson (Pluto. Crazed cult leader); Ken Kesey (Pluto. Leader of the LSD-crazed Merry Pranksters); George W. Bush (Saturn. President—war against Iraq).

28 Cancer

A Native American girl introduces her college boyfriend to the tribe.[22] *He gives a short speech and then cautiously responds to objections from his girlfriend's mother.*

Descriptive Phrases

Insistent attempt to get through to others (alienated); power of the heart to bridge human differences; seeking understanding and acceptance of one's viewpoint (insecure); eliciting feedback; keeping close tabs on public opinion; pushing the bounds of the socially acceptable into new territory and thus changing social attitudes (hidden cultural agendas); breaking down national or cultural barriers by refusing to respect them (social gaffes, get off on the wrong foot); winning an argument by being able to see both sides (cultural arrogance may lead to ostracism); using a talent or skill to gain acceptance in an otherwise closed society (wowing the public); putting one's own peculiar ideas into a language people can understand; speaking from the heart.

Examples

John F. Kennedy (Saturn. First Catholic president); Woody Allen (Pluto. Filmmaker, one of America's most visible Jews); Billy Holiday (Neptune, Stationary direct. Blues singer); C. V. Wedgwood (Sun. Historian, hid the fact that she was a woman by using only her initials); Julie Andrews (Pluto. Actress, singer—*Victor, Victoria*); Jesse Owens (Neptune. Black runner who showed up Nazi racial theories at the 1936 Olympics in Berlin); Frantz Fanon (Sun. Writer on the destructive effects of colonialism); Joseph Conrad (Saturn. Writer—*Heart of Darkness; Lord Jim*); Luciano Pavarotti (Pluto. Popularized opera in U.S.); Carlos Santana (Sun. Singer); Sammy Davis, Jr. (North Node. Black entertainer, converted to Judaism, received death threats for his relationship with a white woman); Carl Stokes (Sun. Cleveland's first Black mayor); Maria Montessori (Mars, Uranus. Progressive educator); Civil Rights Act (Uranus. 3/1/1872, puts Blacks on juries, and gives them equal legal rights in public).

29 Cancer

Peering over the scales of justice, a judge listens intently as the prosecuting attorney outlines his case.

Descriptive Phrases

Penetrating to the heart of a matter; seeing the turning point of an issue; argumentation; intellectual sparring; penetrating questions and quick retorts (too sure of their own position, blind spots leave them vulnerable); pressing one's advantage vs. backing away from unproductive disputes; seizing one's destiny by acting with courage and decisiveness at life's crossroads (dramatic swings of fortune, attempts to get one's emotional life and career back on an even keel); seeing the larger pattern in a cultural conflict; being an articulate spokesperson for one side of an issue; refocusing public debate (alienate others by championing unpopular positions); weighing and comparing the value of two positions; penetrating intellectual or spiritual judgment.

Examples

Dick Cavett (Pluto. Talk-show host); Hayley Mills (Mars. Quizzical actress); Bertrand Russell (Uranus. Philosopher, mathematician—*Why I Am Not a Christian*); Judy Blume (Pluto. Controversial author of children's books—*Blubber*); Diana Rigg (Mars. Actress—Emma Peel on *The Avengers*); Bill Cosby (Pluto. Comic, TV dad); Herman Wouk (Neptune. Author—*The Caine Mutiny*); Earl Warren (Chiron. Liberal chief justice of the Supreme Court); William F. Buckley (North Node. Conservative political commentator); William Tallman (Neptune. Hamilton Berger on *Perry Mason* series); Vaclav Havel (Pluto. Dissident playwright, first post-Communist president of Czechoslovakia); Mary Travers (Pluto. Singer—Peter, Paul, and Mary; political activist); Albert Brooks (Sun. Film director—*Defending Your Life*); Melvin Belli (Mercury. Showboat lawyer who relishes confrontation); Learned Hand (Uranus. Highly insightful federal judge); Robert F. Kennedy (North Node. Attorney general who fought for racial equality before the law).

30 Cancer

After delivering a lecture on reincarnation, a guru fields a question from a skeptic in the audience.[23]

Descriptive Phrases

Updating a spiritual tradition in light of one's own observations and research; putting new spins on old truths (hip); learning from spiritual adepts but being wary about being sucked in (gullibility vs. skepticism); spiritual self-reliance; sharing one's truths (pretend to more knowledge than they have); exposing misinterpretations; uncovering facts that change one's worldview (unsettled beliefs); venturing into murky speculative realms vs. giving practical attention to one's own problems; differentiating the true from the probably true, the possibly true, and the false; suspending judgment until one gets the facts (at sea, don't know what to believe); achieving clarity in meditation vs. collecting spiritual techniques; finding some audience, however small vs. being isolated by one's beliefs; open-mindedness vs. confused uncertainty.

Examples

Jean Houston (Pluto. Founder of the Foundation for Mind Research); John Lilly (Neptune. LSD experimentation, sensory deprivation tanks); Martin Luther (Moon. Leader of the Reformation); John Dee (Sun. 16th-century mathematician and occultist, victim of a supposed angel conjuror); Sally Priesand (Mercury. First female rabbi in the U. S.); Rose Kennedy (Sun, Mercury. Ruling-class matriarch); Jane Fonda (Pluto. Notable critic of the Vietnam War, actress—*The China Syndrome*, remade herself several times); Eugene McCarthy (Neptune. Ran for president to stop the war in Vietnam); Robert Darnton (Pluto. Hip historian—*The Great Cat Massacre*, mass psychology or *mentalité*); Christina Crawford (Pluto. Author of *Mommy Dearest*); Lucien Febvre (Sun. Historian—*The Problem of Unbelief in the Sixteenth Century*); Immanuel Velikovsky (Mars. Controversial cosmologist who wrote *Worlds in Collision*); Alan Watts (Neptune. Popularizer of Zen Buddhism); Fred Hoyle (Neptune. Astronomer, held out for the steady-state theory over the "big bang").

1 Leo

A lion tamer faces a roaring, rampant lion and brings him under control with a bellowed command.

Descriptive Phrases

Establishing control; governing oneself and others; reining in one's passions vs. undermining one's position by blowing up or by being too sexually aggressive (strong urges to express oneself, even when socially inappropriate); pursuing one's business with quiet confidence vs. causing an uproar with an emotional outburst; mastering a personal or political situation and turning it in a positive direction (take the bull by the horns); righteous political leadership (imperious, high-handed); winning a confrontation vs. backing down; courageously speaking one's mind vs. biting one's tongue; channeling animal passions (strongly sexual, controlling oneself when aroused vs. sexual self-display); fully mobilizing one's energies; dominating one's field.

Examples

Annie Oakley (South Node. Sharpshooter); Portia Porter (Neptune. Female bullfighter); Jackie Gleason (Neptune. Comedian—"To the moon, Alice! To the moon!"); Madonna (Venus. Crotch-grabbing pop singer—*Truth or Dare*); Hunter Thompson (Pluto. Writer—*Fear and Loathing in Las Vegas*); Girolamo Savonarola (Uranus. Fiery Renaissance preacher who gained great political power, but was eventually burned at the stake); Margaret Thatcher (North Node. Iron-willed British prime minister); Peter Benchley (Pluto. Author—*Jaws*); Alexandre Dumas (Sun. Author—*The Three Musketeers*); Churchill's "Blood, Toil, Tears, and Sweat" speech (Pluto. 5/13/1949); Monica Lewinsky (Sun. Sometime mistress of President Clinton); Jon King (North Node. Porn star); John Foster Dulles (Saturn. U. S. statesman who saw the containment of world communism as his mission); Bill Maher (Uranus. Talk-show host—*Politically Incorrect*); Daniel Radcliffe (Sun. Plays the title role in the *Harry Potter* films).

2 Leo

Having arrived at the site of an epidemic, a doctor gives a press conference on the nature of the disease and procedures for containment.

Descriptive Phrases

Disseminating vital information; promoting sexual, mental, and emotional health; injecting potent information into the body politic to boost its resistance to dangerous ideas or desires vs. infecting the public with insidious but seemingly harmless cultural forms; focusing in on a problem; journeying boldly into the belly of the beast to discover its workings vs. quarantining oneself from virulent ideas or desires (letting a fever run its course—indulging perverse or destructive desires); strictly following a personal code of conduct; examining the purity of one's motives before beginning a new venture vs. acting out of lust or resentment (sexual rebelliousness, let no one else dictate their behavior); getting something out in the open.

Examples

Philip Agee (South Node. Exposed the horrors of the CIA's cover operations); Betty Furness (Neptune. Consumer affairs spokesperson); William Ruckelshaus (Sun. First head of the Environmental Protection Agency); Don Herbert (Saturn. TV's popular science host, *Mr. Wizard*); Josef Goebbels (South Node. Nazi propaganda minister); Tokyo Rose (Neptune. Taunting radio announcer during World War II); Ken Russell (Mercury. Filmmaker—*Lair of the White Worm*); Liv Ullmann (Pluto, Rising. Star of Ingmar Bergman films—*Through a Glass Darkly*); Gore Vidal (North Node. Leftist gadfly—*Julian, Burr*); William Masters (Neptune. Sex researcher); Theodore Reik (Saturn. Psychoanalyst—*Masochism in Modern Man*, claimed to cure homosexuality); Jill Ireland (Neptune. Actress, wrote a book on surviving breast cancer); Peter Fonda (Pluto. Actor—*Easy Rider*, and *Ulee's Gold*, in which he plays a father who must help his drug-addicted daughter); Welles' *War of the Worlds* broadcast (Pluto. 10/31/1938).

3 Leo

Having done up her hair in a fashionable twist, a woman smiles confidently at her reflection in the mirror.

Descriptive Phrases

Learning to project one's personality with confidence and warmth; maintaining a positive self-image; grooming oneself for success; courting the public; passionate involvement in life versus withdrawing due to personal insecurity (too sensitive to criticism, especially about their looks, focus on negatives rather than positives); fashionable attitudes; working at the cutting edge of modern social sensibilities (trendy, hip); putting one's finger on the key problem in a tangled situation (the barrette as a Chiron-like key); unlocking social energies; getting people to laugh and let down their hair; telling it like it is (political humor); enthusiastic self-creation vs. uptight poses; playing a supporting role vs. going for star status (feel unappreciated).

Examples

Goldie Hawn (Mars. Actress—*Private Benjamin, The Banger Sisters*); Mick Jagger (Sun. Androgynous rock star once married to mirror-image Bianca Jagger); James Dean (Mars. Charismatic actor who represented a new generation of "troubled youth"); Cass Elliot (Pluto. Fat, beautiful, and charismatic singer for The Mamas and the Papas); Jackie Kennedy (Mercury. First Lady, fashion plate); Judy Blume (Moon. Children's book author—*Blubber*); Carson McCullers (Neptune. Wrote books about misfits and freaks); Troy Perry (Pluto. Gay pastor); Ringo Starr (Mars. Ugly but cute drummer for The Beatles); Spalding Gray (Pluto. Monologuist); Melvin Belli (Sun. Showboat lawyer); Raymond Burr (Neptune. Actor—*Perry Mason*); Jon Stewart (North Node. Topical and political humorist); John F. Kennedy (Neptune. Charismatic president); Glenn Gould (Mars. Classical pianist, *enfant terrible*).

4 Leo

A guest at a prestigious men's club, having tired of all the social games, grabs a hat off of a moose head being used as a hatrack and wittily pronounces on the pretensions and status of its owner.

Descriptive Phrases

Sharp observers of people and society; playing social games vs. exposing the game (don't really fit in—feel awkward and funny-looking); maintaining social composure vs. acting like a bull in a china shop; acid-tongued exposure of social hypocrisy; taking aim at discrepancies between people's true character and their social personas; trying out various "hats" to develop lesser "points" in one's personality vs. developing a dominant or trademark character trait (lack psychological integration, need to do transformative inner work to balance various elements in the personality; interest in human psychology, especially character typology); changing one's costume and social persona in order to explore new aspects of one's personality; impish genius.

Examples

Frank Zappa (Pluto. Trenchantly satirical rock singer—The Mothers of Invention); Barbara Streisand (Pluto. Singer, comedienne—*Funny Girl*); George Bernard Shaw (Sun. Atheist philosopher, playwright—*Pygmalion*); Sandra Bullock (Sun. Actress—*While You Were Sleeping*); Georg Grosz (Sun. Satirical antibourgeois artist); Phil Ochs (Pluto. Leftist folk singer); Voltaire (Pluto. Outrageous Enlightenment satirist—*Candide*); Carl Jung (Sun. Psychologist who posited four human types—feeling, thinking, intuitive, and sensate); Bette Midler (Mars. Singer, comedienne, actress—*Big Business, First Wives' Club*); Bette Davis (Jupiter. Actress—*Jezebel* and *Now, Voyager*); Erica Jong (Pluto. Author—*Fear of Flying*); Aldous Huxley (Sun. Author—*Brave New World*); Spike Lee (Uranus. Filmmaker—*Do the Right Thing*); C. Wright Mills (Neptune. Leftist sociologist—*The Power Elite*).

5 Leo

A master climber deftly ascends a series of invisible handholds. Having attained the summit of the cliff, he turns and exhorts the climbers below.

Descriptive Phrases

Ambition; rugged determination to come out on top; never letting up or letting go (clawing one's way up); shoring up one's position vs. taking potshots at those above (insubordinate); solid reliability of character, which makes one fit to run things (organization managers); keeping one's mind on the business at hand vs. getting involved in everyone else's business (personalize public concerns, publicize private concerns); sure-footed leadership vs. talking others into following a risky plan that hinges on successfully navigating some iffy maneuvers (cliffhangers); scoping out a new terrain; extending previous knowledge to new situations; preaching the truth (rants); being assured and giving assurance; serving as a shining inspiration to the race.

Examples

The Beatles (Paul McCartney—Pluto; Ringo Starr—Moon; John Lennon—Pluto. Rock stars); Alene Duerk (Moon. First female rear admiral); Mohandas Gandhi (North Node. Political and spiritual leader of the Indian independence movement); George Wallace (Jupiter. Southern politician who attempted to blockade desegregation efforts); Petrarch (Sun. Inspired leader of the Renaissance who wrote *The Ascent of Mount Ventoux* about his personal spiritual struggles); Dorothy Brett (Jupiter. Landscape artist of Taos, NM); George Rogers Clark (Neptune. Explorer of the Northwest Territory); Sly Stone (North Node. Rock singer—"Stand," "You Can Make It if You Try"); Muhammad Ali (Pluto. Boxer—"The Greatest"); Harrison Ford (Pluto. Actor—*Indiana Jones* cliffhangers); Betty Ford (Neptune. Set up alcohol treatment center to give a hand to those who have not yet surmounted their problem); Peggy Fleming (Sun. Champion skater); Le Corbusier (Saturn. Architect).

6 Leo

An old flapper and an up-to-date young woman exchange glances of admiration.

Descriptive Phrases

Confident embodiment of new styles in thought, music, and dress; making an unmistakable statement; displaying one's talents; strutting one's stuff (vain, flirtatious, court the admiration of the public); exuberance; playfulness (like a kid dressing up in her parents' clothing); creating and enjoying a scene (organizers of social events); seeing one's own pivotal place in the broad sweep of history; appreciating and preserving the values of the past but taking the next evolutionary step; savvy evaluation of other people's assets (competitive—put people into categories); changes in external fashions that help catalyze changes in consciousness vs. mere trendiness; getting in step with a new beat; harmonious progression; dramatic flair.

Examples

Cass Elliot (Pluto. Lead singer for The Mamas and the Papas—"Words of Love"); Alexis de Tocqueville (Sun. French historian—*Democracy in America*); Bella Abzug (Mercury. Radical politician famous for her big hats); Joe E. Brown (Sun. Comic famous for his tango scene in *Some Like It Hot*); Jacqueline Kennedy Onassis (Sun. Trendsetting First Lady); Alex Haley (Mars, Mercury. Author—*Roots*); Jerry Garcia (Pluto. Rock musician—The Grateful Dead, brought the spirit of the 1960s to a new generations); Joe Namath (Pluto. Fashion-conscious quarterback); Geena Davis (Uranus. Actress—*Earth Girls Are Easy*); Chubby Checker (Pluto. Popularized the Twist and the freeing of the American pelvis); Carl Sagan (South Node. Popularizer of science, debunker); Petrarch (Mercury. Poet, writer, philosopher who initiated the Italian Renaissance); Alphonse Mucha (Jupiter. *Art nouveau* poster artist).

7 Leo

A man contemplates the Great Pyramid on a clear and starry night.

Descriptive Phrases

Sense of wonder in the face of universe; coming upon or seeking out experiences of the magical and the timeless; endowing the natural world with subjective meaning through poetry or art; tuning in to a new vibration or getting into an exciting new groove; zoning in vs. spacing out; macrocosm-microcosm issues; world empire—expanding one's country's boundaries vs. seeing that even the most glorious civilizations eventually return to sand; fear of being obliterated by the sands of time; trying to make a permanent name for oneself for services rendered to one's country vs. realizing that the timeless is entirely transcendent to the physical; being impressed vs. being impressive; appreciating life's unlimited potentiality vs. seeing life as a glorious dream.

Examples

Napoleon Bonaparte (Mercury. Emperor—conquered Egypt and much of Europe but ended a prisoner on a small island); Leo X (Saturn. Renaissance pope, generously patronized the arts to make Rome the most splendid of all cities); Boris Karloff (Saturn. Actor—*The Mummy*); Georgia O'Keeffe (Saturn. Painter); Antionio Gaudi (Venus. Architect of amazing tiled structures); Garth Hudson and Richard Manuel (Pluto. Musicians—The Band); Jerry Garcia (Mercury. The Grateful Dead lead guitarist—played an open-air concert next to the pyramids); Janis Joplin (Pluto. Hippie blues singer); Arthur C. Clarke (Neptune. Sci-fi writer—*Childhood's End*); Lisa Kudrow (Sun. Space-cadet actress on *Friends*); George Lucas (Pluto. Director—*Star Wars*); Kim Deitch (Pluto. Underground cartoonist); Nikki Giovanni (Moon. Poet); Guglielmo Marconi (Uranus. Developer of radio-telegraphy).

8 Leo

Speaker at a demonstration passionately denounces the injustices of the political system.

Descriptive Phrases

Making a passionate case for one's beliefs; raging against injustice and oppression; recounting stories of human heroism and human villainy in the ongoing struggle to redeem humanity (folk and protest music); tenderhearted empathy for human suffering (the Sacred Heart surrounded by the thorns of human suffering); fighting for the underdog; working for the benefit of humanity vs. self-immolation in sexual activity (reject sexual repression as a form of oppression); giving one's all to a cause vs. suffering burnout; demanding immediate change vs. getting hung up in the procedural mechanisms of government (join the ruling elite, sell out); being completely up front vs. having a hidden agenda; inciting others to stand up for their rights.

Examples

Angela Davis (Pluto. Communist professor); Mario Savio (Pluto. Leader of the Free Speech movement); Paul Soglin (Pluto, Stationary. Sixties radical, reformist politician); Declaration of Independence (North Node. 7/4/1776); Larry Flynt (Pluto. Publisher of *Hustler* magazine, fought several court battles over free speech); Alice Walker (Pluto. Writer—*The Color Purple*); Christopher Isherwood (Mars. Gay writer—*Goodbye to Berlin*); Marianne Faithfull (Saturn. Soulful folk-rock singer, one-time heroin addict); R. Crumb (Pluto. Underground cartoonist, the age's greatest political and cultural ranter); Tristan Tzara delivers the Dada Manifesto (Saturn. 3/23/1918); Brigitte Bardot (South Node. Sex-kitten actress, animal-rights activist); Gloria Steinem (Moon. Feminist leader); Lauren Bacall (Venus. Slinky actress—*Cactus Flower*, went to Washington D. C. to protest the McCarthy witch hunt); Bolshevik Revolution (Neptune. 11/7/1917); Julian Beck (North Node. Organizer of The Living Theater, an improvisatory collective).

9 Leo

A police officer asks pointed questions of a sweating, muscular blacksmith who, by way of answer, increases the force of his hammer blows.

Descriptive Phrases

Holding one's own in a confrontation (violent, combative); having the courage to fight for one's beliefs or reputation, and the wisdom to withdraw when the fight can't be won (iron-willed resolve, non-negotiable demands); adjusting physical or emotional forcefulness to the situation: moving between utmost forcefulness and utmost delicacy of touch (overkill vs. underkill); hammering away at one's point (attempt to indoctrinate others or mold them to one's own ways of seeing things, browbeating); self-application to the task at hand vs. nosy intrusiveness; developing mastery in some craft (independent workers, don't like to be bossed); absolute absorption in the creative process (the alchemical alembic); forging a sexual identity; developing one's sexual style and sexual rhythm; inner confidence vs. intimidation and bluster.

Examples

Toshiro Mifune (Neptune, Jupiter. Actor—Samurai movies); Jack Webb (Jupiter, Neptune. Actor—*Dragnet*); Sally Field (Saturn. Actress—*Norma Rae*); Malcolm X (North Node. Black Muslim leader); Amy Lowell (Uranus. Lesbian poet); John Holmes (Pluto. Porn star with an oversized hammer); Ingrid Bergman (Saturn. Actress—*Suspicion*); Adrienne Barbeau (Pluto. Actress—*Escape from New York*); Herman Melville (Sun. Writer—*Moby Dick*); Howard Cosell (Jupiter, Neptune. Sportscaster with a jackhammer vocal style); William Kunstler (Mercury, Neptune. Defense attorney for the Chicago Seven and other political dissidents); Penny Marshall (Pluto. Actress—*Laverne and Shirley*, director—*Big*); Jerry Garcia (Sun. Lead guitarist of The Grateful Dead); William Holden (Saturn. Actor—*Stalag 17*).

10 Leo

In front of a marble temple, wide-eyed Isis holds up a golden ankh, from which shining rays of light fan outward. Next to her stands the stern priest of Re, his eyes closed.

Descriptive Phrases

The power of universal love, expressed by God in the light of the sun; the sun's power to bestow life vs. the sun's power to expose evil; unconditional love vs. harsh judgment; spreading the Word (the Golden Rule); opening people's eyes to the world's love and beauty vs. spiritual blindness and destructive egotism; grasping material things vs. using one's gold for the greater good; high living vs. sharing kindness and hospitality even with the undeserving; holding to external forms vs. centering oneself in eternal spiritual forms; registering strong impressions vs. putting one's personal stamp on all that one does (impeccable taste and style, love of luxury goods); discovering ancient secrets of life and death shining in one's soul (mysticism).

Examples

Lana Turner (Neptune. Played a high priestess in *The Prodigal*); Lauren Bacall (Ascendant. Stylish actress—*How to Marry a Millionaire*); Cher (Pluto. Singer, actress—*Isis Productions*); Yul Brynner (Mercury. Played Pharaoh Rameses in *The Ten Commandments*); Rosalynn Carter (Mercury. First Lady); Myrna Loy (Sun. Stylish actress—*The Thin Man* series, worked for the U.N.); John Tyndall (Sun. Physicist, studied the magneto-optic properties of crystals); Josephine Baker (Ascendant. Cabaret star who raised a tribe of adopted children in a French chateau); Donovan (Pluto. Folk-rock singer); Justin Green (Pluto. Cartoonist—*Binky Brown Meets the Virgin Mary*, where he reveals his childhood hallucinations of "rays" coming from the Virgin's hands); Mozart (Neptune. Classical composer, *bon vivant*); Evalyn McLean (Sun. *Nouveau riche* hostess and *bon vivant*).

11 Leo

Lit by a sunbeam, a beautiful little girl is swinging from the branch of a huge old oak tree. In the darkened foreground, one of the "wee folk" is leading others into a natural door at the base of the tree.

Descriptive Phrases

The eternal child (unwilling to grow up, spiral back in time through the magic door of memory); preserving the communion with nature one enjoyed as a child (Druidic animism—see the world as boundless, magical, and fully alive); innocent playfulness (bossy—insist on controlling the game and the rules; may lead others into dangerous adventures); the ability to become entirely immersed in play or other imaginative, creative activities; the innate, intuitive wisdom of children; using the natural language of symbols (symbolic art as a spell or enchantment); protecting others by herding them back to a more rooted view of life (treat others like children); drawing from the strength and wisdom of nature; stout-hearted embrace of the life-force.

Examples

Gilda Radner (Pluto. Comedienne—*Saturday Night Live*); Patty McCormack (Pluto. Child actress—*The Bad Seed* and *Twilight Zone* episode "Do You Remember Now?"); Jay North (Sun. Child actor—*Dennis the Menace*); Marie Antoinette (Neptune. Consort of Louis XVI, liked to dress up as a shepherdess); Dolly Parton (Pluto. Country singer); Ian Anderson (Venus. Rock singer—*Songs from the Wood*); Morris Berman (Sun. Critic of scientism—*The Reenchantment of the World*); Van Morrison (Pluto. Folk-rock singer); Andy Rooney (Neptune. Folksy commentator, storyteller); Frank Lloyd Wright (North Node. Architect); James Hilton (Ascendant. Writer—*Lost Horizon*); Martha Stewart (Sun. Yuppy crafts mogul); Carroll O'Connor (Sun. Irish-American actor—*Archie Bunker*); Satyajit Ray (Neptune. Indian film director—*The World of Apu*, Indian life as seen through the eyes of a child).

12 Leo

An otherworldly costume party in a grove hung with Japanese lanterns. Nature spirits dance and carouse under the half-moon, each wearing a mask painted with the face of a human being.

Descriptive Phrases

Developing a fascinating public persona that both conceals and reveals one's spiritual identity; letting one's light peek out in order to connect socially with others of one's "tribe"; connecting with different nationalities or types of people by putting forth different sides of one's personality (cosmopolitan); the child's confident knowledge of his own essential nature, which allows him the freedom to play with different personas (only play at being adults, look down on the "act" from above, philosophical detachment vs. campy self-mockery); feeling the host's responsibility for harmonizing a group vs. detachedly checking out a scene; feeling stifled under social conventions vs. stirring things up with probing remarks and public unmaskings (mischief-makers).

Examples

Bette Midler (Pluto. Singer, actress—*Hocus Pocus*, does environmental work); Fred Astaire (Mars. Elf-like dancer); Hans Grimm (Uranus. Fairy-tale collector); Elton John (Pluto. Leprechaun-like rock singer); David Lander (Pluto. Squiggy on *Laverne and Shirley*); Goldie Hawn (Pluto. Sprite-like actress); Theodore Roosevelt (Saturn. U. S. president, conservationist); Arnold Schwarzenegger (Saturn. Bodybuilder, actor, politician); John Lithgow (Pluto. Actor—*The Adventures of Buckaroo Banzai*, *Third Rock from the Sun*); Ray Bradbury (Neptune. Science fiction writer); Alfred Hitchcock (Venus. Hammy movie director); Catherine Burns (Pluto. Actress—fairy in *Legend*); Doug Henning (Pluto. Stage magician); William Butler Yeats (Mars. Irish poet, occultist, compiled fairy stories in *The Celtic Twilight*).

13 Leo

An old sea captain sits on the porch of
his island home and watches a ship's approach,
its golden hull gleaming in the afternoon sun.

Descriptive Phrases

Steadfastness; remaining true to one's spiritual or archetypal nature; faithfully pursuing long-range spiritual goals (sense of divine mission); developing strength of personality by standing up to the tests of experience; going off on adventures vs. renewing oneself through rest and meditation (solitary reflection on life's serious issues); rock-solid faith in one's vision, shaken by periodic doubts as to whether one can manifest this vision (may change tack if they feel this will get them further); maintaining one's mobility vs. getting bogged down in mundane affairs (fiercely independent); the solar hero, who expects the world to revolve around his vision; gaining momentum vs. running into obstacles and resistance; making an impact.

Examples

Amelia Earhart (Mercury. Trans-Pacific aviator); Jacques Cousteau (Moon. Underwater researcher); Lotte Lenya (Mars. Singer—Pirate Jenny in *The Three-Penny Opera*); Thomas Merton (Moon. Christian mystic, seeker who visited Tibet); Pablo Picasso (Ascendant. Artist); Thomas Mann (Uranus. Writer—*Death in Venice, The Magic Mountain*); Penny Marshall (North Node. Actress, director—*Big, Awakenings*); Ian Anderson (Saturn. Rock musician—Jethro Tull); Albert Brooks (Pluto. Filmmaker—*Defending Your Life*); Alfred Lord Tennyson (Sun. Poet); Guy de Maupassant (Sun. Short-story writer); Fannie Lou Hamer (Saturn. Endured beatings and jailings to secure desegregation); Marianne Faithfull (Pluto. Folk singer); James Taylor (Pluto. Folk-rocker); Queen Elizabeth II (Moon. Long-reigning monarch); Debbie Reynolds (Jupiter. Actress).

14 Leo

A beautiful young woman lost in a dream of love. Around her face float images of soft clouds and winged cherubs.

Descriptive Phrases

Flying off on the wings of fantasy; seeing life as a waking dream, where fantasy and reality intertwine (adolescent belief that anything can happen vs. being saddened by ugly, disillusioning experiences); compassionate forgiveness that protects one's innocence of heart after bad experiences; pursuing an adventurous sex life (sensualism); belief in the immanence of the spiritual world (weird encounters); opening people up to the spiritual origin of love and beauty vs. seducing the public by playing into their fantasies (intense need for love and acceptance); openness of the unconscious to angelic or demonic influences; being aware of the divine as it incarnates through one's personality vs. grieving for the unnecessary departure of people and the world from the ideal.

Examples

Marilyn Monroe (Ascendant. Comic actress—*Seven Year Itch*); Jack Kerouac (Neptune. Beat writer—*On the Road*); R. Crumb (Jupiter. Comic artist known for his sexual obsessions); Bernadette Peters (Pluto. Dancer, actress—*Pennies from Heaven*); Art Spiegelman (Pluto. Wrote *Maus*—a history of Nazi concentration camps in comic-book form); Cher (Mars. Actress—*Moonstruck, Mask*); Pier Paolo Pasolini (Neptune. Filmmaker—*Arabian Nights, The Gospel According to Saint Matthew*); Piers Anthony (Sun. Sci-fi writer—*The Macroscope*); Ann Landers (Saturn. Advice columnist); Charlie Chaplin (Saturn, Stationary direct. Comedian); Walt Kelly (Mercury. Cartoonist—*Pogo*); Robert Altman (North Node. Disillusioned filmmaker—*Nashville, The Player*); Judy Garland (Neptune. Actress—*The Wizard of Oz*); Lucille Ball (Sun. Comedienne); Art Garfunkel (Ascendant. Folk-rock singer).

15 Leo

Amid a riot of music and costumes, the host of a variety show introduces the next act.

Descriptive Phrases

Acting as the ringmaster of one's own reality (waggish arbiters of culture); playing to an audience that follows one's progress and cheers one on; fully participating vs. holding back (crabby, rain on other folks' parades); seeing life as a party vs. using entertainment as a way of getting across a serious cultural message; slipping the real story into everyday conversation vs. flummoxing people with a torrent of semiserious nonsense; keeping people guessing; multifaceted personalities whose several public masks both hide and reveal their inner selves; life as a predictable drama vs. stumbling upon scary subplots; keeping culturally vital story fragments alive by embodying them in one's life; polishing one's act vs. topping oneself with something new.

Examples

Ed Sullivan (Mars. Variety show host, introduced The Beatles and other culturally important figures); Andy Warhol (Ascendant. Cultural kingpin who presided over The Factory); Josephine Baker (North Node. Outrageous Black dancer at the Folies Bergères); Florenz Ziegfeld (North Node. Impresario of the Ziegfield Follies); Federico Fellini (Jupiter. Surrealistic filmmaker—*Variety Lights, Ginger and Fred*); Helen Gurley Brown (Neptune. Editor of *Cosmopolitan*); R. Crumb (North Node. Underground cartoonist—Mr. Natural); Stephen King (Pluto. Horror writer); Jacqueline Susann (Neptune. Schlock writer—*Valley of the Dolls*); Kathryn Murray (Moon. Dance teacher); Barbara Walters (Jupiter. Talk-show host); Patrick MacNee (Neptune. Actor—*The Avengers*).

16 Leo

On a lofty throne, the lion king roars in defiance. He holds a sunflower scepter, its spiral geometry prominently emphasized.

Descriptive Phrases

Taking on all comers; standing up to an enemy vs. caving in; rushing boldly into the breach (ferocity, temper); gaining public recognition or political prominence; righteous alignment with the life force vs. dallying with forces of darkness (dishonorable alliances); exposing and purging what is unwholesome, unhealthy, or perverted; expressing and imposing the divine or natural order (dictatorial—"might makes right" as the law of the jungle); seeing the geometry and "fearful symmetry" of nature; concentrating all of one's vital energy on the task at hand vs. having undeveloped potentials in reserve (the sunflower in bud); making a forceful and energetic personal statement; robust physicality; hearty friendliness vs. ferocious enmity.

Examples

Ludwig von Beethoven (Saturn. Composer); Annie Oakley (Mercury. Markswoman, circus performer); Angie Dickinson (Jupiter. Rough-em-up actress); John Belushi (Pluto. Roaring comedian, involved in sordid drug scene); Esther Williams (Sun. Glamorous Hollywood star—synchronized swimming); John Addey (Jupiter. Astrologer who developed the use of harmonics); Shirley MacLaine (South Node. Actress, spiritual seeker); Neville Chamberlain (Mars. English prime minister—policy of appeasement to Hitler); Winston Churchill (Uranus. Took on Hitler); Aubrey Beardsley (Jupiter. Decadent fin-de-siècle illustrator); T. E. Lawrence (Mercury. Lawrence of Arabia); Ted Kennedy (Jupiter. Champion of justice for South America, sordid personal life); William Blake (Neptune. Visionary poet—"Tiger, tiger, burning bright").

17 Leo

A gentle Sunday-school teacher uses current events to demonstrate the importance of spiritual ideals.

Descriptive Phrases

Unflagging persuasiveness (propagandists); securing the future by educating the young in things that really matter; inciting others to participate in political or spiritual concerns; infusing established organizations with one's own ideals vs. starting one's own organization (get completely off-track in speculative heresies); unofficial spiritual leadership; gently guiding some group to work for cultural reform; using one's influence respectfully vs. hammering away at weaker, more immature minds with forceful, well-developed arguments; escaping a rigid ideology vs. slipping into an ideology of one's own (demonize opponents, "holy wars"); debunking beliefs based on faulty facts or interpretations; having a real vocation for teaching.

Examples

John Dewey (South Node. Progressive educational theorist, philosopher); Howard Zinn (Neptune. Author—*A People's History of the United States*); Susan Oliver (Jupiter. Actress—*Father Knows Best*); Carol Weissleader (Neptune. Prison guard); Roger Waters (Saturn. Lead singer of Pink Floyd—*The Wall*); Karen Carpenter (Pluto. Inspirational pop singer); Ian Anderson (Sun. Lead singer of Jethro Tull—"Thick as a Brick"); Jane Goodall (South Node. Integrated herself into a group of apes); Ramsey Clark (North Node. Ex-attorney general, progressive foreign policy activist); Lyndon La Rouche (Neptune. Left-wing activist turned right-wing activist); Jim Jones (Mars. Cult leader—mass suicide); Barbara Mikulski (Moon. Populist Baltimore politician); Paul Ehrlich (Jupiter. Ecologist—*The Population Bomb*); Sargent Shriver (Mars. First director of the Peace Corps).

18 Leo

Having finished with the physical examination, a doctor questions his patient about emotional and spiritual issues.

Descriptive Phrases

Squarely facing the fundamental realities of the world and of one's own state of being (depressive, worriers); engaging one's friends in heart-to-heart talks about life and the world situation; tackling serious problems; seeking feedback for one's perceptions; pushing an argument to get to a deeper level of truth; taking other people's ideas to the next step by probing and questioning (Socratic method); breaking down the elements of an argument or the stages of a process; piecing together an accurate picture by gathering and assembling the evidence (scientific analysis); cultivating health of body, mind, spirit, and emotion; nurturing others in their quest for health and sanity; questions and answers about what's really going on.

Examples

Geraldo Rivera (North Node. Talk-show host); Jack Anderson (Neptune. Muckraking reporter); Roseanne Barr (South Node. Television comedienne who is unusually grounded in reality); Jackson Browne (Pluto. Folk singer, former heroin addict); Stevie Nicks (Saturn. Rock singer); Henry Miller (Chiron. Author—*Tropic of Cancer, Black Spring*, devotee of astrology); Stephen King (Saturn. Horror writer—*Carrie, The Shawshank Redemption*); Gillian Anderson (Sun. Actress—Scully on *The X-Files*); Jodie Foster (Mars. Actress—*Silence of the Lambs*); George Sand (Venus. Presided over an artistic salon); Jonathan Kozol (Mars. Writer—*Death at an Early Age: The Destruction of the Hearts and Minds of Negro Children in the Boston Public Schools, Prisoners of Silence: Breaking the Bonds of Adult Illiteracy*); Gay Talese (Jupiter. Author—*Working, Thy Neighbor's Wife*); Peggy Cass (Neptune. Actress, panelist on *What's My Line*).

19 Leo

The captain of a cruise ship chats casually with passengers and directs them to their destinations, turning momentarily to bark orders at the crew.

Descriptive Phrases

Life as a glamorous and exciting adventure; entertaining oneself and others (hedonism vs. chaperone-like moralizing); giving people more slack vs. running a tight ship; personableness; helpfulness; warmhearted schmoozing; keeping track of where one is going in the midst of life's hubbub (being the captain of one's own soul); living into a mythic persona, but knowing where the fiction ends and reality begins (not anchored in consensual reality); launching some new myth in a sea of popular fantasies to see if it will float (conartists); taking wisdom from faraway places and applying it to the immediate scene; shepherding others along a spiritual journey; seeking out one's spiritual roots (sense of personal relationship to God); congeniality.

Examples

Geraldine Saunders (Neptune. Worked as a hostess for Princess Cruises, then wrote *The Love Boat,* which was the basis for the TV show); Edna Ferber (North Node. Novelist—*Show Boat*); Madame Blavatsky (Sun. Founder of Theosophy—*The Secret Doctrine*); George Hamilton (Sun. The man with the immaculate tan, in his white suit); Alex Haley (Sun. Author—*Roots*); Marcus Garvey (North Node. Black leader—"Back to Africa", started the Black Star steamship line to take Blacks back to Africa); Hulk Hogan (Sun. Wrestling superstar); Jerry Falwell (Sun. Right-wing televangelist); Joseph Smith (Uranus. Mormon leader); Tony Randall (Neptune. Actor—*The Odd Couple*); Dianne Wiest (Mars. Stage and screen actress—*Bullets over Broadway, Radio Days*); Sly Stone (Jupiter. Rock singer—"I Am Everyday People"); Robert Morse (Mars. Actor—*The Loved One, The Boatniks*).

20 Leo

Atop a desert mesa, burning in the afternoon sun,
an Indian medicine man teaches the tribe's youngsters
the complicated steps of a circular sun dance.

Descriptive Phrases

The study of ancient wisdom traditions; mining one's familial, racial, or spiritual heritage for valuable lore, and bringing it up to date; reemphasizing the cardinal principles of some technique or tradition; perfecting the use of rituals or spiritual laws in everyday life; getting off on the right foot (botched timing, comedies of errors—going around in circles); mastering one stage before one can move to another; educational regimens that teach children subjects appropriate to their developmental stage; defining moments that begin a new stage of culture or life; having the interpretive framework of an outsider (dismayed outlook on modern society); guiding and representing one's people; defending one's stomping ground; modern priesthood.

Examples

Edith Hamilton (Sun. Scholar—*The Greek Way, the Roman Way*); Malcolm X (Neptune. Black revolutionary, leader of the Black Muslim movement); Rudolf Steiner (Jupiter. Occultist who founded Waldorf schools, which tailor teaching to developmental level); Jean Piaget (Jupiter. Psychologist who studies phases of child development); Jim Carrey (North Node. Comedian who plays an arrested child who makes the same mistakes over and over—*Dumb and Dumber, Me, Myself and Irene*); Bill Murray (Pluto. Comedian with Buddhist sensibilities—*Groundhog Day*); Aleister Crowley (Uranus. Occultist—ritual magic); Margaret Jacob (North Node. Historian of early Freemasonry); Archbishop Makarios (Sun. Patriarch of the Eastern Orthodox church); Gilbert Grosvenor (Uranus. Explorer, scientist, founder of *National Geographic*); Evonne Goolagong (Pluto. Tennis star, represents Australian aborigines in the world press); Fidel Castro (Sun. Cuban revolutionary, ideologue); Joanne Wickenburg (Mars. Astrologer—*When Your Sun Returns*).

21 Leo

Drunk chickens make giddy
attempts to fly over the barnyard fence.

Descriptive Phrases

Silly antics to lighten things up; playing the fool; attaining a higher state of consciousness through drugs or alcohol; chicken-brained ridiculousness of human behavior as seen from a higher perspective; cultural criticism; stray insights from a higher plane, expressed through humor; having the courage to risk failure or humiliation in some new venture (chickening out); finding a supportive audience for one's fledgling efforts; maintaining inner dignity in undignified situations; accepting one's own and other people's shortcomings (make too much of their handicaps); cutting oneself slack; seeing how high one can get in life vs. accepting a lowly position; rising to meet the needs of the situation vs. attempting the impossible; serious zaniness.

Examples

Bert Lahr (Sun. The Cowardly Lion in *The Wizard of Oz*); Robin Williams (Pluto. Comedian); Lily Tomlin (Mercury. Comedienne—the bag lady who receives messages from another planet); Chevy Chase (Jupiter. Stumblebum comic); Alfred Hitchcock (Sun. Director—*Vertigo*); Jimmy Carter (North Node. President—helicopter fiasco over Iran); Fidel Castro (Sun. Cuban missile crisis—not so funny); Bob Weir (Saturn. Musician—The Grateful Dead); Ruth Gordon (South Node. Actress—*Harold and Maude*); Alice Toklas (Uranus. Maker of famous pot brownies); Hunter Thompson (Mercury. Serious drug abuser—*Fear and Loathing in Las Vegas*); Kathleen Battle (Sun. Black opera star who challenged the odds); Charlton Heston (North Node. B-movie actor—*The Ten Commandments, Planet of the Apes*); Kenneth Koch (Neptune. Poet and writer of silly plays); Oliver North (Jupiter. Iran-contra operative); Lina Wertmuller (Sun. Filmmaker—*Seven Beauties*).

22 Leo

A carrier pigeon with a message alights before its master.[24] *Musing over the missive's contents, the man strokes the bird's feathers and mentally composes a response.*

Descriptive Phrases

Openness of heart; allowing other people and the world to impress a clear image upon the heart (good listeners); learning what one needs to know through intuitive reflection (being open to spiritual inspiration vs. clinging to illusions); receiving new information that puts the world into sharper focus (cultural critics who discuss discrepancies between society's self-image and its reality); continuity in one's sense of self, maintained through self-recollection vs. retooling one's self-image in a new phase of life; controlling one's projected image and the context of one's communications with others vs. allowing other people to set the agenda (passive); spiritual partnerships; coaxing people into more honest and affectionate relationships.

Examples

Penny Marshall (Jupiter. Actress—*Laverne and Shirley*, director—*Big*, *Awakenings*); Steve Martin (Sun. Revived American comedy, acted in *Roxanne* and *The Jerk*); Paul Bindrim (Sun. Ran nude therapy groups); Robert Bly (Moon. Poet, leader in the men's movement—*Iron John*); Jane Fonda (Moon. Actress, activist, exercise guru); Stockard Channing (Jupiter. Actress—*Girl Most Likely To*); Marcello Mastroianni (Neptune. Actor—*8½*, about a surrealistic rehashing of Fellini's life); George Clooney (Uranus. Actor—*O Brother, Where Art Thou?*); Lauren Bacall (Neptune, North Node. Sensual actress, wrote her own autobiography); Thomas Taylor (Mars. Translations and commentaries on neoplatonic texts); Claude Debussy (Ascendant. Impressionist composer, occultist); Jimmy Carter (Neptune. Ex-president); Edgar Cayce (Uranus. The Sleeping Prophet).

23 Leo

A scantily dressed bareback rider
jumps into the ring amid rowdy applause.

Descriptive Phrases

Fearless participation in life; meeting everyday challenges with courage and confidence; making oneself the center of attention; riding the unpredictable horse of public opinion (court the public with lowbrow culture, vulgar displays, and swaggering sexuality); entering into the competitive arena of public life (politics, entertainment); maintaining one's poise in victory or defeat vs. getting on one's high horse; getting things to revolve around oneself (testy demand for respect, sensitive egos that require lots of stroking); making the rounds of society; knowing how to generate energy and excitement (create a storm of controversy); having a worldly, freewheeling self-image; taking control through force of personality (bossy, argumentative); making a big impression.

Examples

Rita Moreno (Jupiter. Dancer, singer—*West Side Story*); Eddie Murphy (Uranus. Vulgar comedian—*The Nutty Professor*); Marilyn Monroe (Neptune. Comedienne, sex symbol—*The Prince and the Showgirl*); Bhagwan Shree Rajneesh (Jupiter. Controversial tantric yoga guru whose ashram was a continual sex orgy); Hugh Hefner (Neptune. *Playboy Magazine* empire); Julia Child (Sun. Comic chef); Bea Arthur (Neptune. Bellowing, opinionated actress—*Maude, Golden Girls*); Steven Spielberg (Saturn. Filmmaker—*E.T., Jurassic Park, Indiana Jones*); Christopher Reeve (Ascendant, Pluto. Star of *Superman*, became paralyzed when he fell off a horse); Ed Wood, Jr. (Neptune. Inept transvestite filmmaker—*Plan Nine from Outer Space*); Jimmy Connors (Mercury. Uninhibited tennis champ); G. Gordon Liddy (Jupiter. Right-wing operative jailed for Watergate involvement, talk-show host); Napoleon Bonaparte (Sun. Conqueror); Blondin walks over Niagara Falls on a tightrope (South Node. 6/30/1859).

24 Leo

In a shabby garret, a writer is at work on the final draft of an antibourgeois novel. His mistress stands behind him and tries to coax him into the bedroom.[25]

Descriptive Phrases

Going after what one really wants from life, no matter what other people think (throw caution to the wind, but end up paying the price); living by one's own rules, but with a strict code of personal honor; Bohemian or semiBohemian lifestyles (artistic luxury amid poverty); perfecting one's craft through diligent application vs. being distracted by fleeting pangs of desire; being able to tune out distractions and focus on one's creative work vs. self-indulgence (marathon sex sessions, substance abuse); cooking up something that will shake up society; keeping a lid on one's negative emotions vs. boiling over with rage; skirting the edge of social toleration (outrageousness); being unshakably self-directed vs. feeling the constant cramp of social pressures; fearless, passionate living.

Examples

Georg Grosz (Mercury. Viciously antibourgeois painter); Eric Idle and Michael Palin (Chiron. *Monty Python* comedians—*The Life of Brian*); Ulrike Meinhof (Mars. Political terrorist); Princess Diana (Uranus. Did international work to disable and remove land mines); Billie Holiday (South Node. Blues singer); Charles Bukowski (Sun. Poet); Frida Kahlo (Ascendant. Painter, wife of Diego Rivera); Fyodor Dostoevski (Mars. Writer—*Crime and Punishment*); James Baldwin (North Node. Writer—*Another Country*); Robert DeNiro (Sun. Actor—*Taxi Driver, Raging Bull*); Thomas Taylor (Moon. Translator, neoplatonist, lived and died poor); Elliot Gould (Mars. Actor—*Bob & Carol & Ted & Alice, M*A*S*H*); Neil Cassady (Neptune. Bisexual hophead beatnik); Antonin Artaud (South Node. Playwright—Theater of Cruelty, modeled himself on Poe and Baudelaire).

25 Leo

Standing next to his camel, an Arab merchant looks out over the desert and considers which oases he will visit to secure food and water.

Descriptive Phrases

Spiritual self-sufficiency and self-reliance; resolved but flexible pursuit of long-range goals; mapping out possible solutions to an intricate problem; having a game plan (taking advantage of unforeseen opportunities vs. encountering obstacles that weren't apparent at a distance); coming to grips with immediate problems vs. futile attempts to arrive at a solution in one's head; coordinating mental and physical effort; trimming one's baggage to necessities (exercising a healthy mind and body); getting a handle on one's vital energies vs. letting some vice run away with you; thinking things through carefully vs. ridiculous, half-baked improvisations (humor based on ineptitude and cluelessness); keeping track of the main line of an argument; shaking people out of stupid mental constructs (argumentative); adventurousness.

Examples

Joe Namath (Chiron. Quarterback); Mark Hamill (Mars. Actor—*Star Wars*); Woody Harrelson (Uranus. Actor—*Kingpin, Wag the Dog*); Melina Mercouri (Neptune. Politician, actress—*Topkapi*); Don Adams (Neptune. Comic star—*Get Smart*); Angela Lansbury (Neptune. Actress—*Murder, She Wrote, The Manchurian Candidate*); Arthur Conan Doyle (South Node. Detective writer—*Sherlock Holmes*); Lindbergh begins flight to Paris (Neptune. 5/20/1927); Gerard d'Aboville (Mercury. Crossed the Pacific Ocean in a rowboat); Davey Crockett (Sun. Pioneer, politician); Juliette Low (Jupiter. Founder of the Girl Scouts); Wayne Gretzsky (Uranus. Hockey champ); Mairead Corrigan (Jupiter. Irish peace activist); Baron Mayer Rothschild (Mars. Financier); Gertrude Ederle swims the English Channel (Neptune. 8/6/1926).

26 Leo

Sitting on a broken-down bridge, a blonde cowgirl strums her guitar and sings a ballad about a battle that took place on that spot. Over her head, a rainbow breaks through the clouds.

Descriptive Phrases

Expanding into life's moments of peace and beauty; looking past today's battles to a time when bridges will be mended and peace restored (polarizing different groups of people vs. harmonizing them); gaining enough distance from human struggles to see their overarching meaning (anthropological objectivity vs. the outlaw's rejection of social laws for natural laws); nostalgic reflection on the past; sensitivity to the moods of nature; beautiful moments captured through art and music; creative flair; finding a job that feels like play; discovering one's natural rhythm; time-efficient workmanship that allows one more free time; penetration of human life by the divine plan; total identification with an idealized self-image; finding grace in everyday life.

Examples

Mae West (Sun. Comedienne, singer—*My Little Chickadee*); Bernadette Peters (Midheaven. Actress—*The Jerk, Annie*); Robert Redford (Sun. Movie star—*Butch Cassidy and the Sundance Kid*); Billy the Kid (Saturn. Outlaw); Joni Mitchell (Jupiter. Singer-songwriter); Scott Joplin (Mars. Ragtime composer); Mary Cassatt (Chiron. Impressionist painter of women and children); Isak Dinesen (Jupiter. Writer—*Out of Africa*); Meriwether Lewis (Sun, Mercury. Explorer—Lewis and Clark expedition); C. Eric Lincoln (North Node. Wrote a book on the Black Muslims); Hart Crane (Mercury. Poet—"The Bridge," "The Broken Arc"); Isadora Duncan (Uranus. Dancer); Sanford Gottlieb (Neptune. Pacifist—head of SANE, author of *The Defense Addiction*); Johann von Goethe (Mercury. Poet, playwright, tried to disprove Newton's theory of white light); Guglielmo Marconi (Moon. Inventor of radiotelegraphy—a new "bridge" in the ether).

27 Leo

After a life-changing event, the sun rises upon a world that looks totally different.

Descriptive Phrases

Revelations about oneself or the world (disillusionment, rude awakenings); seeing a situation in a brand new light; revealing a secret in a grand manner (closely guarding some secret until the right moment, hide their weaknesses and present an image of placid self-assurance); living up to what people have come to expect of you vs. scandalous revelations; working for fundamental change in the cultural or political landscape; trying to awaken people from the grip of a some common myth; attacking people's faith in established institutions through cynical humor; letting go of the past vs. trying to give form to a cherished dream; developing a mythic persona that makes one a focus of public attention (self-inflation); coming into one's own vs. harboring a burning hatred for whatever stands in one's way.

Examples

Bill Clinton (Sun. U. S. president, sexual scandals); Tom Lehrer (Neptune. Purveyor of scandalous ditties); Voltaire (Jupiter. Influential Enlightenment cynic—*Candide*); Hirohito (Mars. Emperor of Japan—Land of the Rising Sun, surprised allies with Pearl Harbor attack, surprised in turn by atomic bomb attack); Judy Chicago (Sun. Modern artist with strong sexual content); Janis Joplin (North Node. Rock singer); Patricia Loud (Neptune. Let a TV crew film and televise her family's household life); St. Francesca Cabrini (Venus. Catholic saint—set up many missions and hospitals); Orville Wright (Sun. Co-invented the airplane); H. R. Haldeman (Neptune. Nixon aide imprisoned for Watergate misdeeds, author of *The Ends of Power*); Elaine Pagels (Chiron. Surprisingly revelatory works on the evolution of Christian doctrine); Fidel Castro (Neptune. Cuban revolutionary, dictator); Lyndon Johnson (Jupiter. Became president suddenly upon Kennedy's death).

28 Leo

A mystic in an underground cell meditates upon the Tree of Life, pictured as a tree with smiling suns and frowning moons as fruit. When he emerges into the light, the world seems strangely transformed.

Descriptive Phrases

Promoting some mystical or imaginative vision (scary interface between dreams and reality—science fiction, horror); gnostic reinterpretations of theological truths (heretical beliefs that undermine normal reality, leading to persecution by the "reality police"); being imprisoned in a false system of values which posits "us against them" vs. leading people out of spiritual darkness into a more universal system of values; universalism vs. tribalism in human society; refounding society on the principles of love and cooperation; recognizing that heaven and hell are states of mind, but far from being "just psychological," have a structural basis in human society; feeling imprisoned by ignorance vs. emerging transformed after a spiritual crisis.

Examples

Paul Foster Case (Jupiter. Expert on the tarot and Cabala); David Duchovny (North Node. Actor—*The X-Files*); H. P. Lovecraft (Sun. Horror writer); Patrick McGoohan (Neptune. Actor—*The Prisoner*); Vladimir Bukovsky (North Node. Activist who exposed Russia's use of mental institutions for political prisoners); Thomas Merton (South Node. Christian mystic); Jane Roberts (Neptune. Author—*Seth Speaks*); Herbert Marcuse (Sun. "Heretical" Marxist with a psychological bent—*Eros and Civilization*); Vivian Robson (Saturn. Astrologer); Peter Weir (Sun. Mystical filmmaker—*Picnic at Hanging Rock*); Robert Duncan (Saturn. Helped found San Francisco poetry scene, deep interest in alchemy); Hans Kung (Neptune. Theologian—reinterpreted damnation, outlined a new "global ethics"); Martin Buber (Uranus. Jewish theologian—*I and Thou*); J. D. Salinger (Saturn. Novelist and recluse—*Catcher in the Rye*).

29 Leo

A mermaid, held prisoner by a prince who demands her love, manages to escape back into the ocean.

Descriptive Phrases

Being out of one's element, and in danger of spiritual or emotional dessication; escaping an oppressive political or emotional situation by physically moving to a freer locale (expatriates); being exotically different from others and thus liable to misunderstanding and persecution (imprisonment); fighting for human rights against cruelty and barbarism vs. making self-preservation one's chief priority; exploring one's more lush or exotic emotional fantasies through art or the imagination (self-indulgent); trying to get a handle on slippery but powerful emotional truths; otherworldly visions or connections to other planes of being; judging which of one's desires are worth actively pursuing, and which lead to death or stagnation; fortitude of spirit that takes one through troubled times.

Examples

Aleksandr Solzhenitsyn (Saturn. Wrote *The Gulag Archipelago* on the institutionalization of political dissidents); Richard Wright (Jupiter. Writer—*Black Boy*); Anne Frank (Neptune. Famous diary describes her life hiding from the Nazis); R. D. Laing (Neptune. Psychologist—*The Divided Self*); John Lilly (South Node. Isolation chamber, communication with dolphins); Kenneth Kaunda (North Node. President of Zambia, often imprisoned for political activity); Lina Wertmuller (Neptune. Filmmaker—*Swept Away*); Jane Fonda and Roger Vadim (Moon and Neptune. Actress and filmmaker—*Barbarella*); Claude Debussy (Sun. Impressionist composer—"La Mer"); Ann Blyth (Neptune. Actress—*Mr. Peabody and the Mermaid*); Jimi Hendrix (Chiron. Musical visionary—"Electric Ladyland," "Bellybutton Window"); Diana Nyad (Sun. Olympic swimmer); Vaslav Nijinsky (Saturn. Ballet superstar); Jane Roberts (Neptune. Channeler—*Seth Speaks*); Aubrey Beardsley (Sun. Libertine illustrator).

30 Leo

Noontide: a little girl sets out to deliver an unsealed letter bearing the embossed insignia of the king.

Descriptive Phrases

Serving the laws of one's divine nature as one's highest duty; cheerfully and humbly accepting one's childlike role in the larger scheme (living up to parental expectations); faith that one has been given all that one needs in order to do what one was put here to do (sense of divine protection); remembering what one is about vs. losing oneself in unthinking routines (misplaced focus, put minor tasks on the same level as important tasks); unhurriedly carrying out one's duties; radiant assurance in the goodness of life (ignore problems under their noses); being cheerfully untroubled vs. being empty-headed; warmth and openness of personality; attunement to life's higher harmony and design (studying life's unvarying cycles vs. lazy and childish fatalism); step-by-step fulfillment of personal dharma; implicit trust in the order of things.

Examples

Cindy Williams (Sun. Actress—*Laverne and Shirley*); Dick York (Neptune. Darren on *Bewitched*); Max Schulman (Moon. Writer—*Dobie Gillis*); Gene Kelley (Sun. Dancer, actor); Barbara Eden (Sun. Actress—*I Dream of Jeannie*); Stan Laurel (Saturn. Comedian—*Laurel and Hardy*); Jerry Garcia (Mars. Rock musician—the Grateful Dead); Sonny Jurgenson (Sun. Football star, sports commentator); Beverly Nichols (Mercury. Writer—*Father Figure*); Shelley Long (Sun. Actress—*Cheers*); Ernie Bushmiller (Sun. Cartoonist—*Nancy*); Rob Hand (Chiron. Astrologer); Betty Furness (Mars. Consumer advocate); Thomas Jefferson (Saturn. Took up the task of writing the Declaration of Independence for the emerging nation of the United States); Billy Joel (Saturn. Singer); Jeff Davis (Sun. 20th-century hobo "king"); Roddy MacDowell (Neptune. Actor—*National Velvet*).

1 Virgo

An idealized portrait in a fancy frame.

Descriptive Phrases

Being true to oneself and one's viewpoint; seeing oneself as one really is vs. false fronts; learning about one's best and worst traits from the reactions of one's friends and enemies; cultivating character through honest self-criticism vs. letting oneself go to seed (*The Portrait of Dorian Gray*); cultivating a dignified self-image vs. moral hypocrisy; the public vs. the private self (secrets come under public scrutiny); looking toward the judgment of posterity—how one will be remembered after death; sincerity and modesty that makes one lovable vs. arrogance that creates enmity; abiding by one's own counsel and sharing one's critiques only if asked (take a direct, pragmatic approach to problems); determination to realize one's innate potentials.

Examples

Louis XVI (Mercury. During the French Revolution, he was recognized from his profile on a coin while escaping and lost his head on the guillotine); Jackie Kennedy (Neptune. First Lady); Robert Hooke (Mercury. 17th-century scientist—microscopy, optics); Jorge Borges (Sun. Self-deprecating novelist, almost blind—*The Library of Babel, The Aleph*); Saint Bernadette of Lourdes (Chiron. Religious visionary); Thornton Wilder (Jupiter. Playwright—*Our Town*); William Kunstler (Venus. Flamboyant lawyer—defended the Chicago Eight); Lance Ito (Mercury. Showboat judge in O. J. Simpson trial); Ingrid Bergman (Venus. Actress—*Casablanca*, controversial love-life); Bob Geldof (Mars. Punk rocker, organized concerts for African famine relief); Ralph Reed (North Node. Front man for the Christian Coalition); Frank Capra (Jupiter. Director—*It's a Wonderful Life*); Martin Luther King, Jr. (Neptune. Civil-rights leader).

2 Virgo

Excluded from a talent show because of her race, a flamboyantly dressed Black girl sneaks in the stage door and successfully pleads her case before the judges.

Descriptive Phrases

Gaining legitimacy; being accepted on one's own terms, whether at work or in one's family (embarrassed by their origins, social climbers); reinventing oneself; living up to one's own expectations but also seeking recognition for one's superior performance (overly self-critical); holding to one's own perspective and values; gaining a voice in society; inserting one's voice, even when it isn't wanted; gaining access to a new social set by dissolving misunderstandings; getting a hearing; bringing fresh air to a stuffy scene (promote a more open and inclusive society); steadfast pursuit of personal goals (will be content later in life only when their struggles serve humanity and not just themselves); suffering insecurity and doubt vs. snatching one's chance; getting one's foot in the door.

Examples

Madonna (Pluto. Pop singer, actress—*Truth or Dare*); Johnny Depp (Uranus. Actor in films about gaining acceptance—*Crybaby, Edward Scissorhands*); Maggie Kuhn (North Node. Grey Panthers leader); Ross Perot (Neptune. Third-party candidate); Leonard Bernstein (Sun. Conductor, composer, civil-rights activist); George Wallace (Sun, Saturn. Racist obstructionist who relented after a change of heart); Alix Schulman (Jupiter. Feminist author—*Diary of an Ex-Prom Queen*); Dr. Vivian Long (Mars. Chiropractor who fought to legalize astrology in California); Noam Chomsky (Neptune. Semiotician, leftist critic of the media); Melanie Griffith (Mars. Actress—*Working Girl, Cecil B. Demented*); Jean Auel (Ascendant. Author—*Clan of the Cave Bear*); Danny Aiello (South Node. Actor—*Do the Right Thing*); Jayne Mansfield (Mars. Actress of high IQ who succeeded in films by playing a dumb sexpot); Wilhelm Reich (Jupiter. Radical sexual psychologist, persecuted and imprisoned for mail fraud).

3 Virgo

A shining angel hovers protectively over a naked couple lost in the wilderness.

Descriptive Phrases

Striving to achieve a balanced, dispassionate overview of one's situation—especially one's relationships; analytical clarity; guidance by the unclouded eyes of the higher self (abandoning oneself to irrational passions); balancing the spiritual and worldly sides of a relationship; seeing the divinity in one's partner vs. sexual attraction; self-recollection and spiritual self-sufficiency that gives the ability to love (worn out by ongoing strains on their romantic ideals); patient, levelheaded sharing of insight; spiritual ideals passed to the next generation; protection that comes to those on the spiritual path (recognize and avoid badly framed situations, reframe problems along more productive lines); faith that there is a way vs. giving in to despair.

Examples

Barbara Hershey (Mars. Actress—*Hannah and Her Sisters,* played Mary Magdalene in *The Last Temptation of Christ*); Steve Martin (Mercury. Comedian—*My Blue Heaven, The Jerk*); Carol Burnett (Mars. Comedienne, daughter was addicted to heroin); Bryan Ferry (Venus. Rock singer—Roxy Music); Enya (North Node. New Age musician); Hazrat Khan (Mars. Sufi guru, musical mysticism); Robert de Niro (Chiron. Actor); Audrey Meadows (North Node. Alice on *The Honeymooners*); Rabindranath Tagore (Saturn. Poet, spiritual interests); Barbara Walters (Neptune. Interviewer); Luc Besson (Pluto. Film director—*The Fifth Element*); Melissa Anderson (Uranus. Child actor—*Little House on the Prairie*); Lina Wertmuller (Venus. Film director—*Swept Away*) Tem Terriktar (Mercury. Editor of *The Mountain Astrologer*); George Sarton (Jupiter. Historian who studied the ongoing evolution of science).

4 Virgo

With the foundation of the new meeting house successfully completed, the leader of a commune discusses further construction with members of his multinational community.

Descriptive Phrases

Social idealists who work for the general welfare; finding grounds for mutual agreement; ministering to universal human needs vs. feeling contempt for individual differences; creating a new plan for one's country or community; allowing a new creation to emerge organically from the collective consciousness vs. shoveling everything into preconceived categories; recognizing and nurturing one's own and other people's surprising potentials; openness to new ideas vs. reluctance to reexamine basic assumptions; creating "cells" that can act as models for social regeneration vs. failing because one falls into power trips embracing ungrounded or extremist ideas, or because one doesn't successfully integrate into the larger community.

Examples

Lyndon Johnson (Sun. President famous for his civil-rights legislation—The Great Society); Lillian Hellman (North Node. Leftist writer, antifascist activist—*Scoundrel Time*); Joseph Stalin (Moon. Russian premier with many "five-year plans"); George Orwell (North Node. Critic of Stalinism—*Animal Farm*); Yasir Arafat (Sun. Chief negotiator for a Palestinian state); William Shatner (Neptune. Actor—*Star Trek* captain who examines the galaxy's many cultures); Eleanor Roosevelt (Venus. First Lady, key author of the U. N. Universal Declaration of Human Rights); Irish Land League founded by Parnell (Uranus. 10/21/1878); David Koresh (Pluto. Idealistic religious cult leader); Sally Priesand (Mars. First female rabbi in the United States); Emiliano Zapata (Uranus. Revolutionary leader who fought for land reform in Mexico, killed by the government);

5 Virgo

Sleeping under an old willow tree, an Irishwoman dreams of a meeting with a sly old leprechaun. When she awakes, she tries to remember their conversation.

Descriptive Phrases

Stubbornly holding to one's instinctual, childlike view of the world (the unsocialized or natural man); attunement to unconscious imagery, especially collective sexual imagery; living in a dream world vs. waking up to objective conditions; belief in participatory magic—playing with the boundaries between the physical and the imagined world (difficulties translating the language of another realm); collecting odd facts that mark out the borders of one's reality; sucking others into one's reality; living out fantasies in a positive way vs. going beyond the bounds of acceptable behavior; getting past sexual or psychological hang-ups vs. getting stuck; playful examination of a problem from various angles; having a droll and mischievous outlook on life.

Examples

Wolfgang von Goethe (Sun. German romantic writer—*Faust, The Metamorphosis of Plants*); Caroline Casey (Moon. Shamanic astrologer); Wyndham Lewis (Jupiter. Symbolist poet, editor of *Blast*, a magazine of "vorticism"); Morning Glory Zerr (Mars. Neopagan witch, astrologer); Augustus Owsley III (Moon. Chemist, dispenser of huge quantities of LSD in the sixties); Mike Judge (Uranus. Cartoonist—*Beavis and Butthead, King of the Hill*); Andy Warhol (Neptune. Artist, filmmaker); Dorothy Parker (Mars. Writer of corrosive wit, made suicide attempts); George Kuchar (Sun, North Node. Underground filmmaker—*Hold Me While I'm Naked, Thundercrack!*); Kay Parker (Sun. Porn actress); Philip Roth (Mars. Writer—*Portnoy's Complaint*, on obsessive masturbation); Kate Millett (Venus. Sculptress, feminist author—*Sexual Politics*); Allen Funt (South Node. Television host—*Candid Camera*).

6 Virgo

Amid the roar of the crowd, a brightly clad jockey swerves around the last curve to make a daring run from behind.

Descriptive Phrases

Daring; leaving a secure position in order to attain one's desires (insecure—constantly trying to prove themselves; defending their choices and beliefs, or trying to stay on top of their game); taking gambles; bondage to the ups and downs of the wheel of fortune; going around in circles vs. staking out a new direction in life; all-out efforts; perfecting one's skills through disciplined practice (chaotic personal life can undermine their professional reliability); never-ending search for fun and excitement; life in the fast lane; active sports; having fun with one's clothes and appearance; controversial stances on issues of morals and taste (combative); pushing the envelope of permissible public behavior (scandalous); getting people to think about cultural norms vs. mechanically following the crowd; making a splash.

Examples

Mickey Rooney (Jupiter. Acted in many "let's put on a show" films with Judy Garland); Madonna (Mercury. Constantly reinvented pop star, actress—*Truth or Dare*); Dennis Rodman (Neptune. Outrageous basketball star—*Bad as I Want to Be*); Phranc (Sun. Butch lesbian folk-rock singer); Richard Blackwell (Sun. Columnist who started a "worst-dressed women of the year" column); James Hunt (Sun. British World Racing champion); Pete Townsend (Moon. Hyperkinetic guitarist of The Who, composer of *Tommy*); Vaclav Havel (Mars. Playwright, first president of Czech Republic, erstwhile friend of Frank Zappa); Willie Shoemaker (Neptune. Jockey); Jimmy Breslin (Neptune. Earthy sports commentator); Jeanette Rankin (Uranus. Pioneering feminist agitator); Andy Kaufman (Saturn. Competent comedian, incompetent wrestler); Ilona Stoller (South Node. Porn star who became a popular Italian politico); Elmer Sperry (Sun. Inventor of the gyroscope).

7 Virgo

An exquisitely beautiful woman in a luxurious harem, holding a pomegranate in one hand and a lute in the other.

Descriptive Phrases

Physical beauty that veils a jewel-like beauty of the soul; being a prisoner of the senses vs. glimpsing and escaping into the supersensual realm (Persephone trapped in the underworld, Scheherazade escapes defilement by elaborating an ongoing allegorical story); refinement of the senses through sublimation vs. coarsening the senses through gross sensual indulgence (the dance of the seven veils); using drugs for mental expansion vs. sinking into drug abuse; making the compromises necessary to earthly existence vs. prostituting one's talents for selfish gain; giving oneself in tender lovemaking vs. shy withdrawal behind personality screens; sensual dallying; awareness of emotional undercurrents (intrigues); emotional discretion.

Examples

Diana Rigg (Venus. Actress—*The Avengers*); Robert Von Gulik (Mercury. Dutch ambassador, expert on Chinese erotic art, writer of the intricate Judge Dee mysteries); Myrna Loy (Moon. Actress—*The Thin Man*, worked for the United Nations); Shirley MacLaine (Moon. Actress—played a prostitute in fourteen different films); Princess Diana (Pluto. Beloved English royal); Georges Simenon (Moon. Mystery writer who claims to have had sex with 10,000 women, 8,000 of them prostitutes); Deborah Kerr (Mars. Actress—*The King and I*); Ted Kennedy (Moon, Neptune. Womanizing politician, advocate for the poor and downtrodden); Philip Roth (South Node. Author—*Portnoy's Complaint*); John Phillips (Sun. Singer-songwriter—The Mamas and the Papas, heroin addict); Roger McGuinn (North Node. Lead singer of The Byrds); Evangeline Adams (North Node. Astrologer); Jean Ingres (Sun. Painter—"The Turkish Bath"); Brigham Young approves polygamy for Mormons (Sun. 8/29/1852).

8 Virgo

A little girl performs a spinning dance at her first recital.

Descriptive Phrases

Showing off one's talents vs. merely showing off; joyous self-expression; command performances; coordinating mind and body; deportment—learning how to move in public and in private (casting aside a prim persona for the unbridled instinctuality of the bedroom, shaking one's booty); injecting fun into every situation; getting an education vs. "getting an education"; learning correct behavior vs. hoody rebelliousness; standing on one's own two feet vs. tottering dependence on social approval (learning to stand up to public criticism); basic individuality as it is discovered in joyous, spontaneous responses to life; being absolutely true to oneself; the dance of life; being and becoming as the two strands of life; DNA; the seed self; developing self-confidence vs. shy self-consciousness; dance.

Examples

Lily Tomlin (Sun. Comedienne); Louis Armstrong (Venus. Trumpeter); Roger Ebert (North Node. Film critic, screenwriter for *Beyond the Valley of the Dolls*); Rita Hayworth (Saturn. Actress—*Gilda*); Billy Ray Cyrus (Pluto. Country singer); Ginger Rogers (Venus. Actress—Fred Astaire and Ginger Rogers movies); Betty Jane Rowlands (Moon. Vaudeville performer, stripper); Maria Montessori (Sun. Educator, educational philosopher); Rudolf Steiner (Uranus. Occult philosopher, educator—Waldorf Schools); George Kuchar (Sun. Underground filmmaker—*Hold Me While I'm Naked*); Huey Long (Sun. Populist Louisiana demagogue); Juliette Low (Saturn. Founder of the Girl Scouts); Hank Ketcham (Saturn. Cartoonist—*Dennis the Menace*); Sally Rand performs a nude fan-dance at the Chicago Exposition (Neptune. 5/30/1933); Walter Matthau (Jupiter. Actor—*The Odd Couple*).

9 Virgo

Leaning against a rail, a sheriff of the old West looks fixedly toward the center of town.

Descriptive Phrases

Tough customers who take a no-nonsense approach to difficult situations; dominating one's situation through power of personality (belligerent); power of command (tyrannical, bulldoze opponents); getting one's way even if it takes a fight (pecking orders); never backing down vs. learning to walk away from no-win situations; viscerally grasping the gist of the situation; contemplating a set of options and acting decisively on the best of them; independent perspective and analysis (unmoved by established opinion); having a life whose stages are defined by job changes; extreme self-reliance (untrusting, have difficulty letting down their guard); creating a dramatic persona that catches the public imagination; earthy populism vs. demagoguery.

Examples

Ann Richards (Sun. Feisty governor of Texas); Peter Fonda (Moon. Actor—*Easy Rider*, other biker roles); Anjelica Huston (Moon. Model, actress, film director); Joseph Stalin (Uranus. Soviet dictator—bloody purges); Rosie O'Donnell (Pluto. Talk-show host, wisecracking comedienne); Will Rogers (Uranus. Homespun cowboy storyteller); Patsy Cline (Neptune. Country singer); Camille Paglia (Moon. Take-no-prisoners social commentator); Ruth Bader-Ginzburg (Neptune. Supreme Court justice); Marcia Clark (Sun. Prosecuting attorney—O. J. Simpson case); Huey Long (Mars. Populist Louisiana governor and senator, demagogue); W. C. Fields (Uranus. Irascible comedian); James Coburn (Sun. Actor—*The Great Escape, The Magnificent Seven*); Douglas MacArthur (Uranus. General who commanded U. S. forces in the Pacific during World War II).

10 Virgo

Balancing on a high rocky outcropping, a master surveyor argues with his apprentice about what they are actually seeing. Pulling the apprentice to his own position, the master surveyor hands him a pair of binoculars.

Descriptive Phrases

Sharp observers; getting a quick fix on a problem; gathering enough evidence to construct a coherent inner picture of the world (critical new facts change one's views); stereoscopic vision that balances logic and spiritual vision and adds a new dimension to people's view of reality (integration and self-mastery vs. imbalances between mind, body, and soul); compensatory aspects of relationships; sharing one's strengths and getting others to buttress one's weaknesses; seeking out expert opinions (two heads are better than one); being sure of one's position vs. scrambling to correct dangerous errors in judgment (cliffhangers); convincing others of one's passionately individualistic vision of the world; workmanlike pride and technical mastery paired with genuine superiority of perspective.

Examples

Bill Moyers (Neptune. Wide-ranging and innovative journalist); Shirley MacLaine (Neptune. Actress, spiritual interests—*Out on a Limb*); George Lucas (Chiron. Filmmaker—*Star Wars*); Cosimo de'Medici (Venus. Renaissance politician and patron of philosophy and the arts); Teilhard de Chardin (Uranus. Geneticist, philosopher); R. D. Laing (Venus. Psychologist—*The Politics of Family*); Elaine Pagels (Neptune. Dissident historian of gnosticism and Christianity); Susan Sontag (Neptune. Literary critic, novelist); Martha Stewart (Venus. Martha Stewart home-and-garden empire); Nicholas Cage (Uranus. Actor—*Raising Arizona, The Rock*); Lucille Ball (Mercury. Comic actress—*I Love Lucy*); Andrei Sakharov (Jupiter. Russian nuclear physicist, dissident); Gillian Anderson (Jupiter. Actress—*The X-Files*); Daniel Egan (Sun. Extreme skier—near-vertical slopes).

11 Virgo

Boy in a high-school play delivers a soliloquy, while his mother watches proudly from the wings.

Descriptive Phrases

Living up to expectations; making good on early promise; learning one's craft through steady application vs. failing to carry through (may subvert their own success if the track they're on doesn't feel right); taking stock of one's assets and parlaying them into worldly success (beauty, money, talents); presenting an attractive package to employers or potential mates (self-conscious, tongue-tied); seeking recognition and support for one's talents, but also nurturing the efforts of one's friends; aspiring to inner standards of excellence vs. conforming to purely external standards; finding one's true voice (confident analysis, speechifiers); listening to others, but staying in tune with one's inner voice; suiting other people vs. suiting oneself; writing one's own script vs. following other people's scripts.

Examples

Jimmy Connors (Sun. Tennis pro, threw childish tantrums); Melissa Anderson (Moon. Child star—*Little House on the Prairie, The Brady Bunch*); Kenneth Branagh (North Node. Shakespearean actor); Penny Marshall (Venus, Chiron. Director, actress—*Laverne and Shirley*); Sean Penn (Venus. Brat-pack actor—*Fast Times at Ridgemont High, Sweet and Lowdown*); Ayn Rand (North Node. Political novelist—*The Fountainhead*); Sam Donaldson (North Node. Newscaster); Curt Ducasse (Uranus. Philosophy professor with an interest in parapsychology); Robin Williams (Venus. Zany and voluble comedian—*Good Morning, Vietnam* and *Jumanji*); Barbara Streisand (North Node. Singer, actress—*Yentl*); Rajiv Gandhi (Moon. Corrupt Indian politician who took over after his mother, Indira, died; assassinated); Alan Freed (Neptune. Rock promoter who discovered Bob Dylan, Bruce Springsteen, and others); Vanessa Williams (Pluto. Miss America, deprived of the title because she had posed nude; made it as a singer and film actress).

12 Virgo

A bride removes her veil and her crown of wildflowers, and passionately kisses her husband.

Descriptive Phrases

Gentle, playful courtship as a way of naturally lowering emotional barriers; giving direct and honest expression to one's thoughts and feelings (emotionally and sexually demanding); modesty vs. immodesty; hiding delicate feelings vs. brazening it out; seeing through people's defenses; confirming conjectures by coaxing people to open up (gossip-mongers vs. being victims of gossip); waiting for the right moment to unveil a hidden talent or a hidden side of oneself (timorous); secretiveness (closeted bisexuality); role reversals (men tend to be shy, women very sexually direct); living out one's romantic fantasies vs. harsh comedowns (unfulfilling sex, rape); making progress in a relationship vs. fear of making a commitment; virginity vs. marriage.

Examples

Cass Elliot (Moon. Singer—The Mamas and the Papas); Dustin Hoffman (Mercury. Actor—*The Graduate, Tootsie*); Brian Wilson (Moon. Singer—The Beach Boys, emotional problems); Twiggy (Saturn. Virginal waiflike model); Sun Myung Moon (Saturn. Cult leader—organizes mass weddings between strangers); Alan Bates (Neptune. Actor—*Women in Love, Butley*); Ralph Nader (Neptune. Consumer advocate, unmarried); Sophia Loren (Venus. Actress—*Two Women*, longtime affair with married director Carlo Ponti—eventually married him); Christo (Neptune. Artist—immense fabric wrappings of buildings); Robert Downey, Jr. (Uranus. Actor—*Chaplin, Soapdish*, bisexual); Emily Brontë (Mars. Author—*Wuthering Heights*); John F. Kennedy, Jr. (North Node. Longtime eligible bachelor, editor of *George*); Catherine Deneuve (Chiron. Actress, had children with Mastroianni and Vadim without marrying them, successfully sued *Paris Match* for invasion of privacy).

13 Virgo

Clenching his fist and pounding the table, a charismatic statesman brings a hysterical mob under control.

Descriptive Phrases

Handling the people and situations one encounters with confidence; coolness under fire vs. losing one's grip, especially emotionally (overreact to perceived threats); acting boldly and decisively to bring order to an unstructured situation (control freaks); waiting for the right moment to act vs. panic-stricken fumbling; long-range contingency planning vs. shortsighted focus on momentary exigencies; seizing, holding, and using power; working one's way into the power elite; exercising conscious control over one's scene and one's relationships (resist emotional manipulation but may manipulate others); knowing what one wants sexually vs. going with the flow (uptight); charismatic sexual presence; self-possession and self-determination.

Examples

Sandra Bullock (Pluto. Actress—*Speed,* in which she takes control of a booby-trapped runaway bus); Brian Epstein (Neptune. The Beatles' manager, responsible for refashioning their public image); Dwight D. Eisenhower (Saturn. General and president); Barbara Howar (Neptune. Newswoman); Janeane Garofalo (Uranus. Comedienne, actress); Napoleon Bonaparte (Mars. Military conqueror, despot); Phil Jackson (Mercury. One-time coach of Chicago Bulls); Jack Valenti (Sun. Devised a rating system for movies); Kate Millett (Neptune. Feminist—*Sexual Politics*); Sophia Loren (Neptune. Actress—*Two Women*); Earl Warren (Saturn. Chief justice of Supreme Court); John Mitchell (Sun. Attorney general under Nixon); Jimmy Swaggart (Neptune. Right-wing Christian televangelist); Russians invade Czechoslovakia to crush Prague Spring (Jupiter. 8/21/1968); Anjelica Huston (South Node. Tough actress—*The Royal Tenenbaums, The Witches*); Larry King (Neptune. Talk-show host).

14 Virgo

A producer of B movies uses a flowchart to explain production and distribution to his managers and assistants.

Descriptive Phrases

Promoting oneself or one's product; organizing a business around a product that the public really wants or needs (panderers—play into a social role that people hunger for); pursuing long-term game plans; perfecting a process or an act by working through a series of problems (get down the basics before perfecting the details); consolidating one's position; running a tight ship; honoring one's commitments; keeping personal and business relationships in order (self-undoing through sloppy behavior); fruitful mergers (marriage as a merger of assets); loosening things up culturally vs. corseting one's energies and saving them for more productive endeavors (sublimation of sexual energy into work vs. sensual dissipation); capitalizing on people's desire for pleasure.

Examples

Steve Wozniak (Mercury. Entrepreneur—Apple Computers); Carol Burnett (Jupiter. Comedienne); Traci Lords (Moon. Porn star, revealed she was underage in early movies only after she founded her own porn company, thus making her earlier movies illegal); Max Reinhardt (Jupiter. Big-time theatrical producer); Dalai Lama (Moon. Representative of Tibetan Buddhism and also the people of Tibet); Carl Sagan (Mars. Propagandist for science); Chris Farley (Pluto. Fat-guy comedian who died in a binge of sensual dissipation); Margaret Morris (Saturn. Founder of the Celtic Ballet Company); Linda Evangelista (Pluto. Supermodel); Mick Jagger (Venus. Rock star—The Rolling Stones, fabulously wealthy); Willie Nelson (Jupiter. Country-folk singer, organized Farm Aid, went bankrupt); Gould and Vanderbilt form Western Union (Uranus. 1/19/1881); Gianni Agnelli (Jupiter. Owner of Fiat empire); George C. Marshall (Uranus. Chief of Staff in World War II, Marshall Plan to rebuild Europe).

15 Virgo

A woman in her boudoir turns a faceted, crystal bottle of perfume in the light. In a reverie, she returns to the night her boyfriend solemnly gave it to her and the whirlwind romance that followed.

Descriptive Phrases

Form vs. content in relationships; looking for honest emotional reciprocation; sincere expressions of affection vs. buying someone's favor with gifts (bend people to their will in a charming way); cosmetics as self-expression vs. hiding oneself in a gaudy package; gallantry; attentiveness to others' needs or wishes; living one's life so that one can collect a store of wonderful memories (fantasize about impossibly romantic adventures); clarity of thought vs. being dazzled or fascinated; intelligent, thoughtful observations; straight-shooting honesty about one's views; seeing things from different viewpoints (chaotic kaleidoscopic visions vs. putting it all together in a meaningful whole); aesthetic and cultural refinement; cultivating one's manners and personal style.

Examples

Nicholas Cage (Pluto. Actor—*Moonstruck*); Jackson Browne (Saturn. Romantic singer-songwriter); Janeane Garofalo (Pluto. Stand-up comic, actress—*Romy and Michelle's High School Reunion*); Gene Wilder (Neptune. Comic actor—*Blazing Saddles*); Ken Kesey (Neptune. Author—*One Flew Over the Cuckoo's Nest*, acid-dropping Merry Prankster); Dean Jones (Neptune. Actor in Disney fantasy movies); Charlie Manson (Neptune, Mars. Hypnotic cult leader); David Copperfield (Jupiter. Stage magician); Julie Kavner (Sun. Actress in Woody Allen movies); Michelle Pfeiffer (Moon. Glamorous romantic actress); Quentin Crisp (Jupiter. Ground-breaking drag queen); Melanie Griffith (Mercury. Actress—*Cecil B. Demented*); Catherine Deneuve (Venus. Actress, perfume salesperson); Michael Douglas (Mercury. Actor—*Fatal Attraction*); Jackie Kennedy (Mars. First Lady).

16 Virgo

An aborigine seeking food and companionship enters the crumbling outskirts of a modern Australian city.

Descriptive Phrases

Awareness of humanity's deeper problems; seeing the primitive underside of other people or of society; listening with an uncensored ear to others; thoughtful observers of human behavior (sociology, anthropology); adapting to social expectations vs. being natural and relaxed; insider-outsider issues; standing up to racism, classism, or sexism vs. holding prejudices of one's own; maintaining one's human dignity (indulging in shameful behavior); refusal to sublimate basic drives (sexual primitives, take what they want); following one's instincts and desires; fighting to square human law with the laws of nature; finding the strength to slog along despite inhospitable conditions.

Examples

Jean Auel (Neptune. Writer—*Clan of the Cave-Bear*); Danny Aiello (Jupiter. Actor—*Do the Right Thing*); Ralph Ellison (South Node. Writer—*Invisible Man*); Evonne Goolagong (Venus. Tennis pro, Australian aborigine); Peter Sellers (Sun. Actor—*The Pink Panther, The Magic Christian*); Jerzy Kosinski (Jupiter. Writer—*The Painted Bird*); Hendrik Verwoerd (Sun. South African leader, Nazi ally, anti-Semite, anti-Black); Bernard Sanders (Sun. Socialist congressman from Vermont, a Jew originally from Brooklyn); Jeanette Rankin (Uranus. Suffragette leader); Philippe Aries (Mars. Writer—histories of attitudes toward children and death); Grace Metalious (Sun. Writer—*Peyton Place*); Marion Barry (Neptune. Disgraced coke-head mayor of Washington, D.C.); Chastity Bono (Moon. Gay rights activist, daughter of Sonny and Cher); Muhammad Ali (North Node. Boxer); Yoko Ono (Mars. Artist, wife of John Lennon).

17 Virgo

A stern admiral in a peacoat looks out over the ocean. Behind him, a mutineer scrambles into a packing crate that is about to be lifted onto the dock.

Descriptive Phrases

Chains of command between the superego, ego, and id; the ego as it organizes thought and life vs. the eruption of ideas and impulses from the unconscious (use of subconscious imagery in art); running a tight ship—in the military or in some other organization; trying to control a situation vs. taking desperate measures to secure one's freedom of thought and action (refuse to be put in a box by social or familial expectations; repressiveness provokes rebellion and mutiny; ego-controls are thrown overboard); securing one's social position vs. fear of being undermined; following a strict regimen in life vs. blowing off steam through comic antics; envisioning oneself as a dramatic lead in the historical tragicomedy (self-important); rising within the system vs. escaping the system.

Examples

William Bligh (Sun. Tyrannous captain of the Bounty); Isabella d'Este (Pluto. Renaissance aristocrat who was married off in various dynastic ploys, patron of the arts); Henry Kissinger (North Node. U. S. foreign policy architect); Cardinal Richelieu (Sun. Statesman); Seymour Hersh (Neptune. Investigative reporter—publicized the My Lai massacre); General DeGaulle (Saturn. French general, leader of Free French forces during World War II); Bernadine Dohrn (North Node. Radical—the Weather Underground); Pedro Almodovar (Mercury. Filmmaker—*Women on the Verge of a Nervous Breakdown*); Jacqueline Susann (Mercury. Sleazy seventies pop novelist—*Valley of the Dolls*); Woody Allen (Neptune. Comedian, film director—*Play It Again Sam, Zelig*); R. Crumb (Venus. Underground cartoonist—*Mister Natural, The Sewer Snoids*, and the scammy astrologers known as the *Lighter-Than-Air Boys*); Rosanna Arquette (Venus. Actress—*Desperately Seeking Susan*).

18 Virgo

A group of people are gathered around a table to consult the Ouija board. After a few meaningful glances, a young woman begins to play footsie with the young man seated across the table.

Descriptive Phrases

Subliminal or overt hints that one wants to get to a deeper level of communication; connecting the dots; making sense of assorted bits of data vs. arriving at premature conclusions; astute readings; seeing beyond social facades or official stories (don't take anything at face value, suspect ulterior motives); knowing the score; cluing other people in (working one's way out of some illusion by exposing "funny business" going on under the surface vs. taking people in through some scam, may have a secret double life); knowing what other people want (manipulative crowd-pleasers); seeking experiential proof of one's hunches (seeing what one wants to see vs. skeptical debunking); seeking more profound levels of truth vs. dabbling in the mysteries.

Examples

Cybil Shepherd (Saturn. Actress—*Moonlighting*); John F. Kennedy (Moon. Famed as a speed-reader); Richard Nixon (Ascendant. Famous for Watergate intelligence-gathering escapade); James Joyce (Uranus. Author—*Finnegan's Wake*); Jim Gross (Neptune. Astrologer, inventor of Astro-Dice); Georges Cuvier (Mars. Founder of paleontology, could reconstruct a whole animal from a few bones); Jessica Mitford (Sun. Wrote an exposé on the American funeral business); Stephen Jay Gould (Sun. Evolutionary biologist, author of a book on racist anthropology—*The Mismeasure of Man*); Johann Zahn (Moon. Professor of art, supervised the excavation of Pompeii); Reverend G. Vale Owen (Mars. Medium—automatic writing); Rudolf Steiner (Moon. Occultist, Waldorf Schools); Bruce Hershensohn (Sun. Television and media commentator—*Gods of Antenna*); Karen Horney (Jupiter. Psychologist).

19 Virgo

Well-built swimmer prepares to dive off a high promontory into the sea. Below, a crowd watches with a mixture of admiration, attraction, and resentment.

Descriptive Phrases

Embodying a socially recognized ideal of physical beauty; desire to outshine others; winners (sour resentment of the beautiful people, Baldur vs. Loki); being a good role model vs. rebelling against social expectations and following one's inner impulses; coming to terms with one's sexuality (consciously eliciting sexual responses vs. repelling unwanted advances, diving into a life of Dionysian pleasure vs. prudishness, innocence vs. sexual knowingness); freeing oneself from sexual hang-ups; integrating mind and body; physical coordination (too identified with the body or the mind); confident, uninhibited approach to life (risky adventures); sharing one's love of life with others, especially children; strong solar presence; looking and feeling on top of the world.

Examples

Troy Donahue (Neptune. Movie idol); Pamela Lee (Pluto. *Baywatch* babe); Brad Pitt (Pluto. Handsome movie idol); Mary Tyler Moore (Neptune. Actress who "lights up the world with her smile," in *The Dick Van Dyke Show, The Mary Tyler Moore Show*); Richard De Mont (Moon. Olympic swimmer, disqualified for drug use); Cindy Crawford (Uranus. Fashion model, once married to Richard Gere); Linda Tripp (Saturn. Plotter who encouraged Monica Lewinsky to tape phone calls to Clinton); Kenneth Starr (Mars. Special prosecutor—Monicagate); Danny Thomas (South Node. Entertainer—*The Danny Thomas Show*, promoted St. Jude Children's Hospital); D. H. Lawrence (Sun. Writer—*Women in Love, Lady Chatterley's Lover*); Jerry Rubin (Neptune. Yippie—*Do It*); Alix Schulman (South Node. Feminist—*Diary of an Ex-Prom Queen*); Kevin Corcoran (Jupiter. Disney child star—Moochy); Gunther Gebel Williams (Sun. Lion tamer).

20 Virgo

A longstanding critic of a manufacturing company has been hired to thoroughly reorganize it. He looks down at the circular production line and shakes his head.

Descriptive Phrases

Implementing improvements; seeing through a host of minor problems to the problems that are actually preventing progress; advantages of the outsider's perspective vs. problems particular to outsiders who become insiders; perfecting a routine by analysis and testing; getting the kinks out of one's act; solving problems before they become serious obstacles; seeing life as an ongoing process whose goals and routes are provisional; keeping one's eyes on one's goals vs. forgetting one's priorities or getting off-track (need to withdraw occasionally in order to reconnoiter); getting out of a rut vs. going around in circles; feeling unappreciated or left behind vs. getting a scene to revolve around you; achieving success through longstanding competence of performance; modernism—being at the forefront of the human enterprise.

Examples

Robert Redford (Moon. Actor, heads the Sundance Festival, which from outsider status has become a new conveyor of status); Lewis Mumford (Venus. Cultural analyst—*Technics and Civilization*); Paul Kennedy (Jupiter. Economic historian); Ruby Keeler (North Node. Actress—*42nd Street*, in which the understudy gets her big break); Liliana Cavani (Mars. Filmmaker—*The Story of the Third Reich*); Peter Jennings (Neptune. Newscaster); Spock (Uranus. *Star Trek* character introduced on 9/8/1966); Aldo Garzanti (Uranus. Publisher); William Ruckelshaus (South Node. First head of the EPA); Antoine Lavoisier (Jupiter. Groundbreaking chemist); Rube Goldberg (Uranus. Cartoonist—insane, useless machines); Ben Stiller (Uranus. Outsider actor, now Hollywood royalty); Helen Caldicott (Neptune. Anti-nuclear activist); Aung San Suu Kyi (Jupiter. Human rights advocate); Wilson Goode (Neptune. First Black mayor of Philadelphia); Janet Reno (Neptune. President Clinton's attorney general).

21 Virgo

An anarchist with wild, curly hair throws a bomb into a government building.

Descriptive Phrases

Creating shock waves in the public mind; stirring up discussion, often by sensational means; broaching a social or political taboo; forcing people to confront an ugly truth (Perseus holding up Medusa's head); exposing the source of some social evil vs. blowing a problem out of all proportion; crazy scramble to secure the future (fallout from half-baked plans); handling a difficult situation smoothly vs. emotional blowups and self-defeating tactics; teamwork vs. annoying grandstanding; seeing the humor in life's crazy situations; integrating elements of novelty, change, and chaos into the overall rhythm of life (nonplussed, hip); introducing a shocking cultural element that throws the situation off-kilter; cultural radicalism; destabilization.

Examples

Christina Crawford (Neptune, Stationary. Author—*Mommie Dearest*); Timothy McVeigh (Pluto. Oklahoma City bomber); Diane Arbus (North Node. Photographer—disturbing subjects); Benigno Aquino (Jupiter. Philippine opponent of Ferdinand Marcos—assassinated); Judy Collins (Neptune. Radical folk-rock singer—"Marat Sade"); Karen Black (Neptune. Actress—*Nashville, Plan Ten from Outer Space*); Timothy Leary (Saturn. Acid guru); Ricki Lake (Pluto. Trash-TV talk-show host, actress in John Waters' *Hairspray*); Graham Greene (Mercury. Novelist—*The Ministry of Fear, The Confidential Agent*); Edward G. Robinson (Chiron. Movie star—gangster roles); Yoko Ono (Jupiter. Annoying avant-garde artist); Marcel Marceau (North Node. Mime); Fourth International formed (Neptune. 9/3/1938); José Orozco (Moon. Revolutionary muralist); Mort Sahl (Moon. Topical humorist—obsessed with the JFK assassination).

22 Virgo

A coat of arms over the stone gateway of a manor with a prominent Latin motto. Standing in the gateway, the woman of the house gives a warm welcome to a visitor.

Descriptive Phrases

Standing firmly behind what one says; clearly and concisely outlining one's beliefs; fully integrating one's moral philosophy into one's life; viewing and analyzing the world through a framework of unchanging values; upholding worthwhile traditions vs. inheriting the bad habits of one's parents; working toward a well-ordered society (activism, social correctives); mental orderliness reflected in the orderliness and beauty of one's home; old fashioned hospitality; welcoming others into one's home; projecting an honest self-image; happy recognition of other people's spiritual signatures; loyalty to family and friends; keeping an ideal image of one's friends and country in one's heart (hold friends and country to high standards); setting an example in matters of values or style; inner aristocracy.

Examples

Mary Tyler Moore (Neptune. Actress); Jim Nabors (South Node. Actor on *The Andy Griffith Show*, gospel singer); Vivien Leigh (South Node. Actress—*Gone with the Wind*); Michael Learned (Neptune. Actress—matriarch on *The Waltons*); Jimmy Carter (Mercury. U. S. president, works for Habitat for Humanity and other humanitarian concerns); Kate Millett (Sun. Radical feminist—*Sexual Politics*); René Cassin (Venus. President of the U. N. Human Rights Commission); Jesse Jackson (North Node. Preacher, civil-rights activist); Louis XIII (Mercury. King of France, consolidated power); Isaac Bashevis Singer (North Node. Witty, wise Yiddish writer—*In my Father's Court, The Manor*); Bela Lugosi (Uranus. Actor—*Count Dracula*); Grace Metalious (Mercury. Author—*Peyton Place*); Mao Tse Tung (Chiron. Revolutionary, author of *The Little Red Book* of aphorisms); Charlton Heston (Mars. Actor—*The Ten Commandments*).

23 Virgo

Amid cheers and boos, a prizefighter stands panting over his fallen opponent.

Descriptive Phrases

Indomitability; standing up for oneself and one's beliefs; brashness, scrappiness; physical and emotional aggressiveness (coarse loudmouths); marshaling one's forces; mastering animal passions of desire and fear (sexual voraciousness vs. sexual self-control); harnessing emotions to some conscious end; thrusting oneself into the public arena (muscling in on a scene); self-promotion; strutting one's stuff; individualism (need emotional space); standing up to social pressure; attacking other people's worldviews; getting others to look critically at their social conditioning or social assumptions; promoting a new philosophy or attitude toward life; mastering each situation as it arises; defeating one's enemies.

Examples

General Patton (North Node. Self-willed World War II general); Rush Limbaugh (South Node. Right-wing talk-show host); Norman Mailer (North Node. Novelist—*Armies of the Night*, amateur boxer); Maria Callas (Moon. Tempestuous opera diva); Nancy Sinatra (Neptune. Singer—"These Boots Are Made for Walking"); Cass Elliot (North Node. Singer—The Mamas and Papas); Danny De Vito (Jupiter. Actor—*Ruthless People*); Oliver Stone (Sun. Director—*JFK*, *Platoon*); Waylon Jennings (Moon. Country-western singer, definitive "outlaw"); Jacqueline Susann (Jupiter. Trash writer—*Valley of the Dolls*); Michelle Pfeiffer (Jupiter. Actress—*Batman*, *Dangerous Minds*, *Wolf*); Evel Knievel (Neptune. Motorcycle stunt jumper); Tom Jones (Neptune, Stationary. Sexy singer); Jack Kramer (Saturn. Tennis champ); Anne Francis (Sun. Actress—*The Blackboard Jungle*).

24 Virgo

Having built a playhouse out of odds and ends,
a group of children decide upon the characters
they'll play in their improvised drama.

Descriptive Phrases

Playfulness; trying out various personas to see which one is the most fun; being who one wants to be rather than who others want one to be; irrepressibility (mischief-makers); developing an open-ended persona vs. feeling trapped in socially-imposed roles (rebel against sex roles and other social rules); trying to live out an adventurous fantasy, but knowing just what is needed to make it come true; pragmatic idealism (flaky; gullible); being too romantically trusting vs. being too cynical; resourcefulness; taking what life has provided and turning it into something interesting and exciting (capitalize on misfortunes—make broken eggs into omelettes); thankfulness for the many gifts one has vs. constantly looking to new projects and possibilities.

Examples

Cassandra Peterson (Sun. Horror show host—Elvira); Bill Murray (Saturn. Comic actor); Patrick Stewart (Neptune. Actor—*Star Trek*); Johnny Weismuller (North Node. Swimmer, *Tarzan* star); Lucille Ball (Venus. Comedienne—*I Love Lucy*); Troy Perry (Neptune. Gay pastor—*The Lord Is My Shepherd and He Knows I'm Gay*); Germaine Greer (Neptune. Feminist author—*The Female Eunuch*); Barbara Steele (Neptune, Stationary. Actress—horror movies); Louis Aragon (Mercury. Dadaist, surrealist poet, communist); Lili Taylor (Uranus. Actress—*I Shot Andy Warhol*); Bauser Bauman (Venus. Lead singer of Sha-Na-Na); Stewart Brand (Neptune. Editor of *The Whole Earth Catalog*); Phil Proctor (Neptune. Comic—*The Firesign Theater*); Ringo Starr (Neptune. Beatles drummer, actor—*The Magic Christian*); Jerzy Grotowski (Jupiter. Experimental dramatist—*Towards a Poor Theater*).

25 Virgo

At a family dinner, a retired general frankly relates a dishonorable event in his past, whereupon his wife refutes him by bringing up an instance of his bravery.

Descriptive Phrases

Being entirely honest with oneself and others (brutal revelations about society, other people, or oneself); recognizing that shameful secrets will pollute a close family environment and will eventually come out anyway; putting old issues to rest vs. feeling that an important matter is hanging in the air; living up to one's own expectations (overly modest and self-critical); valuing one's own judgment vs. being obsessed with one's public reputation; commitment to achieving one's personal goals vs. being of service to the community; being on top of one's "to-do" list and ready to deal with whatever comes up; putting together the life one wants by dint of hard work; going forward despite setbacks; cultivating a pleasant family life; matter-of-fact acceptance of reality.

Examples

John Sayles (Saturn. Filmmaker—*Matewan, Brother from Another Planet*); John Ritter (Sun. Actor—*Three's Company*); Donna Reed (Saturn. Perfect TV wife); Nora Ephron (Neptune. Confessional writer, screenwriter—*Crazy Salad, Father of the Bride*); Spalding Gray (Neptune. Confessional monologuist); Martha Stewart (North Node. Home-and-garden guru); Justin Green (Jupiter. Confessional comic-book artist—*Binky Brown Meets the Virgin Mary*); Rosalynn Carter (Venus. Jimmy Carter's wife and helper, Habitat for Humanity); Jane Austen (Neptune. Author—*Sense and Sensibility*); Elizabeth I (Sun. Queen of England at the height of the English Renaissance, multiple accomplishments); Phil Jackson (Sun. No-nonsense Chicago Bulls coach); Harry Truman (Uranus. Plain-speaking president); Jacqueline Susann (Saturn. Schlock novelist—*Valley of the Dolls*).

26 Virgo

At her first communion, a girl stares into the flame of the candle she is cradling while the priest recites the liturgy.

Descriptive Phrases

Childlike reverence and gratefulness for the gift of life, apart from any system of belief; seeing the immortal beauty in oneself and others; sincerity; sharing one's insights; illuminating a situation; tending to the spiritual vitality of a relationship or institution rather than its outer form (go through the motions, mechanical detachment from unvalued tasks); selfless service; sense of political or spiritual mission; taking one's part in the larger scheme; sense of personal dignity (easily offended, shut people out); transience of the physical vs. immortality of the spirit (unhealthy detachment from the body—physical problems); keeping one's head up high, even when one is being dragged through a difficult or degrading ordeal; lessons in purification.

Examples

Greta Garbo (Sun. Reclusive star, "I want to be alone."); Jessye Norman (Sun. Opera diva); D. H. Lawrence (North Node. Author— *Women in Love, Lady Chatterley's Lover*); Rossano Brazzi (Sun. Actor—*South Pacific*, was implicated in gun-running for the Palestinians); Liv Ullman (Neptune. Actress in Bergman films—*Cries and Whispers*); Edward Bulwer-Lytton (Jupiter. Fin-de-siècle author—*Zanoni*); Ralph Waldo Emerson (Jupiter. Poet with spiritual sensibilities—"Nature"); Brian Epstein (Sun. Manager of The Beatles); Twiggy (Sun. Waif-like model); Harold Nicholson (South Node. CIA agent who sold secrets to the KGB); Odette Samsone (Moon. Secret agent, resistance fighter, suffered torture without revealing any information); Sylvia Tyson (Neptune. Folk singer); Stokely Carmichael (Neptune. Civil-rights leader); Zane Stein (Saturn. Astrologer who specializes in Chiron); Ron Karenga (Neptune, North Node. Black-nationalist, invented the Black holiday of Kwanzaa).

27 Virgo

An African guest at an English high tea is getting on fine, until a racist remark goads him into an impassioned speech.

Descriptive Phrases

Adjusting one's behavior when one enters an established scene without sacrificing one's integrity (overly self-effacing vs. overly touchy); bridging two cultures; meeting others halfway vs. holding stubbornly to one's position (educating a hostile audience); smoothing out differences vs. angry showdowns (feel like outsiders who are under constant scrutiny, inclusion-exclusion issues, may stand out in a crowd due to their striking appearance); finding common ground through cross-cultural comparisons (racism, jingoism, guarding established privileges); striving to improve one's social position (civil-rights activism); self-acceptance independent of social status that leads one to stand up for one's human dignity; reconciliation based on social justice.

Examples

Spike Lee (Jupiter. Film director—*Do the Right Thing*); Miriam Makeba (South Node. South African singer); Andrew Young (South Node. Civil-rights activist); Stokely Carmichael (North Node. Civil-rights activist); Emancipation Proclamation (Saturn. 9/22/1862); Mary Travers (Mars. Political activist, folk singer—Peter, Paul, and Mary); Lech Walesa (Mercury. Polish labor leader—first president of newly-democratic Poland); James Spader (North Node. Actor—*Stargate*); Sophia Loren (Sun. Rags-to-riches actress); Celine Dion (Uranus. French-Canadian pop singer); George Lincoln Rockwell (Mars. American Nazi Party leader); Carol MacElvoy (Jupiter. Newscaster who uses sign language); Dorothy Brett (Uranus. Socialite and artist in D. H. Lawrence's circle); Jean-Baptiste Lamy (Jupiter. Early Santa Fe archbishop, set up Indian school).

28 Virgo

At a meeting of important personages, a bald-headed man interjects a penetrating observation.

Descriptive Phrases

Injecting new ideas into public discourse (argumentative); thought-provoking opinions that get people to a deeper level; serving as a focal point for collective decision-making; orchestrating (dominating) group projects; wrangling agreement from others by using soft or hard sells; finding the consensus vs. redoubling one's efforts if the balance of public opinion turns against one; confidence in one's position vs. private misgivings; prodding people into seeing the dark side of something (playing devil's advocate vs. hostile deviltry); puncturing illusions vs. promoting weighty truths through one's art; being an agent of justice vs. letting one's emotions destroy one's objectivity (dominate others intellectually, emotionally or physically).

Examples

Bernard Sanders (Neptune. Hard-hitting socialist politician in Vermont); Albert Brooks (Moon. Renegade director—*Defending Your Life*); Liz Taylor (South Node. Actress—*Cleopatra, Who's Afraid of Virginia Woolf?*); Roger Ebert (Neptune. Film reviewer, opinion shaper); Friedrich Nietzsche (Mars. Philosopher of the will to power); George Wallace (Venus. Racist demagogue); Barbara Streisand (Neptune. Singer, actress—*Funny Girl, Yentl*); Joan Baez (Neptune. Folk singer, antiwar activist); Jesse Helms (Venus. Powerful reactionary senator); Stephen Jay Gould (Neptune. Evolutionary biologist, public propagandist for science); Stephen King (Sun. Horror writer); Joseph Campbell (North Node. Academic expert on mythology, successful television popularization); Steve Martin (Jupiter. Fast-talking comedian); Rick Klimczak (Sun. Astrologer, rock musician); Gillian Anderson (Uranus. Actress—*The X-Files*); Frank Zappa (Neptune. Trenchantly satirical rock star).

29 Virgo

A man with a lantern has found an old diary in the basement, full of beautiful poems and illustrations.

Descriptive Phrases

Confessional honesty about one's thoughts and feelings; sharing personal insights about life through literature and art; resonance between the personal and the universal or archetypal levels of experience; unraveling the larger themes of one's life by deciphering one's dreams or visions (the universal language of symbols, symbolic and allegorical readings); learning to understand the personal language of the soul; making important connections vs. losing the main thread; casting new light on obscure truths; wrapping up one's past and stepping boldly into the future; the historical record interpreted in light of mankind's spiritual evolution; hopefulness vs. haplessness in the face of a complex fate; working in obscurity out of deeply held inner values vs. being discovered for one's talents; voicing undying truths.

Examples

Paul Simon (Neptune. Folk singer—Simon and Garfunkel); Joni Mitchell (Chiron. Folk-rock-jazz singer and poet); Bob Dylan (Neptune. Singer, poet); Pierre de Ronsard (Sun. Influential 16th-century poet, leader of the Pléiade); H. G. Wells (Sun. Novelist—*The Time Machine, The Shape of Things to Come*); Peter Coyote (Neptune. Actor, author of a memoir of the sixties called *Sleeping Where I Fall*); Thomas Moore (Neptune. Jungian therapist, author—*The Care of the Soul, The Planets Within*); Edna St. Vincent Millay (Saturn. Poet—"The Harp Weaver"); Nora Ephron (North Node. Writer—*Crazy Salad*); Jean Cocteau (Moon. Symbolist filmmaker); Bill Murray (South Node. Actor—*Groundhog Day, The Razor's Edge*); Aretha Franklin (Neptune. Soul singer); Ethan Hawke (Pluto. Actor—*Reality Bites, Waking Life*).

30 Virgo

A writer, unable to work because a group of hoodlums is blasting a radio on the street, pulls out a pistol and walks to the window. Thinking better of it, he puts the pistol away and sets off to find a quieter place.

Descriptive Phrases

Keeping long-term goals in mind vs. losing one's head (thoughtless actions with serious consequences, guns, violence); recognizing that worldly conditions are unstable and that it is best to find one's footing in one's inner purpose (unsettled, restless, scatter themselves in multiple projects); having a game-plan; abiding by one's priorities vs. nerve-wracking immersion in superficial crises; learning to tune out irrelevant people or events; giving things their proper weight vs. overreacting; good-natured toleration of people's faults vs. failing to react until it's too late (damage-control); keeping things under control vs. shaking up society by challenging false beliefs or values (antisocial behavior, act as if the rules don't apply to them); retaining one's focus even in the midst of chaos.

Examples

Richard Lester (South Node. Film director—*Help*); Sissy Spacek (Mars. Actress—*Badlands*); Ice Cube (Uranus. Rap star); Robert Anton Wilson (South Node. Writer—*The Cosmic Trigger of the Illuminati*); Charlton Heston (Mercury. Actor, president of the National Rifle Association); Sarah Brady (Neptune. Gun-control activist); Malcolm McDowell (Neptune. Actor—*A Clockwork Orange*); Jack Nicholson (Moon. Actor—*Easy Rider*); Herbert Hoover (Venus. U. S. president, presided over the stock market crash); Danny DeVito (Chiron. Actor, director—*Ruthless People, Death to Smoochy*); Charles IX (Uranus. French king who ordered the St. Bartholomew's Day massacre); Christine Keeler (Neptune. Call-girl who precipitated the fall of the British government); Cathy Guisewite (South Node. Cartoonist—*Cathy*); John Cage (Venus. Avant-garde composer—the sound of things falling apart).

1 Libra

A white butterfly being chased by a child with a butterfly net is suddenly transfixed by a beam of light.

Descriptive Phrases

Spreading one's wings; unfolding a more mature and expansive image of oneself vs. getting trapped in one's own or someone else's idealized view of oneself; holding to crystallized memories of perfect moments vs. being open to the changeable, unpredictable nature of life (whimsical, fickle); living within an idealized image of the world vs. the spirit's entrapment in a lower plane of reality (live in a dream world, poor reality-sense); discontented search for the ideal within the manifest; sudden recognition of archetypal truths that manifest in everyday life (spiritual "flashes"); symbolic and allegorical thinking; spiritual insights revealed in dreams, visions, or the imagination; self-absorbed egotism vs. ego-loss and spiritual enlightenment.

Examples

J.R.R. Tolkien (Saturn. Author of *The Lord of the Rings*); Lewis Carroll (Midheaven. Author of *Alice in Wonderland*); Judy Garland (Saturn. Actress, singer—*The Wizard of Oz*); Billie Burke (Uranus. Actress—Glinda in the *The Wizard of Oz*); R. Crumb (Neptune. Underground cartoonist and spiritual seeker of a sort); Mother Teresa (Mercury. Catholic missionary who worked with the dying); Leonardo da Vinci (Neptune. Renaissance inventor with many "bright ideas"); Renee Zellweger (Uranus. Actress—*Nurse Betty, Me, Myself and Irene*); Bruce Springsteen (Sun. Rock singer); Alice Bailey (Moon. Mystic, metaphysician, Theosophist); Martin Niemoller (Saturn. Theologian); Johann Strauss, Jr. (Saturn. Waltz king—"Tales from the Vienna Woods"); José Silva (Venus. Silva mind-control method); Marcello Mastroianni (Moon. Actor in Fellini films); Suzanne Valadon (Sun. Artist's model, artist, mother of Maurice Utrillo).

2 Libra

Odysseus and his men are sailing through a channel to an unknown sea when they come upon a whirlpool and, behind it, a beautiful siren playing a lyre.

Descriptive Phrases

Following out vague intimations of the marvelous; being onto something new that drags one in (vortexes—either positive or negative); going with the flow when one is going in the right direction vs. resisting dangerous undercurrents, especially risky erotic attractions; following one's heart-strings (emotional drifting, promiscuity); knowing when one's heart is resonating to someone, or merely one's body; looking for excitement and adventure (travel); picking up on new ideas and running with them, to the benefit of the whole race; venturing beyond the point of no return (shipwrecks, debacles); artistic, and especially musical, innovation that introduces humanity to a new level of vibration; sensitivity to ideas or inspirations that are floating in the wind; susceptibility.

Examples

Carol Lynley (Neptune. Sexpot actress); George Harrison (Neptune. The Beatles' bass guitarist); Shelley Winters (North Node. Actress—*The Poseidon Adventure*, slept with half of Hollywood); Van Morrison (Jupiter. Rock musician); Juliette Lewis (Pluto. Actress—*Natural Born Killers*); Chester Nimitz (Uranus. Admiral); D-Day invasion of France (Neptune, Stationary. 6/6/1944); Jim Henson (Sun. Puppeteer—*The Muppets*); Alain Robbe-Grillet (North Node. Novelist who believed that we live only through the physical senses); Jimi Hendrix (Neptune. Psychedelic rock guitarist); Larry Flynt (Neptune. Founder and editor of *Hustler*); Meredith Monk (Neptune. Avant-garde musician, choreographer); George Lucas (Neptune. Film director—*Star Wars*); Michelle Phillips (Neptune. Singer—The Mamas and the Papas).

3 Libra

A boy lies in bed in his new home and recalls the wondrous sights of his cross-country journey. He rises and looks out on the new town, faintly illumined in the light of dawn.

Descriptive Phrases

Seeing the world differently after a life-changing event; turning points where one leaves behind old assumptions and adopts a new stance toward the world (make-or-break situations); reinterpreting what is important; freeing oneself from assumptions and developing a new analysis; new beginnings vs. bridging the past and future (try to hold on to what has already worked, in terms of character, behavior, or beliefs; may live in the past or future through science fiction or historical romance, pondering the mysteries of time); being open and attuned to what's in the air (gain fame as representatives of some "happening" thing); disgust with one's own era vs. wholeheartedly embracing life's new possibilities; dawning realizations vs. rude awakenings.

Examples

Janis Joplin (Neptune. Rock singer who exemplified the sixties sensibility of living in the moment); John Lennon (Mars. Rock star—The Beatles); F. Scott Fitzgerald (Sun. Author—*The Great Gatsby*, paragon of the Roaring Twenties); Norman Lear (North Node. Director—*All in the Family, Maude*); Steve Zahn (Mars, Uranus. Comedian—*Happy, Texas*); Barbara Feldon (North Node. Actress—*Get Smart*); Gwyneth Paltrow (Pluto. Actress—*Sliding Doors*); Michael Douglas (Sun. Actor who specializes in nasty yuppie roles); Lech Walesa (Neptune. Polish labor leader, first prime minister after the fall of Communism); H. G. Wells (North Node. Author—*The Time Machine*); Thomas Kuhn (Saturn. Historian—*The Structure of Scientific Revolutions*); Kitty Hawk flight (North Node. 12/17/1903); Ursula LeGuin (Venus. Sci-fi novelist—*The Beginning Place*).

4 Libra

Campers gather around a campfire, drawn by a woman playing the guitar and singing a political folk song.

Descriptive Phrases

Having an important message to share and finding a platform from which to share it; intimate meetings of the minds; reaching out to others emotionally and dispelling confusion and despair; bringing "lost souls" into a more centered emotional space; emotional inclusiveness; grappling with the difficulties of modern society and coming up with some real answers; drawing the human community together and inspiring them to solve their collective problems; well-articulated views or carefully honed artistic talents that have a powerful and long-lived influence; showing moral courage in everyday life; pulling oneself together vs. letting oneself fall apart; patient forbearance vs. forcing others to come to grips with uncomfortable truths (confrontational); having an impact.

Examples

Joni Mitchell (Neptune. Rock singer—"Court and Spark"); Stephen Stills (Moon. Musician—Crosby, Stills, and Nash); Pete Townsend (Neptune. Rock star—*Tommy*); Alice Walker (Neptune. Writer, poet—*The Color Purple, Meridian*, civil-rights activist); Dick Cavett (Mars. Talk-show host); Norman Lear (Saturn. Director—*All in the Family, Maude, Good Times*); Yasir Arafat (Mars. Palestinian leader who has been a key figure in the peace talks); Gore Vidal (Mars. Politico, novelist—*Burr*); Madalyn Murray O'Hair (Moon. Atheist opponent of prayer in school); Lynn Anderson (Sun. Country singer); Cass Elliot (North Node. Singer—The Mamas and the Papas); Maria Montessori (Mercury. Educator—the Montessori method); George Gershwin (Sun. Composer—*Porgy and Bess, Rhapsody in Blue*); Vaclav Havel (Mercury. Czech playwright, first president of democratic Czechoslovakia); T. S. Eliot (Sun. Poet); John Sayles (Sun. Filmmaker).

5 Libra

A professor of aesthetic philosophy expounds upon his beliefs. Met with a critical question from the audience, he responds with a detailed rebuttal.

Descriptive Phrases

Sincere, impassioned exposition of the truth; getting across a pressing cultural message or an original artistic vision; paying heed to one's internal conversation until one finds an explanation that intuitively clicks; noodling around vs. getting into a groove; exploring the ramifications of an original intellectual or aesthetic idea; thinking off the top of one's head vs. rehearsing one's arguments and organizing them in a pleasing form (utter their opinions like proclamations, cultivate eccentricities as part of their act); winning over an audience with impelling truths vs. relying on emotional arguments or slippery rationalizations; having a strong cultural impact vs. expecting mere words to regenerate society; argumentative skill vs. quarrelsomeness.

Examples

Amédée Ozenfant (Uranus. Cubist artist, founder of Ozenfant School of Fine Arts); Friedrich Nietzsche (Mercury. Highly original philosopher—*The Genealogy of Morals, The Birth of Tragedy*); Francesco Petrarca (Saturn. Invented the neo-Latin aesthetic that began the Italian Renaissance); H. L. Mencken (Mars. Satirist, editor); Angela Davis (Neptune. Professor, communist); Shana Alexander (Mars. Political commentator); Ben E. King (Sun. Rhythm-and-blues singer); Pablo Picasso (Venus. Abstract artist); Andy Warhol (Mars. Seminal pop artist); Bill Griffith (Neptune. Cartoonist—*Zippy the Pinhead*); Al Capp (Sun. Cartoonist—*L'il Abner*); Mary Margaret McBride (Chiron. Radio and talk-show personality); Steve Martin (Neptune. Comedian who has a degree in philosophy); Herbert Marcuse (Jupiter. Philosopher—*One-Dimensional Man*).

6 Libra

A woman of luminous beauty holds out a half-opened rose to her lover and leads him through a gateway into a garden.

Descriptive Phrases

Winning and holding the affection of those one desires (seducers); mystical commitment to the ideals of love and beauty beyond any single relationship (disappointed in love); making practical compromises vs. pursuing unrealistic ideals; sincerity and purity of emotion; the unfolding of refined, intimate emotions (self-revelations, love poetry); letting things progress naturally vs. trying to make things conform to one's desires; sexual attraction as it leads one toward the higher side of love; being true to one's inner ideals vs. straying to pursue some shiny new love interest; guiding others to the spiritual or intellectual realms; inward expansiveness; wisdom drawn directly from spiritual intuition; art suffused with mystical truth; way-showers.

Examples

Joan Baez (North Node. Folk singer); Jack Kerouac (Saturn. Writer—*On the Road*); Jessye Norman (Neptune. Opera singer); Marcello Mastroianni (Sun. Actor—Fellini films); Lew Ayres (Ascendant. Actor, pacifist, spiritual seeker); Ann Landers (Mars. Advice columnist); Sting (Saturn. Rock star); Twyla Tharp (Moon. Innovative dancer); Van Morrison (Neptune. Rock musician—*Into the Music*); Rita Mae Brown (Neptune. Lesbian writer—*Rubyfruit Jungle*); Pier Paolo Pasolini (Saturn. Gay film director—*The Gospel According to St. Matthew*); Debbie Reynolds (Ascendant. Actress—*The Unsinkable Molly Brown, My Six Lovers*); Jennifer Aniston (Jupiter. Actress—*The Good Girl*); Edgar Degas (Saturn. Impressionist painter—ballet themes); Nathaniel West (North Node. Writer—*Miss Lonelyhearts*); Gwyneth Paltrow (Sun. Actress—*Shakespeare in Love*); Sylvia Kars (Sun. Sensuality therapist); Rosalyn Bruyère (Moon. Healer who sees auras).

7 Libra

A witch stands next to her chicken coop and chats with a neighbor, keeping one eye peeled for a hawk that has been attacking her chickens.

Descriptive Phrases

Issues of trust; turning a blind eye to people's minor faults vs. dragging serious evils to light and attacking them (project their own evil onto other people, may scapegoat innocent people); awareness that sinister forces are at work behind the scenes (secret enemies, conspiracies); exaggerating dangers, like Chicken Little vs. investigating one's suspicions and getting an accurate fix on the situation; facing down social ridicule with *outré* behavior vs. protecting one's weak spots; projecting a funny, exaggerated image that makes a feared or rejected archetype seem harmless and acceptable; knowledge of unseen forces and laws vs. ungrounded conjecture or flights of fantasy; educating and protecting the innocent against evil people or false ideas; penetrating perception of human motivation.

Examples

Sybil Leek (Saturn. Self-professed witch); Senator Joseph McCarthy (Jupiter. Paranoid, anticommunist witch hunter); Simon Wiesenthal (Ascendant. Tracked down Nazis); Madeline Kahn (Sun. Comedienne—*Young Frankenstein*); Truman Capote (Sun. Openly gay writer—*In Cold Blood*); Fletcher Knebel (Sun. Writer—*Seven Days in May*); Divine (Neptune. Drag queen in John Waters' movies); Bryan Ferry (Jupiter. Musician—Roxy Music); Frank Zappa (North Node. Rock singer, hawkeyed social critic); Bill Clinton (Mars, Neptune. U. S. president who was under constant attack by his enemies); Mia Farrow (Neptune. Actress—*Rosemary's Baby*, Woody Allen's lover until she discovered he was having sex with her adopted daughter); Cher (Neptune. Actress, singer); J. B. Rhine (Sun. ESP researcher); Herman Kahn (Saturn. Defense analyst—*On Thermonuclear War*); Maila Nurmi (Saturn. Actress—*Vampira*); Marc Bolan (Sun. Fey rock musician—T-Rex).

8 Libra

A stranger investigates an abandoned old house. He sees a fireplace blazing and another person's shadow on the wall, but no one else in the room.

Descriptive Phrases

Tracking down dark, hidden forces in society, beyond the façade; combating social decay (reformers); passionate desire to educate the public about their sociopolitical situation; debunking false reality constructs (need to put their own house in order or they will project their own problems); dragging a mystery to light at the scene of the crime; difficulty in pinning down reality beyond subjective viewpoints, since we tend to find confirmations of our own beliefs (false first impressions); realizing that a vital piece of the puzzle is missing; uncovering obscure facts vs. accepting the mysteriousness of the structure of reality, especially concerning time; the unfolding of karma from an internal source (can't escape their fate); tentative analyses; criticizing the foundations of society.

Examples

Desmond Tutu (Sun. Preacher who crusaded for social justice in South Africa); Annie Besant (Sun. Occultist; crusader for birth control, labor unions, and home rule in India); Girolamo Savonarola (Sun. Preacher who gained power in Renaissance Florence through accurate prophecies and then instituted a thoroughgoing reform program); Kate Millett (Mercury. Feminist writer); Gore Vidal (Mercury. Political analyst, novelist—*Burr*); George Stanhope (North Node. Funded the exploration of Tutankhamen's tomb); Joan Cusack (Mercury. Actress—*Addam's Family Values* with its haunted house); Werner Herzog (Mercury. Director—*Every Man for Himself and God Against All, Fitzcarraldo*); Patrick MacNee (Saturn. Actor—*The Avengers*); Oliver Stone (Neptune. Film director—*JFK*); Georg Grosz (Saturn. Artist—political themes); Neil Young (Neptune. Rock musician); Dionne Warwick (North Node. Singer, host of *Psychic Friends Network*); H. L. Mencken (Venus. Journalist, satirist of the American "booboisie"); Sinclair Lewis (North Node. Writer—*Babbitt*).

9 Libra

A famous actress strikes and holds a pose in the final scene of a play.

Descriptive Phrases

Fully entering a self-created public role (larger-than-life personas); dramatizing collective ideals of love and beauty; participating in and promoting widely cherished dreams; inviting others to enter into one's fantasies; using artistic symbolism to channel timeless truths; penetrating to a deeper level of meaning vs. being stuck in superficials (empty posing, false fronts); moments of spiritual decision vs. getting stuck on the horns of a dilemma (unable to adequately focus a problem without the feedback of others; find themselves playing the same scene over and over); having a clear image of personal success and the ideal relationship vs. being disillusioned by hard realities; manifesting a personal ideal and selling it to the public; forceful projection of personality.

Examples

Mary Pickford (Saturn. Early movie heartthrob); Leonardo DiCaprio (Pluto. Actor—*Romeo and Juliet, Titanic*); O. J. Simpson (Neptune. Football star); Richard and Karen Carpenter (Neptune and Mars respectively. Songwriter and singer of dreamy ballads); William Shakespeare (Moon. Playwright—*Romeo and Juliet*); Heather Graham (Uranus. Actress—*The Spy Who Shagged Me*); Albert Brooks (Neptune. Film director—*Lost in America, Defending Your Life*); Marianne Williamson (Saturn. Spiritual teacher—*A Course in Miracles*); Spanky McFarland (Sun. Child actor—*Little Rascals*); Dolly Parton (Neptune. Country singer); Ian Anderson (Neptune. Lead singer of Jethro Tull); Marc Edmund Jones (Sun. Astrologer, facilitator for the Sabian symbols); Mia Farrow (Neptune. Actress—*Radio Days, Alice*); Judy Garland (Jupiter. Actress, singer—*Meet Me in Saint Louis*).

10 Libra

At a summer camp, boys in swim suits leap into the water and clamber into canoes for a race. From the outset, one boy sets off on a course entirely different from the others.

Descriptive Phrases

Having the confidence to energetically pursue one's own goals vs. standing on the sidelines or feeling left behind; being self-directed vs. needing social validation; juvenile competitiveness; physical pride vs. feeling like a wimp; physical competence acquired through training; keen sense of where various courses of action are leading; going with the flow vs. alerting others that they are pursuing the wrong course; spiritually leading the way; displaying one's values in one's dress and speech; creating a unique social role; creating a cultural vehicle and seeing how far it gets with the public; holding to a plan vs. quick-witted improvisation; coming through in a pinch (narrow escapes);[26] scrappily navigating life's challenges vs. drifting through life.

Examples

David Hasselhoff (Saturn. Producer, singer, actor—*Baywatch*); Margaret Thatcher (Mars. British prime minister—gunboat diplomacy); Joan Crawford (Mars. Scary actress—*Mildred Pierce*); Gore Vidal (Sun. Writer, cultural critic—*Burr, Myra Breckinridge*); Jack Kerouac (North Node. Beat writer—*On the Road*); Robin Williams (Saturn. Comic—*Good Morning, Vietnam*); Billy Crystal (Neptune. Comedian—*City Slickers*); Walt Disney (Moon. Cartoonist; creator of Disneyland); Elizabeth Arden (North Node. Cosmetics empire); Donna Karan (Sun. Fashion designer); Bob Newhart (Mars. Comedian, wrote *The Button-Down Mind Strikes Back*); Florence Entwistle (Uranus. Portrait photographer); Ferdinand Foch (Sun, Venus. Supreme commander of Allied troops in World War I); Mohandas Gandhi (Sun. Crusader for a free India, pacifist, activist); Tazio Nuvolari (Saturn. Daredevil auto racer).

11 Libra

After showing a film in class, a kindly old professor peers over his bifocals and opens a discussion of the film's meaning, illustrating various points with episodes from his own life.[27]

Descriptive Phrases

Object lessons; chatty discussion of issues of general concern; breaking down barriers between people by demonstrating the universal nature of human problems (self-involved, exaggerate the importance of their own struggles); revealing one's interior process, and thus showing others how to focus on the spiritual or emotional dimension of life; sensitivity to the symbolic dimension as it operates in one's own life or the life of society; teaching through symbols; expressing a spiritual message through film, literature or drama; taking a closer look vs. blurry impressions; clear insight into the psychology of others, and especially their problems (droll commentary on the human zoo); empathy vs. bathetic sentimentality; nourishing other people's spiritual understanding.

Examples

Patti Smith (Neptune. Morose rock singer—"Horses"); Andrei Codrescu (Neptune. Humorist, cultural commentator); Kathy Bates (Neptune. Actress—*Dolores Claiborne*); Charlton Heston (Sun. Actor—*The Ten Commandments*); Ursula LeGuin (Mercury. Science-fiction writer—*Earth-Sea Trilogy*); Ingmar Bergman (Mars. Director—*Through a Glass Darkly*); Joseph Conrad (Mars. Writer—*Heart of Darkness, Nostromo*); Paul Foster Case (Sun. Writer on the tarot); John Lennon (North Node. Confessional rock star, songwriter—The Beatles); Pier Paolo Pasolini (North Node. Director—*The Gospel According to Saint Matthew*); Stendhal (Neptune. Writer—*The Red and the Black*); Patty Duke (Neptune. Actress—*The Miracle Worker*); Susan Sarandon (Sun. Actress, activist—*Dead Man Walking*); Akira Kurosawa (Jupiter. Film director—*The Seven Samurai*).

12 Libra

A beaming coal miner drags some of his fellow workers into the light and shows them a large diamond he has just found.

Descriptive Phrases

Discovering and cultivating one's inner gifts and presenting them to the public (rags-to-riches success stories); trying to live up to one's higher potentials, while struggling to escape the dark maze of one's baser nature (become habituated to bleak, restrictive conditions); toiling for a brighter future where one will be free to explore one's personal development; holding on to one's hopes; personal struggles that parallel the struggles of humanity; inspiring others to take their lives in hand; dogged efforts to raise humanity to a higher level; deep empathy for the downtrodden and oppressed; crusading for a more just society, where people can move beyond basic subsistence values; restructuring society around humane, egalitarian values.

Examples

Madame Curie (Mars. Codiscoverer of radium); Giovanni Piranesi (Sun. 18th-century artist whose works feature maze-like prisons); H. Rider Haggard (Mars. Author—*King Solomon's Mines*); Huey Long (Saturn. Populist politician from Louisiana); American Federation of Labor established (Uranus. 12/8/1886); Fran Drescher (Jupiter. Actress—*The Nanny, The Beautician and the Beast*); Julia Child (Moon. *The French Chef*); Richard Dreyfuss (Neptune. Actor—*Close Encounters of the Third Kind*); Michael Dukakis (Jupiter. Liberal politician, presidential candidate); Kevin Kline (Neptune. Actor—*Dave*, about a look-alike who becomes president); Tiger Woods (Pluto. Pro golfer); Denis Diderot (Sun. Leading intellectual of 18th-century France—*Jacques the Fatalist*); Bob Geldof (Sun. Punk rocker who organized a charity concert for famine relief); Annie Besant (Venus. Occultist, champion of birth control and home rule in India).

13 Libra

At a glittering costume ball, some of the guests are blowing soap bubbles while others are engaged in more adult games.

Descriptive Phrases

Playfulness and whimsy; taking delight in each passing moment; fooling around to release tension (loopy antics); temporarily letting go of one's constant efforts to define reality; fancifulness—taking as trivial what is normally seen as important, and important what is normally seen as trivial; renegotiating the sphere of cultural values to make it more livable and interesting (see everything as a game or diversion, amoral relativists); playing around with one's social persona (may adopt a shocking persona); seeing under the plausible mask of reality (run from the ugly, dark side of life); appreciating the convex and concave side of every polarity (gender-benders); being socially and sexually sophisticated without losing one's innocence and sense of fun.

Examples

Emma Thompson (North Node. Actress—*Sense and Sensibility*); Frédéric Chopin (Moon. Composer); George Sand (Uranus. Author, Chopin's lover); Alice Cooper (Neptune. Shock-rocker); Elvis Presley (Mars. Rock idol, star of many frivolous movies); Alexander Woollcott (Uranus. Critic, raconteur); Vaclav Havel (Sun. Playwright, political leader of reconstructed Czechoslovakia); Michel Foucault (Venus. Literary deconstructivist theoretician—*The Order of Things*); Norman Lear (Jupiter. Taboo-breaking producer—*All in the Family* and *Mary Hartman, Mary Hartman*); Raquel Welch (North Node. Silly sexpot—*The Magic Christian, Legally Blonde*); Blake Edwards (Jupiter. Producer—*Arthur, The Pink Panther*); Luis Borges (Mars. Author of fantastic tales); Roald Dahl (Mercury. Writer of children's stories—*The Witches, James and the Giant Peach*); Margaret Geller (Neptune. Physicist—postulated the "soap-bubble theory" of the structure of the universe).

14 Libra

A man wrapped in a serape takes a siesta on a hammock and dreams pleasant dreams.

Descriptive Phrases

Knowing how to unwind; taking advantage of slack-time to compose oneself emotionally; respecting the rhythms of the body; tuning out unpleasant aspects of reality and tuning in to one's own rhythm of life (unconscious—refuse to look at reality as it is; cling to their beliefs like a security blanket, or, alternately, force others to look at hard truths); rich fantasy life; trying to live out romantic or adventurous fantasies in real life (lose themselves in a fantasy role, purveyors of lightweight culture); refusing to deal with reality on any terms other than one's own (trendsetting social postures); friendly, easygoing charm; savoir-faire vs. evading life's harder questions; putting together a pleasant life for oneself vs. rude awakenings.

Examples

Dwayne Hickman (Jupiter. Actor—*Dobie Gillis*); Bob Denver (Mars. Actor—*Dobie Gillis, Gilligan's Island*); Valerie Harper (North Node. Television actress—*Rhoda*); Henry Winkler (Chiron. Actor—The Fonz); Carole Lombard (Sun. Actress, comedienne); Bill Moyers (Jupiter. Commentator, cultural researcher); Niccolò Machiavelli (Uranus. Author of *The Prince*, which shattered the age's pleasant fantasies about the politics of rulership); Shari Lewis (Moon. Puppeteer—*Lambchop*); David Niven (Jupiter. Actor, *bon vivant—The Pink Panther*); Douglas Adams (Saturn. Writer—*A Hitchhiker's Guide to the Galaxy*); Erik von Daniken (Mars. Sensationalist author on aliens); Oliver North (Sun. Sleazy patriot); Robert Louis Stevenson (Jupiter. Writer—*Treasure Island*, moved to Samoa for his health); Laraine Newman (Saturn. Comedienne—*Saturday Night Live*); Kookie Byrnes (Mars. One-time teen idol who epitomized "coolness").

15 Libra

A man cranks a hurdy-gurdy, while a trained monkey dressed in a red cap juggles three balls in the air.[28]

Descriptive Phrases

Physical and mental agility; keeping track of a number of independent factors; competent multitasking vs. dropping the ball; deciding what needs attention and what can be allowed to slide; keeping one's eyes on long-term goals while having fun in the moment; being ahead of the curve vs. being blindsided; being the contact point between otherwise unrelated people or events; getting things to revolve around you; focusing an organization around its central purpose; developing an interconnected analysis of reality that takes account of neglected factors; summary judgments based on complex calculations; thinking or talking circles around other people (fast, clever conversationalists); cheeky rejection of false analyses (witty comebacks, zingers, pranks, monkeyshines); processing information rapidly vs. confused mix-ups.

Examples

Chevy Chase (Sun. Comedian—*Saturday Night Live*); Vicki Lawrence (Neptune. Comedienne); Larry King (Jupiter. Talk-show host); Rona Barrett (Sun. Talk-show host); Art Buchwald (Mars. Political humorist); Lola Falana (Mercury. Performer with multiple talents); John Gardner (Sun. President of Common Cause); Pamela Aden (Moon. Market analyst); Mary Boyd (Sun. Astrologer—*Financial Astrology Techniques*); Ken Uston (Mars. Gambler who developed a winning blackjack system); Nikola Tesla (Moon. Inventor, genius); John Baird (Uranus. Inventor of television); Phil Proctor (North Node. Manic comedian—The Firesign Theater; Elijah Muhammad (Sun. Founder of the Black Muslims); Pierre Trudeau (Sun. Canadian prime minister).

16 Libra

After a hurricane, a man assesses damages to a wrecked boat landing and begins repairs.

Descriptive Phrases

Having a good handle on one's situation; recognizing pivotal factors so one can act in a timely and intelligent fashion (confusion, indecision); attacking a problem from an odd but effective angle; tackling a major project oneself vs. enlisting able helpers and inspiring them with one's energy and a "can-do" attitude (frazzled overexertion vs. drawing upon spiritual reserves); resilience—bouncing back after setbacks; knowing when to salvage a compromised project and when to let it go and launch a new project (hanging on too long vs. giving up too soon); reexamining one's long-range goals vs. attending to matters at hand (get lost in trivia, actions don't tally with goals); fortitude in the face of life's problems, including physical problems; recognizing that destructive and constructive forces are always balanced in nature; pluck.

Examples

Lee Iacocca (Mercury. CEO who rebuilt the Chrysler company); Queen Elizabeth I (Mercury. Consolidated English power, successfully navigated England's religious conflicts); Benjamin Disraeli (Saturn. Prime minister under Queen Victoria); Tony Garnier (Mars. City planner of Lyon, France); Georgia O'Keeffe (Uranus. Painter); John Lennon (Sun. Member of The Beatles); Winona Ryder (Uranus. Actress—*Girl Interrupted, Edward Scissorhands*); Greg Morris (Mercury. Actor—*Mission Impossible*, had his face rebuilt after an auto accident); Stevie Wonder (Neptune. Blind singer-songwriter); Albert Schweitzer (Ascendant. Medical missionary, organist); Ruby Dee (Mercury. Actress—*A Raisin in the Sun*, civil-rights activist); Ruth Ellis (Sun. Murdered her abusive husband); John Belushi (Neptune. Anarchic comedian—*Animal House*); Al Lewis (Saturn. Anarchic actor—Grandpa Munster, ran for Congress as a Green).

17 Libra

In a dressing room full of various costumes, an actress removes her makeup and costume. When her boyfriend arrives, she meets him at the door dressed only in a bathrobe.

Descriptive Phrases

Developing a stagy public persona, which is put aside in one's personal life (personality inflation caused by too close an identification with a role, may play into an image their lover finds attractive and live in fear that they will be disillusioned); intimate communication that dispels false impressions vs. sad sense that one will never be understood (complex relationship problems); private struggles over issues of spiritual identity; psychological understanding of different personality types or "masks"; having to take up a dramatically different role in life; penetrating observation of the human drama; facing life bravely; wrapping up old business and meeting the future with a naked but resolute spirit (vulnerability); navigating a changing emotional landscape with intelligence and honesty; using the arts to bring matters of spiritual concern to the public.

Examples

Robert Bly (Midheaven. Poet, author of *Iron John*, about different archetypes of male psychology); Liz Greene (Mars. Archetypal astrologer); Christopher Reeve (Saturn. Actor—*Superman*, paralyzed); Craig Russell (Moon. Female impersonator); Bonnie Raitt (Neptune. Bluesy singer); Rudolf Serkin (North Node. Sublime classical pianist); Meryl Streep (Neptune. Actress—*Sophie's Choice, Out of Africa*); Bill Murray (Neptune. Actor—*Groundhog Day, Lost in Translation*); Karen Carpenter (Neptune. Singer, died of bulimia set off by a magazine article that called her "chubby"); Helen Hayes (Sun. Actress); Johnny Carson (Mars. Talk-show host with a line of men's clothing, many marriages); John Sayles (Neptune. Film director—*Return of the Secaucus Seven, Brother from Another Planet*); Jack Kerouac (Jupiter. Personally troubled beat writer—*On the Road*); Charles Schulz (Saturn. Cartoonist—*Peanuts*); Anaïs Nin (Mars. Erotic diarist); Prince Charles (Venus. British royal).

18 Libra

Testifying in a court of law, a witness tries to make himself clear to both judge and jury.

Descriptive Phrases

Bearing witness; standing by what one knows to be true (obstinate, argumentative); telling it like it is (impudent, in-your-face); weighing the pros and cons of a problem and coming to a conclusion; forcing a decision; legally negotiating the rights of competing social groups vs. relying on physical force when discussion fails and the rule of law breaks down; planning one's battles and playing to win; accountability to society; defending or expanding social limits (push the limits of individual rights, including the limits of good taste); tailoring one's style to one's audience (cultural elitism vs. panderers who aim at the lowest common denominator); practicality; understanding the law of cause and effect; being an agent of justice (vindictive).

Examples

Howard Zinn (Jupiter. Historian—*A People's History of the United States*); Rosie the Riveter (North Node. Symbol of women in the war effort); Rudyard Kipling (North Node. Author—*Captains Courageous*); Sissy Spacek (Neptune. Actress—*Carrie, In the Bedroom*); Redd Foxx (Saturn. Obstinate comedian who used lots of profanity in his stand-up act); Marla Gibbs (Jupiter. Nasty character actress); Randy Shilts (Neptune. Gay-rights activist); Jesse Helms (North Node. Reactionary senator especially adamant on sexual issues); Thirteenth Amendment abolishes slavery (North Node. 12/18/1865); KKK founded (North Node. 12/24/1865); Joyce's *Ulysses* declared not obscene (Jupiter. 8/7/1934); Joe Valachi (Mercury. Mafioso, turned informer for the Justice Department); Jean Cocteau (Uranus. Shocking surrealist filmmaker); Bill Mauldin (North Node. Political cartoonist during World War II); Cybill Shepherd (Neptune. Actress—*The Last Picture Show, Moonlighting*); R. D. Laing (Mars. Psychologist—politics of family); Georgie Ann Geyer (Mars. Conservative columnist).

19 Libra

Hiding in a starlit forest, a masked robber spies upon a heavily laden caravan snaking along the road. From a sedan chair in the caravan, a richly clad woman gazes straight at him.

Descriptive Phrases

Astral perception or psychism—on a lower level, attunement to other people's sexual desires, on a higher level, tuning into ideas or energies and materializing them in artistic forms; catching glimmerings from a higher level; stealing divine gifts (Jack in the Beanstalk); bringing a stream of secret knowledge to the public (snake-oil salesmen, hokey spiritual trips); consciously developing one's personal magic (romantic allure); masking one's true self vs. accentuating one's magical persona through dress or behavior; getting into the public eye by bold but underhanded means; skirting the edge of the legal or the legitimate; getting a thrill from clandestine or undercover activities (detective work, romantic and sexual intrigues, voyeurism); suspenseful expectation.

Examples

Cagliostro (Moon. Alchemist, soothsayer, procurer); Cher (Jupiter. Singer, actress—*Moonstruck*); Kurt Russell (Neptune. Actor—*Stargate*); Giuseppe Tornatore (Moon. Director—*Night of the Shooting Stars*); Goldie Hawn (Jupiter. Actress—*Everyone Says I Love You; Death Becomes Her*); First release of *Time Bandits* (Saturn. 11/20/1981); Alfred Kinsey (Saturn. Sexual psychologist); Helen Gurley Brown (Jupiter. Founder of *Cosmopolitan* magazine); Edgar Allen Poe (Mars. Author who created the modern detective story—*Murders in the Rue Morgue*); Georges Simenon (North Node. Detective stories); Harold Nicholson (Neptune. CIA officer who sold secrets to the Russians); J. S. Bach (Jupiter. Composer who was a master at building emotional suspense); Wolfgang Amadeus Mozart (Jupiter. Classical composer); Sybil Leek (Jupiter. Witch); Marianne Williamson (Neptune. *Course in Miracles* teacher); Darryl Anka (Sun. Channeler of "Bashar"); Richard Crenna (Moon. Actor—*Wait until Dark*); Cassandra Peterson (Neptune. Actress—Elvira).

20 Libra

A rabbi shares a moral fable with his congregation that is based on his struggles with personal demons.

Descriptive Phrases

Preachers or propagandists who stir people's emotions (manipulative); instigators who force people to confront subconscious truths (browbeating dogmatists); facing up to evil (project their own evil onto others, identify problems of modern life but apply childish solutions); moral tests—listening to one's conscience vs. listening to desires for power, sex, or money (the ego as the devil, playing devil's advocate); extracting moral lessons from modern situations and fitting them into a framework of traditional values; bringing esoteric knowledge into the language of everyday human experience; sexual integration that provides a stable base for one's psychological structure; listening to or arguing with one's moral conscience; straining to get across one's beliefs.

Examples

Robin Williams (Neptune. Comic actor—*Good Morning, Vietnam, The Fisher King*); Joan Armatrading (Neptune. Socially conscious folk singer); Paul Simon (Sun. Poet, folk singer—Simon and Garfunkel); Girolamo Savonarola (Saturn. Renaissance religious zealot); Adolf Hitler (Uranus. Viciously anti-Semitic Nazi dictator); Lenny Bruce (Sun. Foul-mouthed stand-up comic in constant trouble with the law, died of an overdose); Vincent Bugliosi (Jupiter. Lawyer who prosecuted Charles Manson); Sally Field (Ascendant. Actress—*Norma Rae*); Jane Austen (Saturn. Writer—*Emma*); Ken Kesey (Mercury. Writer—*One Flew over the Cuckoo's Nest*); Rosalyn Bruyère (Chiron. Healer, guru—Healing Light Center); Dick Gregory (Sun. Comic, activist, paranoid); Roberto Benigni (Sun. Comic actor, director—*Life is Beautiful*); Hans Christian Andersen (Uranus. Author of fairytales); Aleister Crowley (Sun. Black magician); Al Pacino (North Node. Actor—*The Devil's Advocate*); Miguel de Unamuno (Saturn. Writer—*The Tragic Sense of Life*).

21 Libra

At a public beach, a crowd is engaged in a rowdy tug-of-war. A cheer rises when a local tough joins one of the teams.

Descriptive Phrases

Throwing oneself wholeheartedly into life; holding one's own in the struggles of everyday life; scrappy, down-to-earth characters with the courage of their convictions (brawlers); giving as good as one gets (may overestimate their powers and take on more than they can handle, refuse to accept defeat, don't know when to let go); joining in a group enterprise without relinquishing one's autonomy or losing sight of one's personal interests; letting other people know where one stands; shrewd understanding of what makes the average person tick (cynical, streetwise); clearing the air by exposing hidden motives; physical or sexual prowess; showing off one's talents; throwing one's weight behind a cause; superhuman efforts alternating with timeouts; earthy populism.

Examples

Roseanne Barr (Saturn. Rowdy comedienne); Norman Mailer (Saturn. Writer—*Armies of the Night, The Presidential Papers*); Bette Midler (Jupiter. Comedienne, actress—*For the Boys*); David Carradine (Moon. Actor—*Kung Fu*); Brendan Behan (Saturn. Irish playwright, runner for the IRA); Maria Callas (Moon. Temperamental opera diva); George Meany (Saturn. Labor leader); Christopher Reeve (Neptune. Actor—*Superman*, spokesperson for the paralyzed); Henry Ford (Jupiter. Inventor, industrialist—Ford Motor Company); Paddy Chayevsky (Saturn, Stationary. Playwright—*Marty*); Jean Stapleton (Saturn. Actress—Edith Bunker in *All in the Family*); John F. Kennedy (Ascendant. U. S. president); Sonny Jurgenson (Jupiter. Famous football quarterback, sportscaster); Tuli Kupferberg (Saturn. Impudent singer—The Fugs); Judy Canova (Venus. Raucous comedienne); Whoopi Goldberg (Mars. Worldly wise comedienne); Elliott Gould (Venus. Actor—*Bob & Ted & Carol & Alice*).

22 Libra

Standing next to a circular marble fountain, a little girl is giving two birds a drink from a cup.

Descriptive Phrases

Peacemakers; finding common ground between living things; appeals for kindness and compassion; cooperative efforts; emotional inclusiveness (popularity seekers); getting people to open up (coaxing familiarity); offering spiritual nourishment to less advanced souls; adapting one's message to other people's capacities (patronizing); finding opportunities to awaken others to the immanence of the divine; living out one's spiritual principles in everyday life; dissolving the barriers between the personal and the collective; full-bodied participation in life vs. sitting on the fence; seeking fun and adventure vs. complacent satiety; infectious enthusiasm for life (robustly sensual); mirthful optimism; expansive generosity of spirit; seeking a wider harmony.

Examples

Hayley Mills (Jupiter. Actress—*Pollyanna, The Parent Trap*); Dwight D. Eisenhower (Sun. General, president who presided over the peaceful fifties); Carolyn Casey (Sun. Shamanistic astrologer); John Waters (Jupiter. Ultratolerant underground film director); Kathie Lee Gifford (Neptune. Talk-show emcee tarnished by sweatshop scandal); Alex Haley (North Node. Author—*Roots*); William Penn (Sun. Quaker religious leader, peacemaker, founder of Pennsylvania); Penny Marshall (Sun. Actress—*Laverne and Shirley*, film director—*Big*); Dolly Parton (Chiron. Country singer); Dr. Bernie Siegel (Sun. Holistic doctor); James Jones (Venus. Author—*From Here to Eternity*); Douglas Adams (Neptune. Writer—*Hitchhiker's Guide to the Galaxy*); Roberto Benigni (Neptune. Actor, director—*Life is Beautiful*); Richard Carpenter (Sun. Singer-songwriter—The Carpenters); Marie Bashkirtsett (Venus. Became famous for her diary of romantic and sexual awakening).

23 Libra

A gnomelike man in a dinner suit entertains his guests with a talking rooster, which perches on his shoulder.

Descriptive Phrases

Taking a fresh look at one's scene and offering sharp, pithy observations on what one sees (refreshing honesty vs. outrageous bluntness); commenting on the absurd and incongruous elements of human society (may act as if they are above the rules of human society); droll, mischievous humor; foolish wisdom vs. wise foolishness; self-deflating wit vs. acting like the sun rises with one's pronouncements; playing out a fanciful role on the stage of life (love of costume, dandies and fashion-plates, "cocks-of-the-walk"); playing the crowd; developing some aspect of the self that delights the public (cartoonlike self-exaggeration); effective self-promotion (social climbers); spellbinding conversationalists with the gift of gab (blarney); educating while entertaining.

Examples

Ed Wynn (Jupiter. Comedian); Stan Laurel (Uranus. Comic actor); Henry Kissinger (Moon. Policymaker); Friedrich Nietzsche (Sun. Self-inflated moral philosopher); Mickey Rooney (Venus. Actor); Oscar Wilde (Sun. Playwright, dandy, aesthetician); Woody Allen (Venus. Filmmaker and sharp observer of the human comedy); Shari Lewis (Jupiter. Puppeteer); Roseanne Barr (Neptune. Comedienne); Margaret Hamilton (North Node. Character actress); Jimmy Swaggart (Mars. Televangelist); Aimée Semple McPherson (Uranus. Showboat evangelist); Lee Iacocca (Sun. Self-made man, headed Ford, then Chrysler); Gunther Gebel-Williams (Moon. Lion tamer); Noel Coward (Ascendant. Witty playwright); Suzanne Somers (Sun. Self-deprecating bimbo actress); Stephen Jay Gould (Ascendant. Self-important science educator, radical materialist); Hulk Hogan (Saturn. Wrestler).

24 Libra

At a public meeting, a mayoral candidate reads a position paper on his plans to beautify and politically reorganize the city. After the meeting, a crowd of converts signs up to work on the campaign.

Descriptive Phrases

Developing blueprints for a far-reaching program of social, political, or religious reform; setting armies marching in service of an ideal; eliminating corruption, poverty, and other social ills (Utopianism vs. Puritanical zealotry); evolution toward a social ideal; turning over a new leaf; writing a new chapter in history; putting one's ideals into practical action; balancing contemplation and action; sizing up the changing situation, and making a strategic move; anchoring one's character in unchanging moral principles; steeping oneself in the lessons of history, religion, or moral philosophy; moral fortitude and solidity of character which allows one to stand up to enemies who seek to destroy one's position; persuasiveness; effectively communicating one's vision of the future.

Examples

Mao Tse Tung (Saturn. Chinese political and cultural revolutionary, author of *The Little Red Book*); Elizabeth Gurley Flynn (Uranus. Early activist for women's suffrage); Winston Churchill (Jupiter. British prime minister, moral bastion during World War II); Lewis Mumford (Mars. Author—*Story of Utopias, Technics and Civilization*); Henri Bergson (Sun. Philosopher—*Creative Evolution*); Henry van de Velde (Jupiter. Leader of the Art Nouveau movement); Martin Luther (Jupiter. Initiated the Protestant Reformation); Frances Willard (Jupiter. Women's Christian Temperance movement); Margaret Thatcher (Mercury. Conservative British prime minister); Joseph McCarthy (Mars. Senator—head of the House Un-American Activities Committee); Desiderius Erasmus (Venus. 16th-century religious reformer, satirist); F. Scott Fitzgerald (Venus. Author—*The Great Gatsby*); Donald Sutherland (Mars. Actor—*M*A*S*H, Start the Revolution Without Me*).

25 Libra

Having skipped school, a boy puts down his Gothic horror novel and walks to the window, where he watches townspeople scurrying through a sudden shower of rain and falling leaves.

Descriptive Phrases

Letting go of artificial, ephemeral values; giving things their proper weight; clearheaded judgment; sharp commentary on the parade of human folly; having one foot firmly planted in the changeable material world, and one in the unchanging values of the inner realm; transience of human reality constructions vs. the permanence of the natural world and its cycles; learning from books vs. learning directly from life; detaching oneself from unrewarding scenes; following out some daydream or line of thought vs. knowing when to come back to earth (disastrous blurring of the line between reality and fantasy); finding amusing pastimes; taking breathers; meditation—clearing the mind of mental clutter; watching thoughts come and go; idle daydreaming vs. self-forgetful immersion in nature.

Examples

F. Scott Fitzgerald (Mercury. Author—*The Great Gatsby*); Susan Sarandon (Mercury. Actress—*Rocky Horror Picture Show*); Tim Burton (North Node. Filmmaker—*Beetlejuice, The Nightmare Before Christmas*); Jerry Seinfeld (Neptune. Comedian); Julie Brown (North Node. Comedienne—*Because I'm Blonde*); Terry Gilliam (Venus. *Monty Python* comic, filmmaker—*Brazil, Adventures of Baron Munchausen*); Laura Nyro (Sun. Singer—"Stoned Soul Picnic"); Inger Stevens (Sun. Actress); Agatha Christie (Uranus. Mystery writer); Jackie Chan (Saturn. Martial arts silliness); Petrarch (Uranus. Poet, cultural innovator); Roman Polanski (Mars. Filmmaker—*Repulsion, Fearless Vampire Killers*); Edgar Bergen (Moon. Ventriloquist who used Charlie McCarthy to mock social foibles); Meher Baba (Saturn. The silent guru); Percy Shelley (Jupiter, Mars. Lyric poet, drowned in a sudden lake storm); Erik Menendez (Mars. Killed his parents).

26 Libra

A glamorous movie star enters a Hollywood party from a lofty staircase, her producer-husband in tow.

Descriptive Phrases

Worshipful relationship with a person who serves as a muse and connects one to divine beauty and love; relationships where one person works in the background, and the other is a public figure; knowing when to withdraw into the background and when to come forward in one's glory; confident display of one's talents; masterful exercise of one's various abilities (like many-armed Shiva); self-mastery; command performances; dazzling display; drawing other people into one's vision; controlling the illusion; playing a lead role in life's drama; maintaining the dignity of one's higher self in potentially degrading situations (cold, aloof); manifesting one's divinity vs. self-caricature; deciding whether to play a scene modestly or whether to take it by storm.

Examples

Sophia Loren (Jupiter. Actress, paired with director Carlo Ponti); Madonna (North Node. Brazenly sexual pop singer); Peter Max (Sun. Psychedelic artist); John Lennon (Ascendant. Rock singer, songwriter—The Beatles); Brian Epstein (Jupiter. The Beatles' manager); Guru Maharaj-ji (Jupiter. Guru); Madeline Kahn (Mercury. Comedienne in Mel Brooks films—*Blazing Saddles*); Diane Keaton (Jupiter. Actress in Woody Allen movies); Divine (Sun. Fat transvestite in John Waters' films); Toulouse-Lautrec (Saturn. Artist who specialized in dancehall scenes); King Mongkut (Sun. King on whom *The King and I* was based); Kareem Abdul Jabbar (Ascendant. Basketball superstar); Nijinsky (Uranus. Ballet superstar); Federico Fellini (Mars. Filmmaker, was married to Giulietta Masina, who starred in many of his films); Howard Stern (Neptune. Off-color talk-radio host, paired with Robin Quivers); Tom Hulce (Neptune. Actor—*Amadeus*).

27 Libra

After a sordid political battle, a legislator takes a flight home. Looking down through a hole in the clouds, he can see the dome of the capitol building.

Descriptive Phrases

Overview; being above it all vs. being down in the fray (sordid entanglements); seeing the larger picture; shining a light on a situation (channeling the light of the divine mind); pointing out facts that others are trying to ignore vs. having one's head in the clouds; seeing a way out of one's current difficulties—a "hole in the clouds"—and guiding others toward this escape route vs. getting trapped in a no-win situation (judging when to fight and when to bail out); trying to establish ideals of freedom, justice, and truth at the highest level of society; arguing for one's political and social ideals (spiritual passion vs. argumentativeness); trying to influence public policy; being guided by firmly held beliefs throughout the entire trajectory of one's life; promoting a higher level of civilization; imperturbable high-mindedness.

Examples

Art Buchwald (Sun. Political cartoonist); Marjorie Claprood (Moon. Politician—women's issues); Alan Alda (Midheaven. Actor—*M*A*S*H*); Dwight D. Eisenhower (Uranus. U.S. President); Mamie Eisenhower (Mars. First Lady); Mary Tyler Moore (Mars. Actress—*The Mary Tyler Moore Show*); Cicely Tyson (North Node. Actress—*The Autobiography of Miss Jane Pittman*); Christopher Wren (Sun. Architect of St. Paul's Cathedral); Joseph Smith (Saturn. Mormon leader); Lewis Mumford (Sun. Author—*Technics and Civilization*); Satyajit Ray (North Node. Indian filmmaker—*Pather Panchali*); Leon Uris (Saturn. Author—*Exodus*); Daniel Berrigan (North Node. Priest, peace activist); Ruth Benedict (Jupiter. Anthropologist who studied racism in *Race: Science and Politics*); James Baldwin (Saturn. Black writer and activist—*Go Tell It on the Mountain*); John Adams (Pluto. Led the debate in favor of declaring independence from England, U. S. president after Washington).

28 Libra

A man stands at a crossroads; behind him, unseen, a good and a bad angel.

Descriptive Phrases

Exerting an ongoing influence behind the scenes, for good or for ill (working through intermediaries or front men); seeing oneself as an agent of invisible spiritual powers (the human personality as it extends into the realms of the angelic and the demonic); shining a light on a moral crossroads being faced by the public; guiding others along a path of light; moral accountability (see the long-range spiritual consequences of their actions, aware that good and bad actions have a snowballing effect); convergences of causal factors (synchronicity vs. scary brushes with occult forces); tracking down an external problem to its spiritual source; trying to solve complex problems on an inner level; faith in the efficacy of benevolent forces vs. paranoid entanglement.

Examples

Scott Bakula (Neptune. Actor—*Quantum Leap*); Mia Farrow (Jupiter. Actress—*Rosemary's Baby, Alice*); Oliver Stone (Jupiter. Film director—*JFK*); Bela Lugosi (Sun. *Dracula*); Bruce Willis (Neptune. Actor—*The Fifth Element, The Sixth Sense*); Jim Jarmusch (Saturn. Film director—*Mystery Train, Dead Man*); Tom Hanks (Neptune, Stationary direct. Actor—*Forrest Gump*); Roz Chast (Neptune. Loopy cartoonist); H. R. Haldeman (Venus. Nixon henchman); Brigitte Bardot (Jupiter, Mercury. One-time sexpot, animal-rights activist); Gerard Croiset (Moon. Psychic who helps police track down criminals); Karen Silkwood (Jupiter. Killed while investigating radioactive polluters); William Butler Yeats (North Node. Poet, occultist, kept Crowley out of the Order of the Golden Dawn); Martin Luther (Jupiter. Religious reformer, several sightings of Satan); Sir Thomas More (Mars. Chancellor beheaded by Henry VIII, author of *Utopia*); Seth Green (Uranus. Actor—Scott Evil in *Austin Powers* films).

29 Libra

A white-robed priestess stands in front of her congregation. In one hand, she holds a serpent; in the other, she holds a chalice containing a consciousness-expanding drug.

Descriptive Phrases

Striving to reach an entirely new level of consciousness; freeing oneself from the psychological assumptions of the dominant society like a snake shedding its skin (radical social critiques); seeing through collective delusions vs. seducing others with groundless promises into one's own speculative belief-system (spiritual gurus vs. cult leaders); storming heaven's gates vs. losing one's moral footing (sexual lawlessness); gnostic demand for direct spiritual experience (sacramental use of drugs vs. drug abuse); impatient demand for a radical transformation of consciousness that will lead, in turn, to a radical restructuring of society; revealing hidden powers; rising through one's talents; living fully within one's own myths.

Examples

Deepak Chopra (Sun. Guru—*Mastering the Forces That Shape Personal Reality*); Leni Riefenstahl (North Node. Nazi film propagandist—*Triumph of the Will*); Timothy Leary (Sun. Psychedelic guru); Martin Luther (South Node. Leader of the Reformation who broke from the Catholic Church; many of his innovations concerned the nature of the Eucharist); Grace Slick (North Node. Lead singer—Jefferson Airplane, promoted drug use with "White Rabbit"); Carrie Fisher (Sun. Actress—Princess Leia in *Star Wars*, ex-coke-head); Franklin Jones (North Node. Guru—Bubba Free John); Ellen Degeneres (Jupiter. Gay TV comedienne); Martin Heidigger (Mercury. Philosopher); Derek Jacobi (Sun. Actor—*I, Claudius, Brother Cadfael*); Ursula LeGuin (Sun. Utopian science fiction writer); Kevin Costner (Neptune. Actor—*Dances with Wolves, Waterworld*); Elijah Muhammad (Mars. Black Muslim leader).

30 Libra

A turbaned mind reader surreptitiously hides something in the sleeve of his robe.

Descriptive Phrases

Keeping tabs on other people's underhanded maneuvers vs. subtle control of people's emotions and desires (temptation to base actions, sleazy behavior); gleaning underlying motives from a person's body language or from lapses in their speech; probing people's psychology through subtle insinuation vs. knowing when to keep a secret under wraps, especially in a relationship; playing one's cards close to the chest; humorous and astute commentary on the foibles of human behavior (pretend to be wiser and more worldly than they are—marvelous humbugs who affect droll disreputability under a veneer of decorum); wary attentiveness vs. failing to heed various warning signals; getting the lowdown; sniffing out the facts (occult or scientific research).

Examples

Johnny Carson (Sun. Comedian—Karnak the Magnificent); Jonathan Winters (Mars. Comedian—The Blessed Reverend); Jon Lovitz (Neptune. Comedian who plays a compulsive liar); Henry VIII (Pluto. Bluebeard king); George Adamski (Uranus. UFO enthusiast); Larry Flynt (Mars. *Hustler* magnate, battles for freedom of the press); Tama Janowitz (Neptune. Author—*Slaves of New York*); Grace Metalious (Saturn. Author—*Peyton Place*); Jay Gould (Saturn. Made a fortune through railroad stock manipulation); Ruth Ellis (Mercury. Murdered abusive husband, acquitted); Michael Crichton (Sun. Author—*The Andromeda Strain*); Fritz Lang (Uranus. Filmmaker—*Metropolis*); Cheri St. Cyr (Sun. Tarot reader, masseuse, artist in painted silks); Eric Hoffer (North Node. Writer—*The True Believer*); Robert Mapplethorpe (Chiron. Photographer of gay S and M); Desiderius Erasmus (Mercury. German humanist—*In Praise of Folly, Adagia*); Al Jaffee (North Node. *Mad* magazine cartoonist).

1 Scorpio

Chinese emperor interviews a barbarian princess. Finding her obstinate, he resorts to threats, whereupon she whistles, summoning a giant dragon, which flies down and alights beside her.

Descriptive Phrases

Power struggles; sly diplomacy vs. showing one's teeth (resort to threats or physical violence); forcing a despot or a corrupt official out of power; standing up for one's side vs. falling in with the dark force and betraying one's principles; being locked in an unending battle vs. seeing the underlying unity of male and female, desire and fear, good and evil, creation and destruction; dragonish musings on the paradoxes of the cosmos; metaphysical imagination vs. escapist fantasy; hunger for fantastic adventure (reckless); boldly examining a new scene; getting one's mind around the full parameters of one's situation; having the greater reality on one's side; forcing people to come to grips with something they'd rather not look at.

Examples

Mark Twain (Saturn. Writer—*Connecticut Yankee in King Arthur's Court, Letters from the Earth*); Lauren Bacall (Saturn. Actress—*Designing Women*); C. S. Lewis (Jupiter. Fantasy writer—*Perelandra Trilogy*); D. W. Griffith (Jupiter. Ambitious silent-film director—*Intolerance, Birth of a Nation*); George S. Patton (Saturn. General); Melanie Griffith (Neptune. Actress—*Working Girl, Cecil B. Demented*); Uma Thurman (Neptune. Actress—Poison Ivy in *Batman*); George Harrison (Moon. Rock musician—The Beatles); Deborah Kerr (Mercury. Actress—*The King and I*); Carrie Fisher (Neptune. Actress—*Star Wars*); Jim Morrison (Venus. Lead singer—The Doors); Heinrich Himmler (Mercury. Head of the S. S., ordered the death of millions); Immanuel Velikovsky (Saturn. Controversial scientist—*When Worlds Collide*); Cyril Ritchart (Jupiter. Played Captain Hook, who was constantly pursued by a crocodile).

2 Scorpio

Pretty waitress banters jokingly with an insolent customer, while setting a vase of flowers on the table. When he steps over the line, she accidentally tips a glass of wine onto his pants.

Descriptive Phrases

Maintaining emotional equilibrium in difficult situations; learning to roll with the punches; ignoring or forgiving annoying behavior vs. carrying a grudge (emotional sticking points); learning to release emotional toxins in a socially acceptable way; witty repartee vs. irritating insistence on one's personal obsessions; having fixed romantic expectations vs. good-naturedly accepting love's mixture of beauty and ugliness; trying to give concrete form to one's values and aesthetic ideals in every situation; attending to important details vs. unrealistic perfectionism; displaying one's beauty, charm, and talent to best advantage; self-containment vs. pouring oneself out for others; humbly doing a good job vs. wanting to be placed on a pedestal.

Examples

Fran Drescher (Neptune. Comedienne—*The Nanny, The Beautician and the Beast,* in which she does a makeover of a backward country); Michelle Pfeiffer (Neptune. Beautiful actress); Marcello Mastroianni (Saturn. Handsome romantic lead in Fellini movies—*Ginger and Fred*); Claudia Schiffer (Jupiter. Stunning model, very private); Brett Butler (Jupiter. Hard-bitten comedienne—*Grace under Fire,* alcohol problems); Lili Taylor (Jupiter. Actress—*I Shot Andy Warhol*); Graham Greene (Venus. Writer—*The Quiet American,* served in British Intelligence); Andie McDowell (North Node. Model, actress—*Groundhog Day; sex, lies, and videotape*); Bruce Lee (Venus. Martial arts superstar); Martin Luther (Mars. Reformer who broke from the Catholic Church, in part because of his insistence on his own view of the Eucharist); Jimmy Carter (Saturn. President); Dr. Bernie Siegel (Mercury. Alternative physician—self-healing); Gerard Depardieu (South Node. Coarse-faced romantic lead).

3 Scorpio

A newly married couple and their friends are hammering up the frame of the couple's new home, while a radio plays cheerfully in the background.

Descriptive Phrases

Teamwork; working to make one's home or workplace a loving and harmonious place; giving concrete form to one's dreams (lost in romantic fantasies—hearts floating around their heads); having a concrete plan vs. letting things fall into place; getting ahead of oneself vs. patiently attending to the work at hand; learning to compromise vs. demanding agreement; emotional persuasiveness vs. hammering away at a point (believe their superior understanding gives them the right to control a project); working on a relationship; patching up disagreements (being constructive or at least being quiet—giving one's partner breathing room); the importance of getting off on the right foot, with the blessing of one's family and the community; group efforts.

Examples

Ed Asner (Venus. The boss on *The Mary Tyler Moore Show*); Cloris Leachman (South Node. Actress—*The Mary Tyler Moore Show, Young Frankenstein*); William Powell (Uranus. Actor in *The Thin Man* series, paired with Myrna Loy); Audrey Meadows (Saturn. Alice on *The Honeymooners*); Tony Randall (Saturn. Actor—*The Odd Couple*); Howard Kaylan (Chiron. Satirical singer—Flo and Eddie); Mae West (Uranus. Often paired with W. C. Fields); Kevin Bacon (Neptune, Stationary. Actor—subject of a game in which all people are related to each other through intermediary people); John Cleese (Sun. *Monty Python* comedian); Geena Davis (Neptune. Actress—*Thelma and Louise, A League of Their Own*); Keenen Ivory Wayans (Neptune. Heads up family comedy team on *In Living Color*); Bill Monroe (South Node. Bluegrass great); Angela Bassett (Neptune. Actress—*What's Love Got to Do with It?*).

4 Scorpio

Holding a lit candle, a young woman investigates the spooky castle she has just inherited.

Descriptive Phrases

First entry into "the spirit world," with all its scary projections (the astral light, ghosts and spirits); probing into the darker corners of the mind in order to dispel negative influences; cultural housecleaning; throwing away outworn elements of a tradition, and bringing new blood to what is still relevant (cultural influence that lasts beyond one's death, much as the light of the soul survives the decay of the body); throwing a fresh new light on a situation vs. getting drawn into an unwholesome tradition; removing political or spiritual abuses; severing morbid alliances; seeing things that are invisible to others or pretending to (trading in shadows and illusions, shady dealings); storytellers (Gothic tales); initiating others into a tradition; acting as a guide to the dream world or the underworld; purification and refinement of spiritual energies.

Examples

Margaret Rutherford (Uranus. Actress—Miss Marple); Evelyn Waugh (Sun. Writer—*The Loved One*, a farcical attack on Forest Lawn cemetery); Francesco Petrarca (Neptune. Medieval poet who was the first to attack medieval culture and promote a revived Roman culture); Pietro Aretino (Pluto. Attacked humanist culture as fusty); Sybil Danning (Chiron. Actress—*Bluebeard*); Friedrich Murnau (Moon. Director—*Nosferatu*); Joseph McCarthy (Mercury. Tried to clean Communists out of government); Ruth Gordon (Chiron. Actress—*Harold and Maude*, *Rosemary's Baby*); Kurt Vonnegut (Jupiter. Sci-fi writer—*Welcome to the Monkey House*); Eleanor Smeal (North Node. President of National Organization for Women); Sonia Gandhi (Chiron. Italian wife of Sanjay Gandhi who became a Congress Party politician after he was assassinated); Robert Chaney (Sun. Spiritualist reverend); Alfred Hitchcock (Jupiter. Film director—*Psycho*); Tina Brown (Saturn. Took over *Vanity Fair* and livened it up); Harry Hamlin (Moon. Actor—*Andromeda and Jason*); Ethel Waters (Chiron. Singer, actress—*A Member of the Wedding*).

5 Scorpio

A wild party on a boat moored near a rocky cliff. A guest arrives by way of the steep and dangerous road down the side of the cliff.

Descriptive Phrases

Getting to know one's own limits by testing them (excesses may lead to catastrophe); stony self-possession even in the midst of risk-taking activity; living close to the edge; taking risks because it makes one feel more alive vs. fearfully clinging to safe routines; participating fully in life (don't want to miss out on the party); getting others to participate vs. pointing out hidden dangers; learning from one's passionate involvements and teaching what one has learned; finding a stable emotional bedrock under temporary mood swings; discovering permanent heart values that transcend the storms and shipwrecks of passion; refusing to be diverted from one's more serious ends; self-possession and cultural refinement vs. abandoning oneself to base pleasures.

Examples

Hunter Thompson (North Node. Radical writer and journalist who lives life at a breakneck pace, drug and alcohol abuser—*Fear and Loathing in Las Vegas*); Cindy Williams (Chiron. Actress—Laverne in *Laverne and Shirley*); Kevin Spacey (Neptune. Actor—*American Beauty*); Victoria Abril (Neptune. Actress in Almodovar films—*Women on the Verge of a Nervous Breakdown*); Ann Richards (Mars. Texas politician, alcohol problems); Steve Martin (Moon. Comedian, actor—*The Jerk*, *Pennies from Heaven*, problems with depression and isolation); Marjorie Merriweather Post (Jupiter. Socialite, high liver); Maria Montessori (Moon. Innovative educator); Dave Brubeck (North Node. Jazz pianist); Sylvia Plath (Sun. Poet—*The Bell Jar*, suicide); Steve McQueen (South Node. "Force of nature" actor—*The Great Escape*); Salvatore Giuliano (Jupiter. Italian bandit chief who lived in a mountain hideout); Terry Thomas (Jupiter. Comedian in cliffhangers like *The Perils of Pauline* and *Make Mine Mink*).

6 Scorpio

Pistol in hand, a detective stands by a door and listens to a gang of thieves hatching a plot.[29]

Descriptive Phrases

Confronting other people's underlying motives (psychological acuity); investigating fishy explanations (eavesdropping, prying); unmasking deceit and half-truths; circling in on a hunch; identifying a key piece of a puzzle; testing one's hunches by seeing if they have the power to stir others; taking potshots and setting off a chain reaction vs. trying not to rock the boat; getting the full scoop vs. acting too quickly and making a mess of things; critically examining one's own desires; being hip to one's own game vs. scamming oneself or others, or betraying one's ideals; dodging other people's agendas and protecting one's own interests (cynical, suspicious, need total honesty in relationships); learning who one's real friends are (always testing others); exposing some mystery.

Examples

Adam Carolla (Jupiter. Panelist on *Loveline* who tries to get at people's underlying sexual problems); Jamie Lee Curtis (Neptune. Actress—*Halloween, True Lies*); Kim Basinger (Saturn. Actress—*L.A. Confidential*); R. D. Laing (Mercury. Psychologist who tries to unravel repressive family dynamics); Sidney Toler (South Node. Actor—*Charlie Chan* series); Vivian Vance (Jupiter, South Node. Actress—*I Love Lucy*); Emma Thompson (Neptune. Actress—*Sense and Sensibility*); Charles Nordhoff (Jupiter. Writer—*Mutiny on the Bounty*); Jerry Seinfeld (Saturn. Comedian—*Seinfeld*); George Stanhope (Saturn. Bankrolled the expedition to find Tutankhamen's tomb); Deepak Chopra (Jupiter. Holistic healer); J. Edgar Hoover (Saturn. Paranoid head of the FBI who kept files on everybody); Ngaio Marsh (Jupiter. Detective writer); Larry Flynt (Venus. Founder of *Hustler*); Winona Ryder (Sun. Actress—*Heathers*); Ray Merriman (Chiron. Stockmarket astrologer).

7 Scorpio

Decked out in a top hat, a cane, and a precariously hanging diaper, a toddler mugs for a crowd of appreciative adults.

Descriptive Phrases

Strutting one's stuff; uncovering and parading one's native gifts; presenting the public with a surprising new truth; self-exploration vs. self-exploitation; standing on one's own vs. being a big baby (expect people to take care of them); giving the public what it wants vs. revealing too much; exploring all of one's gifts vs. learning that one doesn't have to embrace all of one's desires or impulses; trusting and elaborating upon one's first instinctive take on a situation (distrust consensual reality); offering fresh solutions to preexisting problems; thinking things through before presenting them vs. blurting out one's first thought; secretiveness vs. spilling one's guts; making a strong first impression; fun-loving antics played off against natural dignity.

Examples

Fanny Brice (Uranus. Vaudeville comedienne—Baby Snooks); David Schwimmer (Venus. Actor—*Friends*); Lucille Ball (Jupiter. Actress—*I Love Lucy*); Benito Mussolini (North Node. Italian fascist dictator); Christina Crawford (North Node. Confessional writer—*Mommy Dearest*); Henry Winkler (Sun. Actor, director, Fonzie on *Happy Days*); Charles Schulz (Jupiter. Cartoonist—*Peanuts*); Bella Abzug (Mars. Flamboyant radical politician); Marquis de Sade (Pluto. Shocking pornographer with a political agenda); Tiger Woods (Uranus. Golf superstar); Spencer Brown (Uranus, Stationary. Andy Brown on *Amos and Andy*); Oscar Levant (Mars. Pianist and actor with a confessional neurotic persona); Grace Slick (Sun. Lead singer of The Jefferson Airplane); Mark Volman (Chiron. Impudent rock singer—The Turtles, Flo and Eddy); Sarah Ferguson (Neptune. High-living British duchess).

8 Scorpio

In a dark stream bathed by moonlight, a cobra swims to shore. On discovering another snake there, it stands erect and displays its hood.

Descriptive Phrases

Being aware of dangerous sexual or political undercurrents, without feeding them with too much psychic energy (tangled up in dark forces, especially the desire to dominate others); taking a stand when faced with life's challenges (evasive maneuvers vs. grappling with enemies in a win or die situation); directing others in some bold enterprise; managing power responsibly vs. controlling others through force of personality or menacing displays (hypnotic or psychic powers); feeling potent vs. feeling impotent (feel steamrolled by people whose will is at cross-purposes to their own); slick, sophisticated navigation of subtle undercurrents in social situations (discerning the interior landscape); kundalini's power to expand the astral body; machismo.

Examples

Huey Long (Uranus. Charismatic populist demagogue); Eva Le Gallienne (Jupiter. Influential drama teacher, lesbian); Toshiro Mifune (Mars. Macho actor in Kurosawa films—*The Seven Samurai*); Camille Paglia (Chiron. Cultural critic who takes on political correctness and deconstructionism with deadly aim); Niccolò Machiavelli (Neptune. Renaissance political theorist—*The Prince*); Charles Manson (Jupiter. Insane cult leader, apparently with hypnotic powers); Charles Atlas (Sun. Bodybuilding entrepreneur—"Don't let them kick sand in your face."); Beverly Nichols (Jupiter. Gardening writer who also wrote *Father Figure*, about his abusive father); Hugh Grant (Neptune. Actor whose forte is stammering ineffectuality); Ruth Gordon (Sun. Actress—*Rosemary's Baby, Harold and Maude*); Amelia Earhart (Chiron. Pilot, disappeared over the South Pacific); Wolf Messing (Jupiter. Psychic with remarkable hypnotic powers); Chiang Kai-shek (Sun. Chinese nationalist military leader).

9 Scorpio

A dentist shows a patient an X-ray of his cavities before drilling and filling his teeth.

Descriptive Phrases

Insistently pointing out a personal or social problem that needs immediate attention, before it gets out of hand; timely diagnosis vs. frenetic stopgap remedies; accurate and detailed observation vs. reading too much or too little into a situation (may fixate on issues that are not of particular personal importance, need to develop mental discipline to avoid paranoid vortexes of thought); making people deal with issues they'd as soon ignore; protecting the body-politic from malign influences; exposing and rooting out political, social, or moral corruption (Puritanism vs. prurient libertinism); hitting a nerve; pushing people's buttons in order to see if one's intuitions are correct (rude); lashing out irrationally vs. clinically examining a problem's deeper roots.

Examples

Martin Luther (Sun. Catalyzed the Protestant Reformation by attacking the corruption of the Catholic Church); Catherine MacKinnon (Mars. Antipornography feminist activist); Oliver Stone (Venus. Muckraking film director—*JFK*, *Platoon*); Agatha Christie (Venus. Mystery writer); Howard Cosell (Mars. Grating sports commentator); David Rorvik (Sun. Writer—*The Cloning of Man*); Princess Diana (Neptune. Jet-setter, worked to ban land mines); Marco Furlan (Neptune. Serial killer of prostitutes, gays); Lavrenty Beria (Jupiter. Head of Stalin's secret police); Robert Mapplethorpe (Jupiter. Homoerotic photographer whose extreme work threatened funding for the arts); Sigmund Freud (Ascendant. Founder of psychoanalysis, dealt mainly with patients suffering from hysteria); Howard Stern (Saturn. Abrasive talk-show host); Franz Kafka (North Node. Paranoid writer—*Metamorphosis, The Penal Colony*); Mary Shelley (Neptune. Writer—*Frankenstein*).

10 Scorpio

At a family dinner, the son negotiates with his father for the use of the car, while his younger sister is grounded for having sassed her father.

Descriptive Phrases

Asserting one's individuality, but respecting the basic requirements of the group (rebellious, bratty, stretching the rules); conflict between one's own desires and one's duty to family and society; being carefree vs. stepping into one's parent's shoes; taking responsibility for the well-being of the group; parenting; being authoritative vs. being authoritarian; preserving old values without sacrificing good will for external facades; negotiating or arguing about social or political rules; policy-making (want to be on top, resent having to subordinate their will to others); shaping public opinion; working for society; reorganizing group or corporate enterprises along more functional lines; reintegrating problem areas; promoting a rich family life.

Examples

Matt Groening (Saturn. Cartoonist—*The Simpsons*); Hank Ketcham (Mars. Cartoonist—*Dennis the Menace*); Ron Howard (Saturn. Opie on *The Andie Griffith Show*, later a famous producer-director); Anne Francis (Venus. Actress—*The Blackboard Jungle*); Desmond Tutu (Mars. Freedom-fighting reverend in South Africa); Dale Evans (Mars. Cowgirl TV star on the *Roy Rogers Show*, advocacy work for abused children); John F. Kennedy, Jr. (Neptune. Editor of *George* magazine, died in plane crash); Sally Field (Jupiter. Comic actress—*Soapdish*); Matt Damon (Jupiter. Actor—*Good Will Hunting, The Talented Mr. Ripley*); Beverly Nichols (Moon. Writer—*Father Figure*, which exposes his abusive father); Patti Hearst (Saturn. Kidnapped heiress who held up a bank with the Symbionese Liberation Army, later acted in John Waters' films); Jawaharlal Nehru (Mercury. Freedom fighter, first president of independent India); Abraham Lincoln (Uranus. U. S. president who freed the slaves).

11 Scorpio

A man at the seaside watches a beautiful young woman swimming toward the reef on which he is sitting. When she has difficulty pulling herself out of the water, he reaches down and aids her, his eyes meeting hers.

Descriptive Phrases

Prowling around for sex and romance; abandoning oneself to sexual or emotional impulses (get in over their heads); betraying old commitments by plunging into murky affairs vs. finding oneself by losing oneself; merging energies with someone; baring one's soul; knowing oneself emotionally vs. floundering around and hoping to be "rescued"; taking a chance on something more emotionally vital vs. standing on the sidelines, feeling like one is drying up; sensitivity to people's underlying needs (meddlers); reaching out to give or receive aid; finding a worthy mate vs. attraction to the needy or suffering (sensitive, empathetic); merging of mind and body in sexual expression (obsess over their physical attractiveness or fitness); brave and passionate living.

Examples

Daryl Hannah (Neptune. Actress—*Roxanne, Splash*); Marvin Gaye (North Node. Soul singer—"Sexual Healing"); Paul Goodman (Jupiter. Educational critic, into the gay pick-up scene); Lili Taylor (South Node. Actress—played a deranged stalker in *I Shot Andy Warhol*); Ang Lee (Saturn. Film director—*Crouching Tiger, Hidden Dragon* and *Sense and Sensibility*); Martin Scorsese (Mars. Film director—*Raging Bull*); Bernardo Bertolucci (Moon. Film director—*Last Tango in Paris*); John Cassavetes (South Node. Film director—*Love Streams*); Gertrude Stein (South Node. Author of *Three Lives*, headed a literary and painting salon in Paris); Franz Schubert (Neptune. Highly romantic classical composer, suffered from syphilis); Ursula Le Guin (Mars. Sci-fi writer—*The Left Hand of Darkness*); André Malraux (Sun. Author—*Man's Fate*, fought in various wars of liberation).

12 Scorpio

A frontier woman, dressed in a tiara and an evening gown, makes an entrance at a high-society embassy ball.

Descriptive Phrases

Remembering one's self-worth no matter what one's social status; creative interaction with the best and brightest; hobnobbing with the elite, but keeping one's individual integrity (*Unsinkable Molly Brown* archetype); maintaining strong loyalties to one's own class vs. social climbing (party crashers); maintaining good relations with people in inferior positions; being a subservient "satellite" in some elite scene vs. being the king or queen of one's own scene (expect everything to revolve around them); sociopolitical maneuvers—giving proper weight to every factor and waiting for the right moment to act; adhering to a personal code of honor that supersedes social norms and gives a moral center to one's group (outlaws); strong sense of personal dignity.

Examples

Mae West (South Node. Comedienne); Arthur Treacher (Uranus, Stationary. Actor—butler roles); Roseanne Barr (Sun. Working-class sitcom star—*Roseanne*); Marie Antoinette (Venus. Consort of Louis XVI, "Let them eat cake," guillotined); Bob Rubin (Sun. Amway kingpin at the top of the pyramid); Art Carney (Sun. Ed Norton in *The Honeymooners*); Henry Kissinger (Jupiter. Policymaker); Bela Lugosi (Mars. Actor—Count Dracula); Salvatore Giuliano (Mercury. Italian bandit chief); Bella Abzug (North Node. Flamboyant Jewish leftist politician); Sam Wagstaff (Sun. Museum curator, Robert Mapplethorpe patron); Manuel Irabarne (Mercury. Spanish ambassador to England, opposition party leader); King Mongkut of Siam (Jupiter. Regent after whom *The King and I* was modeled); Erasmus (Moon. Renaissance humanist); Goldie Hawn (Venus. Screwball actress—*The Banger Sisters*).

13 Scorpio

Amid a clutter of wires and equipment, the host of a radio talk show holds a frank discussion with an extremely controversial guest.

Descriptive Phrases

Independence of thought; supplying correctives to public discussions, often through mass media (flaunt eccentric views); cultural provocateurs (gain attention by extreme or vulgar opinions and behavior, but may end up suffering for it); jolting people out of their complacency vs. amping down high-voltage ideas to make them palatable; getting the lowdown; assembling overlooked facts into a new synthesis; running through possibilities till one finds an explanation that clicks (overly excited by new but unproven connections, spout opinions to see whether they have public resonance); uncompromising commitment to one's vision vs. getting valuable correctives; using charm, charisma, and wit to promote one's ideas or one's art; unique but compelling worldviews.

Examples

Will Rogers (Sun. Raconteur); Tina Brown (Venus. Controversial *Vanity Fair* editor); Whoopi Goldberg (Moon. Standup comic, actress); Henry Miller (Moon. Author—*Tropic of Cancer, Black Spring*); Tammy Faye Bakker (Moon. Televangelist, makeup saleswoman); Mary Margaret McBride (Mercury. Popular radio talk-show host from 1934 to 1954); Fran Drescher (North Node. Comedienne, flashy dresser—*The Nanny*); Gore Vidal (Saturn. Radical political analyst, author—*Burr, Myra Breckenridge*); Martin Luther (Venus. Protestant reformer, used obscene broadsheets in his campaign against Rome); Harpo Marx (Uranus. Marx Brothers comedian, harpist); Paul Harvey (Mars. Radio host with lots of conspiracy theories); Imogen Cunningham (North Node. Strange photographer); Mike Judge (Neptune. Cartoonist—*Beavis and Butthead, King of the Hill*); Jean Renoir (Uranus. Film director—*The Rules of the Game*).

14 Scorpio

Telephone linemen have almost reconnected a tornado-stricken town to the outside world. While one worker taps into the line to request more cable, another taps in to phone his girlfriend.

Descriptive Phrases

Keeping sight of one's mission in life vs. getting distracted; setting up attainable goals; getting from point A to point B (leave things hanging); leaving behind a scene that is irremediably wrecked vs. hanging tough come hell or high water; channeling one's energy to escape a dire situation (enjoy living close to the edge); putting survival first, but also knowing how to enjoy life; home as a place to hang one's hat vs. making time for luxury; putting one's own house in order vs. meddling in everyone else's problems; policymaking; calling the shots politically; communicating one's truth in condensed form (must adapt to other people's wavelengths); spiritual progress in spite of external conditions; losing track of one's purpose vs. reconnecting.

Examples

Harold Lloyd (Uranus. Clock-hanging comedian); J. R. Ullman (Mercury, Stationary. Author of the mountaineering thriller—*Third Man on the Mountain*); Johnny Depp (Neptune. Actor—*What's Eating Gilbert Grape?*); Willa Cather (South Node. Author—*Oh, Pioneers!*); Margaret Thatcher (Saturn. Iron-willed conservative British prime minister); Nikita Khrushchev (Uranus. Russian leader); Jimmy Carter (Moon. U. S. president, Habitat for Humanity activist); The Dalai Lama (Jupiter. Exiled Tibetan leader); Joni Mitchell (Mercury. Meditative folk singer—*Hejira*); Sebastian Junger (Neptune. Author of *The Perfect Storm*); Sally Field (Sun. Actress—*Norma Rae, Places in the Heart*); Maria Tallchief (Saturn. Dancer); Antonio Gaudi (Jupiter. Architect of bizarrely beautiful, unstable-looking buildings); Israel is founded and on the following day is attacked by Arab states (South Node. 5/14–15/1948); Ronald Reagan (Jupiter. U. S. president—The Great Communicator); Chogyam Trungpa (North Node. Tibetan Buddhist teacher, linked two worlds).

15 Scorpio

A poolside poker game is perfectly ordinary until someone starts "reading the cards "for the other players.[30]

Descriptive Phrases

Pointing out the extraordinary within the ordinary; staying this side of normal reality vs. sticking one's foot into the waters of the unknown; the immanence of the invisible realm in even the most workaday situations; sticking with the information of the five senses vs. using the sixth sense to perceive life's hidden patterns; invisible rays that connect the macrocosm to the microcosm; the astral body as the bridge between the physical and spiritual planes; symbols as a bridge between the invisible and visible realms; exciting research into the physical and supraphysical universe (science); breaking through to a more meaningful level that engages the soul vs. the boredom of the cynical or literally minded.

Examples

Edith Randall (Chiron. Occultist—*Sacred Symbols of the Ancients*); Hans Bender (Moon. Psychic and parapsychological research); Colin Wilson (Moon. Author of *The Occult*, posited "Factor X"); Roz Chast (Saturn. Whimsically existentialist cartoonist—*The New Yorker*); Johnny Carson (Saturn. Comic noted for tidbits culled from the news); Jon Stewart (Neptune. Mordantly analytical comedian); Conan O'Brien (Neptune. Comedian, early writer for *The Simpsons*); Carl Sagan (Venus. Pop astronomer, radical materialist with an interest in extraterrestrial life); Marie Curie (Sun. Research into radium and X-rays); Billy Graham (Sun. Christian evangelical preacher who came to a belief in reincarnation later in life); Bernard Lyot (Chiron. Astrophysicist who invented the coronagraph); Erin Sullivan (Chiron. Astrologer); Françoise Sagan (Jupiter. Existentialist feminist writer—*Bonjour Tristesse*); Albert Camus (Sun. Existentialist philosopher); Paul Foster Case (Mars. Expert on the tarot cards); Cheiro (Saturn. Occultist, palm reader).

16 Scorpio

Torches in hand, a revolutionary and his followers fight their way down the corridor of a state prison, intent on freeing their imprisoned comrades.

Descriptive Phrases

Total mobilization of personal powers in reaching one's goals, either in politics or in love; testing one's mettle; offering inspiring leadership vs. taking people for a ride (dominate others through force of personality); rallying people around a cause; bringing the light of freedom to the downtrodden; challenging illegitimate authority (political and cultural revolutionaries); figuring out an opponent's weaknesses and breaching their defenses; planning a campaign in stages vs. dealing with unforeseen obstacles; commandeering a situation (bully people when they can't get their way through charm); determination to win vs. arrogant overextension or selling out for lesser goals; trying to control external situations vs. learning to control one's own passions.

Examples

Thomas Jefferson (Pluto. Revolutionary leader, president, architect of Monticello); Leon Trotsky (Sun. Communist revolutionary); Sandra Bullock (Neptune, Stationary. Actress—*Speed, The Net*); Michael Jordan (Neptune. Basketball superstar); Loretta Swit (Mercury. Actress—*M*A*S*H*); Bruce Lee (Mercury. Martial arts superstar); Barbara Steele (North Node. Queen of horror); Keanu Reeves (Neptune. Actor—*Speed, The Matrix*); Basil Rathbone (South Node. Actor—the sheriff of Nottingham in *Robin Hood,* also Sherlock Holmes); Buckminster Fuller (Uranus. Utopian thinker who invented the geodesic dome); Margaret Seddon (Sun. Astronaut, surgeon); Napoleon Bonaparte (Jupiter. French general and emperor who conquered much of Europe); Cardinal Mazarin (Saturn. First minister to Louis XIII); Sun Yat-sen (Saturn. Chinese revolutionary who overthrew the Manchu dynasty); William Kunstler (Moon. Radical lawyer who wrote *The Case for Courage*).

17 Scorpio

Having entered the dragon's cave, a knight warily questions the beast in order to discover its weaknesses. Behind the dragon is a miniature city under a glass dome, painted with the stars of heaven.

Descriptive Phrases

Looking squarely at an evil that is close at hand vs. lashing out in ignorant misunderstanding (project their own evil onto others); fighting one's inner demons (in the grip of powerful lusts); psychoanalysis—talking out one's inner struggles; purifying one's will and desires; containment of evil forces; protecting the young by fighting political or cultural corruption; working on society from within vs. being assimilated and corrupted (hold to a static picture of an ideal society, violently defend unexamined assumptions); careful examination of a problem vs. being unwilling to look at an issue from both sides; modesty about one's knowledge that allows room for further enlightenment; listening with the heart vs. loving the sound of one's own voice (pompous moralizing).

Examples

Esther Rolle (Sun. Played the mother on *Good Times*); J.R.R. Tolkien (Mars. Fantasy writer—*Lord of the Rings*); Jodie Foster (Venus. Actress—*The Silence of the Lambs, Taxi Driver*); Martin Scorsese (Mercury. Filmmaker—*Taxi Driver, Angel Heart*); William Friedkin (Jupiter. Producer—*The Exorcist*); Petra Kelly (Chiron. Human-rights activist, Green Party leader); Snoop Doggy Dog (Venus. Gangsta rapper); Althea Flynt (Moon. Deceased wife of *Hustler's* Larry Flynt, heroin addict); Thomas Szasz (North Node. Psychologist—"the insane are sane"); Carl Sagan (Sun. Science popularizer—ignorant attacks on astrology, author—*The Demon-Haunted World, The Dragons of Eden*); Erin Sullivan (Sun. Astrologer); Jesse Helms (Mercury. Reactionary senator who is antipornography and antigay); Bruno Bettelheim (Moon. Psychologist who wrote a book on spiritual survival in the concentration camps); Jamie Lee Curtis (Jupiter. Actress—*Halloween, True Lies*); John Cleese (Venus. Comic actor specializing in self-righteous bluster).

18 Scorpio

After visiting the grave of her husband, a woman walks alone through autumnal woods and finds inspiration in the brightly colored leaves dancing down all around her.

Descriptive Phrases

Sense of life's preciousness in light of one's inevitable death; accepting the strange, beautiful, and tragic dance of life; letting go of an old life pattern; awakening to a unique and colorful vision of life after a period of withdrawal; finding inspiration in the beautiful forms of nature; meditative retreats vs. feeling hemmed in by society and its lies; clarifying larger patterns in political or social life (overwhelmed by life's complexities—can't see the forest for the trees); escaping stifling situations vs. abandoning worthwhile projects; serious reflection on the meaning of one's experience; detached observation of the patterns and trajectories of one's life; expressing one's true colors.

Examples

Georgia O'Keeffe (Jupiter. Meditative painter of Southwestern landscapes); Nicholas Cage (Neptune. Actor—*Moonstruck, Raising Arizona*); Jimi Hendrix (Mars. Psychedelic rock guitarist); Jeddu Krishnamurti (Uranus. Guru who promoted meditation); Kahlil Gibran (North Node. Inspirational writer); Tracy Chapman (Neptune. Black folk singer, social critic); Mary Travers (Sun. Folk singer, political activist); Albert Brooks (Jupiter. Film director—*Defending Your Life*); Norman Mailer (Jupiter. Author—*Armies of the Night, The White Negro*); George Santayana (Jupiter. Spanish-American poet, philosopher—*The Sense of Beauty*, unexpectedly resigned from the Harvard faculty); Patty Duke (Jupiter. Actress—*The Miracle Worker, The Patty Duke Show*); John Leguizamo (Neptune. Confessional stand-up comic); Callista Flockhart (Neptune. Actress—*Allie McBeal*); Jean Seberg (North Node. Actress—*St. Joan*, committed suicide after the loss of a child).

19 Scorpio

An imp with curly hair and short horns holds up a magic mirror that provides a mercilessly critical reflection of his morally squalid surroundings.[31]

Descriptive Phrases

Critical observation of other people and of popular culture; holding up a mirror to social hypocrisy (cynical of religion and other common beliefs, play devil's advocate); imprinting of early childhood experiences on the soul (mirroring the sins of one's surroundings vs. consciously deciding which aspects of culture should be rejected and which should be emulated and reproduced); scornful parodies of soulless culture (impish hooliganism, nihilism); compassion for others that allows one to see people as they really are vs. allowing hatred to make people into monsters; seeing beauty and innocence amid ugliness vs. spotting the fatal flaw in a perfect picture; cartoonlike exaggeration of reality that brings out its essential features; witty and penetrating social commentary.

Examples

Eugene Ionesco (Saturn. Absurdist playwright); Diane Arbus (Jupiter. Photographer of human grotesques); William Hogarth (Sun. Satirical lithographer); Tuli Kupferberg (Jupiter. Lead singer of the obscene rock group The Fugs); Winona Ryder (Mercury. Actress—*Girl, Interrupted, Heathers*); Leonardo di Caprio (Sun. Actor—*The Gangs of New York*); Bob Denver (Jupiter. Actor—Maynard G. Krebs on *Dobie Gillis*); Clara Bow (Mars. Silent-movie star); Kurt Vonnegut (Sun. Sci-fi writer—*Welcome to the Monkeyhouse, The Sirens of Titan*); Andrei Codrescu (Jupiter. Satirical writer, filmmaker—*Roads' Scholar*); Wassily Kandinsky (Saturn. Colorful abstract artist); Anne Perry (North Node. Muckraking detective fiction, murdered someone in her teen years); Jean Dubuffet (North Node. Artist, "art brut," often obscene); Mark Twain (Mercury. Humorist—*Huck Finn, Letters from the Earth*); Jackie Coogan (Mars. Actor—*The Addams Family*).

20 Scorpio

A sultry woman glances backward and disappears behind red velvet drapes. Following her, a man suddenly finds himself spinning through space.

Descriptive Phrases

Remaining self-possessed no matter what bizarre adventures life throws one's way; gamely plunging into a vortex-like situation, hoping it might lead to an interesting new reality or state of consciousness (drug use); giving birth to an alternate reality by taking action within it; identifying "real" elements within the fantastic and unreal elements in "waking" consciousness; eruption of dreamlike elements into everyday life (subvert normal reality, throw others for a loop); leading timid souls into new territory vs. attaching oneself to a charismatic "guide"; being an expert in weird reality zones vs. losing one's footing in reality; living into a personal mythology with the knowledge that outer reality will bend itself to inner reality (lost in their own world).

Examples

Elisabeth Kubler-Ross (Saturn. Writer—*On Death and Dying*); Ken Kesey (Jupiter. Writer—*One Flew over the Cuckoo's Nest*, leader of the LSD-crazed Merry Pranksters); Alice Liddell (Jupiter. Lewis Carroll's Alice); Jurgen Habermas (Moon. Political philosopher—*Knowledge and Human Interests*); Scott Bakula (Saturn. Actor—*Quantum Leap*); Grace Kelly (Sun. Actress—*Rear Window, Dial M for Murder*, became the Princess of Monaco); Charlie Manson (Sun. Scary charismatic cult-leader); Vicki Morgan (Mars. S & M mistress of Alfred Bloomingdale); Neil Young (Sun. Innovative rock musician); Demi Moore (Sun. Actress—*Ghost*); Brandon Lee (Neptune. Actor—*The Crow*); John Carpenter (South Node. Director of horror movies—*They Live*); André Breton (Saturn. Dadaist surrealist, political radical); Boris Karloff (Jupiter. Horror star—*Frankenstein*).

21 Scorpio

During the dress rehearsal of a high-school play, an actor breaks into an improvised dialogue with an imaginary character. Some of the cast are enthralled; others are irritated.[32]

Descriptive Phrases

Bravery in creating and living out an imaginative social identity; boldly following the impulses of the moment; tuning out the criticisms and expectations of others vs. loss of nerve (overstep social bounds); challenging oneself to break through inhibitions; surprising oneself; learning to trust one's intuitive insights; playing along with vague perceptions of the spiritual realm and giving them physical expression; accepting realities invisible to others, while rejecting normally accepted realities as insubstantial (ghosts and other spiritual entities); identifying the spiritual issues behind social problems; getting in back of one's own reality grids; playful rebellion against imposed realities; opening up the bounds of what is possible.

Examples

Dick Van Dyke (Mars. Comic actor—*The Dick Van Dyke Show, Mary Poppins*); Whoopi Goldberg (Sun. Comic actress—*Sister Act, Ghost*); Bill Cosby (Mars. Comedian—*The Bill Cosby Show, Ghost Dad*); Carol Burnett (Jupiter. Television comic); Bruce Willis (Saturn. Actor—action movies, *The Sixth Sense*); Vera Caspary (Sun, Jupiter. Leftist, fiction writer—*Laura*); Robert Louis Stevenson (Sun. Fiction writer—*Kidnapped, Treasure Island*); Gore Vidal (Venus. Leftist writer of historical fiction—*Burr, Lincoln*); Ivan Illich (Saturn. Anarchist theorist—*Deschooling America*); Ernesto Montgomery (Venus. Jamaican psychic who worked for allied intelligence during World War II); Deepak Chopra (Mercury. Holistic health guru—"mind power"); Girolamo Savonarola (Venus. Fanatical Renaissance preacher, prophet); Patti Smith (Jupiter. Influential proto-punk rocker).

22 Scorpio

Soldier, home from war, sees his sweetheart standing by the calm waters of the mill pond. Dropping his gun, he runs to embrace her.

Descriptive Phrases

Emotional responsiveness and vulnerability; wearing one's heart on one's sleeve (bosomy embraces); stilling the heart so one's real desires become clear; sensitivity to the emotional environment (pained by human suffering); being emotionally open vs. knowing when someone can't be trusted; being sexually targeted vs. sidestepping danger in a tricky situation; going after what one wants on a romantic level; making sacrifices for love's sake; emotional loyalty; biding one's time; steadfast pursuit of noble goals (peacemakers—try to bring others into the wider harmony); powerful and direct expression of emotion; expansive romanticism (musical expressiveness); spiritual attunement; speaking directly to the situation; creating ripples of recognition.

Examples

Roger Waters (Jupiter. Musician—Pink Floyd); Loretta Lynn (Jupiter. Country-western singer with a troubled personal life); Marilyn Monroe (Saturn. Bosomy movie star); Steven Spielberg (South Node. Sentimentalist filmmaker—*E.T.*, *Indiana Jones* series); Sandy Denny (Jupiter. Lead singer of Fairport Convention); Andy Griffith (Saturn. Actor—*The Andy Griffith Show*); Audrey Hepburn (South Node. Actress—*Breakfast at Tiffany's*, *My Fair Lady*; worked for poor children); Miles Davis (Saturn. Meditative jazz musician); Federico Fellini (North Node. Poetic filmmaker—*Amarcord*, *Nights of Cabiria*); Burt Bacharach (North Node. Romantic songwriter); Claude Monet (Sun. Impressionist painter); Sylvia Plath (Mercury. Depressive poet—*The Bell Jar*); Victor Hugo (Neptune. Romantic writer—*The Hunchback of Notre Dame*); F. Scott Fitzgerald (Uranus. Writer—*The Great Gatsby*); Johnny Mathis (Jupiter. Crooner).

23 Scorpio

A seated elf, one arm around a large book, looks quizzically at the viewer, then turns into a hare and hops through a stone wall.

Descriptive Phrases

Jumping to a new level of awareness by stepping outside of an old reality framework; falling into unconscious mental ruts vs. waking up from self-delusions; detached overview vs. fervid projections that lock one into a false reading of reality (ideologues); following up one's hunches; having one's ears out for clues ; finding wisdom in imaginative, gnostic musings (escapist sci-fi); closely examining life's magical possibilities vs. living in an bookish dream world (self-isolation); teachers and students of the metaphysical and theosophical structure of reality; getting others to transcend limited analytical frameworks; jarring people out of their complacency vs. glum resignation to human somnolence; elfin mischief; mind games; Wonderland's rabbit hole.

Examples

Timothy Leary (Mercury. LSD guru, flaky gnostic); Winona Ryder (Venus. Actress—*Girl Interrupted, Beetlejuice*); Mary Martin (Mercury. Actress—*Peter Pan*); Carlos Castaneda (Saturn. Writer on shamanism—*The Adventures of Don Juan*); David Mamet (South Node. Dramatist, filmmaker—*House of Games*); Matt Damon (Venus. Actor, screenwriter—*Good Will Hunting, The Talented Mr. Ripley*); Nicole Kidman (Neptune. Actress—*Eyes Wide Shut*); Kevin Spacey (Jupiter. Actor—*American Beauty, The Usual Suspects*); Julie Andrews (Jupiter. Actress—*Mary Poppins, Victor, Victoria*); Spike Lee (North Node. Filmmaker—*Do the Right Thing*); John Carpenter (Chiron. Filmmaker—*Halloween, They Live*); Margaret Geller (South Node. Physicist—soap-bubble structure of the universe); Burgess Meredith (Sun. Actor—The Penguin on *Batman*); Hans Geiger (North Node. Inventor of the Geiger counter).

24 Scorpio

A gate crasher at a garden party holds forth on a controversial point. Some of the guests are interested; others leave in confusion.

Descriptive Phrases

Demanding to be taken exactly as one is (bulldoze their way through life); unwillingness to conform to other people's realities; humorous disregard for social niceties (trespass social bounds, party crashers); entering new scenes with friendly but presumptuous intimacy (nosy snooping); finding an audience that is ready to receive one's truths (gain attention through brazen publicity stunts); confronting others with unwelcome truths; turning people's world upside down (radicals); facing life squarely, without fear or expectation; authority that comes from staying on one's own wavelength and sticking to one's own experience; reckless adventurousness vs. losing one's stride and becoming too cautious; delivering the unvarnished truth with wit and gusto.

Examples

Ricki Lake (Neptune. Talk-show host, actress—*Hairspray, Mrs. Winterbourne*); Jerry Rubin (North Node. Yippie activist); Whoopi Goldberg (Saturn. Comic actress—*Sister Act, Jumpin' Jack Flash*); George Burns (Uranus. Comic); Warren Beatty (Moon. Leftist actor—*Bulworth, Shampoo*); Diana Rigg (North Node. Actress—*The Avengers*); Ruth Gordon (Uranus. Actress—*Harold and Maude*); Max von Sydow (South Node. Actor in Bergman films—*The Magician, The Seventh Seal*); Gillian Anderson (Neptune. Actress—*The X-Files*); Drew Pearson (Chiron. Journalist—*The Case against Congress*); Eugene Schoenfeld (Jupiter. Hip medical columnist—*Dr. Hippocrates*); Patricia Loud (Saturn. Opened her home to TV surveillance, which led to the dissolution of her marriage); Tristan Tzara (Uranus. Dadaist, surrealist); Jennifer Aniston (Mars. Actress—*Office Space, The Good Girl*).

25 Scorpio

A husband and wife are locked in argument. He makes a number of assertions based on logic, while she tries to bring the argument to the level of underlying motivations.[33]

Descriptive Phrases

Confrontation between emotion and reason; trying to nail down a suspected underlying reality by asserting it strongly (invite others to refute them); pushing one's examination to a deeper level vs. making snap judgments marred by emotional presuppositions; reexamining underlying motivations and assumptions vs. suffering reversals when one builds on a faulty foundation; trusting one's intuition vs. needing to get an education in matters of logic and procedure; standing up to arbitrary authority vs. trying to usurp authority without adequate training; attacking faulty foundations of the social order, especially prejudice and sexism (unbending postures cause rifts in relationships); skirmishes in the war of the sexes (violence); pushing an argument too far vs. heartfelt reconciliation.

Examples

Danny DeVito (Mars. Actor—*Ruthless People*, about a man who pays to have his wife kidnapped); Lili Taylor (Neptune, Stationary. Actress—*I Shot Andy Warhol*); Helen Gurley Brown (Moon. Editor of *Cosmopolitan*, purveyor of shallow analyses of the male psyche); Bette Midler (Venus. Actress, singer—*First Wives' Club, Outrageous Fortune*); Henry Miller (South Node. Controversial writer—*Tropic of Cancer*); Michel Foucault (Saturn. Deconstructionist theorist—*The Order of Things*); Pablo Picasso (Mercury. Modern artist, deconstructor); Frances Yates (Jupiter. Historian of the Western occult tradition who gets a lot of pseudorational criticism from the academic establishment); Billy Crystal (Chiron. Comic, actor—*When Harry Met Sally, Deconstructing Harry, Throw Mama from the Train*); John Wayne Bobbitt (Neptune. Abused his wife for years, so she cut off his penis while he slept); Patrick Swayze (Mars. Actor—*Dirty Dancing, Ghost*); Martin Scorsese (Sun. Director—*The King of Comedy, The Last Temptation of Christ*).

26 Scorpio

Before dawn, a Native American chieftain oversees the silent dismantling of an encampment of tepees.

Descriptive Phrases

Team efforts; competent vs. incompetent execution of group projects (snafus that result from a contested hierarchy of authority; too many chiefs, too few Indians; anarchic comic antics); selecting the most competent member to lead (lazily conform to other people's authority and use it as a crutch, rather than exercising self-reliance); practicality and competence in tight situations; *sang-froid*; resourcefulness; behind-the-scenes preparations for anticipated opportunities and events (get the jump on the opposition, surprise attacks); creating a working bridge between two different cultures or peoples; anticipating others' objections (psychic power based on attunement to the group mind); subordinating oneself vs. taking matters into one's own hands.

Examples

Bernard Montgomery (Sun, Mercury. World War II military hero—North Africa); Marie Curie (Venus. Physicist who collaborated closely with her husband); Sir David Yule (Mars. East India Company merchant and entrepreneur); Moe Howard (Saturn. Comic—leader of The Three Stooges); Groucho Marx (Venus. Comedian—The Marx Brothers); Jerry Lewis (Saturn. Comic paired with Dean Martin); Geena Davis (North Node. Actress—*Thelma and Louise*); Farrah Fawcett (Jupiter. Actress—*Charlie's Angels*); Squeaky Fromm (Chiron. Mansonite); Carl Barks (North Node. Cartoonist—Donald Duck); Barbara Stabiner (Mars. Renowned psychic); Robert Louis Stevenson (Mars. Author—*Treasure Island, Kidnapped*); Christiane Vasse (Venus. Studies parapsychology and does ESP experiments with kids); Will Durant (Mercury. Historian who collaborated with his wife, Ariel); Kareem Abdul Jabbar (Jupiter. Basketball superstar); H. R. Haldeman (Saturn, Mercury. Nixon aide).

27 Scorpio

At a rehearsal, the guest conductor discusses a piece with the various members of the orchestra.

Descriptive Phrases

Leading cooperative efforts for the betterment of society; sober reflection that leads to emotional maturity and soundness of judgment; having a full range of life experiences that allows one to connect with different kinds of people; harmonizing with others vs. forcing people to march to one's own tune; bravura performances vs. tiresome grandstanding; being familiar with the public's feelings and expectations without getting caught up in them; giving the public what it wants vs. marching to a different drummer (oppose the narrow prejudices of the masses; offer a "voice of reason" when the human community falls out of harmony); getting oneself across; turning up the volume so one's voice can be heard (shrill); inborn authority and persuasive eloquence.

Examples

George Szell (Saturn. Conductor); E. G. Marshall (South Node. Actor—*Twelve Angry Men, Town Without Pity*); Katie Couric (North Node. Newscaster, advocate of colon testing after her husband died of colon cancer); Doris Lessing (North Node. Psychoanaltyical writer—*Persons We Choose to Live Inside, The Golden Notebook*); Tom Hanks (Saturn. Actor—*Apollo 13, Castaway*); Peter Yarrow (North Node. Folk singer in Peter, Paul, and Mary); George and Ira Gershwin (Chiron and Uranus respectively. Composer and his lyricist collaborator); Alan Greenspan (Saturn. Head of the Federal Reserve Board, the most powerful unelected U. S. official); Stephen King (South Node. Horror fiction—*Misery, Carrie, Needful Things*); Ignaz Paderewski (Sun. Classical pianist with a rock-star persona); Billy Sunday (Sun. Flamboyant revivalist); Jane Curtin (North Node. Comedienne who worked in the original *Saturday Night Live* ensemble); Sonia Gandhi (Mercury. Replaced her assassinated husband as a Congress Party leader and performed admirably).

28 Scorpio

The king of the fairies bends affectionately over the sleeping figure of Puck and sprinkles him with pixy dust. The shining sparks form a whirl of images that enter into Puck's dream.

Descriptive Phrases

Receiving teachings from a higher level through dreams and fantasies; symbolic or occult thinking (escapist fantasy trips); the immanence of the spiritual world; sense that God's wisdom is immediately available and that one is loved by God as a child by his parent (isolation, difficulty sustaining sexual love); sharing one's spiritual wealth; gently shaking others awake from some dark illusion and pulling them into a more centered, natural place; enchantment—spinning fantasies that contain spiritual teachings; nature mysticism—the cloaking of the divine spirit within the forms of nature; pagan devotion—seeing the One in the All; Puckish humor that displays the superior attunement of the child; spiritually recentering oneself.

Examples

Hans Christian Andersen (Neptune. Fairytale writer); Elton John (Jupiter. Rock singer with a Puckish persona); Carol Channing (Moon. Loopy Broadway singer—*Hello Dolly*); Walt Disney (Mercury. Cartoonist—Mickey Mouse and a host of other "invisibles"); Mike Judge (Venus. Cartoonist—*Beavis and Butthead, King of the Hill*); Grace Slick (Mercury. Lead singer of Jefferson Airplane); Dick Cavett (Sun. Talk-show host); Tom Smothers (Sun. Pixyish comedian); *The Twilight Zone* premieres (Saturn. 9/2/1956); Gian Carlo Menotti (Moon. Composer—*Amahl and the Night Visitors*); Sean Young (Sun. Actress—*Bladerunner, Dune*); David Livingstone (Uranus. Explorer, missionary); Helen Pyke (Moon. Palmist, astrologer); Kaye Ballard (Sun. Vaudevillian who sang with Spike Jones' band); Cindy Williams (South Node. Actress—*Laverne and Shirley*).

29 Scorpio

Beautiful folk singer, with a baby in her arms, leads a group of singing demonstrators through a police cordon up the stairs of a government building.

Descriptive Phrases

Giving birth to an idealistic new movement; pulling people together around an intoxicating vision of the future; crusaders who immolate themselves, phoenixlike, in a cause (seduce others into flaky trips); facing danger, sacrifices, and persecution in order to secure the future; walking down one's own road, however narrow; nimble maneuvering; deft footwork in sidestepping obstacles and dangers (recklessness vs. slippery attempts to evade one's karma); disciplining oneself to accept the obstacles in one's path without resentment or envy; making a heartfelt appeal to the public; hitting a spiritual chord—reminding people of a truth they already know in their hearts; musical and oratorical powers (intoxicating beauty); moving into a position of spiritual leadership within a counterculture.

Examples

Marsilio Ficino (Mercury. Leader of a Hermetic neoplatonic movement during the Renaissance); Dorothy Day (Uranus. Catholic Worker's Union leader—pragmatic idealist); Robert F. Kennedy (Sun. Champion of civil rights as U. S. attorney general, martyred); Odetta (Venus. Black folk singer in beat scene); Phil Ochs (Venus. Protest singer); Assassination of John F. Kennedy (Sun. 11/22/1963); David Frost (Moon. Host of political talk shows—*That Was the Week That Was*); Goldie Hawn (Sun. *Laugh-In* comic, actress in *The Banger Sisters*); Billy Graham (Mercury. Christian revivalist with immense following); Luc Jouret (Jupiter. Gnostic cult leader—mass suicide of followers); Igor Stravinsky (North Node. Composer—*The Firebird Suite*); Paolo Rossi (Saturn. Soccer superstar); Michele Maffei (Venus. Olympic swordsman); Claudia Schiffer (Neptune. Model); Bob Weir (Jupiter. Lead singer of The Grateful Dead); Timothy Leary (Venus. LSD guru, space-case).

30 Scorpio

At a Halloween costume ball, a criminal walks among the revelers wearing the mask of a boar.

Descriptive Phrases

The treacherous, shifting ground of reality, where things are not what they seem; manipulating semblances to subtly change reality-perceptions; mischievously undermining reality's boundaries; pig-headed insistence on seeing things to one's best advantage; giving one's antisocial impulses enough rein that they don't become inflated (loss of moral compass; seek power in the underworld or the demimonde; criminals who live in a hell-world of their own creation, even in this life); dehumanization through the loss of solid values vs. committing oneself to spiritual values that will have existence even beyond one's present incarnational mask; getting trapped in a social persona vs. maintaining the child's playful, improvisational attitude towards social roles.

Examples

René Magritte (Sun. Surrealist artist); Helen Gurley Brown (Mars. Magazine publisher—*Cosmopolitan*); Jamie Lee Curtis (Sun. Actress—*Halloween*); Rocky Dennis (Venus. Deformed child, real-life protagonist of *Mask*); Mel Gibson (Saturn. Actor—*Mad Max, The Patriot*); Dr. John (Sun. Voodoo-influenced blues musician, ex-heroin addict); Cindy Crawford (South Node. Mask-faced fashion model); Terry Gilliam (Sun. Monty Python comedian who directed *Time Bandits*, with its dwarflike trick-or-treaters); George Wallace (North Node. Racist politician who renounced these views after he was shot and paralyzed); George Eliot (Sun. Writer—*Silas Marner*); Vito Genovese (Uranus. Mobster); Jean Genet (Mars. Homoerotic writer, criminal); Matt Damon (Neptune. Actor—*The Talented Mr. Ripley*); Lucky Luciano (Uranus. Mobster); Dortha Fretz (Sun. Spiritualist reverend); Dr. Franz Hartmann (Sun. Theosophist); Albert Brooks (South Node. Director—*Defending Your Life*).

1 Sagittarius

On a steep bluff, army veterans reminisce around a dying campfire while their leader surveys the countryside by the light of the rising sun.

Descriptive Phrases

Looking toward new possibilities when an old trip is burnt out; setting clear goals that challenge one's best talents; figuring out which life battles really matter; ignoring unimportant problems and strengthening one's heart for the fights ahead; superhuman efforts; daring adventures; willingness to suffer for one's ideals; social vision; individual effort that inspires the group; lighting a fire under people; instigating collective action based on a clear vision of the future; cooperation and comradeship based on shared ideals; enlisting the aid of others (confederacies, working alliances); team efforts versus sturdy self-reliance; long-range plans; foresight; periodically reassessing one's progress toward grander goals; signal success (difficulty living up to early promise); the path of glory.

Examples

John Glenn (Ascendant. Astronaut); Lindsay Wagner (Ascendant. Actress—*The Bionic Woman*); Sai Baba (Venus. Guru, healer, "physical manifestations"); Dustin Hoffman (Mars. Played an idiot savant in *Rain Man*); Emma Thompson (Jupiter. Shakespearean actress, director); Margot Kidder (Mars. *Supergirl* role); Ken Kesey (Mars. Writer—*One Flew Over the Cuckoo's Nest*, Merry Pranksters); George Gershwin (Uranus. Composer); Eric Remarque (Uranus. Writer—*All Quiet on the Western Front*); Rough Riders assault San Juan Hill (Uranus. 7/1/1898); William Blake (Jupiter. Mystical poet, artist); Jules Verne (Mars. Author—*20,000 Leagues Under the Sea*); Otis Chandler (Sun. Newspaper executive); Richard Byrd (Venus. Explored Antarctica); Charles DeGaulle (Sun. General, leader of the Free French in World War II); Sally Field (Venus. Actress—*Norma Rae*); Isaac Newton (Neptune. Groundbreaking scientist); Margaret Chase Smith (Uranus. First woman to be elected to either house of Congress).

2 Sagittarius

A man in a diving suit is lowered into the ocean from a ship while, closer to shore, a surfer rides the waves.

Descriptive Phrases

Moving between different levels of involvement; entanglement vs. self-extrication; playfully surfing the waves of life's changing surface phenomena vs. getting caught up in some deeper mystery (reject superficial perspectives in favor of a more multileveled view of reality); having fun with a self-created persona vs. viewing oneself detachedly from a higher level; pulling one's own strings vs. being jerked around by others; keeping one's sense of identity fluid vs. being trapped in a rigid self-conception; swimming easily within life's complex currents and rhythms vs. getting out of synch (wild, stir things up for fun); celebrating life's giddy extravagances vs. seeing it all as a sand castle by the sea.

Examples

Murray Rose (Venus. Surfer, star of *Ride the Wild Surf*); Spike Jones (Jupiter. Crazed bandleader); Ethel Waters (Mercury. Jazz singer, actress); Harpo Marx (Sun. Comic harpist—The Marx Brothers); Tony Sarg (North Node. Puppeteer); Zazu Pitts (Jupiter. Actress, played wallflowers in crazy comedies); Neil Simon (Saturn. Playwright—*Come Blow Your Horn*); Ishmael Reed (North Node. Autho—*Mumbo Jumbo*); Winona Ryder (Neptune. Actress—*Edward Scissorhands; Girl, Interrupted; Heathers*); Holling C. Holling (Jupiter. Children's book author and illustrator—*Paddle-to-the-Sea, Minn of the Mississippi*); Richard Dreyfuss (Jupiter. Actor—*Jaws, Close Encounters of the Third Kind*); Florence Chadwick (Mercury. Swam English channel); Tama Janowitz (Saturn. Author—*Slaves of New York*); Max Planck (Mars. Physicist, abandoned Newtonian principles and proposed the quantum theory); Fritjof Capra (Mars. Author—*The Tao of Physics*); Garson Kanin (Sun. Author—*The Smile of the World, Blow Up a Storm*); Art Tatum (Venus. Jazz pianist, composer).

3 Sagittarius

A young prince and his tutor concentrate on a game of chess. Around the board, an inlaid design depicts black and white dragons biting each other's tails.

Descriptive Phrases

Vying for top honors within a limited field; playing to win, no holds barred vs. doing one's best and playing like a gentleman; strategy; anticipating one's opponent's next move vs. losing one's objectivity through negative emotional projections; detachment and mental discipline vs. playing out a mindless power game to the bitter end; mentoring; helping others, especially children, to mature in judgment; learning from an older person (don't listen, impatiently dismiss contrary evidence); sorting out issues internally through active fantasy; reality grids; getting a fix on one's situation; knowing where one stands in the scheme of things (pawns vs. kings); ongoing battles between liberals and conservatives over governmental policies; power games.

Examples

William F. Buckley (Sun. Conservative commentator); Steve Allen (Moon. TV comic, outspoken critic of sex and violence on TV); Andrew Carnegie (Sun. Steel mogul); Golda Meir (Uranus. Former prime minister of Israel); Lucrezia Borgia (Uranus. Pawn in the power games of her family, patron of the arts); Robert Bly (Saturn. Men's movement author who examines male archetypes in *Iron John*); Lewis Carroll (Ascendant. Author—*Through the Looking Glass*); E. R. Eddison (Sun. Fantasy writer—*Queen of Spades, A Fish Dinner in Memison*); Nostradamus (Pluto. Seer); Mary Queen of Scots (Venus. Treacherous queen who was eventually beheaded at the command of Queen Elizabeth I); Milton Friedman (Jupiter. Conservative economic theorist); Martin Balsam (Mercury. Actor—*Twelve Angry Men*); Laura Flessel (Venus. Olympic fencer); John F. Kennedy, Jr. (Sun. Editor of *George* magazine); Margaret Thatcher (Venus. Conservative British prime minister).

4 Sagittarius

A brash youngster persuades his friends to undertake a daring adventure, but insists that a frightened younger child be left behind.

Descriptive Phrases

Mustering the courage to strike out on a new path, despite dangers and lack of guarantees; trusting one's instincts and desires; seeking out new experiences (moral lapses, fall into sordid scenes); inner battle between one's adventurous side and one's fearful side; getting the group to play along with something one has dreamed up vs. waiting for someone else to take the lead; independent stances (creating a bold new role vs. empty posturing); being on the cutting edge (get more conservative with age); leaving behind a more childish stage of development vs. getting stuck; callowness vs. worldly sophistication; acerbic criticism of social behavior, particularly conformism; pushing the envelope of the socially acceptable; taking a brave step forward.

Examples

Spanky McFarland (South Node. Child actor—leader of the *Little Rascals*); Roseanne Barr (Mercury. Comedienne); Matt Groening (Mars. Cartoonist—*The Simpsons*, with Bart, the archetypal brat); Kate Millett (Moon. Feminist); Erwin Rommel (Mercury. Nazi general—the Desert Fox); Kon Tiki begins its voyage (South Node. 4/29/1947); John Lilly (Venus. Cutting-edge experimentation with psychedelics); Charles Schulz (Sun. Cartoonist—*Peanuts*); Lotte Lenya (North Node. Actress—Pirate Jenny in *The Threepenny Opera*); Woody Allen (Mercury. Comedian); Alan Watts (Venus. Introduced Zen teachings on TV); Marlon Brando (Ascendant. Actor—leader of the pack); Quentin Crisp (Venus. Drag as a statement rather than entertainment); Tina Turner (Sun. Risqué rock star); Abraham Lincoln (Saturn. U. S. president, as a young man he led a band of youths that volunteered to fight in the Black Hawk War).

5 Sagittarius

On a desolate seashore, an owl watches a ship's approach.

Descriptive Phrases

Watchfulness—knowing when to strike (sneak attacks); zeroing in on a problem; incorrect first impressions, as of objects when one enters a darkened room; constant refocusing; incongruous details that give away a false reality-construct; fitting the fragmented images of experience into a coherent picture; collecting and sharing vital information; oblique approaches to truth; being at sea vs. coming to earth; foreign travel; getting the lay of the land (unseen dangers); curious perspectives; weird interface between myth and reality; finding real underpinnings in resonant myths and stories (flaky beliefs, fear trips); experientially based knowledge of occult forces; learning to "see."

Examples

Jorge Luis Borges (Uranus. Writer of occult fiction); C. S. Lewis (Uranus. Writer—*Narnia* books); Marilyn Ferguson (Ascendant. Writer—*The Aquarian Conspiracy, Brain-Mind Bulletin*); Rod Serling (Venus. Writer and director of *The Twilight Zone* and *Night Gallery*); William Butler Yeats (Midheaven. Poet, practicing magician); Chogyam Trungpa (Mars. Tibetan guru); John Travolta (Mars. Actor—*Pulp Fiction, Phenomenon*); Woody Allen (Jupiter. Filmmaker—*Alice, Selig*); Günter Grass (Saturn. Writer—*The Tin Drum*); Eric Sevareid (Sun. News commentator); Dionne Warwick (Mercury. Singer, psychic hotline entrepreneur); Jimi Hendrix (Sun. Visionary rock guitarist); Harry Houdini (Moon. Magician who exposed fake mediums, but had real psychic experiences); E. B. White (Uranus. Children's writer—*Stuart Little*); Steven Forrest (Chiron. Astrologer); Dale O'Brien (Ascendant. Astrologer); Lin Luttrell (Jupiter. Astrologer, occultist); Jane Fonda (North Node. Actress—*The China Syndrome*).

6 Sagittarius

An old coach jokes around with the team and critiques their game before they run back on the field.[34]

Descriptive Phrases

Promoting teamwork and group morale; developing winning routines vs. getting stuck in a rut; pausing to reappraise one's approach; playing fair vs. using underhanded tactics; taking the command position vs. working in a team; chains of command; rising through the ranks by perfecting one's skills; playing one's natural position vs. filling in where one is needed; bolstering morale through humor vs. sabotaging morale with nasty jibes (blunt, rude); uniting people against a common obstacle; diligent pursuit of long-range goals vs. frustrated demands for immediate results (rash, violent); long-term campaigns to achieve social, political, or military objectives; smuggling in major social changes by challenging the ground rules; life as a game (playing at life); physical coordination and bravery.

Examples

Ty Cobb (Mercury. Baseball star); Knute Rockne (Jupiter. Football coach); Elizabeth Gurley Flynn (Mars. Feminist organizer); Cicely Tyson (Mercury. Actress—*The Autobiography of Miss Jane Pittman*); Colin Powell (Mars. General in the Gulf War and the War in Afghanistan); George Patton (Mercury. General, tank warfare); John Belushi (Chiron. Comedian—*Animal House*); Bruce Lee (Sun. Martial arts star); Jojo White (Mars. Basketball star); Jack Nicholson (Mars. Actor—*As Good as It Gets, Chinatown*); Ernst Roehm (Sun. Headed the *Sturmabteilung*, an organization of Nazi street thugs); Julia Child (Jupiter. *The French Chef*); Edith Cavell (Mars. Nurse); Art Linkletter (Jupiter. TV host—*People Are Funny*); Franklin D. Roosevelt (North Node. U. S. president who coordinated America's war effort); Robert Carradine (Moon. Actor—*Revenge of the Nerds*); Ed Harris (Sun. Actor—*The Right Stuff*).

7 Sagittarius

A man and woman at a cocktail party exchange flirtatious remarks. Unseen by them, Cupid takes aim with his bow and arrow.

Descriptive Phrases

Flirtatiousness; amorousness; mischievous hijinks; going beyond accepted boundaries, but all in good fun; sexual awakening—being ambushed by one's own desires or desirability; direct and piercing appeal for love (adolescent awkwardness); double-edged nature of Eros, which can resurrect a person in a new love or emotionally wound them; sly pretense that lust is love vs. entering wholeheartedly into an idealistic romance; rambunctious playfulness; witty observations on the human comedy; probing the desires of the human heart, its loves and hates; stirring up excitement in one's life vs. disasters that arise from giving free rein to one's passions; love of the chase as distinctly human, yet containing a strong animal element; romping, high-spirited fun.

Examples

Shirley Temple (Ascendant. Child star); Amy Fisher (Neptune. The Long Island Lolita); Tom Hanks (North Node. Actor—*Big, Forrest Gump*); Jane Austen (Mercury. Author—*Emma*); Jacqueline Susann (Midheaven. Author—*The Love Machine*); Randy Newman (Sun. Comic singer—"Short People"); Nancy Mitford (Sun. Witty novelist); Peter Bergman (Sun. Comedian in The Firesign Theater); Fred Astaire (Uranus. Actor and dancer in romantic comedies); John Belushi (Chiron. Comedian—*Animal House*); Roberto Benigni (Venus. Comedian—*The Monster*); Don Adams (Saturn. Comic actor—*Get Smart*); Mikhail Bulgakov (South Node. Author—*The Master and Margarita*); René Girard (Jupiter. Anthropologist who wrote *Violence and the Sacred*, on the relationship of sex and violence in religious myth and ritual); Al Capone (Uranus. Cherubic mobster); Jimmy Hatlo (Saturn. Cartoonist—*They'll Do It Every Time*); William Shakespeare (Neptune. Playwright—*Romeo and Juliet*); Beatrice Lilly (Uranus. British stage comedienne).

8 Sagittarius

In the forge of the gods, a cauldron of molten metals with the figure of a king rising to the surface.

Descriptive Phrases

Inner alchemy; humanity as an unfinished product; forging a unified self out of various components of the personality; things coming together vs. things falling apart; integrity vs. critical flaws of character (Achilles' heel); intrepid resolve to succeed despite all obstacles; enlisting in some great struggle; surviving the tests of life (suffering); iron-willed self-discipline; power of command (military service); burning desire for deep-rooted personal and social transformation; recognizing the noblest elements in self or society and sacrificing everything else as dross (intolerance of weakness vs. sardonic commentary on human frailty); issues of racial or cultural superiority (bronze age vs. iron age mentalities); creative intensity and concentration; celebrating the birth of a new order.

Examples

Winston Churchill (Sun. Military leader—World War II); Sidney Poitier (Saturn. Black actor—*Look Who's Coming to Dinner, Lilies of the Field*); Queen Elizabeth I (North Node. Inspirational political leader who had a relation executed for the good of the state); Mark Twain (Sun. Author, satirist—*Huckleberry Finn, Life on the Mississippi*); Ernie Pyle (North Node. Folksy war correspondent, alcoholic); Louisa May Alcott (Sun. Author—*Little Women*); Phranc (Saturn. Lesbian singer); Toulouse-Lautrec (Jupiter. Artist of the Paris demimonde); Gloria Swanson (Uranus. Actress—*Sunset Boulevard*); Heinrich Himmler (Jupiter. Head of Nazi S.S. who set up the death camps); Gerald Wasserburg (Saturn. Geophysicist); Baba Ram Dass (Saturn. Guru, suffered a debilitating stroke); Thomas Huxley (Moon. Champion of evolutionary theory—survival of the fittest); Ayatollah Khomeini (Jupiter. Purist Moslem leader who took over Iran after the fall of the Shah); Tina Turner (Mercury. Rock singer).

9 Sagittarius

A woman helps her children up a ledge on a winding path through the forest. From their new perspective, the morning star can be seen in the soft glow of dawn.

Descriptive Phrases

Way-showers; leading people into the light of higher understanding; following one's political or spiritual ideals; blazing a trail vs. having to cover one's tracks (escape from persecution); spiritual guides; intuitive grasp of archetypal or symbolic signposts along the spiritual path (astrological or New Age interests); arriving at a new level of consciousness (reinvent themselves at crucial junctures); taking a problem step by step vs. getting ahead of oneself; picking one's way through a tricky situation vs. dangerous muddle-headedness (snares, ambushes); keeping one's followers from straying into error vs. misleading people; establishing bonds of trust; spiritual or political support groups; giving and receiving aid; helpful insights; Antares as Isis.

Examples

Sir Baden-Powell (Midheaven. Founder of the Boy Scouts); Deena Grier (Mercury. Canadian astrologer); Dick Clark (Sun, Mars. Emceed a teen dance show); George Rogers Clark (Pluto. Frontiersman, trailblazer); Frances Yates (Uranus. Trailblazing historian of the Western occult tradition—*Giordano Bruno and the Hermetic Tradition*); Hayley Mills (Ascendant. Actress—*The Parent Trap*); Anne Bancroft (Moon. Actress—*The Miracle Worker, The Graduate*); Georgette Robinson (Sun. World War II secret agent, ferried over 1000 people through an escape route); Ho Chi Minh (Mars. Revolutionary leader in Vietnam); Dale Evans (Venus. TV cowgirl, did advocacy work for abused children); Peter Malsin (Ascendant. Astrologer, author of *The Eyes of the Sun*); Eva LeGallienne (Chiron. Acting teacher, counselor, founder of the American Repertory Theater); Jean de Brunhoff (Uranus. Children's book author—*Babar*); John Calvin (Jupiter. Protestant reformer, tried to create a godly city in Geneva).

10 Sagittarius

After a prologue of witty stage patter, a magician levitates his female assistant with the aid of a very visible wire.

Descriptive Phrases

Rising to fame and influence; faith that one's efforts, charm, talent, and genius will be crowned by success; finding an arena where one can express oneself without restraint; grabbing the limelight (outrageous attention-getting displays); taking one's personality or one's shtick as far as it will go; enthusiasts, extremists (exaggerated claims, fraud); rambunctious puncturing of polite social fictions; exposing the sham or phony through humor; rising above everyday life through flights of fantasy ("get high" with drugs); trying to create a stable private life vs. being "hooked" on the acclaim of the public; delivering messages as if from on high (preachy); jumping into some public controversy; teaching through humor or art; dedicated efforts to realize one's dreams vs. frazzled attempts to do the impossible.

Examples

Mary Martin (Sun. Actress—*Peter Pan*); Woody Allen (Sun. Filmmaker—*Everyone Says I Love You, The Curse of the Jade Scorpion, Alice*); Bette Midler (Sun. Entertainer, singer); Dr. Ruth Westheimer (South Node. TV sex counselor); Franz Liszt (Neptune. Genius of the classical piano with a rock-star persona); Friedrich Nietzsche (Moon. Aphoristic anti-Christian philosopher); Whoopi Goldberg (Venus. Actress—*Ghost, Sister Act*); Uri Geller (Mercury. Spoon-bending stage magician); Harriet Beecher Stowe (Neptune. Author of *Uncle Tom's Cabin*, which helped fuel the Civil War); Martin Luther (Mercury. Anti-papal theologian, leader of the Reformation); Antoine de St. Exupéry (North Node, Uranus. Aviator, author—*The Little Prince*); Richard Pryor (Sun. Comedian—racial issues); Alan Cumming (Moon. Comic actor—*Spy Kids*); Timothy Leary (Ascendant. LSD guru); Adolphe Sax (Mercury. Inventor of the saxophone).

11 Sagittarius

An explorer examines an archaic idol shaped like a crouching panther, set high above a village square. In the flickering light of a votive candle, its eyes appear alternately laughing and ominous.

Descriptive Phrases

Encountering life in the raw; finding one's own truths, apart from the idols of one's culture; lynx-like acuity of perception; integrating human intelligence with the instinctive perceptions of the animal; studying human character and behavior, from the noblest to the most savage (travel); anthropological detachment vs. satirical caricaturing of human foibles (judgmental, condescending; pessimistic assessment of humanity); looking at things playfully, from a variety of perspectives vs. becoming hypnotized by some negative thought-form; prowling around for excitement and adventure; connecting with one's instincts, but keeping dangerous passions on a leash; propitiating an urge vs. being consumed by a dangerous passion; distinguishing between true and false beliefs; cultural relativism vs. rigid belief-systems.

Examples

John Philip Law (North Node. Actor in *The Golden Voyage of Sinbad,* in which he fights a giant six-armed statue of Kali that has come to life); James Baldwin (Jupiter. Gay Black writer—*Another Country*); Hallie Burnett (Sun. Writer—*This Heart, This Hunter*); Tama Janowitz (North Node. Writer—*A Cannibal in Manhattan*); Tex Watson and Patricia Krenwinkle (Sun. Mansonite murderers, jailed for life); Barbara Tuchman (Jupiter. Historian—*The March of Folly*, on the American misadventure in Vietnam); Jack Kerouac (Mars. Author—*The Dharma Bums*); Patti Smith (South Node. Anguished rock star and poet); Erich Fromm (Jupiter. Psychologist—*Escape from Freedom*); Pablo Picasso (North Node. Primitivist painter); Golda Meir (Saturn. One-time prime minister of Israel); Noam Chomsky (Mercury. Leading critic of media control of public discourse); Voltaire (Sun. Influential satirist—*Candide*); Lotte Lenya (Uranus. Actress—Pirate Jenny in *The Threepenny Opera*).

12 Sagittarius

*An eagle perched atop a flagpole
screams at the crowd forming below.*

Descriptive Phrases

Joining a social group that is centered around political or social ideals, and rising to become a spokesperson of that group; translating one's ideals into concrete policies or actions; knowing what a situation requires and voicing these opinions in a strong voice that resonates with the public; providing a symbolic focus for important issues (symbolic gestures without practical follow-through); gathering enough public support to win one's battles vs. knowing when to walk away from a lost cause; far-sighted sociopolitical analysis; keeping an eye on distant goals; living up to one's public image (change their self-image in different phases of life as their goals change); inspiring others to live up to their ideals (meddlesome); patriotic oratory (power-hungry flagwavers).

Examples

Barry Goldwater (Venus. Hawkish presidential candidate); George McGovern (Mars. Antiwar presidential candidate); Linda Tripp (Chiron. Right-wing squawker in Monicagate); Grace Metalious (Jupiter. Author of the notorious *Peyton Place*); Norman Lear (North Node. Producer of *Maude, All in the Family*, liberal crusader—People for the American Way); Dustin Hoffman (North Node. Actor—*The Graduate, All the President's Men*); Robert Redford (North Node. Actor—*All the President's Men*); Patty Duke (South Node. Actress—*The Miracle Worker*); Charles Duke (Mars. Apollo 16 astronaut); Sandy Koufax (Jupiter. Baseball great); Simon Wiesenthal (Venus. Nazi hunter); Maria Callas (Sun. Operatic diva); Geena Davis (Saturn. Actress—*Thelma and Louise*); Eugene Ormandy (Mars. Orchestra conductor); Admiral Hyman Rickover (Uranus. Tireless propagandist for a nuclear navy).

13 Sagittarius

Seen against the orb of the sun, the winged horse Pegasus flies over a battlefield.

Descriptive Phrases

Spiritual self-knowledge that allows one to appreciate the larger trajectory of one's life; rising above one's immediate problems by putting them in a wider spiritual perspective; riding the wings of fantasy into the realm of one's heart's desire; realizing one's dreams through focused creative efforts (imaginative art, leave behind a legacy of magic); romanticism; love that transcends the boundaries of time and space; living within a romanticized vision of the past vs. living in the moment, from which all true possibilities spring; deciding on a bold course of action and sticking with it; robust faith that one will surmount life's obstacles (belief in happy endings); achieving great things vs. falling on one's face when one lacks a solid footing in reality; worldly savvy joined with unshakeable spiritual idealism; zest for life.

Examples

Steven Spielberg (Jupiter. Filmmaker—*E.T.*, *Jurassic Park*); Lauren Bacall (Jupiter. Actress—*Cactus Flower*, Bogart's widow); Walt Disney (Sun. Cartoonist, theme park entrepreneur); United States of America (Ascendant? 7/4/1776); Ethel Waters (Jupiter. Hot jazz singer, actress); Fred Astaire (Ascendant. Actor, dancer, singer); Charles Dickens (Moon. Writer—*Oliver Twist, A Christmas Carol*); Carlos Castaneda (Mercury. Author of *Don Juan* books); René Magritte (Saturn. Surrealist artist); Joan Blondell (South Node. Actress—*Gold Diggers of 1933*); Jeff Bridges (Sun. Actor—*The Big Lebowski*, *K-Pax*); Mohandas Gandhi (Saturn. Led the fight for Indian independence); Jean Stapleton (Venus. Actress—Edith Bunker on *All in the Family*); Mickey Rooney (Mars. Trouper, actor, married many times); Maurice Jarre (Jupiter. Wrote film scores for *Lawrence of Arabia* and *Dr. Zhivago*); Christopher Reeve (Moon. Actor—*Superman*, paralyzed in riding accident); Elvis Presley (Ascendant. Rock and roll star, acted in many fantasy movies, had a poor grasp of reality).

14 Sagittarius

A tourist and an Egyptian guide argue in front of the entrance of the Great Pyramid.

Descriptive Phrases

Travel; meeting another culture on its own terms vs. superficial encounters of tourists or colonialists (close-mindedness—racial or cultural prejudice); difficulties entering into a world in which the whole matrix of assumptions is different; systems analysis—examining interlocking factors as part of an integrated whole; building a mental edifice on solid facts vs. ungrounded speculation based on personal tastes and specious arguments; patiently collecting and connecting various clues vs. forcing the facts into a preexisting belief structure; invigorating an old tradition by modernizing it vs. acknowledging nonnegotiables; step-by-step revelation of life's enduring mysteries vs. being a tourist in life.

Examples

Lawrence Durrell (Jupiter. Author of the *Alexandria Quartet*); Idries Shah (Jupiter. Writer on Sufism); Robert Hand (Sun. Astrologer—Project Hindsight); Baruch Spinoza (Sun. Original metaphysician who was condemned by both Christians and Jews); Claudette Colbert (Mars. Actress—*Cleopatra*); Gertrude Lawrence (Uranus. Actress—*The King and I*); Thalmus Rasulala (Mercury. Actor—Kunta Kinte in *Roots*); Bob Crane (Saturn. Actor—*Hogan's Heroes*); Barbara Hutton (Mercury. Heiress, married seven times, lived in Tangiers); Alan King (Mars. Acerbic Jewish comedian); Michelle Pfeiffer (Saturn. Actress—*Dangerous Minds*); A. P. Sinnett (Venus. Theosophist, editor of *Hong Kong Daily Press*); Hans Kung (South Node. Renegade Catholic theologian); Henry Morton Stanley (Jupiter. African explorer); Sabu (Jupiter. Indian stable boy who became a star—*Elephant Boy, The Thief of Baghdad*); E. C. Krupp (Mercury. Archaeoastronomer—*Echoes of Ancient Skies*); Joan Didion (Sun. Writer—*Panic in Needle Park*); Milton Caniff (Mars. Cartoonist—*Terry and the Pirates*).

15 Sagittarius

Groundhog, out of its winter sleep, looks for its shadow[35].

Descriptive Phrases

Open-mindedness; registering a situation and trying to make sense out of it (bumbling around as if half asleep); interpreting life as if it were a dream (feel overwhelmed by a chaos of symbolism); facing the music vs. letting problems slide; inescapability of basic human problems, which are always "still there in the morning"; withdrawing after failure and coming up with a more workable approach (optimists—take life as it comes); being a man or a mouse (standing up for human freedom); balancing the needs of the situation with what one can handle (withdraw to rest, gather strength, and clarify one's social purpose); gambling on a hunch vs. acting out of true conviction; reconsidering whether what one is seeing is actually there.

Examples

Art Carney (North Node. Comedian, sewer-worker Ed Norton in *The Honeymooners*); Eve Arden (Jupiter. Actress—*Our Miss Brooks*); Marcello Mastroianni (Jupiter. Actor—*8½*); Marjoe Gortner (Venus. Ex-evangelist, scam artist); Honoré de Balzac (Moon. Writer—*The Human Comedy*); Billy Graham (North Node. Evangelist); André Malraux (Mars. Philosopher, fighter in freedom movements); Emancipation Proclamation takes effect (North Node. 1/1/1863); Albert Einstein (Moon. Theoretical physicist—relativity); Spike Lee (Saturn. Film director—*Do the Right Thing*); Odette Samsone (Jupiter. Spy who withstood torture); Jimmy Carter (Jupiter. U.S. president, diplomat); Susan Sarandon (South Node. Actress—*Thelma and Louise*); Mary Todd Lincoln (Mars. Lincoln's wife, tried to contact her dead husband through mediums); Dave Brubeck (Sun. Jazz great); Wally Cox (Sun. Low-key comedian); Tom Hulce (Sun. Actor—*Animal House, Amadeus*); Tom Waits (Sun. Gruff-voiced bluesy singer, actor—*Down by Law*).

16 Sagittarius

In an amateur production of The Pirates of Penzance, *the pirate king gets carried away and sets fire to the admiral's plywood galleon.*

Descriptive Phrases

The ragged edge between art and life; playing a role to the hilt vs. stepping outside a boring social scene and treating it like a shabby construct; choosing how much of oneself to invest in a scene (going overboard vs. bailing out); living life as a romantic adventure (developing enough detachment to alter a bad script); making it up as one goes along (rudderless); getting carried along or carried away; unpleasant surprises vs. serendipity; stirring things up; incendiary statements; staging a cultural revolution (champions of the poor and enemies of boring respectability); overwhelming one's opposition with sheer energy (balls of fire); clowning around vs. buckling down; rash abandon vs. awaiting the right moment to act (missteps, destructive debacles); swashbuckling bravado (fiery temper).

Examples

Roseanne Barr (Venus. Bawdy comedienne, infamous for her obscene rendition of "The Star Spangled Banner"); Tim Matheson (Jupiter. Actor—*Animal House*, with its climactic destruction of the college parade); Sissy Spacek (Chiron. Actress—*Carrie*, with its incineration of the school prom); Red Grooms (North Node. Artist—cheesy constructed cityscapes); Ed Wood, Jr. (Jupiter. Transvestite director of *Plan 9 from Outer Space*); Alexandre Dumas (Chiron. Writer—*The Three Musketeers*); Louis Farrakhan (Moon. Black Muslim leader, incendiary racist statements); Mao Tse Tung (Mercury. Revolutionary general, leader of the Cultural Revolution); Pearl Harbor attacked (Sun. 12/7/1941); Dr. Ruth Westheimer (Saturn. Television personality—advice on sexual problems); Jim Morrison (Sun. Lead singer of The Doors); Ethel Merman (Uranus. Out-of-control Broadway singer); Oliver Stone (South Node. Film director—*JFK*, *Platoon*); Francesco Petrarca (North Node. Cultural revolutionary, waged an all-out attack on medieval culture).

17 Sagittarius

Worshippers at an Easter sunrise service are awed by a glorious ring of light on the horizon.

Descriptive Phrases

Renewal of hope; seeing the cloud's silver lining (having faith in the light force vs. succumbing to despair); resignation to the cyclical ups and downs of fortune; making the best of one's situation; viewing a problem in a higher, more spiritual light; confronting the public with some problem and guiding them toward a spiritual solution (portentously laying down the "gospel"); atonement for one's errors; spiritual purgation; rising to a spiritual challenge; tests of faith; waiting for an answer, in whatever form or at whatever time it may appear; seeing the "writing" of God in nature; spiritual wisdom concentrated in symbols; Christian mysteries—forbearance, faith, and the triumph of immortal spirit over the forces of death; immanence vs. transcendence.

Examples

Simone Weil (Mars. Mystic, social philosopher); Diego Rivera (Sun. Murals with political and spiritual themes); Phoebe Snow (Chiron. Singer, became a mystic after the birth of a child with birth defects); Herman Melville (Moon. Author—*Moby Dick*); Guru Maharaj-ji (Saturn. Guru); John Sayles (Chiron. Film director—*Brother from Another Planet*); Lee Iacocca (Jupiter. Turned around the fortunes of Chrysler; there are many entrepreneurs with planets on this degree); Elisabeth Schwarzkopf (Sun. Opera singer, forced to join the Nazi Party, but exonerated after the war); Bill Murray (Chiron. Comedian, actor—*Lost in Translation, The Razor's Edge*); Roger Zelazny (Midheaven. Science fiction writer—*Lord of Light*); René Magritte (Mercury. Surrealist painter); Emperor Hirohito (Uranus. One-time ruler of the "Land of the Rising Sun"); David Carradine (Sun. Acid-head actor—*Kung Fu*); Patricia Neal (Mars. Actress—*The Day the Earth Stood Still*, recovered from paralysis).

18 Sagittarius

In a flashy dress parade, a foreign ambassador in a fez is driven down the street in an open car. On the sidelines, an observer dressed in a quilted bathrobe and a nightcap makes cynical observations to his neighbor.

Descriptive Phrases

Seeing through superficial trappings to what is really going on (the Emperor's New Clothes); bravely voicing unspoken truths; seeing things from promising new angles; putting a funny spin on events (irreverent); penetrating commentary; sharing the wisdom of another perspective or another culture vs. rigidly adhering to local cultural criteria; differences in perspective that depend on the different "hats" we wear; cynically judging the unending parade of successive political leaders, who are preceded by their promises and followed by disillusioning revelations (mustn't forget that they too will be judged by their accomplishments rather than their promises); standing aside rather than getting caught up in dubious endeavors vs. finding one's place in life's parade; adopting a relaxed, unpretentious attitude vs. striking pompous poses.

Examples

Redd Foxx (Mercury. Comedian—*Sanford and Son*); Alfred Hitchcock (Saturn. Director—*Vertigo, North by Northwest*); Joan Rivers (Sun. Chatty comedienne); Tip O'Neill (Sun. Speaker of the House, driving force behind Nixon's resignation); Natalie Davis (Saturn. Historian—*The Return of Martin Guerre*, about the uncovering of a great deception); Ed Sullivan (Uranus. Variety show host, introduced The Beatles and other big acts); Guru Maharaj-ji (Sun. Youthful guru); Shelley Winters (Mars. Actress); Paul Harvey (North Node. Talk-radio host); Tony Randall (Jupiter. Actor—*The Odd Couple*); Wolfgang Amadeus Mozart (Moon, Pluto. Composer, improvised readily on any musical theme, expert billiards player); James Thurber (Sun. Humorist); Alan Alda (Jupiter. Actor—*M*A*S*H*); Mayor Jimmy Walker (North Node. Mayor of New York City during the twenties, a notably sharp dresser known as Beau James).

19 Sagittarius

A refugee camp for children comes under the crossfire of war. A woman snatches one of the children to her breast and runs for safer ground.

Descriptive Phrases

Deep concern about the state of the world—trying to make it a safer place for future generations; knowing when to make a stand and when to escape an imminent danger; spiritual shepherding; taking others under one's wing and teaching them the inner truths of the heart, beyond the hatred and divisiveness of the world (vengeful cruelty); the pelican[36] as an alchemical symbol of Christ's sacrificial love; the Red Tincture—potent but mysterious spiritual influence; living on society's fringe vs. successfully influencing the context of public discussion; political or cultural activism (may be forced onto the sidelines by disturbing developments, but never give up); finding, after much restless travel, that one's true home is where one is most needed; abiding presence; protectiveness.

Examples

Princess Diana (Ascendant. Activist against land mines, inexplicable worldwide influence); Seymour Hersh (North Node. Journalist who wrote on the massacre of civilians at My Lai); Sally Struthers (Moon. Actress, activist concerned with feeding the world's children); Tom Hayden (Sun. Antiwar activist, California legislator); Teddy Roosevelt (Venus. President, conservationist); Neil Young (Midheaven. Rock singer, devoted father of two children with cerebral palsy); Shirley Temple Black (Saturn. Child star, ambassador to Africa); Aleksandr Solzhenitsyn (Sun. Soviet dissident—*The Gulag Archipelago*, lived on a secluded Vermont estate); Anwar Sadat (Mercury. President of Egypt, Nobel Peace Prize for negotiations with Israel); Steven Spielberg (Sun. Director—*E.T.*, *Schindler's List*); Jane Fonda (Venus. Peace activist, actress—*The China Syndrome*, about a nuclear meltdown); E.T.A. Hoffman (Venus. Fairytale writer—*The Nutcracker, The Golden Flower Pot*); Odumegwu Ojukwu (Mars. Biafran political leader, fled into exile); Marlene Dietrich (Uranus. Actress who fled Nazi Germany).

20 Sagittarius

Off-duty soldier chats up a woman over iced drinks, then asks her if she wants to dance.

Descriptive Phrases

Engaging others in conversation or argument; breaking the ice; warming someone up vs. getting the cold shoulder; going after a romantic vision of life and seeing whether it receives the support of others; seeing how far one can live into one's unique vision of life (pander to the expectations of the public); backing up what one projects; setting the record straight vs. creating glamorous myths about oneself or others; bringing romance into everyday life; hunger for experience; accumulating experiences to be savored and digested later in life (follow the law of desire—sexual adventurers); seeing what one can get away with vs. treading on thin ice; life as dance; finding a pleasant rhythm vs. feeling out of synch; repeating the same old scene vs. trying a new spin; being centered in the here and now; physical presence; sexual charisma.

Examples

Frank Sinatra (Sun. Singer, dancer, movie star); Doris Day (Mars. Actress—*Pillow Talk*); Marlon Brando (Jupiter. Actor); Madonna (Saturn. Singer, sexpot); Fiorello La Guardia (Sun, Mars. Charismatic ex-mayor of New York); Sylvester Stallone (South Node. Actor—*Rocky*); Susie Quatro (Chiron. Black-leather-clad rock and roller); Angela Bassett (Saturn. Black actress); Xavier Cugat (North Node. Bandleader—*The Rumba King*); José Greco (Mercury. Flamenco dancer); Gene Markay (Sun. Naval officer, married three top Hollywood stars); Rona Barrett (Jupiter. Gossip maven); Mark Spitz (Chiron. Olympic swimmer); Noel Coward (North Node. Chatty, humorous playwright); Virna Lisi (Venus. Actress—*Casanova*); Sarah Vaughn (Jupiter. Jazz singer); Humphrey Bogart (North Node. Suave actor—*To Have and Have Not, Casablanca*).

21 Sagittarius

In an oral examination, a rabbinical student and his professor pull down their glasses in an angry face-off, the student arguing from Scripture and the professor arguing from personal experience.

Descriptive Phrases

Sincere attempt to communicate in spite of differing perceptual frameworks (ideologically rigid, don't listen to those they consider social inferiors); beginning to see how higher spiritual realities and everyday life experiences interpenetrate; seeing the archetypal and symbolic meaning of one's experience; examining a belief from all sides; correcting mistaken assumptions; learning from a mentor who has tested abstract theories in the school of hard knocks (half-baked theories; may adopt the role of a teacher before they are intellectually mature); clarifying one's spiritual intuitions by reflecting on them and by bouncing them off of other people (eccentric spiritual beliefs, flaky gnosticism); growing into the role of the spiritual teacher vs. being marginalized by the intellectual elite or remaining a perpetual student in life's classroom.

Examples

Bob Dylan (Ascendant. Folk-rock musician—"Like a Rolling Stone"); Noam Chomsky (Saturn. Linguist, radical analysis of the role of the media in controlling discourse); Barbara Jordan (Jupiter. Professor of law); Ingmar Bergman (North Node. Film director—*Fanny and Alexander, Wild Strawberries*); Frances Yates (North Node. Historian who exposed the importance of the occult tradition); Ed Koch (Sun. Ex-mayor of New York City, TV judge); Bill Griffith (Venus. Existential cartoonist—*Zippy the Pinhead*); Antoine de St. Exupéry (Chiron. Pilot, author—*The Little Prince*); L. Ron Hubbard (Ascendant. Founder of Scientology); Alan Watts (South Node. Taught Zen on TV); Paracelsus (Venus. Physician whose medicine was based on correspondences between the macrocosm and microcosm); Gail Sheehy (Mercury. Pop psychologist—*Changes*); Teilhard de Chardin (North Node. Philosopher, mystic); Julie Walters (Chiron. Actress—*Educating Rita*).

22 Sagittarius

A retired Chinese gentleman is writing a damning memoir of his experiences as a government official. Behind him hangs a red silk tapestry picturing a dragon flying downward and breathing fire.

Descriptive Phrases

Savagely independent perspective; exposing lies foisted upon the public by government and organized religion; railing against cultural prejudices and the setup of society (satire); uncovering and confronting evil; seeing universal natural Law behind differing cultural norms (despise local customs, feel like a stranger in a strange land); living life boldly, without concern for petty social taboos; conforming to the dictates of reason (atheism) vs. carrying a mythic tradition within oneself (Eastern wisdom); holding oneself to high standards of truth; examining a case carefully vs. swift summary judgments (demonize people who disagree with them, use violent solutions); teaching people hard truths taken from one's own experience; Lucifer's pitchfork prodding humanity to higher moral awareness; Promethean fire.

Examples

Mark Twain (Venus. Novelist—*Letters from the Earth*); Voltaire (Mars. Enlightenment provocateur—*Philosophical Letters*); Frances Yates (Mercury. Historian of the occult—*The Rosicrucian Enlightenment*); Margaret Hamilton (Uranus. Actress—the Wicked Witch in *The Wizard of Oz*); Rainer Fassbinder (South Node. Filmmaker—*The Marriage of Maria Braun*); Jamie Lee Curtis (Mercury. Actress—*Halloween* slasher films); Emile Zola (Saturn. Led movement to exonerate Dreyfus); Bette Midler (Mercury. Singer, actress—*First Wive's Club*); Carl Jung (Mars. Archetypal psychologist—*Answer to Job*); Alice Cooper (Moon. Shock-rock star who guillotines himself); Carl Sagan (Moon. Scientist, propagandist against astrology, antinuclear activist); Vanessa Redgrave (North Node. Leftist actress); Gurdjieff (Jupiter. Guru); M. Scott Peck (Jupiter. Pop psychologist who deals with the problem of evil—*Children of the Lie*); Theodore Adorno (Uranus. Social theorist); Tom Wolfe (Ascendant. Journalistic novelist—*The Bonfire of the Vanities*, on the corrupt culture of New York in the eighties).

23 Sagittarius

From the shining crown of the Statue of Liberty, immigrants look out upon their new country.

Descriptive Phrases

Fighting for and defending one's personal and political freedom; standing up for high personal and national ideals; Promethean man, urging humanity to attain its full stature; joining with others who share one's aspirations; elevating group morale; nobility of character—living up to one's promises; shining a light on hypocrisy and skulduggery (being exposed for one's dirty deeds); openheartedness vs. dignified reserve; romantic idealism (unrealistically optimistic expectations); emotional loyalty vs. betrayal (demand to be treated with honesty and respect); feeling shackled vs. busting loose (need lots of psychological space, but may take liberties); sense of unbounded horizons—seeing beyond limitations and setbacks to ultimate victory.

Examples

Drew Pearson (Sun. Political journalist—*The Case Against Congress*); Winston Churchill (Venus. Prime minister of England during World War II); Ludwig von Beethoven (Jupiter. Composer—*The Eroica*); Patty Duke (Sun. Actress—*The Miracle Worker*); Gustave Courbet (Uranus. Realist artist, joined the Paris Commune); Henrik Ibsen (Mars. Writer—*A Doll's House*); Joan Armatrading (Chiron. Folk singer); Maxfield Parrish (Saturn. Illustrator, artist); Maximilian Robespierre (Pluto. Ideological leader of the French Revolution, called The Incorruptible); Kathy Bates (Jupiter. Actress—*Dolores Claiborne, The War at Home*); Sammy Davis, Jr. (Mercury. Rat-pack singer who crossed the color line); Barbara Hershey (Jupiter. Actress—Mary Magdalene in *The Last Temptation of Christ*); Kemal Ataturk (North Node. Overthrew the Ottoman Empire and established the secular Republic of Turkey); Nero (Pluto. Decadent Roman emperor); Aleksandr Sozhenitsyn (Venus. Dissident writer—*The Gulag Archipelago*).

24 Sagittarius

A man in overalls returns to his sunny little cottage after a good day's fishing and finds a bluebird singing on the gatepost.

Descriptive Phrases

Attunement to nature; cheerfulness; optimism; looking at the bright side of life ("Mr. Bluebird's on my shoulder"); looking for happiness in life's simple pleasures (playful subversion of coolness and sophistication); laying aside one's cares and letting one's spirit take flight; attunement to the song of life; music and singing; seeing the good in others, no matter how rough their exterior; sociability; warmth and hospitality; finding one's soulmate; marriages made in heaven; feeling at home anywhere on God's green earth; being comfortable and at home with oneself (careless neglect of mundane affairs); making one's bed and lying in it vs. peevish squawking; putting one's spiritual estate in order; turning a deaf ear to criticism and pursuing one's own goals; getting on a good wavelength.

Examples

Hayley Mills (South Node. Actress—*Pollyanna, The Parent Trap*); Domenico Modugno (Mars. Pop singer—"Volare"); Walt Whitman (Uranus. Poet); Albert Finney (Jupiter. Actor—*Tom Jones*); Glenda Jackson (Jupiter. Actress—*Women in Love*); Peter Falk (South Node. Actor); Grace Brumbry (North Node. Opera singer); Duke Ellington (Saturn. Jazz great); Thomas Merton (Venus. Spiritual seeker—*The Seven-Storey Mountain*); James Doolittle (Sun. Air Force general, stunt pilot); Paramhansa Yogananda (Mercury. Spiritual guru); Michael Landon (Jupiter. Actor—*Bonanza, Little House on the Prairie*); Harriet Beecher Stowe (Saturn. Abolitionist writer—*Uncle Tom's Cabin*, had seven children); Tom Waits (Mercury. Down-home bluesy singer); Gertrude Berg (North Node. Television's Jewish mother).

25 Sagittarius

A little boy on a rocking horse imagines himself flying to a multicolored candyland.

Descriptive Phrases

Flights of fancy; working oneself up into a creative frenzy; lofty artistic ambitions; experimenting intelligently with a medium vs. playing around; establishing a life-rhythm that includes work and play vs. waiting for inspiration (substance abuse, gluttons for sensory stimulation); finding one's own wavelength and going with it; drawing others into an exciting new vision (psychedelic or empyrean vistas); intoxicating *joie de vivre* (extreme mood swings, manic-depression, being on an even keel vs. going over the edge); tempering the spirit through life's trials (moderation replacing excess); enthusiastic participation in life; sexual adventures (unbridled passion); excitement for living.

Examples

Jimi Hendrix (Ascendant. Psychedelic guitarist—"Electric Ladyland"); Vincent Van Gogh (Jupiter. Post-impressionist painter); Ludwig von Beethoven (Sun. Daemonic romantic composer); Patti Smith (Mercury. Seminal dirge-rock singer); Janis Joplin (Mars. Psychedelic blues singer); Eugene O'Neill (Mars. Playwright, drunk); Bob Guccione (Sun. *Penthouse* mogul; produced *Caligula*); Henry VIII (Neptune. Glutton for women, but helped revive the arts); Margaret Mead (Sun. Anthropologist—*Coming of Age in Samoa*); Philip K. Dick (Sun. Acidhead, visionary science fiction writer—*Do Androids Dream of Electric Sheep?*); Emily Brontë (Neptune. Writer—*Wuthering Heights*); William Butler Yeats (Jupiter. Visionary poet, occultist); Rudyard Kipling (Mars, Mercury. Poet, writer—*The Jungle Book*); Jackie Kennedy (Saturn. Horsey First Lady); Kees van Dongen (Jupiter. Fauve artist); John Greenleaf Whittier (Sun. Quaker poet).

26 Sagittarius

A flag bearer leads a spearhead attack.

Descriptive Phrases

Taking a stand; having the courage of one's convictions (reckless); faith in a better future that makes one willing to fight for one's beliefs; crusaders; agitators; getting people psyched about a cause vs. solitary pursuit of personal goals; following the beat of one's own drummer; taking a pursuit as far as it will go (enthusiastic, tickled by life's limitless possibilities); spearheading a cause; stump speeches (inflammatory rhetoric); clearly articulating the issues; driving home a point; skewering hypocrisy and bullshit and promoting honest discussion (restless, jumpy, try to get energies moving, upbraid people who have sunk into indifference); holding oneself and others to high standards; inspiring others by embodying an ideal.

Examples

Martin Luther King Jr. (Saturn. Civil-rights leader, assassinated); Mother Teresa (Ascendant. Ministered to the poor and dying, Catholic ideologue); Stephen Crane (Mars. Journalist in the Spanish-American War, author of *The Red Badge of Courage*); Mary Travers (Jupiter. Folk singer—Peter, Paul, and Mary); Abbie Hoffman (North Node. Activist, yippie prankster); Willy Brandt (Sun. Chancellor of Germany, opposed Hitler from the start, served as a journalist during the Nuremberg trials); Jeddu Krishnamurti (Moon. Spiritual philosopher); Keith Richards (Sun. Guitarist for The Rolling Stones); Rudyard Kipling (Venus. Poet, author—*Captains Courageous*); Nancy Walker (Mars. Comedienne, Broadway singer); Holly Hunter (Saturn. Actress—*Raising Arizona*); Queen Ida (Saturn. Zydeco superstar); Newt Gingrich (Moon. Conservative firebrand); Sun Yat-sen (Venus. Led the overthrow of the Manchu dynasty); Mary, Queen of Scots (Sun. Fanatical Catholic monarch, beheaded by Elizabeth).

27 Sagittarius

A woman guides the hands of a youngster as he shapes a large platter on a potter's wheel.

Descriptive Phrases

Retaining contact with the immature, formative side of the personality (overly malleable, may get "worked over" when they try to conform to others' expectations); being socially adaptable, yet retaining a firm inner knowledge of who one is (slaves to the ups and downs of circumstance, until they learn to live from their core); first tentative grasp of a situation that presages a more mature and solid understanding; teaching people to examine their lives from a higher, more detached perspective; serendipity—letting life emerge as it will vs. imposing an ordered vision onto life (rebels—throw monkey wrenches into the spokes); drawing out people's creativity through gentle coaxing (sensual exploration); developing a skill through apprenticeship; the galactic center.

Examples

Betty Grable (Sun. Actress, swimsuit pinup girl); Isaac Bashevis Singer (Uranus. Storyteller—*Gimpel the Fool*); Ursula LeGuin (Saturn. Writer—*Earth-Sea Trilogy*); Steven Spielberg (Sun. Director—*Jurassic Park, E.T.*); Shirley Jones (Midheaven. Actress—*The Partridge Family*); Deena Grier (Sun. Canadian astrologer); Edith Piaf (Sun. *Chanteuse*, her life was a total mess, from beginning to end); Julie Kavner (Chiron. Actress—*Rhoda*, Woody Allen films); Cosimo de'Medici (Jupiter. Quintessential patron of the arts); Alfred Hitchcock (North Node. Film director); Claus Oldenburg (Saturn. Sculptor—"Soft Toaster"); Dada Manifesto released by Tristan Tzara (North Node. 3/23/1918); John Whitney (Uranus. Heir, polo player, gambler, coproducer of *Gone with the Wind*); Claude Levi-Strauss (South Node. Anthropologist); Dwayne Hickman (Ascendant. Actor—*Dobey Gillis*).

28 Sagittarius

A peasant leads a mob armed with pikes and torches across a stone bridge spanning the crocodile-infested moat of the castle.

Descriptive Phrases

Leading humanity in a vital new cultural direction, against formidable opposition; grim determination to have one's views prevail (constant struggle); scathing attacks on stifling traditions (barbarians at the gates guided by destructive passions); unflinching examination of monstrous problems (hell-raisers who flirt with the dark side); puncturing political or religious myths; exorcizing cultural demons by bringing them to light in a palatable cultural form (art with a message); appealing to the masses vs. appealing to the *cognoscenti* and losing one's impact; the ability of institutions to survive violent change vs. the inevitable crumbling of traditions that have outlived their usefulness; showdowns; burning one's bridges in a major confrontation.

Examples

Norman Mailer (Midheaven. Writer—*Armies of the Night*); Mary Shelley (Moon. Writer—*Frankenstein*); Friedrich Engels (Uranus. Communist theorist, author—*The Peasant War in Germany*); Gustave Courbet (Neptune. Realist artist who joined the Paris Commune); Cassandra Peterson (Chiron. Horror show host—Elvira); Jean Genet (Sun. Homoerotic writer, criminal); Victoria Sackville-West (Mars. Writer, sexually licentious, lived in Sissinghurst Castle); Pedro Almodovar (Chiron. Film director, sexual anarchist); Michel de Montaigne (Jupiter. Groundbreaking essayist); Walt Whitman (Neptune. Poet—*Leaves of Grass*); Roger Vadim (Venus. Film director—*Barbarella*); Phil Ochs (Sun. Political folk singer, committed suicide); Marisa Berenson (Moon. Actress—*Holocaust, Cabaret, A Death in Venice*); Marshal Henri Pétain (Moon. Hero of the Battle of Verdun in 1916—"They shall not pass"); Tycho Brahe (Saturn. Astronomical researcher who worked out of the castle of Uraniborg).

29 Sagittarius

Stripped to the waist, a farmer cuts grain with a sickle.

Descriptive Phrases

Deciding on a course of action and following through with ruthless efficiency; uncompromising integrity of thought and action (wrestling with doubts); sharp, unflinching analysis; getting down to the bare bones of the situation by clearing away irrelevancies (naïve oversimplification); mowing down one's opponents in debate; doing away with outmoded ideas in order to clear a path for the new (revolutionary, violent); harvesting the hard lessons of experience at the end of a cycle; harmonizing oneself with powerful historical or evolutionary forces (survival of the fittest, contempt for flabbiness of thought or action); physical regimens; learning to perform a physical task with strength and grace; making great strides through practical, disciplined action.

Examples

Herbert Spencer (Uranus. Darwinist—survival of the fittest); Petra Kelly (Venus. Ecologist, cofounder of the Greens); Francis Galton (Moon. Anthropologist, founder of the eugenics movement); Will Durant (Venus. Popular historian); Vladimir Lenin (Saturn. Communist revolutionary leader); Angela Davis (Venus. Communist activist); Ed Asner (Saturn. Actor—*The Mary Tyler Moore Show*); Mary Tyler Moore (Venus. Actress); Ed Koch (Jupiter. Ex-mayor of New York); G. Gordon Liddy (Venus, Mercury. Watergate scandal, talk-show host); Chris Evert (Sun. Tennis pro); Johnny Weismuller (Uranus. Actor—*Tarzan*); Anjelica Huston (Chiron. Actress, director); Francisco Franco (Mercury. Leader of the Spanish fascists); Saint Valentine's Day Massacre (Saturn. 2/14/1929, mafia massacre); Peter Criss (Sun. Rock star—Kiss); David Lynch (South Node. Sicko filmmaker—*Dune, Blue Velvet*); Dianne Wiest (Jupiter. Actress—*Bullets over Broadway*).

30 Sagittarius

A man pores over the cover of an ancient book of wisdom, whose sinuous designs are outlined in jewels and gold leaf.

Descriptive Phrases

Studying the curious mysteries of life and nature; looking at what is in front of one's nose in a new light (distrust old approaches, notice anomalies in the established worldview and use these as keys to unlock a new understanding); framing one's situation in an inventive, open-ended way; italicizing overlooked but important pieces of the puzzle (taste for the whimsical and bizarre; lose basic meanings in baroque elaborations); tricking people into seeing fallacies in their worldview (mindgames); opening up a chink in Plato's cave; penetrating insights into reality; truths hidden in the curious images of the subconscious; unpacking the meaning of symbols or parables; reducing situations to adages, quips, parables, or scientific formulas.

Examples

Joseph Campbell (Uranus. Mythologist—*The Masks of God*); Dr. Seuss (Uranus. Bizarre children's book author—*The Cat in the Hat*); Salvador Dali (Uranus. Surrealist artist who did a remarkable tarot deck); Sulamith Wulfing (Chiron. Illustrator—occult overtones); Rod Serling (Moon. Director—*The Twilight Zone*); Jane Roberts (Saturn. Writer—*Seth* books); Art Garfunkel (Venus. Folk-rock musician of Simon and Garfunkel—"Parsley, Sage, Rosemary and Thyme"); Adelle Davis (Uranus. Natural foods advocate); Frank Zappa (Sun. "Noodling" musician—"Peaches en Regalia," "Absolutely Free"); Jean-François Champollion (Venus. Deciphered Egyptian hieroglyphics); Andrea Alciati (Neptune. Author of a Renaissance book of emblems); Enrico Fermi (Chiron. Invented the first atomic reactor); Franz Cumont (Mercury. Scholar of ancient religions); Alexander Blok (North Node. Symbolist poet); Charubel (Venus. Clairvoyant, astrological degree symbols).

1 Capricorn

Native American chief stands atop a rocky crag and demands the attention of the assembled tribe.

Descriptive Phrases

Sense of personal authority; confidence in one's position and one's cause (need constant validation); realistic appraisal of the situation and its needs; addressing the needs of the public (political reformers); leading people in some new direction (do not accept opposing views gracefully, may bully others to get their way); devising a practical game plan to reach one's goals; persevering despite ongoing obstacles in one's path (overestimation of their powers may cause their downfall, need to listen to the advice of people they trust); sincere and honest communication of one's feelings and needs (being sexually playful and up-front vs. being overly demanding, mischievous hijinks); developing personal strengths; power of leadership; integrity and backbone.

Examples

Maggie Kuhn (Uranus. Champion for the rights of the elderly—Grey Panthers); Richard Nixon (Mercury. U. S. president brought down by scandal); Leon Jaworski (Uranus. Watergate special prosecutor, demanded the Nixon tapes); Robespierre officiates as priest at the Temple of Reason (Jupiter. 6/8/1794, he was eventually guillotined); Sandra Bullock (South Node. Actress who made the big time with *Speed*, a film about a boobytrapped bus); Moe Howard (Sun. Pint-sized dictatorial comedian—*The Three Stooges*); John Belushi (Ascendant. Comedian—star of *Animal House*); Maria Callas (Venus. Temperamental operatic diva); Battle of the Monitor and Merrimac (North Node. 3/9/1862, first armored ships in the Civil War); Georg von Békésy (North Node. Physicist who studied human hearing; this degree has a lot to do with the ability to listen to others); Dag Hammerskjold (Uranus. Secretary-General of the United Nations); Myrna Loy (Uranus. Live-wire actress in *The Thin Man* series, U. N. activist); Ramsey Clark (Jupiter. Activist in the arena of foreign policy); Howard Dean (Jupiter. Democratic politician).

2 Capricorn

Seeking refuge from the raging war outside, citizens are gathered within a Gothic cathedral. The mass continues even as one of the church's two rose windows is destroyed by a blast.

Descriptive Phrases

Surviving the blows of fate by spiritually fortifying oneself; feeling embattled vs. putting one's problems in a higher perspective; seeing the big picture vs. getting lost in fragmentary truths (the rose window); abiding by values that will survive the rise and fall of nations; seizing worldly power in order to preserve social institutions (selfishness causes blind spots that may undermine their efforts, can overestimate their understanding and resolve); seeing historical events as moral parables (preachy); seeing eternal archetypes shining through ordinary events; emotional roots that spiral down through time to feed on the immortal truths of an embattled spiritual tradition; standing firm in one's beliefs (propagandists).

Examples

Joseph Smith (Sun. Gnostic Christian, founder of Mormonism); Rush Limbaugh (Mercury, Stationary. Antigovernment talk-show host who lost much credibility after the Oklahoma City bombing); Lyndon Johnson (South Node. Withdrew from office due to weakening resolve over the war in Vietnam); Francis I of France (Neptune. Attacked Renaissance Italy, gravely weakening its political stability); Linda Blair (Saturn. Actress—*The Exorcist*); Nostradamus (Sun. Astrologer, seer, quatrains predicting events in world history); Kevin Spacey (Saturn. Actor—*American Beauty*, with its themes of thwarted desire and karmic comeuppance); Marcia Starck (Sun. Medical astrologer, inner dousing); Warwick Deeping (Jupiter. Wrote a novel based on his World War I experiences); Ermingildo Florit (Chiron. Archbishop of Florence); Bloody Mary (Pluto. Fanatical campaign to reestablish Catholicism in England); Aimée Semple McPherson (Jupiter. High-living evangelist); David Carradine (Jupiter. Actor—*Kung Fu*, seeker).

3 Capricorn

By the light of a lantern, a man toils over an unfinished work of philosophy.

Descriptive Phrases

Working out the full implications of one's philosophy or beliefs; deep reflection; taking an important idea to its logical conclusion (paint themselves into a corner, overgeneralize from a few facts); looking at life's deeper problems with intelligence and insight (suspicious of easy answers, make life difficult for themselves); foresight—seeing how a certain line of thought will play itself out; taking a chance on expressing some new facet of oneself vs. clinging to a safe but limited self-image; existentialism (feel isolated and weird, may withdraw emotionally); learning the hard lessons of love vs. jumping from one disillusioning relationship to another; holding high personal standards (social critics, illuminate social hypocrisy); shining the light of understanding on the human condition.

Examples

Voltaire (Saturn. Enlightenment philosopher, satirist); Lillian Hellman (Uranus. Author—*The Little Foxes*); Jean-Paul Sartre (Uranus. Existentialist philosopher); Ayn Rand (Uranus. Philosopher of individualism—*Atlas Shrugged*); George Orwell (Uranus. Political novelist—*Animal Farm*); Charles Hermite (Sun. Mathematician—devised the formula for continuous reduction); Robert Musil (Moon. Author—*The Man without Qualities*); Karen Bolander (Jupiter. Jungian psychologist, astrologer); Jean Anouilh (Moon. Writer whose characters choose isolation over traditional life); H. H. Kung (North Node. Liberal theologian); Tom Robbins (North Node. Writer—*Even Cowgirls Get the Blues*); Thomas Mann (Mars. Writer—*The Magic Mountain*); Ngaio Marsh (North Node. Mystery writer—*Overture to Death*); George Santayana (Mercury. Philosopher—*The Life of Reason*).

4 Capricorn

Pandora stands with her back to a mysterious black chest, her hand resting on its lid. Later, she is seen on her knees, looking through the chest's keyhole.[37]

Descriptive Phrases

The fascination of the forbidden or the unknown; being drawn into something negative vs. putting a lid on unwholesome desires; distaste for whatever "smells bad" vs. attraction to decadent or curious lore; prying out people's secrets, yet knowing how to guard a secret for perpetuity if need be; respecting others' privacy vs. creating mistrust by prying; picking up on occult or sexual subcurrents; navigating the dark waters of the subconscious (shamanism, magic); getting one's bearings by nailing down emotional or occult truths vs. being taken in by plausible stories; examining flaws in one's reality-set; needling other people's hollow assumptions; stealing glimpses of a hidden reality (louche or off-color art); social trespass.

Examples

Rod Serling (Sun. Writer and director of *The Twilight Zone*); Carlos Castaneda (Sun. Modern-day shaman, author of *Don Juan* books on Mexican sorcery); Annie Lennox (Sun. Fiercely private lead singer of The Eurhythmics, made the charts with "Sweet Dreams Are Made of This"); Sir Richard Burton (Uranus, Neptune. Adventurer who disguised himself and penetrated the brothels of the Near East, writing an explicit account of their sexual practices); Goethe (Mars. Poet, author of *Faust*, where the principal sells his soul to the devil to gain knowledge); Alice Toklas (Jupiter. Lesbian lover of Gertrude Stein, aficionado of hash brownies); Régine (Saturn. Disco entrepreneur); J. Edgar Hoover (Ascendant. Longtime head of the FBI who collected stories on practically everyone, may have been a closeted homosexual); Arnold Schwarzenegger (Moon. Actor—*Conan the Barbarian*, murky sexual history, governor of California); Karl Abraham (Jupiter. Freudian psychologist); Dick Cavett (Venus. Inquisitive talk-show host, social gatekeeper).

5 Capricorn

Indian brave in a war bonnet watches the tribe's children playing cowboys and Indians. He joins them momentarily, raising his tomahawk and leading a wild charge.

Descriptive Phrases

The untamed or natural man, who is at one with his instincts and impulses (moral childishness); following the law of one's own being (uncompromising in who they are and what they believe); bold decisiveness; leading some political or spiritual cause; knowing, through keen foresight, which battles can be won (on the warpath, decisive and sometimes violent removal of obstacles to progress); looking to the future (concern for children); preparing for a social role, especially a leadership role, through imaginative play (children's games, silly shticks, blowing off steam); emotionally psyching a crowd to join in a major enterprise; keeping one's mind on the task at hand vs. splitting off into side issues (fascistic demand for unity); studying the laws of history or the laws of nature, and living by them.

Examples

Milton Berle (South Node. Variety-show comic); Steve Allen (Sun. Comedian—*The Steve Allen Show*, activist who tried to remove sex and violence from television); Shari Lewis (Venus. Puppeteer for a children's TV show); Joe E. Ross (Uranus. Comic actor—Sgt. Toody on *Car 54, Where Are You?*); Ru Paul (Jupiter. Ultrasuccessful Black drag queen); Ronald Reagan (Mars. Cowboy actor, cowboy president); Ed Gein (Uranus. Savage serial killer); Kevin Costner (North Node. Actor—*Dances with Wolves*); Charles Dickens (Saturn. Writer—*Oliver Twist, David Copperfield*); Hannah Arendt (Uranus. Radical political philosopher—*Origins of Totalitarianism, On Violence*); Henry Miller (Sun. Sexual primitive, writer—*Tropic of Cancer, Crazy Cock*); Mao Tse-tung (Sun. Communist revolutionary, political and cultural dictator); Robin Rose (Moon. Actress—*An Enemy of the People*).

6 Capricorn

From under a brick archway, a hunter peers into an ancient forest. A strange little man appears beside him and gives him tips about the maze of paths through the forest.

Descriptive Phrases

Venturing into dangerous new territory and having to learn a new set of rules; aiding those who are ill-prepared for life in either the material or spiritual realms (Chiron as the guide beyond Saturn's wall to more unconscious outer-planetary energies); clowning around—humorously puncturing rigid belief systems (dirty tricks, lead people in circles); adapting to different psychic environments, as at work, at home, or in foreign countries; using one's animal instincts in new situations without being led around by them (dubious companions goad one beyond one's bounds; extricating oneself from some vortex, sexual misadventures); examining an anomaly that may be the key to some new breakthrough; problem-solving vs. going over the same bumpy road again and again.

Examples

Ella Young (Saturn. Writer—*Celtic Wonder Tales*); Johannes Kepler (Mercury. Astronomer who figured out that planetary orbits are elliptical from deviations in his data); Anne Francis (Saturn. Actress—*The Blackboard Jungle, Twilight Zone* episodes); Sean Connery (Saturn. Actor—*James Bond* movies, *Time Bandits*); Marlene Dietrich (Sun. Vamp actress—*The Blue Angel, Touch of Evil*); Dennis Hopper (North Node. Actor—*Easy Rider, Waterworld*); Edward Peters (North Node. Historian of the witch hunts); Giles Healey (Chiron. Astrologer who discovered Mayan ruins in Bonampak); Jerry Seinfeld (Mars. Comedian who lives comfortably in the midst of crazy complications); Groucho Marx (Mars. Zany comedian); Gracie Fields (Mars. Zany comedienne); William James (Mars. Psychologist—*Varieties of Religious Experience*); Jacques Lacan (Chiron. Psychoanalyst, deconstructionist); Marcel Proust (Saturn. Writer—*Remembrance of Things Past*).

7 Capricorn

Populist hero, being tried for a capital offense, delivers a resonating, emotional appeal. The executioner looms in the background, a black hood over his face.

Descriptive Phrases

Standing one's ground and proving oneself; taking up one's destined role in life and playing it as if one's life depended on it; charisma based on physical and psychic domination (dictatorial, bully others into submission); doing whatever is necessary to prevail (immoral expedients); picking up on and voicing the passions of the public; forcing people to admit what they already feel (may give people what they want rather than what they need, may even manipulate mass fear and hatred); sincere oratory vs. sly humbuggery; heart-to-heart talks vs. sardonic detachment (depressive, emotionally negative); ability to project not only one's role, but the whole reality behind it (use costume to elicit a desired response); getting on top and staying on top; heroic grandstanding.

Examples

Denzel Washington (Sun. Actor—*Hurricane, Malcolm X*); Yukio Mishima (Jupiter. Ultranationalist writer—*Confessions of a Mask*); Aimée Semple McPherson (South Node. Glamorous preacher with a wild private life); Mobutu (Saturn. President of Zaire who came to power through a military coup and headed a corrupt government); Helen Keller (North Node. Blind and deaf but became a socialist propagandist); Tracy Chapman (South Node. Folk singer, political themes); Adolf Hitler (Moon. Dictator who played upon the resentments of the masses); Dietrich Bonhoeffer (Uranus. Lutheran minister, actively opposed Nazis, died in a concentration camp); Stephen Dorff (North Node. Actor—*Cecil B. Demented, Blade*); Steve Martin (South Node. Glib-tongued comedian in the mold of a phony preacher, white suit and lots of props); Karen Black (Moon. Scary actress—*Eternal Evil, Nashville, Night Angel*); Federico Chabaud (Jupiter. Historian—Machiavelli expert); Lorne Greene (Venus. Actor—*Bonanza, Battlestar Galactica*).

8 Capricorn

A Chinese gentleman holds a birdcage within a beam of sunlight. Inside, a canary sings cheerfully oblivious to the cage's open door.

Descriptive Phrases

Circumspection; choosing one's options carefully; joy that accompanies freedom from guilt and worry; assessing one's talents carefully before boldly pushing oneself forward (lack of resolve); finding an appreciative audience (parlor acts—songbirds with beautiful voices); being self-defined vs. worrying about others' opinions; cleverly evading society's attempts to confine one to a single role, while successfully performing one's duties to family and society (hemmed in by self-imposed responsibilities); making oneself comfortable in one's environment, including one's body; expressing one's spiritual identity within everyday situations; spreading one's wings vs. finding a comfortable landing spot; attending to one's spiritual wellbeing.

Examples

Lucille Ball (Moon. "Tweety Bird" actress—*I Love Lucy*); Amos Bronson Alcott (Moon. Leader of an intellectual salon that included Emerson and Hawthorne); Emma Thompson (Saturn, Stationary. Actress—*Sense and Sensibility*); Jeanette Rankin (North Node. Women's rights leader); Mary Tyler Moore (Sun. Actress—semiliberated housewife on *The Dick Van Dyke Show*); Del Shannon (Sun. Singer—"Runaway"); Ulysses S. Grant (Uranus. Union general); Woodrow Wilson (Sun. U. S. president during World War I); Emma Destinn (Moon. Operatic soprano); Elisabeth Schwarzkopf (Venus. Operatic soprano); Don Johnson (Mercury. TV actor—*Miami Vice*, married to "canary" Melanie Griffith); Suffragettes arrested while picketing the White House (North Node. 8/28/1917, their maltreatment in jail was a turning point in the struggle for women's right to vote); Sir William Cecil (Pluto. Lord treasurer, chief minister and mentor to Queen Elizabeth I); Eiffel Tower opened to the public (Jupiter. 3/31/1889—cage-like structure that is finally opened); Meher Baba (Mars. Guru—"Don't worry, be happy!").

9 Capricorn

On a rocky crag backdropped by the stars, a shining woman is standing with a national flag draped over one shoulder and a lyre in her hand. A man is climbing, enraptured, toward the light.

Descriptive Phrases

Political and social visionaries; blazing a path toward a new national ideal (the woman as the soul of the nation); quasi-religious reverence for one's country; bolstering vs. undermining the strength of the nation; joining sensible policy analysis with idealism vs. heading for a fall when one is tempted by ungrounded fantasies (know-it-alls with bad blind spots); following one's ideals, whatever the obstacles; drawing others into one's vision with magnetic personal charm and an attunement to the needs of the time; striking the right chord with the public (offer new role models); sudden glimpses of personal or national destiny; seeing a divine hand in simple events (rise in life by being in the right place at the right time); cosmic attunement; wonder; Lyra and Vega.

Examples

Ross Perot (Saturn. Industrialist who founded the Reform Party); Oscar Romero (North Node. Archbishop critical of human rights abuses in El Salvador; was murdered); Gloria Steinem (North Node. Feminist leader); Robert Bly (Venus. Poet, men's movement leader); Mary Tyler Moore (Mercury. Early representative of the single career woman on TV); Joanne Woodward (Saturn. Actress—*Three Faces of Eve*); Rudyard Kipling (Sun. Poet, fiction writer—*Captains Courageous*); Sulamith Wulfing (Saturn. Illustrator—magical pictures with many angels in them); Johannes Kepler (Uranus. Visionary astronomer); Patti Smith (Sun. Proto-punk singer); Otto von Bismarck (Moon. Visionary nationalist who united Germany); Hugo Black (Moon. Supreme Court justice who championed individual rights); Anthony Blunt (Uranus. Art historian, spy); Thomas Mattingly (North Node. Historian—*The Armada*); Arnold Toynbee (Jupiter. Historian who studied the rise and fall of civilizations); Adolf Hitler (Jupiter. Charismatic German tyrant).

10 Capricorn

Having seen his brother crush the wing of an albatross, a sailor decides to adopt the bird and have its wing put in a splint.

Descriptive Phrases

Squarely facing life's graver problems; indomitability of spirit; perseverance and pluck (depression); empathic identification with other people (meddlesome—try to force people into their own molds); correcting one's flaws through willpower; integrating one's personality vs. sweeping problems under the rug (rejected components form negative personality fragments—Dr. Jekyll and Mr. Hyde); remaking oneself; withdrawing and reemerging with a reconstructed identity (comebacks); developing forbearance and forgiveness vs. blindness to everything but one's own ego-needs; appreciating one's interconnectedness with the rest of the world; uniting the world in mutual forgiveness and aid; humaneness vs. desensitization and emotional coarseness.

Examples

Ernest Hemingway (Moon. Writer—*The Old Man and the Sea*, suicide); Bette Davis (South Node. Actress—*Now, Voyager, Dead Ringer*); Frances Chichester (Saturn, Stationary. Traveled around the world in a small sailboat, authored *The Lonely Sea and the Sky*); Joanne Woodward (Saturn. Actress—*Three Faces of Eve*); Dana Delaney (Mars. Actress who played a military nurse on *China Beach*); Simon Wiesenthal (Sun. Tracked down Nazis who were still at large); Anthony Hopkins (Sun. Actor—*The Elephant Man, Silence of the Lambs*); Patti Smith (Mars. Pained proto-punk rock singer—"Gone Again"); Tom Wolfe (Saturn. Writer—*Bonfire of the Vanities*); Odetta (Sun. Folk singer); Gerard Croiset (Mars. Psychic who finds missing persons); Maureen Reagan (Mercury. Domestic violence activist); André Malraux (Mercury. Novelist—*Man's Fate*, fought in the French Resistance).

11 Capricorn

A group of noblewomen on horseback, unaware that a gentleman is watching them from behind some trees. When the prettiest woman dismounts, he catches sight of her copper petticoats, which are quickly hidden as she meets his eye.

Descriptive Phrases

Keen perceptivity; penetrating beyond surface appearances; catching a flash of something magical from another level (sci-fi, surrealism); developing one's talents; distilling the more significant details of experience in literature or art; artistic veils that both reveal and conceal one's inner world (figure and ground); seductive physical beauty; courtship games (coquetry); disarming candor vs. discrete intimations; discovering if you are both on the same page before making a move (give mixed signals); deciding who one belongs with and who one doesn't belong with vs. being loyal to one's own social set; standing out vs. fitting in (being a variant on an attractive "type"); vain preening vs. developing inner riches; personal distinction; discernment.

Examples

James Frazer (Sun. Mythologist—*The Golden Bough*); Henri Matisse (Sun. Linear painter, leader of the Fauve school); Berthe Morisot (Mercury. Impressionist painter); Robert Heinlein (Uranus. Sci-fi author—*Stranger in a Strange Land*); Rudyard Kipling (Jupiter. Poet, author—*Kim, The Jungle Book*); Ellen Degeneres (Sun. Comic actress who "came out" on her TV show, *Ellen*); Burt Reynolds (North Node. Red-neck actor—*Smokey and the Bandit*, posed seminude); Isabella Rossellini (Chiron. Actress—*Blue Velvet, Death Becomes Her*); Barbara Stanwyck (Mars, Uranus. Actress); Maurice Béjart (Sun. Choreographer); Sarah Vaughn (Moon. Jazz singer); Tracy Cabot (Mars. Self-help author—*How to Make a Man Fall in Love with You*); Elizabeth Montgomery (Moon. Actress—Samantha on *Bewitched*); Erwin Panofsky (Mars. Art historian, expert on Hermetic symbolism).

12 Capricorn

In a speakeasy, a handsome man in a double-breasted suit puts moves on a young flapper.

Descriptive Phrases

Sexual adventurousness; seductive charm (fast, rakish); understanding the psychology of the opposite sex, and its roots in biology; knowing how things operate beneath social façades; being gallant and well-mannered vs. pushing things past the limits of reputability (unscrupulous gamesters in the war of the sexes—tricking someone into marrying you vs. tricking someone into having casual sex with you); being in control vs. being a slave to one's desires (sociopathic tendencies); encountering chaotic situations with aplomb; being open to all of life's crazy possibilities; jumping on opportunities vs. being blindsided by nasty surprises; creative improvisation; living in the moment; getting into a good groove; mischievous hijinks; living the high life.

Examples

Max Fleischer (South Node. Cartoonist—*Betty Boop*); John Astin (Saturn. Actor—Gomez on *The Addams Family*); Steve McQueen (Saturn. Smouldering, violent leading man—*The Great Escape*); Dorothy Provine (Jupiter. Star of TV's *The Roaring Twenties*); Geena Davis (Mercury, Stationary. Actress—*Earth Girls Are Easy*); Jack Lemmon (Jupiter. Actor—*Some Like It Hot*); Jim Bakker (Sun. Televangelist, ruined by sexual affair and later sent to jail); Louis Armstrong (Saturn. Jazz trumpeter, singer, early career in the red-light district of New Orleans); Eva Le Gallienne (Moon. Theater teacher who founded the New York Civic Rep); Frank Sinatra (Mercury. Bobby-sox singing idol with many glamorous wives; mob connections); Mia Farrow (Moon. Actress—*Broadway Danny Rose, Radio Days*); Jane Russell (Moon. Smoulderingly sexual movie star, her autobiography is titled *My Path and My Detours*); Roberto Benigni (Mars. Comic actor—*Johnny Stecchino, The Monster*); Clark Gable (Saturn. Actor—*It Happened One Night*); Dean Martin (North Node. Crooner and *bon vivant*).

13 Capricorn

Standing by a campfire, a general outlines the tactical situation to his aide-de-camp and discusses the upcoming campaign.

Descriptive Phrases

Giving the problem at hand one's complete focus; collecting new data and boiling it down to something usable; analytical clarification based on the elimination of extraneous factors; figuring out how things fit together; being certain of one's conclusions (ideologues); self-consistency of thought and action; physical or intellectual self-reliance vs. finding a good helpmate; apprenticing the best and eliminating the slackers (subordinate others to the execution of their own goals, secure allies by "sacrificing to their gods"); passing the torch of tradition to a new generation (interest in ancient religious traditions); concentrating one's efforts through chastity of life (Vesta as guardian of the fires of inmost conviction); patriotism based on a love of the land; naturalism and environmentalism.

Examples

John Fremont (Saturn. Explorer of the Oregon Trail); Rachel Carson (Uranus. Early environmentalist—*Silent Spring*); Baldur von Schirach (Uranus. Head of Hitler Youth); Virginia Johnson (Jupiter. Sex researcher—"Masters and Johnson Report"); Stonewall Jackson (Uranus. Confederate general); John Wayne (Uranus. Star of cowboy movies); I. F. Stone (Uranus. Radical journalist who did his own research); David Lindberg (Mars. Historian of science who specializes in Kepler's optics); Brett Favre (Mars. Quarterback); Ansel Adams (Chiron. Photographer of wilderness scenes); Vincent Van Gogh (Chiron. Post-impressionist who depicts the fire within natural forms); Charlene Spretnak (Moon. Feminist author—*The Lost Goddesses of Ancient Greece*); First Congress of the Confederate States of America (Uranus. 7/20/1861); Marsilio Ficino (Moon. Renaissance translator of the *Hermetica* and Plato's dialogues); John F. Kennedy (North Node. U. S. president—"The torch has been passed.").

14 Capricorn

Freed from a tangle of overgrowth, an ancient monument covered with hieroglyphics reveals secrets about human civilization.[38]

Descriptive Phrases

Attempts to arrive at the single correct interpretation of underlying reality; language as the basis of one's reality-picture; defining one's terms and clarifying one's meaning; inventing or translating a language; deep vs. superficial readings of reality; cutting through a tangle of attractive myths and illusions to uncover the truth about society; exposing coverups; catching others in lies and inaccuracies; pointing out the flaws in a position; coming up with a new formulation that undermines or overthrows an old cultural paradigm; abandoning shaky, outdated positions and building on a more solid foundation vs. dabbling in unsupported speculations; research in physics, genetics, archaeology, history, or linguistics; deciphering vs. encrypting.

Examples

James Spader (Saturn, Venus. Actor—*Stargate*, about a giant ring of hieroglyphs that opens a door to ancient Egypt on another planet); Baron Georges Cuvier (Pluto. Groundbreaking comparative anatomist, reconstructed fossil skeletons of extinct animals); Napoleon Bonaparte (Pluto. His expedition to Egypt led to the discovery of the Rosetta Stone); Isaac Newton (Sun. Scientific genius, tried to reconstruct ancient history through a study of the Bible); J. R. R. Tolkien (Sun. Fantasy writer—*Lord of the Rings*, invented a language to go with his fantasy world); Louis Braille (Sun. Blind organist, invented Braille as a language for the blind); Sallie Nichols (Uranus. Author of a book on the tarot from the Jungian perspective); Gore Vidal (Jupiter. Radical political analyst); Ivan Illich (radical critic of American education); Chernobyl nuclear power plant meltdown (Mars. 4/26/1986); Vanessa Redgrave (Jupiter. Radical actress); Arlene Dahl (Jupiter. Astrologer, actress—*Journey to the Center of the Earth*); Johnny Depp (Moon. Actor—*The Ninth Gate*, and the bush-trimming mutant in *Edward Scissorhands*).

15 Capricorn

A doctor at a pediatric hospital, sporting a bow tie and a checked suit, does a soft-shoe routine to cheer up a group of recovering children.

Descriptive Phrases

Recognizing the importance of a cheery, optimistic attitude in facing life's crises; recovery; getting back on track after a trauma; emotionally digesting a problem or helping others to do so; dispelling gloom, fear, and self-pity by lifting people's spirits (entertainers); admonishing people to look at the funny side of life's problems (preachy); droll observations on self-defeating attitudes and behavior (play the fool, but to a purpose); bridging misunderstandings between people or nations; patiently working through other people's fearful projections until one makes a connection; dealing with other people's emotional or physical scars with gentleness and compassion; resourcefulness—trying various solutions until one finally succeeds; savvy resilience.

Examples

Diane Keaton (Sun. Actress—*Annie Hall*, director—*Unstrung Heroes*); Claude Steiner (Sun. Pop psychologist—*Scripts People Live By*); Milton Erickson (Saturn. Hypnotherapist); Kaye Ballard (Venus. Singer, vaudeville comic); Shari Lewis (Mercury. Gentle puppeteer on TV's *Shari Lewis Show*); W. C. Fields (North Node. Vaudeville juggler, bumbling film comedian); Konrad Adenauer (Sun. German chancellor from 1949 to 1963 who led the country from reconstruction to prosperity); Charles Dederich (Jupiter. Established Synanon drug rehab program); Alexander Graham Bell (Mars. Inventor of the telephone, taught deaf children); Walt Disney (Saturn. Cartoonist, creator of Disneyland amusement park); Chuck Sewell (Moon. Test pilot who survived five crashes); Claude Levi-Strauss (Uranus. Anthropologist); Hyacinthe Vincent (Moon. Physician who developed serums against typhoid); Jimmy Hatlo (North Node. Cartoonist—*They'll Do It Every Time*).

16 Capricorn

Turbaned guru explains a path to higher awareness, while his assistant walks among the meditating disciples and prods them into the correct yogic posture.

Descriptive Phrases

Spiritual teaching; shedding light on the inner meaning of external events; authoritative analysis and commentary; refining and crystallizing one's intuitive knowledge through concrete tests; working out a complex system of belief (base their views on a belief in God as an omnipresent spiritual intelligence); developing one's insight by exercising one's mind (the mind as a muscle whose powers are largely untapped); discipline of the body that is the foundation for the discipline of the mind (yoga); unfolding innate capabilities through practice; seeking the guidance of the spiritually evolved vs. teaching others what one knows (demand formal recognition for their superior intellectual or spiritual gifts; status seekers); mind-body science.

Examples

Manley P. Hall (Saturn. Leading Theosophist—*Spiritual Centers in Man*); William Gray (Jupiter. Expert on the Cabala—*Ladder of Lights*); Johannes Kepler (Sun. Astronomer and astrologer who solved the problem of the planets by refining a vision of nested Platonic solids); Eusapia Paladino (Vertex. Materializing medium); Bhagwan Sri Rajneesh (Moon. Controversial guru—tantric approach, psychic abilities); Annie Sprinkle (North Node. Porn star, sexual guru); Alexander Scriabin (Sun. Mystical composer—synesthesia); John Lilly (Sun, Mercury. Experimenter with awareness techniques, LSD, and communication with dolphins); Steven Forrest (Sun. Astrologer, astrology teacher); Werner Heisenberg (Jupiter. Physicist—Heisenberg uncertainty principle); Sandy Denny (Sun. Folk singer—Fairport Convention); Milton Erickson (Jupiter. Hypnotherapist); Richard Helms (Jupiter. CIA director, guardian of state secrets); Jane Fonda (Mercury. Radical spokesperson often under government surveillance, created workout videos); Sri Aurobindo (Saturn. Guru, poet).

17 Capricorn

A naked woman bathes in a moonlit woodland pool. Freeing her mind of her daytime concerns and self-image, she begins to see pictures forming in the shining water.

Descriptive Phrases

Nurturing and protecting a private relationship with God; dedicating oneself to an inner vision (saintliness, sacrificing oneself for others); visualization—accessing images from the superconscious mind that feed and refresh the soul; inspiring people by holding forth on their hearts' most cherished images (persuasive political or religious allegory); dramatic invocation of ideals; purifying the emotions; "stripping" the mind by shedding waking preconceptions (ungrounded); seeing the open-endedness of reality vs. being sucked in by convention; knowing what to take seriously and what not to take seriously (satirical attack on superficial conventions, playing the fool); visionary political or spiritual leadership.

Examples

Arthur Rimbaud (Chiron. Symbolist poet—*Letters from the Seer*); Bernadette of Lourdes (Sun. Vision of the Virgin Mary); Eusapia Paladino (Chiron. Materializing medium); Adolf Hitler (South Node. Invoked the German *volkgeist* to become Germany's most powerful leader, crazy); Pandit Nehru (North Node. Nationalist Indian leader); Bob Marley (South Node. Legendary Jamaican reggae singer, very political); Anne Bancroft (Saturn. Actress—*The Miracle Worker, Agnes of God*); Jimmy Stewart (Uranus. Actor—*Shenandoah, Mr. Smith Goes to Washington*); Girolamo Savonarola (Moon. Fire-and-brimstone Renaissance preacher, prophecies, many of which came true); Anna Magnani (Uranus. "Force-of-nature" actress—*Il Miracolo*); Alberto Moravia (South Node. Writer of antifascist allegories); Anita Ekberg (Saturn. Actress—*La Dolce Vita*, famous for a scene in which Ekberg walks fully clothed into a fountain); Girolamo Cardano (Neptune. Renaissance physician and astrologer, entertained himself with hypnogogic visions as a child).

18 Capricorn

Amid heavy shelling, a destroyer bears down on an enemy ship, the captain standing resolutely at the helm.

Descriptive Phrases

Ironclad determination to get what one wants from life (selfish); mobilizing one's energy toward a goal; making one's intentions known vs. sneaky maneuvers (don't buy into the rules of polite society, lawless methods); keeping a cool head amid complete mayhem (panicked chases); coming onto a scene from out of nowhere vs. going off in the wrong direction; battleship diplomacy (personal charm united with physical intimidation); physical self-confidence (brawlers, troublemakers); having "balls" vs. feeling castrated; strong physical or sexual presence (animal magnetism); sexual aggressiveness (led around by their genitals; looking for cheap pickups, like a sailor on shore leave); having an explosive impact vs. being blown out of the water; relentlessness.

Examples

George Washington (Moon. Revolutionary general, first president of United States—Washington crossing the Delaware); Joan of Arc (Venus. Political revolutionary with a religious vision); Boris Yeltsin (Saturn. Russian leader); Marlon Brando (Mars. Macho actor—*On the Waterfront*, *Last Tango in Paris*); Marlene Dietrich (Saturn. Actress—*The Blue Angel*, anti-Nazi, affairs with both sexes); Burt Reynolds (Venus. Macho actor—*Smokey and the Bandit*); Tom Selleck (Mars. Macho actor); Cathy Moriarty (Venus. Actress, comic hard-boiled roles—*Soapdish*); Jimmy Page (Mercury. Lead guitarist of Led Zeppelin, into Aleister Crowley); Tom Laughlin (Saturn. Actor, director of *Billy Jack* films); Herschell Lewis (South Node. Director of gore films); Jeffrey Dahmer (Saturn. Sexual sadist, murderer, cannibal); Elvis Presley (Sun. Highly sexual rock idol); Simone de Beauvoir (Sun. Trailblazing feminist writer—*The Second Sex*); Isabel Peron (Saturn. Dancehall girl who became president of Argentina).

19 Capricorn

An orphan huddles next to a shopping cart containing all of her possessions. She hugs herself and sings a little song.

Descriptive Phrases

Hardy self-sufficiency; looking after oneself physically and spiritually from a very early age (early loss of safe surroundings); rising above fate by competently handling life's low points; realistically sizing up the needs of one's own situation, and of the larger human situation; taking on the problems of the collective (what goes around comes around); nurturing others vs. emotional neediness and insistent begging for affection (adorable mugging, gaminlike antics); knowing what physical and emotional resources one can depend on from one's family and what one needs to get for oneself (feel alone in the world); coaxing people to drop their pretenses and get real emotionally vs. emotional armoring; holding on to one's heart in brutal situations.

Examples

Joan Baez (Sun. Folk singer); Marilyn Monroe (South Node. Comic actress who passed through several foster homes as a child); James Dean (Saturn. Actor—*Rebel without a Cause*); Will Rogers (North Node. Cowboy raconteur, amateur philosopher); Bob Denver (Sun. Actor who played the beatnik on *The Dobey Gillis Show* and Gilligan on *Gilligan's Island*); Cher (Moon. Singer, actress—*Mask*, highly publicized problems with her daughter); Allen Ginsberg (South Node. Poet—*Howl*); Darla Hood (Saturn. Child actress—*Little Rascals*); Andy Griffith (South Node. Actor—*The Andy Griffith Show*); Ann Jillian (Mercury. Actress—*Gypsy*, spokesperson for breast cancer research); Robert Stone (Jupiter. Writer—*Dog Soldiers*, about the misuse of soldiers in the Vietnam War); Mary Martin (Jupiter. Actress—*Peter Pan*); Tyron Marble (Neptune. Baby born on the subway); Trey Parker (Mars. Comic writer—*South Park*); Tom Courtenay (Jupiter. Actor—*The Loneliness of the Long-Distance Runner*).

20 Capricorn

A preacher delivers a sermon to his congregation, but is rattled when he sees his mistress emerge from the door of the basement. He looks toward his wife and inwardly vows to break off the affair.

Descriptive Phrases

Fidelity vs. infidelity to ideals; subordinating ephemeral pleasures to the permanent values of a serious relationship; trying to be an ideal parent or spouse vs. feeling trapped in social roles devoid of true feeling (seek release in adultery or a secret sex life); exercising sensitivity and prudence in human relations vs. sidling by a problem at work or in marriage; sizing up a bad situation and taking action (productive showdowns); facing one's psychological shadow internally vs. encountering it in unexpected forms in one's outer life; integrating one's desires with one's social mask; purging one's life of secret sources of moral guilt vs. being exposed as a hypocrite; reinforcing one's values by preaching them vs. teaching others by the example of one's life.

Examples

Hugh Beaumont (Uranus. Actor—played the ideal father and husband on *Leave It to Beaver*); June Lockhart (Jupiter. Played the ideal mom on *Lassie*); Linda Lovelace (Sun. Porn star—*Deep Throat*); Rock Hudson (Jupiter. Actor—light romantic comedies, closeted gay who continued having sex after he knew he had AIDS); Richard Nixon (Sun. Moralistic president up to many dirty tricks, maintained a good marriage); Matt Cvetic (Uranus. FBI spy who infiltrated the Communist Party, fooling even his wife); Dustin Hoffman (Jupiter. Actor—*The Graduate, Midnight Cowboy*); Lisa Kudrow (South Node. Actress—*Friends, The Opposite of Sex*); Oscar Wilde (Jupiter. Closeted gay playwright—*The Importance of Being Earnest, The Portrait of Dorian Gray*); Anaïs Nin (Chiron. Diarist with a frankly libertine sexuality); Jane Austen (Mars. Novelist of human relations—*Sense and Sensibility*); Beatrice Arthur (South Node. Played a liberated, not-so-ideal wife on *Maude*).

21 Capricorn

After a court battle, a citizen's group listens to an official spokesperson outline the newly reformed government policy.[39]

Descriptive Phrases

Attunement to the ideas, feelings, and needs of the public; articulating the public will in the political or cultural arena; playing to the crowd (demagoguery, blinded by class loyalties); negotiating the rights and duties of the people toward the government and the government toward the people; taking a hard look at the system to see whether it is working, or whether it is just paying lip service to its ideals; fighting for social justice; drumming up working alliances, like labor unions or political movements vs. being a tool of government repression (political hacks); breaking through a political, cultural, or mental obstacle; arriving at a new level vs. backsliding or failing to carry through on gains; dynamic leadership based on competence and expertise.

Examples

Rita Mae Brown (South Node. Lesbian writer—*Rubyfruit Jungle*); Arthur Scargill (Sun. British miner's union president); Robert F. Kennedy (Jupiter. Attorney general under JFK, civil-rights advocate); Orval Faubus (Uranus. Governor of Arkansas, tried to prevent school integration); Russian serfs are freed (North Node. 3/3/1861); Linda Jenness (Sun, Mercury. Socialist Workers' Party candidate for president); Pope John Paul XXIII (Moon. Pope who presided over Vatican II); Odetta (Chiron. Folk and protest singer); Albert Hofmann (Sun. Chemist—discoverer of LSD); Norman Stevens (Moon. Psychic, teaches how to build a bodily light-channel in *The Rainbow Bridge*); André Breton (Mars. Founder of surrealism, radically antibourgeois); Dr. Alfred Wallace (Venus, Mercury. Natural historian—early theory of evolution); Joe Hill (North Node. IWW organizer, framed and executed).

22 Capricorn

In the gladiatorial arena, two men armed with swords are locked in mortal combat, the first a foul-mouthed slave, the second an aristocrat.

Descriptive Phrases

Aggressively forwarding one's own interests without compromising one's moral principles; taking up a social or political cause; jumping into the fray (swashbuckling, devil-may-care self-confidence); rising to the occasion; doing what needs doing or what one wants to do, apart from any thought of further reward (mercenary, need to examine their deeper motives); crossing swords with others in argument (fighting honestly by remaining open and interested in the other side of the argument vs. arrogantly dismissing correctives and advice); playing the situation as it lies; unprejudiced assessment of obstacles and adversaries; getting a handle on a perplexing situation vs. confusion and inability to act; backtracking or trying a new approach when an approach meets with failure; moral decisiveness.

Examples

Kirk Douglas (North Node. Actor—*Spartacus*, *Seven Days in May*, self-made man, fought to end the Hollywood blacklist); Danny DeVito (South Node. Actor—*Mars Attacks*, *Ruthless People*); Gypsy Rose Lee (Uranus. Exotic dancer); Nat Hentoff (Jupiter. *Village Voice* columnist, free speech, education advocate); Golda Meir (North Node. Israeli Prime Minister, social activist, politically ruined by Arab surprise attack in 1973); Robert E. Lee (Jupiter. Confederate general); Rita Moreno (Saturn. Singer, dancer—*West Side Story*); Patrick Oliphant (North Node. Slashing political cartoonist); Bonnie Parker (Uranus. Outlaw—Bonnie and Clyde); Alexander Hamilton (Sun. U. S. treasurer who died in a duel with Aaron Burr); Loretta Swit (Jupiter. Actress—*M*A*S*H*); Judy Collins (Mars. Folk singer, political activist—*Marat Sade*); William Shatner (Saturn. Actor—*Star Trek*); Archie Moore (Jupiter. Light-heavyweight boxing champ, often tricked his opponent by feigning weakness).

23 Capricorn

A respected leader pushes his way to the podium and delivers a rousing oration to a group of citizens.

Descriptive Phrases

Gaining a forum for one's views; having a respected public voice; rising to the top of one's field through competent performance and sober judgment; leadership in the political, social, or spiritual realms; educating the public on issues of general concern; having the answers to people's questions; unifying people around a course of action by sharing a simple analysis, illustrated by moral parables; speaking from the heart in a way that resonates with the public; oratorical ability (resonant singing voice); lighting a fire under people (use or misuse of kundalini energy—get burned when they misuse it (psychism, mysticism); developing and using one's powers without betraying the public trust; deciding whether to seek spiritual or political solutions to man's fallen state; giving voice to one's views vs. being constrained by a hostile public.

Examples

Malcolm X (Jupiter. Black radical leader, Black Muslims); Leni Riefenstahl (Saturn. Nazi filmmaker—*Triumph of the Will*); Dr. Benjamin Spock (Chiron. Influential children's doctor); Paul Robeson (North Node. Black singer—*Showboat*, communist); Leonard Nimoy (Saturn. Actor—Spock on *Star Trek*, *In Search of*); Robert Stack (Sun. Actor—*The Untouchables*, *Unsolved Mysteries*); Jeanne Dixon (Chiron. Pop prophet); Pandit Ji Gopi Krishna (Chiron. Writer and teacher on kundalini); Simone Weil (Venus. Leftist labor organizer, religious mystic); Shirley Verrett (Saturn. Operatic mezzo-soprano); Hermann Goering (Sun. Nazi politician second in command to Hitler); Bessie Smith (North Node. Blues singer); Nostradamus (Neptune. Seer); Richard Gere (Jupiter. Actor, Buddhist spokesperson); Brugh Joy (Mercury. Self-healing advocate—*Joy's Way*); Robert Altman (Moon. Film director—*The Player*, *Gosford Park*).

24 Capricorn

Weary of her disorderly life, a woman enters a nunnery, where she receives instruction from the mother superior. In the background, red roses and white lilies grow along the brick walls of the cloister.

Descriptive Phrases

Truth seekers; making sense of one's worldly and erotic experiences from a higher, more mature perspective; seeking spiritually rich, uncomplicated relationships after tiring of crazy erotic intrigues (jaded front may hide a true romantic); finding answers to life's big questions; putting one's finger on arcane truths; challenging false pictures of reality; telling it like it is (confessional); organizing one's life around one's beliefs; finding one's true calling; calmly and diligently carrying out one's life-work; working out the ramifications of one's beliefs vs. settling for the half-baked ideas of a received tradition; intellectual honesty (scientific research—humbly building upon solid details); serving mankind by cultivating a garden of inner truths.

Examples

Oprah Winfrey (Chiron. Talk-show host—spiritual subjects); Marjoe Gortner (Sun. Actor, preacher, reformed scam-artist); Germaine Greer (Mercury. Feminist theorist—*The Female Eunuch*); Jean Genet (Uranus. Homoerotic writer—*Our Lady of the Flowers*); David Niven (Uranus. Actor—*The Pink Panther*, bon vivant, amateur philosopher); Colette (Mercury. Author of risqué novels); Frida Kahlo (South Node. Painter, communist); Georges Lemaitre (Moon. Priest, astronomer, studied the expanding universe); James N. Davidson (Mars. Biochemist—DNA research); Vladimir Lenin (South Node. Communist revolutionary); the Dalai Lama (North Node. Exiled Tibetan spiritual leader); Rip Torn (Mercury. Badass actor—*Tropic of Cancer*); Marshall Applewhite (Saturn. Crazed cult leader—led group suicide); Martin Buber (Jupiter. Freethinking theologian—*I and Thou*, *Paths in Utopia*).

25 Capricorn

A customer in an oriental rug store jumps over a lump that is moving under the carpet he is standing on. In a moment, the scruffy head of the shopkeeper's son pops out from under the edge of the carpet.

Descriptive Phrases

Joyful, creative participation in the ever-changing patterns of life (life as a funhouse); retaining a childlike appreciation of life's kaleidoscopic happenings vs. overlooking new elements as they enter the picture and suffering one misadventure after another; being too involved in a situation to see what's going on vs. gaining enough distance to recognize its larger pattern; being immersed in a confusing sensory whirl vs. detailed analysis from the sidelines (exotic or curious perspectives); making sense of the whole picture by picking out vital connections or details; bringing an argument back to underlying realities; paying attention to underlying causal patterns vs. diving under the sheets and losing oneself in playful sexual revelry.

Examples

Federico Fellini (Moon. Self-indulgent surrealistic film director); Lily Tomlin (Mars. Comedienne—*The Incredible Shrinking Woman*); Warren Beatty (Jupiter. Actor—*Shampoo*); Dick Van Dyke (Jupiter. Actor—*Mary Poppins*); Rainer Fassbinder (Moon. Tawdry filmmaker—*The Marriage of Maria Braun*); Ben Stiller (Venus. Comic actor—*There's Something about Mary, Zoolander*); Kate Jackson (Saturn. Actress—*Charlie's Angels*); Jacques Cousteau (Uranus. Oceanographer); Paul Bowles (Uranus. Adventurer, writer—*The Sheltering Sky*); Pamela Smith (Jupiter. Illustrator of the Waite tarot deck); Fred Ward (Mercury. Actor—*Tremors*); Cary Grant (Chiron. Actor—*North by Northwest*); Neal Cassady (South Node. Beatnik, instigator of roadtrips and crazy adventures); Jean Anouilh (Uranus. Playwright—*The Madwoman of Chaillot*); Elizabeth Ashley (Mars. Actress—*The Carpetbaggers*); Jim Jarmusch (Mercury. Filmmaker—*Mystery Train*); Howlin' Wolf (Uranus. Blues great); Charo (Sun. Hoochy-coochy girl).

26 Capricorn

A radiant sprite kneels by a hole in a rock through which a lake is emptying into a waterfall. Far below, she observes the sordid but strangely attractive world of human passions.

Descriptive Phrases

Maya—the hide-and-seek of the Self from the Self; projecting parts of oneself onto lovers or enemies vs. epiphanic moments where one calms the mind and experiences oneself fully; facing one's psychological problems squarely vs. living within escapist fantasies; refusing to get immersed in the flow of time-bound events vs. deliberately falling from grace in order to experience something fully; balancing the physical and the spiritual sides of the self; mystical romanticism, which gives the spiritual side of love the highest place vs. falling into sordid sexual affairs (live vicariously by observing others); delighting in the rapid flow of emotions and events, and mischievously redirecting them through timely interventions; glimmering reflections of the eternal within the physical.

Examples

Lewis Carroll (Neptune. Author—*Alice in Wonderland*, shot arty photographs of little girls); Mary Martin (Moon. Actress—*Peter Pan*); John Travolta (Chiron. Actor—*Michael*); Patty Hearst (Chiron. Rich princess who was brainwashed into participating in a terrorist organization); Marco Furlan (Sun. Serial killer who targeted prostitutes and gays, and burned down discos); Richard Lester (Saturn. Film director—*Help*); Robert Anton Wilson (Saturn. Author—*The Illuminatus Trilogy*); David Duchovny (Saturn. Actor—*The X-Files, Return to Me*); Eric Segal (Jupiter. Author—*Love Story*); Jane Austen (Pluto. Author—*Sense and Sensibility*); Louisa May Alcott (Neptune. Author—*Little Women*); Eugene O'Neill (South Node. Playwright—*Strange Interlude, Beyond the Horizon*); Christopher Isherwood (Chiron. Novelist, playwright—*Meeting by the River, Goodbye to Berlin, My Guru and Myself*, converted to Vedanta); Peter Weir (South Node. Mystical filmmaker—*Picnic at Hanging Rock*).

27 Capricorn

About to cross the Rockies, the leader of a group of settlers looks appraisingly toward the pass.

Descriptive Phrases

Rugged determination to reach one's goals; long uphill climbs; assessing the feasibility of one's goals before beginning (knowing one's strengths and weaknesses); setting forth in the right season and the right time (being in synch with nature); pacing oneself; setting timetables; modifying one's course as one achieves a better overview; communicating through actions rather than words (want public admiration before they have really accomplished anything, poseurs); eliciting the support and admiration of others, but depending on no one but oneself (play to the crowd, create a public persona and mischievously play off of it); the simplicity of frontier life, where necessities dictate actions and actions dictate thought; sunny perseverance; being good for the long haul.

Examples

Thomas Jefferson (Uranus. Revolutionary, U. S. president); Juliette Low (North Node. Founder of the Girl Scouts); Dr. Tom Dooley (Sun. Set up a hospital in Laos); Baldur von Schirach (South Node. Founder of Hitler Youth); John Wayne (South Node. Cowboy star); David Carradine (Venus. Actor—*Kung Fu*); Dolly Parton (Venus. Country-western singer); Vanessa Williams (South Node. Miss America, dethroned for nude pictures, later success in movies); Saddam Hussein (Jupiter. Iraqi dictator); Pierre Boulle (Venus. Writer—*Bridge on the River Kwai*); Bonnie Raitt (Jupiter. Boogie-blues singer); Brad Pitt (Mars. Actor—*Seven Years in Tibet*); Rachel Carson (South Node. Early environmentalist—*Silent Spring*); Joe Frazier (Sun. Heavyweight boxer); Toussaint L'Ouverture (Uranus. Haitian revolutionary); Jimmy Hoffa (Mars. Teamsters leader, murdered); Ronald Reagan (Uranus. Cowboy actor, cowboy president).

28 Capricorn

A little girl is practicing a humorous ditty for a vaudeville act. When she adds lines of her own, her mother berates her, but finds herself ignored.

Descriptive Phrases

Tuning out naysayers and bringing one's unique talents to the attention of the public (struggle for recognition); listening to one's inner voice rather than the internalized voices of parents, friends, or enemies; sensitivity to other people's energies and voices; talent for mimicry (sarcasm, parody); seeing through facades to underlying psychological realities; puncturing pretenses; playing the fool; messing with other people's realities; consternation with others' lame behavior (browbeating, sarcasm); surpassing mere competence and achieving an impressive performance; seizing one's opportunity and refusing to knuckle under vs. giving in to inner doubts; disciplined practice; pursuing one's own methods till one reaches one's goal, even if it drives other people crazy.

Examples

Jim Carrey (Sun. Comedian, actor—*Ace Ventura, Pet Detective*, *Man on the Moon*, *The Truman Show*); Danny Kaye (Sun. Comic actor, famous for rapid speech and tongue twisters); Vicki Lawrence (Jupiter. Sharp-tongued comedienne—*Mama's Family*); Mary Tyler Moore (Mercury. Pioneered the role of the single career woman on TV); Rich Little (Moon. Comic impersonations); Pietro Aretino (Uranus. Libertine writer, Renaissance satirist); Susan Butcher (Chiron. Sledding champ in the grueling Alaskan dog race); Robert Anton Wilson (Sun. Metaphysician in the "everything you know is wrong" school); Ruby Dee (Mars. Black actress—*A Raisin in the Sun*); Honoré Daumier (Venus. Satirical lithographer); Vivian Vance (Uranus. Played a put-upon housewife with show-biz ambitions on *I Love Lucy*); Nina Hartley (Saturn. Porn actress, civil libertarian); Marshall McLuhan (Uranus. Brilliant analyst and critic of the mass media); Terry Thomas (Uranus. Comic actor—*The School for Scoundrels*).

29 Capricorn

A tree-lined pond on the grounds of an ancient manor. A young man, absorbed in deep reflection, gazes over the pond while his bloodhound sniffs at the debris on the edge of the pond.

Descriptive Phrases

Passive reflection that allows one's deepest thoughts to come to the surface; sensitivity to psychic undercurrents (acidly morbid humor); grappling with the subconscious mind (morbid obsessions); clearing up fears and doubts by stilling the mind vs. stirring up the muck of one's darker thoughts (mental instability); struggling to achieve psychological integration by working through one's thoughts and feelings in imaginative writing or art; separating mental contents into gold and dross (sniffing out life's secrets, seeking the deathless truths of the invisible realm, Anubis); learning to sequester unhealthy psychic perceptions (emotional complexity can lead to isolation and melancholy); mental clarity vs. anxious projection; contemplative vision.

Examples

Washington Irving (Mars. Storyteller—*The Legend of Sleepy Hollow*); Sylvia Plath (Saturn. Poet—*The Bell Jar*); Carl Jung (Ascendant. Archetypal psychology); Jonathan Winters (South Node. Sardonic comedian who played The Blessed Reverend in *The Loved One*); Janis Joplin (Sun. Hippie blues singer, alcoholic); Tennessee Williams (Uranus. Melodramatic playwright—*Suddenly Last Summer, Cat on a Hot Tin Roof*); Charles Addams (Uranus. Morbid cartoonist—*The Addams Family*); Edgar Allen Poe (Sun, Mercury. Morbid poet and writer—*The Cask of Amontillado, The Gold Bug, The Raven*); Jean Delville (Sun. Symbolist painter); Marcia Starck (Venus. Medical astrologer who uses "inner dousing"); David Techter (Saturn. Parapsychology researcher, museum worker in fossil vertebrate department); Elaine Pagels (Mercury. Scholar—*The Gnostic Gospels, The Origin of Satan*); Amy Tan (Venus. Author—*The Hundred Secret Senses*).

30 Capricorn

A military pilot radios his superiors to tell them he is disobeying orders and leading a squadron of airplanes through a hole in enemy lines. After synchronizing watches, they proceed, and change the course of history.

Descriptive Phrases

Accepting what fate brings vs. seizing one's chance when the gears of the cosmic clock are all in synch (dissolution of normal laws of physics at very high speeds); seeing a trajectory into a possible future that is invisible to others, and having the courage to "wing it" (disastrous errors in judgment); grasping the needs of the greater good, but having to make do with incomplete training or knowledge (overreaching vs. doing something people thought impossible); trying to bring down a high level of awareness in the war for the future, but having a hard time knowing how to connect (teach things they don't fully understand); taking some received tradition to the nth degree vs. going off on a tangent; the promise of physical or spiritual science (astrology); storming the future.

Examples

T. E. Lawrence (South Node. Soldier—Lawrence of Arabia); Margaret Bourke-White (Chiron. Photojournalist who followed Patton into Germany); Napoleon Bonaparte (Moon. Conqueror); Bay of Pigs invasion fiasco (Saturn. 4/17/1961); George Clooney (Saturn, Stationary. Actor—*Three Kings*); Walter Bothe (Mercury. Nobel physicist, established Germany's first cyclotron); Michael J. Fox (Saturn. Actor—*Back to the Future*); Patricia Neal (Sun. Actress—*The Day the Earth Stood Still*); Jules Verne (Uranus. Author—*20,000 Leagues Under the Sea*, with Captain Nemo); Werner Heisenberg (Venus. Physicist—Heisenberg uncertainty principle); Marion March and Joan McEvers (Mercury and Venus, respectively. Astrologers—*The Only Way to Learn Astrology*); L. Ron Hubbard (Mars. Founder of Scientology); Charles Lindbergh (Jupiter. Pioneering aviator).

1 Aquarius

A traveler comes upon an ancient temple in the desert, part of it fallen into ruin and part of it adapted for modern use.

Descriptive Phrases

Recognizing that worldly institutions decay to the degree that they lose their indwelling soul or spiritual *raison d'être*; strengthening one's country's shared ideals by putting them into serviceable (if unrecognizable) modern forms; adopting a life-mission that fits one's inner nature vs. ending up in situations that seem arbitrary or absurd (absurdist humor); fully inhabiting one's immediate situation vs. detachedly observing it; withdrawing into the soul's inner sanctum to find spiritual revitalization; judging people by their inner ideals rather than by superficials; fearless openness of mind and heart (fight against prejudice); shaping the future by studying and refashioning the past; true Masonry—new reality constructs based on timeless spiritual laws.

Examples

Woodrow Wilson (Moon. Key architect of the League of Nations); Rudolf Giuliani (South Node. Controversial mayor who "cleaned up" New York City); Bill Maher (Sun. Host of *Politically Incorrect*, fired for saying Trade Tower terrorists were not cowards); Steve Reeves (Sun. Bodybuilder, actor in sword and sandal movies); Elizabeth Taylor (Saturn. Actress—*Cleopatra*); Lord Carnavon (Jupiter. Egyptologist who financed the discovery of Tut's tomb); Carolyn Dodson (Sun. Astrologer, author—*Horoscopes of U. S. States and Cities*); Charles Harvey (Moon. Mundane astrologer); Jane Fonda (Jupiter. Antiwar protester, actress—*The China Syndrome*); Queen Elizabeth I (Pluto. Imported the neoclassicism of the Italian Renaissance to England, mediated between warring Catholic and Protestant factions); Minoru Yamasaki (Uranus. Modern architect who uses gothic motifs); Milton Erickson (Venus. Leading hypnotherapist); Robert Zoller (Mars. Astrologer, translator for Project Hindsight); Eugene Ionesco (Uranus. Absurdist playwright); Peter F. Davis (Mercury. Documentary filmmaker—*Hunger in America*).

2 Aquarius

Crying for joy, a man stands in the pouring rain outside his girlfriend's window and shouts his love to the rooftops.

Descriptive Phrases

Emotional breakthrough; learning to love oneself as one is loved by God before one can accept the love of others (scramble around looking for love but may feel like unlovable losers); the power of love to melt the fears and defenses of the ego; melting barriers between different nationalities and races; following emotional or sexual energy wherever it leads; being emotionally scattered vs. pouring oneself wholeheartedly into some relationship or endeavor (artistic tours de force); sharp observers of humanity (laugh to keep from crying, alienate others with angry or sarcastic outbursts); seeing where things are heading; channeling events to some desired emotional end vs. heading off some disaster; channeling celestial love in acts of charity and kindness.

Examples

Raoul Wallenberg (Uranus. Swedish businessman, helped many Jews escape the Nazis); Sergei Rachmaninoff (Saturn. Ultraromantic composer who suffered from periodic creative blocks followed by storms of inspiration); Woody Guthrie (Uranus. Folk singer, political activist); Dyan Cannon (Mercury. Actress—*Bob & Carol & Ted & Alice*, about free love in the sixties); Ellen Burstyn (Saturn. Actress—*Alice Doesn't Live Here Anymore*); George Segal (Mercury, Stationary. Actor—*Blume in Love*); Leslie Caron (Moon. Actress who played a waiflike child of nature); John Hurt (Sun. Actor—*The Elephant Man, The Naked Civil Servant*); Augustus Owsley III (Sun. Provided much of the LSD that catalyzed the consciousness revolution of the sixties); Jim Carrey (Saturn. Comedian—*The Mask, The Truman Show*); Elvis Presley (North Node. Rock star, freed the American pelvis); Lady Bird Johnson (Uranus. Well-loved First Lady, worked effectively to beautify America); Victor Hugo (Mars. Writer—*The Hunchback of Notre Dame, Les Misérables*).

3 Aquarius

A deserter from the army follows a rocky path through the wilderness, impelled by a radically different vision of public service.

Descriptive Phrases

Rejecting group expectations, but fusing one's personal goals with the needs of the group (disloyal); nonconformity—following one's own path in life (contrary, off-track, entertain every rebellious impulse); periodically reconsidering one's direction in life (lost); refusing to be categorized or pinned down (dodge others' plans like a chipmunk evading gunshots, maintain relationships only on their own terms); going further by going alone (collect a gang of "fellow travelers"); traveling light, guided by ideals (immersed in egoistic fantasies; head in the clouds; stumble over unseen obstacles; find a rough, disappointing road until they purify their purpose of selfish elements); finding new inspirations; trailblazing; being a leader rather than a follower.

Examples

Steve McQueen (Moon. Rebellious film idol—*The Great Escape*); Babe Zaharias (Uranus. Female golfer); Edouard Manet (Sun. Founding father of impressionism); Richard Nixon (Uranus. President, crook); Jeanne Moreau (Sun. French actress—*Jules and Jim, Eve*); Antonio Gramsci (Sun. Socialist theorist); Agatha Christie (Jupiter. Mystery writer); Richard Christmann (Chiron. French double-agent, sold secrets to Germans, assumed many identities); Jack Fertig (Chiron. Gay activist who dresses as a nun—*Sister Boom Boom*); Lord Byron (Sun. Romantic poet with a club foot and a chaotic sexual life); Franz Werfel (Jupiter. Antimilitarist writer); Jack Lemmon (Mercury. Actor—*Some Like It Hot*); Phil Jackson (Moon. One-time coach of Chicago Bulls, into Zen); Jim Jarmusch (Sun. Film director—*Mystery Train, Down by Law*); Joe Valachi (Saturn. Mafia turncoat); Wernher von Braun (Uranus. Rocket scientist, switched loyalties from the Third Reich to the United States).

4 Aquarius

On the edge of a gushing fountain, a passerby ministers to a man who has fallen and injured his head. Behind them, in the mists of the fountain, appears a shining image of Christ.

Descriptive Phrases

Perceiving the divine in all people and channeling this energy into good works; breaking through emotional blockages that can result in physical problems (healers); reestablishing a flow of pranic energy; washing away ugly emotions through forgiveness (vengeful); having the courage to reach out to others vs. being frozen in an attitude of cold dignity; living out one's ideals; speaking to others from the heart (gushing romanticism); immersing oneself in life vs. cynical, detached observation of the human comedy; wrestling with spiritual blockages; being brought to a point of spiritual revelation by life's drama; finding an overarching meaning to life's suffering (Christ's Passion); responding passionately to life; overflowing humanity.

Examples

Bernadette of Lourdes (Mercury. Had visions of the Virgin, predicted and discovered a holy spring); Michelangelo (Jupiter. Passionate, tormented painter, sculptor); Patricia Neal (Jupiter. Actress—*The Fountainhead,* had a stroke at a young age but fully recovered); Odette Sansom (Uranus. French Resistance member who did not crack under torture); Richard Manuel (South Node. Musician—*The Band*); Albert Camus (Uranus. Existentialist philosopher); Anaïs Nin (Saturn. Diarist); Albert Ellis (Uranus. Humanistic psychologist); David Berkowitz (Moon. Serial killer of young lovers); John Lennon (Moon. Musician and songwriter—The Beatles); Bruno Bettelheim (Saturn. Psychologist who wrote about the survival of humanity in German concentration camps); Oral Roberts (Sun. Televangelist, healings); Tony Perkins (Saturn. Actor—*Psycho,* died of AIDS); Diana Ross (South Node. Lead singer of The Supremes); Richard Wagner (Mars. Operatic composer—*Parsifal,* about the search for the Holy Grail, with its healing powers).

5 Aquarius

Calmly ignoring the ghosts at his side and pushing aside strands of cobwebs, a man marches resolutely out of a crypt into the sunlight.

Descriptive Phrases

Leaving behind nagging doubts and marching into a bright vision of the future vs. having one's will sapped by fear (emotional or occult entanglements); the astral body, which perceives immaterial spirits when it is not adequately grounded in the physical body; discriminating good from bad influences and steeling oneself against the latter; fertile imagination—sunny daydreams vs. spooky nightmares, fantasy writers; (unhealthy fantasies may influence their behavior, since thought-forms, like ghosts, have a life of their own); dragging others into the same hole you're in vs. leading people into a life of fun and romance; developing positive momentum vs. falling into spiritual inertia and misanthropy; awakening to a vital new spirit of living (jaunty inspirational music).

Examples

Petula Clark (North Node. Singer—"Downtown"); George M. Cohan (Jupiter. Songwriter—"I'm a Yankee Doodle Dandy"); E.T.A. Hoffman (Sun. Fantasy writer—*The Nutcracker, The Golden Flower Pot*); Bela Lugosi (Moon. As Dracula, he emerged from the crypt; morphine addict); Gene Wilder (Moon. Comedian—*Young Frankenstein*); John Frankenheimer (Mercury. Film director—*The Manchurian Candidate*, in which a man is commanded under hypnosis to assassinate someone); Mel Gibson (Chiron. Actor—*Road Warrior*); John Sebastian (South Node. Folk-rock musician, The Loving Spoonful—"Do You Believe in Magic?"); John Carpenter (Mercury. Horror film director—*Halloween, They Live*); Francois Rabelais (Uranus. Author—*Gargantua*, which pushed aside stifling conventions for a new and carefree vision of life); Kenneth Ring (Mars. Writer on the near-death experience); Robin, Maurice, and Andy Gibb (Jupiter, Jupiter, and Venus, respectively. Members of the hypnotic disco group, The Bee Gees); Brad Steiger (Mercury. Author—*True Ghost Stories, Unknown Powers*).

6 Aquarius

A filmmaker on the set is surrounded by actors who represent characters in his own internal drama.[40]

Descriptive Phrases

The individual as stagemaster of his own personal reality; recognizing that one creates one's reality through emotional projections; living into one's projections vs. cultivating ironic detachment (see life as a play or a circus, don't take anything entirely seriously, may see others as myth-addled sleepwalkers); realizing that others can never be fully known vs. acting as if one had a right to control them (possessiveness and jealousy vs. emotional benevolence and willingness to cut others slack); forcing others to examine their assumptions; debunking manipulative myths vs. unwillingness to go beyond a particular set of questions; playing one's part in life vs. stepping out of a restrictive role; orchestrating events in an entertaining and edifying way.

Examples

Sigmund Freud (Chiron. Founder of psychoanalysis, dream analysis); Bill Maher (Chiron. Talk-show host—*Politically Incorrect*); Virginia Woolf (Sun. Author of *Orlando*, about a person who lives many lives without dying); Carl Sagan (North Node. Astronomer, propagandist for science, secular humanist—*The Dragons of Eden*); Sissy Spacek (Jupiter. Actress—*Carrie*, *Badlands*); William B. Davis (Jupiter. Actor, plays Cancerman on *The X-Files*); Kreskin (Venus. Stage magician, secular humanist); Gabriel Garcia Marquez (Mars. Magic realist writer—*One Hundred Years of Solitude*); Angela Davis (Sun. Leftist activist, debunks accepted political assumptions); Ugo Tognazzi (Moon. Actor—played the cabaret owner in *La Cage aux Folles*); Roger Vadim (Sun. Film director—*Barbarella*); Jean Paul Sartre (Chiron. Existentialist philosopher); Gebhard Frei (Chiron. Professor of comparative religion at the Jung Institute in Zurich).

7 Aquarius

After a dangerous journey, a youthful aviator lands in front of a crowd of exuberant well-wishers and waves to his parents in the front row.[41]

Descriptive Phrases

Inborn self-knowledge and self-confidence; having a fresh, penetrating vision of one's times and its possibilities; seeing new openings for accomplishment; bold action to break through obstacles to human progress; determination to make one's dreams into realities (headstrong, rush into ambitious projects without adequate groundwork); precocious talent; having one's parents or the public support one's talents vs. having to go it alone (being ignored vs. having one's parents make one jump through hoops); winning public acclaim through some tour de force (need constant praise); assuming that one is smiled on by fate and by the public; purity of impulse and emotion that draws the admiration of the public; sure aim in attaining what one wants from life.

Examples

Amelia Earhart (North Node. Aviator who disappeared over the Pacific); Wright brothers' Kitty Hawk flight (Saturn. 12/17/1903); Judy Blume (Mercury. Author of realistic children's books); Mike Judge (South Node. Cartoonist—*Beavis and Butthead*); Martin Handford (Chiron. Author of children's books—*Where's Waldo?*); Danny Thomas (Uranus. TV dad in *The Danny Thomas Show*, major patron of St. Jude's Children's Cancer Institute); Chevy Chase (Moon. Comedian—*Saturday Night Live*, *Caddyshack*); Amy Lowell (Saturn. Poet); Paul Newman (Sun. Actor—*Butch Cassidy and the Sundance Kid*, with its jump from a high cliff); Dennis Rodman (Jupiter. Hotdog basketball superstar); Michael J. Fox (Jupiter. Actor—*Back to the Future*); Carrie Fisher (Chiron. Actress—Princess Leia in *Star Wars*, daughter of Debbie Reynolds); Mia Farrow (Mercury. Actress who could fly in Woody Allen's *Alice*, adopted many children); James Barrie (North Node. Writer—*Peter Pan*); Franklin D. Roosevelt (Venus. U. S. president, led U. S. through the Depression and World War II, despite being wheelchair-bound).

8 Aquarius

In a shanty made of driftwood, an exiled princess makes lace while singing a song she learned at court.

Descriptive Phrases

Attending to the basic necessities of the outer man vs. nurturing the soul through the cultivation of beauty (value permanent acquisitions of character over worldly comforts); cultivating a higher standard of morality and taste than the surrounding society (cultural critics); redefining the boundaries of good taste (find neglected treasures amid the garbage); taking one's art to a new level by perfecting its outer form vs. getting stuck within old genres; promoting a new ideal of beauty vs. having to sell out to put bread on the table; exemplifying one's values in dress and behavior; refined artifice that appears smooth and natural vs. throwing something together to meet immediate needs (cavalier, slovenly); developing a sane framework of values.

Examples

Sophia Loren (North Node. Movie star from an impoverished Neapolitan background who married a famous producer and won an Oscar for *Two Women*); Leonard Cohen (North Node. Singer, songwriter—"Suzanne"); Brigitte Bardot (North Node. Sexpot actress, animal rights activist); Brad Pitt (Venus. Handsome actor—*Fight Club*); Dorothy Dandridge (Mars. Early Black glamor star—*Porgy and Bess*); Thor Heyerdahl (Uranus. Adventurer who rafted across the Pacific); Wolfgang Amadeus Mozart (Sun. Serene and luminous classical composer); Rudolf Serkin (Saturn. Sublime classical pianist); Sonja Henie (Uranus. Figure skater); Diane Keaton (Moon. Actress in Woody Allen films—*Sleeper*, famous for her "secondhand store" look); Bo Derek (Uranus. Actress—*Ten*); Stendhal (Venus. Perfectionist writer—*The Red and the Black*); Alan Alda and Mike Farrell (Sun and Mercury, respectively. Actors on the long-running TV sitcom *M*A*S*H*, where they brought civility and intelligence to the battlefield).

9 Aquarius

An escaped eagle with the remnants of a blindfold hanging over one eye, screams down at its former captors.

Descriptive Phrases

Fighting for one's freedom of thought and action (refuse to be anybody's pet); scorning the bondage of conventional, earthbound reality and flying skyward on the wings of thought (interest in celestial matters); being a master of one's own reality; sharp analysis of society from a boldly independent perspective (come out of left field); voicing the naked truth (highly visible oppositional stance may make them targets for powerful enemies); bold, aggressive action to secure one's desires (sexually predatory, seize what they want from life); laserlike mental focus; getting a glimpse of a truth and shredding mystifications and coverups until it has been entirely unveiled; attaining a high social position without sacrificing one's independence.

Examples

Malcolm X (South Node. Revolutionary—from criminal to prophet, *Autobiography of Malcom X*); Germaine Greer (Sun. Feminist theorist—*The Female Eunuch*, one-time pornographer); Robert Wise (Uranus. Director of *The Day the Earth Stood Still*); Amy Johnson (Saturn. Solo flight from England to Australia); Kurt Vonnegut (Mars. Writer—*The Sirens of Titan*, secular humanist propagandist); James Earl Ray (Mars. Assassin); George Orwell (Saturn. Writer—*Animal Farm*, *1984*); Tycho Brahe (Jupiter. Foremost research astronomer of the early modern period); Louis Braille (Chiron. Inventor of the Braille language for the blind); Barbara Tuchman (Sun. Historian—*The March of Folly*); Tem Terriktar (Chiron. Editor of *The Mountain Astrologer*); Allen Funt (Uranus. Emcee—*Candid Camera*, an often cruel show featuring hidden cameras); Peggy Cass and Kitty Carlisle (South Node and Uranus, respectively. Regular panelists on TV's *To Tell the Truth*); Konrad Lorenz (Saturn. Scientist who studied animal behavior, especially imprinting).

10 Aquarius

After a revealing argument about the nature of their relationship, a couple decides on a trial separation.

Descriptive Phrases

Deciding how far one should go to please other people, or to please the public (don't feel beholden to other people's desires, would rather withdraw than sell out); expressing what one wants and expects in a relationship (testy squawking); arriving at a workable compromise vs. deciding that a relationship isn't worth the effort; getting others to open up about their problems (mischievous provocation); reflecting and correcting people's perceptions (arguers); psychological insightfulness; living what one knows from subjective experience rather than trying to fit into the agreed-upon "objective" reality of society; being true to one's feelings rather than acting out a socially prescribed sex role (sexually bohemian, experimental); living from the inside vs. reclusiveness.

Examples

Oprah Winfrey (Venus. Talk-show host, actress—*The Color Purple*); J. D. Salinger (Mars. Author—*The Catcher in the Rye*, renowned as a recluse); Ralph Ellison (Uranus. Black writer—*Invisible Man*); Winona Ryder (North Node. Actress—*Heathers* and *Girl, Interrupted*); Richard Brautigan (Sun. Author—*Trout Fishing in America*, withdrew from public life and eventually committed suicide); F. M. Cornford (Saturn. Commentator on Plato's dialogues); Billy Tipton (Uranus. Jazz musician who lived as a man, found to be a woman at death); Sylvia Kars (Saturn. Sensuality therapist, surrogate sex partner); Gertrude Stein (Venus. Writer who founded a salon for artists and writers, prominent lesbian); Tennessee Williams (Mars. Playwright—*A Streetcar Named Desire*); Yoko Ono (Saturn. Artist wife of John Lennon); George Harrison (Mercury. Member of The Beatles who withdrew in later life); Swami Satchidananda (Uranus. Yoga guru); Benjamin Spock (Saturn. Expert on child-rearing); Robert Louis Stevenson (South Node. Author, withdrew to a Pacific island for health reasons).

11 Aquarius

Meditating on a mountaintop, a man receives a powerful vision. Later, he walks down toward the city holding the outlines of a new plan.

Descriptive Phrases

Seeking higher intellectual and spiritual understanding; sudden awakening to a higher level of awareness; "flashing" on the truth; mystical merging of personal consciousness with the consciousness of God; seeing the failures and falsehoods of one's society with startling clarity; receiving a spiritual vision and converting it to the specific needs of one's time (short-lived success based on timely cultural contributions); directorial talent based on an ability to communicate one's vision; setting forth one's plan with exactitude and clarity (manifestos, blueprints, sacred texts); setting the world in order (Moses-like sense of mission); spiritual certainty that encourages one to take charge of a situation; taking one's place in the larger cosmic scheme.

Examples

Thomas Merton (Sun. Christian mystic, author—*The Seven-Storey Mountain*); Alan Watts (Uranus. Teacher of Zen Buddhism); John Lilly (Uranus. Serious experimentation with LSD and isolation chambers, visionary); Vanessa Redgrave (Sun. Actress, political radical); Flora Robson (Jupiter. Best film portrayal of Queen Elizabeth I); Otto von Bismarck (Saturn. Unifier of Germany); Leni Riefenstahl (Jupiter. Nazi filmmaker—*Triumph of the Will*, began her career making "mountain films" that glorified nature); Lorne Greene (Mars. Actor—*Battlestar Galactica, Bonanza*); Norman Mailer (Sun. Writer—*Armies of the Night, Ancient Evenings*); Frank Lloyd Wright (South Node. Architect); Bernadette of Lourdes (Venus. Catholic saint who had visions of the Virgin); Margaret Mead (Venus. Anthropologist, held up Samoa's paradisal culture for emulation); Piers Anthony (North Node. Sci-fi writer—*The Macroscope*); Helen Nearing (Mercury. Author—*Develop Your Psychic Skills*).

12 Aquarius

A politician walks up the broad marble stairs of the senate building, brushing aside lobbyists who have approached him with a deal.

Descriptive Phrases

Having an optimistic, forward-looking stance toward life; enthusiastic belief in social and personal betterment; leadership in the public sphere; discovering a path through social and political problems, especially those involving social inequality; promoting a program that serves everyone vs. being tempted into shady practices in order to advance oneself (social climbers); rushing into things, including relationships, and stumbling into foreseeable obstacles vs. carefully assessing one's direction in life and getting off on the right foot; confident belief in one's cause; strong desire to win (competitive); building on the accomplishments of one's predecessors vs. stepping over the bodies of one's opponents; charming the public vs. neurotic need for admiration and respect.

Examples

Ann Richards (Saturn. Feisty Texas governor); Sam Donaldson (Venus. Newscaster); William Proxmire (Uranus. U.S. senator dedicated to governmental reform); Tony Blair (Moon. Gung-ho labor party prime minister); Phil Donahue (Mars. Liberal talk-show host); Patricia Stevens (Uranus. Model, modeling agency); Martin Luther King, Jr. (Mercury. Civil-rights leader); Alan Greenspan (Venus. Longtime manager of the Federal Reserve, the most powerful unelected official in the U. S.); Wendy Yoshimiro (Venus. Symbionese Liberation Army terrorist, later a successful artist); John Ehrlichman (South Node. Nixon operative in the Watergate break-in); Joe Montana (Chiron. Quarterback); Vance Packard (Uranus. Wrote an exposé on advertising—*The Hidden Persuaders*); Lady Bird Johnson (Venus. First Lady who worked to beautify America).

13 Aquarius

Neighbors have gathered to hear the news in a rural mansion equipped with a short-wave radio. The host fiddles with the antenna to get a better signal.

Descriptive Phrases

Being plugged in to what's going on no matter where one is (live on the fringe, often in rural areas); having one's antennae out (good listeners); networking with people who are on the same wavelength; making quick contacts (slow to commit); psychological insight; winkling out other people's games; getting culturally involved vs. watching from the sidelines; having several irons in the fire vs. limiting one's involvements and concentrating on truly promising projects (scattered); putting together an accurate interior picture of reality; perceiving a situation's positive and negative possibilities and changing one's course accordingly; considering all the angles until one finds a truth that really resonates; giving the public the inside scoop.

Examples

Bill Maher (Mercury. TV talk-show host—*Politically Incorrect*); Judy Blume (Jupiter. Realistic writer on children's problems); Margaret Bourke-White (Chiron. Photojournalist—the rural poor); Robert Altman (South Node. Filmmaker—*Nashville, Short Cuts*); Gennifer Flowers (Jupiter. Singer, Clinton's mistress, Web site with skinny on possible Clinton crimes); Philip Roth (Saturn. Author—*Portnoy's Complaint*); Wilhelm Reich (North Node. Psychologist who wrote on orgastic potency and invented the "orgone chamber"); Tennessee Williams (Moon. Sordid but insightful Southern playwright); Hugh Hefner (Mars. Founder of *Playboy* magazine—one of the only sources of progressive sexual and political information in the fifties and sixties); Hedda Hopper (Jupiter. Hollywood gossip columnist); Jerry Falwell (Saturn. Right-wing TV evangelist); Margaret Hone (Mars. Founder of the British Faculty of Astrological Studies).

14 Aquarius

A detective with a penlight is about to enter a dark window. He thinks he sees a snake emerging from the window, and then realizes that it is just a vine.

Descriptive Phrases

Warily entering a new scene; casting a cool, unblinking eye on fears and suspicions; awareness that the reality envisioned in one's mind's eye may be true, but may also be a fantasy; living in an operative fiction; getting by mental impasses by testing competing versions of reality (scientific analysis, prod others to get their reactions, emotionally cold); investigation; following up a hunch or premonition as a shortcut to knowledge; penetrating cracks in the "official story"; ferreting out secrets of sex, nature, or consciousness vs. being taken in by false fronts; clarifying or debunking a mystery; seeking out esoteric knowledge that allows one to "pass through the spheres" and consciously reincarnate (the pineal gland, psychism, the serpent power); curiosity.

Examples

Virginia Johnson and William Masters (South Node and Uranus, respectively. Sex researchers); Havelock Ellis (Sun. Sex researcher, spiritual alchemist); Anthony Blunt (Chiron. Art historian into hidden gnostic currents; was also a spy); Strom Thurmond (Jupiter. Racist Southern senator, member of States Rights party); Ayn Rand (Sun. Objectivist philosopher—*Atlas Shrugged*); Eric Hoffer (Jupiter. Sociologist who wrote *The True Believer*; was blind for eight years of his childhood and recovered his sight); Sissy Spacek (Venus. Actress—*Carrie*); Allen Funt (Jupiter. Host of *Candid Camera*, a cruel television show that tricked people into believing the impossible); James Joyce (Sun. Multileveled writer—*Finnegan's Wake*); Andrija Puharich (Mercury. Parapsychology researcher who worked with Geller and Hurkos); Laraine Newman (Venus. *Saturday Night Live* comic who specialized in creepy discoveries); Sidney Toler (Saturn. Actor—*Charlie Chan*); Jonas Salk (Jupiter. Developed a vaccine for polio); Robert Woodward (Mars. Reporter who broke the Watergate scandal).

15 Aquarius

Wearing a fillet of braided white ribbons and holding two lovebirds, an angelic woman sings a sentimental song on the stage of a shabby vaudeville theater. She looks down with pity on the drunken, unruly crowd.

Descriptive Phrases

Tuning in to life's higher harmonies (musical talent); embodying one's higher ideals in an accessible, popular form; faith that life's complicated twists will work out vs. seeing an unbridgeable gap between one's ideals and real life (depression); embodying one's romantic ideals vs. making a mess of one's life; holding up one's end of a relationship vs. abandoning it if it gets too complicated (birdlike "free spirits" vs. marital fidelity); emotional and sexual honesty; breaking down mistrust; unraveling misunderstandings; interceding in human dramas that are heading for disaster; being in the right place at the right time, or the wrong place at the wrong time; pity for the human condition vs. impotent rage; the Venusian principle.

Examples

Josephine Baker (South Node. Black dancer who adopted a multiracial brood); John Belushi (Mars. Comic—*Animal House*, life spiraled downwards into a drug overdose); Moss Hart (Saturn. Playwright—*You Can't Take It With You*); Janis Joplin (Venus. Hippie blues singer); R. Crumb (South Node. Outraged underground cartoonist, banjo player); Alan Alda (Mercury. Actor—*M*A*S*H*); Felix Mendelsohn (Sun. Classical composer—*A Midsummer Night's Dream*, with its wedding march); Robert Young (Chiron. Actor—*Father Knows Best*, secret alcoholic); Morgan Fairchild (Sun. Actress who plays scheming villainesses on soap operas); Philip K. Dick (Moon. Distopian science fiction writer who had five marriages); Christopher Durang (Moon. Playwright—outrageous black comedy); Leonard Wibberley (Uranus. Writer—*The Mouse That Roared*); Lewis Carroll (Uranus. Fantasy writer—*Alice in Wonderland*, photographed virginal young girls); Marlis Alt (Venus. Choreographer for Bausch's ballets).

16 Aquarius

Sitting at a desk surrounded by phones, a film director fields calls from several people simultaneously—an actor, a producer, his wife, and an excitable stranger.

Descriptive Phrases

The brain as central data processor; organizing varying elements of experience into a meaningful whole (sense of disjunction or absurdity); the magician or juggler who sees reality as a creation of will and imagination; feeling competent to handle whatever curveball reality may throw vs. feeling overwhelmed; remaining openminded vs. simplifying reality by shutting people out (bigotry); introducing some strange new element into one's environment that throws everything off balance; absurdist humor that deconstructs conventional reality by showing it up as a flimsy construct; emotional detachment from the results of one's efforts that allows one to coolly improvise if one's schemes fall apart (constant crisis); juggling reality.

Examples

Jim Carrey (Mercury. Comedian—*The Mask*, *The Truman Show*); Robert Altman (Venus. Director—*Nashville*, *Short Cuts*); Alice Cooper (Sun. Shock-rock star who uses guillotines, boa constrictors, and various other props); Criswell (Jupiter. Stage magician, prognosticator); Rosie O'Donnell (South Node. Talk-show host, actress); Chogyam Trungpa (Sun. Tibetan guru, metaphysician); John Cleese and Eric Idle (Mars. Comedians—*Monty Python*); Shirley MacLaine (North Node. Actress, spiritual seeker—*Out on a Limb*); D. W. Griffith (Saturn. Film director—*Birth of a Nation*, *Intolerance*); First Dada performance at Cabaret Voltaire (Uranus. 2/5/1916); Dr. Seuss (Saturn. Children's book writer, illustrator—*The Cat in the Hat*); Carolyn Jones (Saturn. Actress—Morticia in *The Addams Family*); Rod Serling (South Node. Writer, director—*The Twilight Zone*); Peter Weiss (Uranus. Playwright—*Marat/Sade*); Julio Cortazar (Jupiter. Wrote *Hopscotch*, in which the chapters are out of order and the reader has to try to make sense of it).

17 Aquarius

An oracular priestess, scantily clad, stands at the door of a temple. A serpent wrapped around the left pillar of the doorway bares its fangs as a man approaches.[42]

Descriptive Phrases

The body as a temple of the spirit; establishing sexual limits vs. emotional frigidity due to fear of defilement or uncontrolled lusts within oneself; exposing one's emotions or ideas as honestly as possible without becoming too vulnerable (penetrating motivational analysis arouses opposition due to its accusatory character); cynicism about people's motives vs. learning to let down barriers; having the mental discipline to hold fear, greed, and lust at bay within oneself, so one can meet them without fear in the outside world vs. projecting one's own lusts onto others or falling into depraved scenes (distrustful, sniff out false fronts); detachment from the body (astral travel, ungrounded beliefs); seeking the instruction of the "inner woman"; gaining entrance to inner realms vs. being stuck in externals through cynicism or venality.

Examples

Eartha Kitt (Mercury. Singer and actress who played Catwoman, blacklisted after blasting LBJ over the Vietnam War); Jane Goodall (North Node. Gained the trust of apes in the jungle); Pearl Buck (Mars. Author—*Dragonseed, The Good Earth*); Mick Jagger (South Node. Snarling rock star); Arthur Miller (Moon. Playwright—*The Misfits*, was married to Marilyn Monroe); Leonardo Da Vinci (Mars. Anatomist, inventor, painter of the Mona Lisa); William Burroughs (Sun. Writer of depraved fiction—*Naked Lunch*); William Blake (Saturn. Metaphysical poet, visionary); Ronald Reagan (Sun. President, promoted the fantastic Star Wars defense program); Rip Torn (Sun. Actor—*MIB II*, violent roles, sued Dennis Hopper for saying that he pulled a knife on him); Lionel Tiger (Sun. Sexist anthropologist—*Man in Groups*); Zsa Zsa Gabor (Sun. Cynical "actress,"—*Queen of Outer Space*); Jackie Gleason (Uranus. Star of *The Honeymooners*, where he regularly had to withdraw from foolish stances).

18 Aquarius

An ominous silence falls as the last man at a masquerade party prepares to unmask. Outside, a thunderstorm is brewing.[43]

Descriptive Phrases

Exposing uncomfortable truths; unwillingness to relate on a phony, masky level (troublemakers, enjoy rattling people); bringing negative undertones to the surface and clearing the air like a thunderstorm; breaking through fears and doubts that isolate people from each other; sweet and vulnerable self-revelation vs. fearful cloaking of secrets; keeping one's own counsel vs. accepting one's duty to illuminate the group mind (strike a powerful chord with the public); introducing neglected but relevant spiritual truths; critically analyzing phony social scenes vs. making them real enough to participate in; serving as unconscious agents of some larger revelation, however unpleasant (making an unpleasant discovery when it's already too late); penetrating revelations vs. the irresponsible use of shock tactics.

Examples

Madame Blavatsky (Jupiter. Seeker, mystic, founder of Theosophical Society, wrote *Isis Unveiled*); Chris Carter (Moon. Creator of *The X-Files*); Grace Slick (Mars. Lead singer of The Jefferson Airplane); Roseanne Barr (North Node. Brought social realism to the TV sitcom); Tupac Shakur (North Node. Rap star, was murdered); Geraldo Rivera (South Node. Sensationalist journalist); Bob Haldeman (Jupiter. Nixon hatchet man); Walt Whitman (Jupiter. Gay poet); Sam Peckinpah (Venus. Director, screenwriter—*Invasion of the Body Snatchers, Straw Dogs*); Frida Kahlo (Chiron. Painter); Joseph Campbell (Saturn. Jungian anthropologist—*The Masks of God*); B. F. Skinner (Saturn. Behaviorist psychologist); Michel Foucault (Jupiter. Confrontational deconstructionist philosopher); Patricia Loud (Jupiter. Opened her home to TV cameras, revealing all the family dirt).

19 Aquarius

A rapt audience watches as a great actor, underlit by stage lights, rehearses the final scene of Macbeth. *Though there is no set, the audience can clearly visualize the burning castles in the background.*

Descriptive Phrases

Creating and living into a personal myth (play out the role of the romantic hero or heroine); confident self-projection; belief in self which engenders the belief of others; drawing others into one's myth; exceptional power of visualization and imagination (literature, drama, voyages of the imagination); jaunty confidence in one's ability to handle any situation, no matter how dangerous; destructive passions brought under control (unbridled egotism or power-lust that leads to the collapse of one's whole world, as with Macbeth); changing reality according to what one visualizes as true (magic); creating visionary art vs. conjuring up empty illusions; using mental will to hold together a certain picture of reality vs. using highly charged imagery to elicit an audience's imaginative projection; the thin line between the visionary and the madman.

Examples

Orson Welles (Moon. Actor—*Macbeth, Citizen Kane*); Marcel Marceau (Venus. Mime); Jules Verne (Sun. Author—*20,000 Leagues Under the Sea*); Rudolf Steiner (Venus. Clairvoyant, spiritual teacher); Wolfgang von Goethe (Uranus. Author—*Faust*); Edward Gorey (Venus. Morbid illustrator—*Amphigorey*); Zoé Oldenbourg (Uranus. Author—*Massacre at Montségur*); Ralph Nader (North Node. Consumer advocate, political gadfly); Katharine Hepburn (Chiron. Actress—*The African Queen*); Sallie Nichols (Chiron. Writer on the Jungian tarot); Jamie Lee Curtis (Chiron. Actress—*Halloween*); James Dean (Sun. Actor—*Rebel Without a Cause*); Tycho Brahe (Venus. 16th-century astronomer who lived in a splendid castle); Gustave Doré (Moon. Illustrator of Dante's *Inferno*); H. Rider Haggard (Moon. Writer—*She, King Solomon's Mines*); Dorothy Lamour (Jupiter. Actress—road movies with Bob Hope); Gerard Majax (Moon. French stage magician).

20 Aquarius

A luminous dove circles and descends, bearing a message.[44]

Descriptive Phrases

Mysticism; the fertilization of the soul by God with the desire to know God; being open to communication from "beyond the veil" (channeling); rituals and prayers designed to strengthen the bond between man and God; raising one's mind from a state of moralistic dualism, which can beget acts of violence, to a gentle meditative state, in which one sees the divine light in all things; sense of spiritual mission; bearing a message of peace and forbearance; translating divine love into humane institutions; fighting for political and social reform (bear witness to society's crimes against the spirit); destructive selfishness vs. repentance and grace; realignment with the light-force; bringing a message to humanity; light bearers vs. ideologues and propagandists.

Examples

Martin Buber (Sun. Jewish theologian—*I and Thou, Paths in Utopia*); Marilyn Monroe (Moon. Actress—in *The Misfits*, she tries to prevent some cowboys from brutalizing a horse); Emmanuel Swedenborg (Sun. Extravagant mystical writings, with an extensive angelic hierarchy); William Butler Yeats (Moon. Poet, magician in the Rosicrucian tradition); Aleister Crowley (Saturn. Black magician); Saint Bernadette of Lourdes (Neptune. Had visions of the Virgin and manifested a spring of holy water); Charles Schulz (Mars. Cartoonist—*Peanuts*); Jane Jacobs (Uranus. Urban planner—*The Life and Death of the American City*); Olivia de Havilland (Uranus. Actress—Maid Marion in *Robin Hood*; also starred in *The Snake Pit*, about asylums); Ivan Illich (Jupiter. Educational reformer—*Deschooling Society*); Robert Stack (Mars. Actor—*The Untouchables, Unsolved Mysteries*); Alison Lurie (Jupiter. Pulitzer-prize-winning author—*The War Between the Tates, Love and Friendship*); Jeddu Krishnamurti (Ascendant. Spiritual teacher).

21 Aquarius

Staring into her dressing-room mirror, a torch singer reflects sadly on her broken romance. When her lover knocks on the door, she asks the maid to send him away.

Descriptive Phrases

The soul as a mirror; embodying the divine aspect of the soul through the perfection of one's art (music, poetry, dance); realizing that the highest emotions can be shared only in art; feeding the higher emotions of the soul in the absence of external support (unrealistically exalted romantic ideals lead to disillusionment in love); realization that purely physical relationships are ultimately empty, since they do not touch the soul (mind-body dualism); trying to maintain harmony between one's projected image and one's inner self vs. being desired for a false but glamorous persona; having to "look oneself in the face in the morning" vs. "putting on one's face" (narcissism, preciosity, self-involved prima donnas); rejecting praise and criticism as external to the true self; compassion vs. self pity.

Examples

Karen Carpenter (Jupiter. Soulful popular singer, lonely, died of anorexia); Leontyne Price (Sun. Black opera singer); Lisa Kudrow (Saturn. Wistful comedienne—*Friends, Romy and Michelle's High School Reunion*); Andy Griffith (Moon. Sitcom actor—*The Andy Griffith Show,* about idyllic rural life); Buffalo Bob (Uranus. Children's show host, puppeteer); Mia Farrow (Sun. Actress who adopted many children); Quentin Crisp (Chiron. Drag queen, writer—*The Naked Civil Servant*); Sarah Bernhardt (Neptune. Great stage actress); Richard Nixon (Moon. Flawed president with a surprisingly good civil-rights record); Hugh Hefner (Jupiter. Founder of the *Playboy* empire, promoter of the Playboy philosophy of easygoing, unemotional sex); Carson McCullers (Uranus. Writer—*A Member of the Wedding*); Fats Waller (Saturn. Jazz great, composer of beautiful romantic ballads); George Gershwin (Moon. Pop and classical composer—"But Not for Me," unmarried); Rainer Maria Rilke (Saturn. Poet—*Sonnets to Orpheus*).

22 Aquarius

Guerrilla group runs along a zigzagging, boulder-strewn mountain ridge in order to head off a munitions train.

Descriptive Phrases

Protesting or attempting to derail repressive social policies; critical sniping from the fringes of society (revolutionary violence vs. playing cat and mouse with the law); avoiding excessive ruthlessness and haste in trying to effect change, but also avoiding excessive hesitation; knowing the right time to act; stirring up the populace (must firmly adhere to principles of social justice if their message is to be heard); getting people on one's wavelength vs. being out of step; fighting for decency and social justice in an uncivilized world (frontier justice vs. anarchic lawlessness); playing "cosmic freeze tag"—liberating people's minds and bodies through charged ideas, charged sex, and charged music; bravely standing in the breach.

Examples

Daniel Berrigan (Saturn. Antiwar activist, priest); Ishmael Reed (North Node. Black poet and writer of *Mumbo Jumbo*, about the liberative powers of voodoo-influenced jazz); Bernadine Dohrn (Venus. Revolutionary in the Weather Underground); Burt Reynolds (Sun. Male sex symbol—*Smokey and the Bandit, Deliverance*); Birgitte Nillson (Saturn. Actress—*Red Sonja*); Pierre Boulle (Mercury. Writer—*The Bridge on the River Kwai*, about wartime sabotage); Angela Davis (Moon. Radical professor, activist); Oscar Romero (Uranus. Guatemalan archbishop opposed to government brutality, murdered by the death squads); Maria von Trapp (Saturn. Leader of the famous singing family that escaped from the Nazis over the mountains); Ten suffragettes arrested at the White House (Uranus. 8/28/1917, their maltreatment was a turning point in securing the vote for women); Bertold Brecht (Sun. Playwright—*The Threepenny Opera*, communist); Ralph Nader (Saturn. Critic, consumer advocate, Green Party candidate for president); Charlie Manson (Saturn. Psycho-killer who planned to start a race war).

23 Aquarius

Waving its arms and legs, a trained bear balances on a chair perched atop a large rubber ball.[45]

Descriptive Phrases

The Little Bear or Little Dipper, which appears to stir the heavens; developing a political platform or social agenda; securing a public platform from which to broadcast one's ideas; grabbing the attention of the public both through one's ideas and through one's physical presence; promoting revolutionary ideas in terms simple enough for the limited intelligence of the masses; stirring up the public vs. steadying them (power lust, can lose their moral compass); harnessing the emotions of the masses to the task of transforming society (feel that bad people and unworthy principles have been enthroned and must be overturned); riding the beast of popular opinion by balancing heavy philosophy and light humor (overbearing ideologues).

Examples

Franklin Roosevelt (Mercury. First president to use the radio masterfully, completely reorganized government); Karl Marx (Ascendant. Theoretical founder of Communism); Ayn Rand (Saturn. Ideological capitalist); Kate Millett (Saturn. Feminist writer—*Sexual Politics*); Robin Williams (North Node. Manic comedian, actor—*Good Morning Vietnam*); Orson Welles (North Node. Actor—*The Third Man*, with its famous Ferris-wheel scene); War of the Worlds broadcast by Orson Welles (Jupiter. 10/31/1938, caused widespread panic with a broadcast asserting that aliens had invaded); Thomas Edison (Sun. Inventor of light bulb and phonograph); Brigitte Bardot (Saturn. Sexpot actress, animal rights propagandist); Phyllis Diller (Uranus. Zany comedienne); Bert Parks (Jupiter. Emcee for the Miss America contest); Robert Novack (Mercury. Conservative political commentator—*Evans and Novack*); Sam Donaldson (Saturn. Controversial TV newscaster).

24 Aquarius

In an address before the general assembly of the United Nations, an elder statesman reproaches members who are standing in the way of international cooperation.

Descriptive Phrases

Implicit unity of all peoples and all life; promoting a higher harmony; facing one's irrational prejudices and fears and acknowledging their negative effects (stuck in racism and xenophobia—us against them); trying to melt the hearts of those who would obstruct peace; attacking destructive but emotionally seductive myths; looking at one's situation without preconceptions vs. living in a fantasy world; focusing people's attention on crucial but difficult issues; giving voice to the collective mind (echoing the subconscious myths of one's people); assimilating many points of view before deciding on a proper course for the collective (hardheaded ideologues); oratorical ability and suave charm (seducers); reaching a deeper level of understanding by considering all the angles.

Examples

John F. Kennedy (Uranus. President, most significant for his civil-rights record); Abraham Lincoln (Sun. President who both divided and reunited the country); Judy Blume (Sun. Juvenile author—*What Kids Wish They Could Tell You*, *Blubber*); Carroll O'Connor (South Node. Actor—played a slowly improving bigot on *All in the Family*); John Lilly (Jupiter. Experimenter with LSD, communication with dolphins); k.d. lang (South Node. Folk-rock singer); Billy Holiday (North Node. Bluesy singer—"Strange Fruit"); Dean Martin (Uranus. Crooner, womanizing movie star); Leonard Nimoy (Venus. Actor—played the emotionless Spock on *Star Trek*); Cyril Harris (Uranus. Acoustician who designed New York's Philharmonic Hall); Larry King (North Node. Talk-show host); George DuMaurier (Uranus. Antisemitic author of *Trilby*, with its evil, sexually dominating Jew, Svengali); Eduardo Molinaro (Moon. Movie director—*La Cage aux Folles*); Marianne Williamson (North Node. Lecturer on *A Course in Miracles*).

25 Aquarius

A scientist pokes a chrysalis with a probe, whereupon it breaks open and a beautiful luna moth emerges, left wing first.

Descriptive Phrases

Catalyzing the unfolding of a mystery; sequential emergence of different faculties of the personality according to innate natural rhythms; integrating different archetypes within the personality (psychological dissociation, lead double lives); giving equal weight to rational thought and symbolic or intuitive thought (weave a personal mythology to help make sense of their situation); finding the key that awakens one from muddled unconsciousness to awakened comprehension vs. getting trapped in a solipsistic belief-system; pulling oneself together and escaping a morally confused situation; seeing through smokescreens; puncturing falsehoods with pointed humor and pithy sayings (argumentative; sarcastic needling); urging others to evolve; continually evolving analysis.

Examples

Robert Bly (Jupiter. Poet, men's movement writer—*Iron John,* which describes various archetypes found in the male psyche); Joanne Woodward (Moon. Actress—*The Three Faces of Eve*); Kim Novak (Sun. Actress—*Vertigo; Bell, Book and Candle*); Dane Rudhyar (Moon. Pioneer of psychologically centered astrology, composer); Woody Allen (Moon. Director, comic—*Annie Hall, Alice*); Ben Hecht (Venus. Screenwriter); Jean Piaget (North Node. Developmental psychologist); Carl Jung (Saturn. Archetypal psychologist); Carl Bernstein (Sun. Reporter who broke open the Watergate scandal); Alexander Solzhenitsyn (Uranus. Soviet dissident—*The Gulag Archipelago*); Elaine Pagels (Sun. Historian—*The History of Satan,* deconstructor of Christian myths); Edward Albee (Venus. Playwright—*Who's Afraid of Virginia Woolf?*); Marilyn Ferguson (Jupiter. Author—*Brain-Mind Bulletin, The Aquarian Conspiracy*).

26 Aquarius

A detective questions a family in the library of an old mansion, making several tentative accusations before turning his finger on the chief suspect.

Descriptive Phrases

Identifying and solving complex problems; staying cool and composed when confronted with a dire problem vs. indulging in hysterics; following correct procedures vs. dangerous hastiness; piecing together a mystery by collecting facts and testing one's hunches vs. jumping to conclusions or accusing a convenient scapegoat; getting people to show their true colors; provoking a reaction by saying exactly what one thinks (testy, confrontational); turning up the voltage in an argument vs. withdrawing into playful banter; working out of provisional analyses vs. painting oneself into a corner (trapped by their own obsessions); catalyzing the unveiling of the truth vs. confronting the inexplicable (psychic phenomena, flashes of insight); the probing, investigative mind.

Examples

Herman Kahn (Sun. Nuclear war strategist); Elaine Pagels (South Node. Researcher on the history of Christian belief); Lauren Bacall (Mars. Actress—*To Have and Have Not, Shock Treatment*); David Koresh (Chiron. Christian cult leader who was killed in a confrontation with the U.S. government); Truman Capote (Mars. Writer—*In Cold Blood*, the reconstruction of a real murder); Kevin McCarthy (Sun. Actor—*Invasion of the Body Snatchers*); Gerard Croiset (Chiron. Professional psychic who does police work); Peter Schaffer (Jupiter. Playwright—*Equus*, about a psychologist counseling a boy who blinds horses); Jimmy Hoffa (Sun. Corrupt Teamsters' Union leader, missing and probably murdered); Beatrice Arthur (Jupiter. Opinionated sitcom star—*Maude*); Paul Harvey (Uranus. Talk-radio host specializing in unexplained phenomena); Robert Stack (Uranus. Actor—*The Untouchables, Unsolved Mysteries*); Patrick McGoohan (Moon. Actor—*The Prisoner, Secret Agent*).

27 Aquarius

At an informal dance party, the host turns to her husband and makes gentle jokes about their friends.

Descriptive Phrases

Being an enthusiastic participant in the dance of life vs. being a wall-flower;[46] having a firm sense of identity, yet staying open to a wide range of people and viewpoints; choosing one's associates carefully vs. throwing some wild cards into the mix; providing a cultural container for vital social energies (party givers); loyalty to old friends vs. making new contacts; sticking with the staid and comfortable vs. giving something new a whirl; making the most of life's potentials; feeling good about humanity vs. feeling alienated; being composed in the face of life's unsettling changes vs. despairing when things go wrong (live each moment as if it were their last); shrewd observation of life and the world; lightening things up vs. skirting serious issues; gentle but penetrating humor; emotional composure vs. letting it all hang out.

Examples

Elliott Gould (Jupiter. Actor—*M*A*S*H*); Billy Crystal (Mercury. Standup comic, actor); Mel Brooks (Jupiter. Comic film-director—*Blazing Saddles*); Shirley MacLaine (Saturn. Actress, spiritual seeker); Allen Ginsberg (Jupiter. Poet—*Howl*); David Byrne (North Node. Lead singer of the Talking Heads); Marjorie Merriweather Post (South Node. Socialite, hostess); Janis Joplin (South Node. Blues singer, alcoholic); Grace Metalious (Mars. Author—*Peyton Place*); Marisa Berenson (Sun. Actress—*Cabaret, Death in Venice*); Terry Jones (Mercury. Comedian—*Monty Python*); Katharine Ross (South Node. Actress—*The Graduate, The Stepford Wives*); Judith Malina (Jupiter. Cofounder of The Living Theater, which confronted the audience with its passivity and sometimes dragged them into the aisles); Frank O'Hara (Jupiter. Humorous poet of everyday life); Mark Twain (Uranus. Author, raconteur).

28 Aquarius

A chauffeur stands over the hood of his car looking perplexedly at the engine. A funny old man walks over and offers his humble opinion on what is wrong and how to fix it.

Descriptive Phrases

Dispensing earthy wisdom based on hands-on experience; pitting the knowledge of the old-timer against the speculative theories of the greenhorn or the arrogant autocrat; collaborative efforts between people with different areas of expertise; respecting the social hierarchy vs. insubordination when one knows something is being done incorrectly; building on a solid foundation by following the prescribed method vs. following through on a hunch; thinking things through from the start vs. rushed efforts that end in disaster; knowing the limits of one's own competence vs. bungling something due to insufficient knowledge; self-reliance vs. seeking out expert advice; willingness to try a new method vs. taking a boneheaded "here goes nothin'" approach; *bonhomie* and lack of pretense.

Examples

Andy Devine (South Node. Character actor, had constant fights with his car, Nellybelle, on the *Roy Rogers Show*); John Candy (Jupiter. Comic actor—*Trains, Planes, and Automobiles*); Dean Jones (Saturn. Disney actor—*The Love Bug*); Eddie "Rochester" Anderson (Saturn. Played the chauffeur on *The Jack Benny Show*); Ann Landers (Uranus. Advice columnist who consulted many experts); Kenny Rogers (Jupiter. Good-ole-boy country-western singer); Albert Einstein (Jupiter. Theoretical mind behind the atom bomb); Jean Marsh (Saturn. Actress—*Upstairs, Downstairs*); Ted Kennedy (Mars. Liberal senator); Stewart Brand (Jupiter. Editor of *The Whole Earth Catalog*, advocating hippy self-reliance); Sonny Bono (Sun. Self-deprecating entertainer, one-time mayor); David Duchovny (South Node. Teamed with Scully on *The X-Files*); June Haver (Jupiter. Actress—*The Girl Next Door*); Franklin D. Roosevelt (Mercury. U. S. president who relied on a Brain Trust).

29 Aquarius

A hare pops its head out of a hole, pauses momentarily and, in a series of hops, zigzags rapidly across a field.[47]

Descriptive Phrases

Receiving surprising flashes of insight from a higher level of reality; looking at life from a weird angle (cartoonlike surrealism); developing an ever-clearer reality-conception; confronting people's dreamlike assumptions from a more awakened perspective vs. belaboring a point with the unreceptive; slipping in radical cultural innovations; experimentalism (promiscuity); promoting social evolution; knowing the next stage that society must go through; clearly visualizing all the stages (or hops) between where one is and where one wants to be; practical, procedural thinking; skillful execution of plans; high-speed mental maneuvering; being one jump ahead of one's opposition; waking up vs. pursuing one's dreams wherever they may lead.

Examples

Lewis Carroll (Jupiter. Author—*Through the Looking Glass*); Dick Clark (South Node. Host of *American Bandstand*); Alan Watts (North Node. TV Zen teacher who stirred up much of the interest in Buddhism in America); Petrarch (Pluto. Lyric poet, social critic, initiated the Italian Renaissance practically single-handedly); Cary Grant (Mars. Leading Hollywood glamor star, especially good in surreal comedies—*Arsenic and Old Lace, The Philadelphia Story*); William Wordsworth (Mars. Poet—*Intimations of Immortality*); Callista Flockhart (Saturn. Star of the surrealistic *Ally McBeal*); Jean Harlow (Mercury. Noirish Hollywood blonde); Michael Jordan (Sun. Basketball superstar, hangs out with cartoon characters in ads); Betty Friedan (Mercury. Groundbreaking feminist—founder of the National Organization for Women, author of *The Feminine Mystique*); Mario Savio (South Node. Leader of the Free Speech Movement at Berkeley in the sixties); John Sayles (Jupiter. Director of highly focused, socially aware films—*Brother from Another Planet, Matewan*); Jean-Baptiste Corot (Pluto. Preimpressionist painter).

30 Aquarius

The ruins of Atlantis viewed from the porthole of a submarine. Giant sea anemones wave in the foreground, while octopuses and sharks swim between broken columns.[48]

Descriptive Phrases

The transience of all cultural forms, which have periods of growth and decay as regular as the tides; letting go of the past vs. shoring up a society that is being engulfed by its collective sins, or is being infiltrated by alien elements (cleanup campaigns); unwillingness to hide the strange mess of modern society or the unconscious drives underlying human behavior (impudent, ironic commentary on modern life from the perspective of an alien observer vs. sense of horror at the monstrous evils thriving in our midst); the futility of conforming to social or sexual roles that have lost their cultural vitality; finding original, if strange, forms of self-expression based on personal values; mutation vs. immersion in soulless and energiless cultural detritus.

Examples

Brad Steiger (Sun. Pop-occultist writer—*Atlantis Rising, Unknown Powers*); Joseph Dechelette (Chiron. Archaeologist who studies early Rome); Roger Corman (Venus. Schlock director—*Attack of the Crab Monsters, Creature from the Haunted Sea*); Karen Silkwood (Sun. Activist—killed while investigating nuclear malfeasances); Yoko Ono (Sun. Avant-garde artist); Princess Diana (South Node. Jet-set royalty, activist against land mines); Jean Auel (Sun. Writer—*Clan of the Cave Bear*); Alcide de Gaspari (Mars. Saved Italy from Communist domination after World War II); Janeane Garofalo (Saturn. Professionally alienated comedienne, political activist); R. D. Laing (Moon. Psychologist—*The Politics of the Family*); Ed Harris (Jupiter. Actor—*The Abyss, Enemy at the Gates*); Seven hundred men are eaten by sharks after a naval battle (South Node. 11/28/1942); John Travolta (Sun. Actor—*Saturday Night Fever, Pulp Fiction*); Frank Norris (Venus. Muckraking author—*The Octopus*); Isaac Asimov (Uranus. Sci-fi writer—*The Foundation Trilogy*).

1 Pisces

An elegantly dressed young woman banters with the grocer while testing the produce.

Descriptive Phrases

Enjoying human relationships, from everyday contacts to sexual intimacy; give and take of erotic energy in everyday life; charm and subtle flirtatiousness; repartee and gossip; discretion and indiscretion; accurate intuitive impressions of others; creating a strong first impression; realistic self-appraisal within the sexual marketplace; embodying an ethos or set of values in one's dress and speech; promoting certain values by making them attractive vs. adopting values because they are deemed attractive (play into the public anima, embody modern ideals of beauty); participating in public discussions concerning values, aesthetics, and sex; testing for real substance beneath superficial beauty and intellectual postures; egalitarian cooperativeness.

Examples

Myrna Loy (Saturn. Charming actress—*The Thin Man*); James Garner (Mars. Charming actor—*The Rockford Files*); Diana Rigg (Jupiter. Master of repartee on *The Avengers*); Prince Andrew (Sun. Son of Philip, Randy Andy); Marlon Brando (South Node. Film star, icon of male sexuality); Anaïs Nin (Jupiter. Diaries with honest sexual content); Havelock Ellis (North Node. Early researcher into sexual practices, alchemist); Shere Hite (South Node. Researches American sexual practices—*The Hite Report*); Susan Brownmiller (Saturn. Man-hating feminist theorist); Steve Gaskin (Saturn. Commune leader, psychic); John Voight (Jupiter. Actor—*Midnight Cowboy, Deliverance*); Tracy Chapman (Saturn. Folk singer, diarist of everyday life); Larry Flynt (South Node. Editor of *Hustler*); Doris Day (South Node. Actress—*Pillow Talk*).

2 Pisces

An angelfish draws its tail across its face. Spying a fisherman, it darts into the shelter of a coral reef.

Descriptive Phrases

Wariness vs. intimacy; identifying one's friends and foes; searching for that beautiful but elusive partnership (team acts); coyness, flirtation; sexiness; wanting to lower one's veils and defenses, but first feeling out one's partner's reactions; weighing risks against rewards; seeking publicity vs. seeking privacy; maintaining a wall between one's public and private life (present a deceptive image to the public, undercover activity, exposure, scandal); being "stalked" by others; being a victim vs. turning the tables on one's persecutors (paranoid, hole up for safety); mad scrambles and hasty retreats; finding a safe haven within existing social structures vs. turning society upside-down; madcap adventures; vortexes; sexual vitality; pizzazz.

Examples

Clara Bow (Saturn, South Node. Sexy actress—the "It" girl); Ann Sheridan (Sun. Actress—the "Oomph" girl); Patty Hearst (Sun. Abducted by the Symbionese Liberation Army, acts in John Waters' movies); Prince (Moon. Masturbatory rock star); Tricia Nixon (Sun. Shy, reclusive First Daughter); Gracie Allen (Saturn, South Node. Wacky, silly comedienne); Patrick McGoohan (Mercury, Venus. Actor—*The Prisoner, Secret Agent*); Iris Murdoch (Uranus. Writer—*Under the Net*); Tristan Tzara (Mars. Dadaist crazy); Paul Terry (Sun. Cartoonist—*Terry Toons*); Tom Lehrer (Mars. Impudently off-color comedy songs); Jerry Rubin (Jupiter. One-time yippy revolutionary); Timothy Leary (Uranus. LSD guru, escaped from prison); Elvis Presley (Moon. Highly sexed rock star); Annette Funicello (South Node. Coy Mouseketeer); Hedy Lamarr (North Node. Actress—*Ecstasy*).

3 Pisces

A downcast woman stands in front of a dead tree from which the body of her husband is hanging. Perched on a branch, a raven looks down, its head cocked, and chatters cheerfully.

Descriptive Phrases

Sober reflections on the deeper meanings of life and death (cynicism, gallows humor); offering an astute opinion after scrutinizing the evidence; looking squarely at the facts, no matter how unpleasant; sharp-tongued criticism; analyzing some aspect of human society; getting to the bare bones of a situation by stripping away falsehoods; seeing life's multileveled complexity vs. falling into simplistic conclusions; dealing with loss (pessimism, depression); having a core personality that survives every vicissitude of fortune; surviving life's trials and helping others with similar problems; getting along with others by accepting the fact that everyone is motivated by private interests vs. squabbling with intimates over petty offenses (vengeful, won't let people off the hook for past misdeeds); stout-hearted steadfastness; stubborn independence of perspective.

Examples

Jean-Paul Sartre (Saturn. Existentialist philosopher); Lionel Trilling (Saturn. Literary critic, leading critic of liberal hypocrisy); Joyce Carole Oates (Jupiter. Neo-Gothic novelist—*By the North Gate*); William Styron (Moon. Author—*Sophie's Choice*, suffered serious depression); Henry Fonda (Saturn. Stoic actor—*The Grapes of Wrath*); Audrey Meadows (South Node. Alice on *The Honeymooners*); Carson McCullers (Mars. Depressive Southern playwright—*The Heart Is a Lonely Hunter*); Jerzy Kosinski (North Node. Wrote about his horrific World War II experiences—*The Painted Bird, The Devil Tree*); Jeffrey Dahmer (Chiron. Cannibalistic serial killer); Leonardo da Vinci (Jupiter. Inventor, artist—painted skeletons first, then put on the flesh); Robespierre (Saturn. French revolutionary who presided over the Reign of Terror).

4 Pisces

In the decayed mansion of an aged eccentric, a wild party is in full swing. The butler stands sentry at the iron-grated entrance, an iron key on his belt.

Descriptive Phrases

Recognizing that the world one inhabits is a creation of one's mind and particularly one's desires; feeling that one's house is one's castle vs. being imprisoned in a hell-world of one's own making; maintaining an orderly existence by locking up one's more anarchic thoughts and desires vs. giving play to one's wilder fantasies; the power of reality grids to limit perception; integrating ideas and emotions deemed dangerous or insane into a reality framework that has become like a prison vs. protecting one's mind or society from irrational elements (serve as gatekeepers to society's power elite); listening empathetically to other people's stories vs. feeling that one is surrounded by madmen; pointing out the irrational setup of society (react with outrageous behavior, shock tactics, *Grand Guignol*); feeling doomed to an ironclad fate vs. walking away from a bad scene.

Examples

Edward Gorey (Sun, Moon. Macabre cartoonist); Charles Addams (Chiron. Cartoonist—*The Addams Family*); George Orwell (South Node. Writer—*Animal Farm*); Jodie Foster (Jupiter. Actress—*Silence of the Lambs*); Werner Klemperer (Uranus. Colonel Klink on *Hogan's Heroes*); Camille Paglia (Venus. Cultural commentator who is considered a genius by some, a madwoman by others); Richard Nixon (Venus. President who lived in an isolated fantasy world); Alice Cooper (Mercury. *Grand Guignol* shock-rocker—"Caught in a Dream"); Tristan Tzara (Mars. Dadaist crazy); Sandra Bullock (Saturn. Actress—*The Net*); Mike Judge (Jupiter. Cartoonist—*Daria, King of the Hill*); Giulietta Masina (Sun. Actress—*Juliet of the Spirits*); Hugh Hefner (Venus. Founder of *Playboy*, lives in mansion full of erotic delights); Julie Walters (Sun. Actress who played a madam in *Personal Services*); Jean-Paul Sartre (South Node. Existentialist philosopher—*No Exit*).

5 Pisces

A cast party after a benefit performance; partiers carouse, tell tall tales, and join in drunken songs.

Descriptive Phrases

Fostering friendship and harmony between people; dissolving social boundaries; cooperation and teamwork; warm-heartedness; creative ferment of the arty set; bouncing ideas off other people; collaborative efforts; promoting good work by making it fun; zest for living (reckless abandon, sensual dissipation); savoring life's pleasures; crazy hijinks; riding a roller coaster of good and bad fortune; emotional buoyancy (refuse to be brought down); reawakening spiritual sources of emotional inspiration (may lean on alcohol or drugs as social lubricants); ministering to the spiritual and emotional needs of the public; popularization of art and culture; broad appeal (schlock); harmonizing with others vs. finding one's own voice (musical talent); spreading good cheer.

Examples

Carol Burnett (North Node. Comedienne); Carol Channing (Uranus. Broadway veteran—*Hello Dolly*); Allen Funt (North Node. Host of *Candid Camera*); Bill Maher (Venus. Talk-show host—*Politically Incorrect*); Julie Andrews (Saturn. Singer, actress—*Victor, Victoria*); Woody Allen (Saturn. Filmmaker—*Annie Hall, Manhattan*); Luciano Pavarotti (Saturn. Operatic superstar); Willie Nelson (North Node. Country singer—Farm Aid); Gay Talese (Moon. Writer—*Working*); Lawrence Welk (Jupiter. Musical schlockmeister for the older crowd); Robert Louis Stevenson (Neptune. Adventure writer—*Treasure Island*); Celia Franca (Moon. Founder of the National Ballet Company of Canada); Carroll O'Connor (Mars. Comic actor—*All in the Family*); Dale O'Brien (Sun. Astrologer); Stevie Wonder (Jupiter. Singer); Jerry Lee Lewis (Saturn. Early rock and roll superstar, out of control); Geena Davis (Venus. Actress—*Earth Girls Are Easy*).

6 Pisces

An inspection of soldiers in dress uniform. A soldier wearing a red bandana instead of his official hat defiantly stands his ground in the face of the angry rantings of his superior officer.

Descriptive Phrases

Having the courage to stand up and be counted; voicing one's beliefs vs. backing down; using life to test one's mettle (virile pride); giving in to conformist regimentation vs. developing the discipline to effectively realize one's own goals; establishing order in one's workplace or household by articulating well-defined rules (bully others into submission); issues of free speech; presenting the "right image" vs. boldly individualistic dress and behavior (cut a colorful figure); voicing social ideals that demand a new direction in life; joining a movement that holds up a visionary goal (misplaced loyalties); struggles between competing visions of society; open challenges to the existing order (thorny contentiousness); subordinating personal will to group goals, but only on one's own terms.

Examples

Bob Dylan (Mars. Folk singer—"The Times They Are A-Changin'"); George Harrison (Sun. Beatles' guitarist, promoted Indian spirituality); Kathryn Lewis (Uranus. Labor leader); Bill Mauldin (Uranus. Cartoonist who depicted life in World War II's foxholes); Ken Kesey (Saturn. Early acid-head, writer—*One Flew Over the Cuckoo's Nest*); Lucille Ball (Chiron. Actress—*I Love Lucy*); Little Richard (Saturn. Flamboyant rock and roll star); Theodore Roosevelt (North Node. U. S. president, colonialist); Foundation of the Nazi Party (Sun. 2/38/1920); Steve McQueen (Mars. Actor—*The Great Escape*); Giancarlo Giannini (South Node. Ladies' man actor—*Seven Beauties*); Gino Severini (Venus. Futurist artist); Alexander Dubcek (Uranus. Czech leader who led the liberalization that sparked the Russian occupation); Ilona Stoller (North Node. Italian porn star elected to parliament).

7 Pisces

A minister invites a dirty urchin into his church for a bite to eat. The boy stares in wonder at the opulent surroundings and at the beautiful woman singing a hymn.

Descriptive Phrases

Heartfelt concern for the less fortunate; reaching out to those in need (collect stray people or animals); humility of heart that allows one to receive aid as it is given (self-pity); putting oneself in God's hands; immersing oneself in the passionate life, but eventually learning that giving love is better than receiving it (throw tantrums when emotionally thwarted); learning to surrender what is inessential and center oneself in the inner light; mysticism—recognizing that God's love and grace are always close at hand; having one's faith restored by life's little miracles; giving people what they need vs. giving them what they want, even when it's unreal; teaching spiritual truths vs. exploiting people's gullibility; wallowing in illusion vs. achieving spiritual clarity; eloquent expression of heartfelt emotions; finding a safe harbor in the loving heart.

Examples

Audrey Hepburn (Moon. Actress—*My Fair Lady*; worked on problems of world hunger through the United Nations); Carlo Ponti (Chiron. Producer—*La Strada*); Johnny Cash (Sun, Mercury. Hard-luck country singer); Princess Diana (Chiron. Championed various humanitarian causes); Winona Ryder (Moon. Actress—*Girl, Interrupted*); Maria Callas (South Node. Operatic prima donna); Leo Buscaglia (Moon. Teachings on love—Dr. Hug); Meher Baba (Sun. Spiritual teacher—The Silent Prophet); Jackie Gleason (Sun. Comic actor—*The Honeymooners*, occult interests); Josephine Stevens (Moon. Mystic, coauthor of *The Rainbow Bridge*, on building up the light-body); Roger McGuinn (South Node. Leader singer of The Byrds); Saint Francesca Cabrini (Neptune. Nun, social worker).

8 Pisces

An emperor on a throne holding a golden orb in his hand.
Next to him sits the empress, holding an open flower in her hand.
She leans over to him and quietly offers him some frank advice.

Descriptive Phrases

Confident, guileless expression of one's opinions (overstep themselves); naturalness of expression vs. adhering to a prescribed role; redefining sex-roles without losing sight of their function; man and woman as they hold up their own ends of the world; imposing an old order vs. portents of a new egalitarian order; marrying mercy and justice, East and West, Black and white (interracial marriages or other odd pairings); dominating others vs. developing an equal, respectful partnership; combining reason and intuition to arrive at a holistic integration of thought; putting the world in order by thinking globally (counselors who prod the conscience of world leaders); boldly dragging a difficult issue into the spotlight vs. gentle admonitions from the sidelines.

Examples

King Mongkut (Pluto. Siamese king upon whom *The King and I* was based); Elizabeth Taylor (Sun, Mercury. Actress—*Cleopatra*); Benjamin Disraeli (Pluto. Jewish prime minister under Queen Victoria, promoted the British conquest of Africa); Nadine Gordimer (South Node. South African political novelist, antiapartheid); Sidney Poitier (Jupiter. Black actor—*Lilies of the Field*); Vernon Jordan (Saturn. Black advisor and friend of President Clinton); Richard Nixon (Chiron. Conservative president under whom many laws were passed that benefited African Americans); Ariel Sharon (Sun. Israeli political leader, intransigently racist toward indigenous Arabs); Karl Pribram (Mercury. Holographic theory of brain function); Fritjof Capra (Jupiter. Author—*The Tao of Physics*); Michael Caine (North Node. Actor—*Zulu, The Man Who Would Be King*); Charles V (Jupiter. Holy Roman Emperor who ruled much of Europe in the 16th century); Alan Brooke (Moon. Chief military advisor to Churchill).

9 Pisces

In a one-room schoolhouse, a pioneer woman teaches a moral lesson from an episode of history.

Descriptive Phrases

Teaching people what they really need to know; insight and knowledgeability vs. boring people with dry facts or moralizing lectures; drawing spiritual lessons from history or current events; maintaining discipline over oneself and others; finding a balance between indulgence and strictness; running a tight ship but keeping up one's clan's morale; deftness of touch vs. heavy-handedness (cruel); disciplining one's emotions and mind; domination of will over desire (puritanical); concentrating on the task at hand; single-mindedness vs. narrow-mindedness; stoic resolve in facing the ordeals encountered in traveling uncharted territory; the pioneer spirit; traveling the distance for the next generation; serving as a model of rectitude.

Examples

Ralph Nader (Sun. Consumer advocate); Jean Marsh (Moon. Actress—*Upstairs, Downstairs*); Alan Alda and Mike Farrell (Saturn and Jupiter, respectively. Actors in TV's *M*A*S*H*); Agnes Moorehead (Saturn. Actress who specialized in prigs and old maids); Rudolf Serkin (Jupiter. Classical pianist); Chuck Connors (Uranus. Actor—*The Rifleman*); Queen Mary (Sun. Bloody Mary, violently persecuted English Protestants); Robert Louis Stevenson (Moon. Author—*Treasure Island*); Joseph Smith (Pluto. Mormon leader); Alex Haley (Uranus. Author—*Roots*); Florence Henderson (Mars. Actress—*The Brady Bunch*); Gavin McLeod (Sun. Actor—*The Love Boat*); William Wilson (North Node. Cofounder of Alcoholics Anonymous); Edward Bulwer-Lytton (Pluto. Writer—*The Last Days of Pompei*); Father Coughlin (Jupiter. Anti-Semitic radio preacher); Emile Coué (Sun. Promoted the power of positive thinking); Gloria Steinem (Mercury. Feminist author).

10 Pisces

The queen's cat scouts around the rooftops of the palace. Through a window far below, it sees a mouse stealing some cheese.

Descriptive Phrases

Having a clear inner picture of what's going on in one's domain vs. gathering more information; looking down on life from a lofty perspective (removed, withdrawn); exploring things from various angles; catching something going on under the surface that doesn't jibe with outer appearances; grilling people when one suspects some sort of ruse; pouncing on dishonesty vs. accepting life as it is; trusting the inner eye of intuition as well as one's outer eyes (psychic flashes); finding out what is going on under the surface (exploring physical or metaphysical causality); translating one's highest self-image into everyday behavior; inner nobility vs. vain posing; finding a secure position that doesn't require too much work; slyly playful knowingness.

Examples

Kenny Kingston (Mercury. Television psychic); Glynis Johns (South Node. Actress—*The Sword and the Rose, The Chapman Report*); Francis Bacon (Pluto, Venus. Early scientific theorist, attorney general and lord chancellor of England, disgraced for accepting bribes); Donald Sutherland (Saturn. Actor—*Start the Revolution Without Me, M*A*S*H, Casanova*); Kurt Vonnegut (Uranus. Sci-fi writer—*The Sirens of Titan*); Helen Gurley Brown (Uranus. Founder of *Cosmopolitan* magazine); Nancy Reagan (Uranus. First Lady, believer in astrology); David Niven (Sun. Actor—*The Pink Panther, The King's Thief,* first wife died at a housewarming party by falling down the stairs); Sam Donaldson (Mercury. Aggressive newscaster, reporter); Julia Child (Chiron. TV chef, wit); Cassandra Peterson (North Node. Plays the heavy-metal horror host Elvira); Edgar Cayce (North Node. The Sleeping Prophet); Rudolf Steiner (Sun. Occultist—Anthroposophy); J. Edgar Hoover (Moon. Head of the FBI, with files on everyone).

11 Pisces

Old childhood friends, on a road trip, are camped by the side of the road and talking over their lives.

Descriptive Phrases

Camaraderie; being "one of the gang"; sharing the brotherly or sisterly intimacy characteristic of undemanding childhood friendships (nostalgic connection to the innocence and simplicity of childhood); letting down one's hair; lending a sympathetic ear; supporting other people's hopes and ideals and sympathizing with their disappointments; finding fellow travelers who share and reinforce one's values; trying to make a soul-to-soul connection with everyone one meets vs. cynicism and disillusionment with humanity; maintaining old loyalties vs. losing a relationship when one fails to bring it to a new level; long-term relationships tested by shared experiences; fun-loving adventurers on the open road (aimless wandering); informal spiritual brotherhoods.

Examples

Jack Kerouac (Uranus. Poet, writer—*On the Road*); Sissy Spacek (Moon. Actress—*Badlands*); Calamity Jane (Neptune. Fearless, hard-drinking, gun-toting frontier scout); Burt Reynolds (Saturn. Actor—*Smokey and the Bandit*); Ben Stiller (Saturn. Actor—*Flirting with Disaster, There's Something about Mary*); Carl Reiner (Uranus. Actor, director—*The Jerk*); Emiliano Zapata (Jupiter. Mexican revolutionary); Alan Alda (Mars. Actor—*M*A*S*H*); Mary Martin (Chiron. Singer, actress—*Peter Pan*); Peggy Seeger (Saturn. Folk singer); Roger Daltrey (Sun. Lead singer for The Who—*Tommy*); Barbara Streisand (South Node. Singer, actress—*What's Up Doc?*, *Yentl*); Bobby Stone (Uranus. Actor—*Dead End Kids*); Larry Storch (Uranus. Actor—*F Troop*); Barbara Billingsley (Uranus. Actress—*Leave It to Beaver*); Tatum O'Neal (Chiron. Child actress—*Paper Moon, Bad News Bears*).

12 Pisces

The veiled door of the inner sanctum, framed by smoking censers. In the foreground, a candidate for initiation is being examined.

Descriptive Phrases

Inclusion vs. exclusion from a group; being initiated into a new view of reality vs. cynical rejection of anything that isn't immediately apparent; Plato's cave: living among the shadows vs. working with the spiritual myths behind cultural manifestations; seeing the fluid nature of reality; using drugs to enter a new reality (ungrounded beliefs); removing obstacles in consciousness before one can connect with a new set of truths; putting one's own house in order by faithfully applying one's ideals before setting out to reform larger groups; living between two worlds and deciphering one for the other; working behind the scenes (skulduggery); inside information; entering into profitable alliances; balancing personal goals with group goals (mavericks).

Examples

J. B. Rhine (North Node. Pioneered the scientific study of ESP); Dr. Albert Hofmann (Mars. Chemist who discovered LSD); Mary McCarthy (Chiron. Writer—*The Group*); Brad Pitt (Saturn. Actor—*Fight Club*); Bruno Seghetti (Moon. Member of the terrorist Red Brigade that killed Aldo Moro); Randy Shilts (North Node. Gay rights activist); Jean Auel (Saturn. Writer—*Clan of the Cave Bear*); Hermann Hesse (Mars. Writer—*Steppenwolf*); Isis-Urania Temple of the Golden Dawn is authorized (Sun. 3/1/1888); Alan Freed (North Node. Discovered and produced unrecognized blues musicians); Marianne Alireza (Uranus. Became a harem wife, then divorced); Louis Lumière (Chiron. Co-invented color cinematography); Lyndon Larouche (Uranus. Right-wing cult leader); St. Francesca Cabrini (Neptune. Initiated into Catholic sainthood); Edgar Cayce (Mercury. Mystic—The Sleeping Prophet); Richard Sorge (North Node. Soviet spy who penetrated Japanese military circles); Tom Wolfe (Sun. Journalistic novelist who is adept at inserting himself into various "in groups"—*The Electric Kool-Aid Acid Test, The Pump-House Gang*).

13 Pisces

A huge dish-shaped radio telescope. Inside the facility, scientists of different nationalities squabble over how to accurately represent the data.

Descriptive Phrases

Trying to establish an objective framework of understanding beyond any one set of assumptions; reconstructing an accurate picture of reality from the data; accurately transmitting information across space, from one culture to another, or from one sex to another; explaining one's position step by step vs. derailing someone else's train of thought when one does not accept their assumptions; penetrating to the crux of a disagreement; adapting to another way of seeing things vs. insisting on one's own interpretation (dogmatic); arguing at close quarters; odd couples; mix-and-match relationships; trying to find a higher harmony (astrology, astronomy, scientific research and invention); putting worldly events and human relationships in a cosmic context; conforming one's life to celestial patterns vs. moral anarchy bred of chronic indecision.

Examples

Alexander Graham Bell (Sun. Inventor of the telephone); Philo T. Farnsworth (Saturn. Inventor of television); Galileo Galilei (Mercury. Fought against Cardinal Bellarmine for the heliocentric theory of the universe); Dr. Bart Bok (Saturn. Astronomer); Erica Jong (South Node. Feminist author—*Fear of Flying*); Henry Miller (Jupiter. Author—*Tropic of Cancer*); Dean Stockwell (Saturn. Actor—*Quantum Leap*); James Clavell (Moon. Author—*Shogun*); Richard Chamberlain (Mercury. Actor—*Shogun, The Last Wave*); Jesse Ventura (North Node. Wrestler, maverick politician); Diana Ross (Venus. Lead singer of The Supremes); John Boswell (Mars. Scholar—*Same-Sex Unions in Early Modern Europe*); Howard Zinn (Uranus. Radical reformulator of U. S. history); Lincoln's "A house divided cannot stand" speech (North Node. 6/16/1858); Joan Grant (Venus. Writer—novels about ancient Egypt).

14 Pisces

At a cocktail party onboard ship, a glamorous starlet in a fox stole motions some revelers toward a private room.

Descriptive Phrases

The moon in its dual role, as artistic muse or as temptress; wariness about being sucked into someone else's trip vs. sliding down a slippery path into drug abuse or sexual sleaze; insouciance and good humor in navigating life's deceptive waters; worldliness; sly sophistication; drawing someone in with a line of patter or with a seductive fantasy (fantasy writers, or artists who paint a tempting picture); embodying an imaginative ideal; life as art (living an illusion); making oneself attractive and desirable; personal magnetism; poise and style; staying on an even keel vs. stumbling through emotional highs and lows (stormy relationships); having a full range of life experiences vs. choosing associates carefully once one has "done all that."

Examples

Blake Edwards (Uranus. Director—*Operation Petticoat, The Pink Panther,* married to Julie Andrews); Carrie Fisher (Mars. Actress—*Star Wars,* cocaine problem); Judy Garland (Uranus. Singer, actress—*The Wizard of Oz, A Star Is Born*); Marion Barry (Saturn. Ex-mayor of Washington D. C., cocaine abuser); Arthur Rimbaud (Neptune. Poet—*A Season in Hell*); Hugh Hefner (Moon. Head of the *Playboy* empire); Conan O'Brien (Chiron. Humorist, talk-show host); Laura Dern (Venus. Actress—*Foxes, Blue Velvet, Jurassic Park*); Pier Paolo Pasolini (Sun. Filmmaker—*The Gospel According to St. Matthew, Arabian Nights;* murdered by gay pickup); Frances Willard (Uranus. Head of Temperance Union); George Reeves (North Node. Actor—*Superman,* suicide at a party); Tennessee Williams (North Node. Playwright—*Cat on a Hot Tin Roof*); Evelyn Waugh (Jupiter. Writer—*The Loved One*); Emile Zola (Venus. Writer who scandalized the public with *Nana,* the realistic depiction of the life of a prostitute).

15 Pisces

A soldier in tattered clothing takes aim during rifle practice, but has trouble keeping his mind off a personal matter.

Descriptive Phrases

Focusing in on a problem; being on target; intellectual penetration; single-minded concentration on the task at hand vs. rethinking one's larger direction in life (rudderless); physical and mental self-discipline; perfecting some skill through practice; submitting to a regimen; trying to balance one's duty to society and duty to oneself (being fully accountable); organizing one's life around private spiritual beliefs vs. obeying an external authority; penetration of personal will by divine will; energetic pursuit of personal goals despite a lack of social support (risk defeat for some glorious objective); keen analysis of self and society (self-absorbed); hard-nosed political analysis vs. following a personal code of honor during some private quest; martial arts; achieving peak performance.

Examples

Margaret Bourke-White (Saturn. Photojournalist, followed Patton behind German lines); Sir Richard Burton (Mars. Adventurer—*The Complete Book of Bayonet Exercises*); Fritz Fischer (Sun. Historian—*Germany's Aims in the First World War*); Camille Paglia (Mercury. Penetrating cultural analyst); Friedrich Engels (Jupiter. Communist theorist); Roger Staubach (South Node. Quarterback—Dallas Cowboys); Johnny Depp (Chiron. Actor—*Don Juan de Marco, Pirates of the Caribbean*); Edmond Rostand (Mercury. Writer—*Cyrano de Bergerac*); Alec Guiness (Mercury. Actor—*Star Wars*, with its "light saber"); Therese Neumann (Mars. Catholic saint—received the stigmata); Errol Flynn (Mars. Actor—*The Charge of the Light Brigade*); Sarah Brady (South Node. Antigun activist); Carmen de Lavallade (Sun. Ballet—interpreted West Indian dances).

16 Pisces

Wine goblet in hand, a composer in his studio stares off into space. Coming back to himself, he begins to write down a new piece.

Descriptive Phrases

Tuning in to one's muse; drinking deeply at the source of inspiration; recognizing that creative work is a sober, isolated process, demanding a special place and a calm and receptive state of mind (use the rosy glow of alcohol to get their creative juices flowing); appreciating the finer things in life and recognizing that their source is internal (music, poetry, art); viewing inner landscapes of the heart and projecting these onto the outer world (fall in love easily, become intoxicated by the idealized image of the beloved); art as a sacred trust; resonating to the pathos of the human condition; the human heart as it rests within the heart of God; the Holy Grail, and the quintessential life-essence it contains; losing oneself in the greater harmony.

Examples

Franz Schubert (Jupiter. Romantic composer); Dick Cavett (Saturn, Stationary. Talk-show host); Betty Ford (Moon. First Lady, set up alcoholism treatment center); Robert Young (Saturn. Actor—*Father Knows Best*, secret alcoholic); Mary Travers (Saturn. Singer—Peter, Paul and Mary); Benjamin Spock (Jupiter. Influential pediatrician); Buckminster Fuller (North Node. Futurist—inventor of the geodesic dome); Miles Davis (Mars. Meditative jazz trumpeter, drug addict); Hugh Grant (South Node. Actor—*Four Weddings and a Funeral*); Audrey Meadows (Uranus. Actress—Alice on *The Honeymooners*); Benny Hill (Uranus. Vaudevillian comic); Frédéric Chopin (Pluto. Lushly romantic composer); Mary Wilson (Sun. Singer—The Supremes); Carl Sandburg (Saturn. Poet); W. H. Auden (Saturn. Poet); Annie Lennox (Mars. Moody singer for The Eurhythmics).

17 Pisces

Crossing a footbridge with a heavy burden, a man falls through some broken slats and finds himself in the stream in a sopping heap. Concerned bystanders rush to his aid.

Descriptive Phrases

Trying to manage a large task on one's own vs. knowing when one should ask for help (recklessness); recognizing the interdependency of the human community; giving and receiving aid; angling for sympathy by explaining the difficulty of one's situation vs. unwillingness to reach out to others; eliciting emotional support from family, friends, or lovers (decency, emotional openness); tenderhearted affection that dissolves boundaries between people; looking after emotional ties in relationships vs. letting them fall through due to unresolved misunderstandings; reaching an implicit understanding that is not threatened by occasional quarrels; humility vs. foolish pride (critical, uncompromising, demand to be taken on their own terms, need to be coaxed); seeing something through vs. giving up in exasperation; looking out for one another; sympathy given and received.

Examples

Tony Randall (Uranus. Actor—*The Odd Couple*); Oliver Hardy (Jupiter. Comedian); Patsy Cline (North Node. Country singer); Tammy Faye Bakker (Sun. Praise the Lord club, husband thrown in jail); Neil Sedaka (Jupiter. Singer—"Breaking Up Is Hard to Do"); Charles Dickens (Venus. Writer with great compassion for the poor—*Great Expectations*); Alcide de Gaspari (Mercury. Saved Italy from Communist domination after World War II); Joseph Heller (Uranus. Writer—*Catch 22*); John Leguizamo (Saturn. Confessional comedian); Mistinguette (Mercury. Music hall singer, Maurice Chevalier's lover until her possessiveness drove him away); Anna Magnani (Sun. Actress—*Il Miracolo, The Rose Tattoo*); Cardinal Joseph Bernardin (Mercury. Accused falsely of child abuse, led Church to an antinuclear stance).

18 Pisces

Inside a huge tent, a populist politician stirs up the crowd with damning facts about government corruption.

Descriptive Phrases

Reformers and public servants; aggressively debating matters of public policy; using galvanizing oratory to build a movement (propagandists, demagogues); staking out the main points of one's argument; collecting one's facts vs. relying on inflated claims that can be easily punctured; attacking a foe's position; uncovering people's true beliefs by getting a rise out of them (honest self-representation vs. false packaging); policing the beliefs and behavior of one's group (intolerant of dissent); insider-outsider issues; tailoring one's message to one's audience vs. refusing to dress up an ugly situation (sharp-spoken); getting the wrinkles out of one's presentation; addressing some public need; getting one's act together and pitching it to the public.

Examples

Frank Serpico (Saturn. Police reformer); Ramsey Clark (Uranus. Ex-attorney general, champion of civil rights and an enlightened foreign policy); John Madden (Saturn. Pompous football coach, sportscaster); Shirley Chisholm (Uranus. Militant Black congresswoman); Ed Koch (Uranus. No-nonsense mayor of New York); Anita Bryant (Mercury. Singer, antigay propagandist); Vaclav Havel (Saturn. Gadfly poet, president of Czechoslovakia after Communist rule); Rupert D'Oyley Carte (North Node. Theatrical producer of Gilbert and Sullivan musicals); Rona Barrett (Saturn. Blunt gossip columnist); Peter F. Davis (Saturn. Producer—*The Selling of the Pentagon*); Hugh Trevor-Roper (North Node. Historian of the great European witch hunt); Shirley MacLaine (Venus. Actress, propagandist for New Age beliefs); Cesar Chavez (Jupiter. Farmworkers' union organizer); Lazaro Cardenas (North Node. Populist president of Mexico, nationalized the oil industry).

19 Pisces

A beautiful and charismatic woman exhorts a crowd of citizens to settle their differences and rebuild a tumbledown cathedral.

Descriptive Phrases

Devoting one's life to setting the world in order; getting people to see one's vision and enlisting them to help materialize that vision (purveyors of empty forms); building a following; preaching important messages concerning the social or spiritual condition of humanity; elevating the mind above petty squabbles and focusing on the more important things in life (religious concerns); conscious leadership vs. infantilizing one's followers by making decisions for them (collect disciples or even minions); persuasiveness; exceptional personal charm and charisma, used either for selfish ends or for the betterment of society (sexual narcissism); getting people on one's wavelength (musicality, emotional lushness); cleaning up society vs. cleaning up one's own act; passionate pronouncements.

Examples

Martin Luther King, Jr. (Moon. Civil-rights activist); Charlton Heston (Uranus. Actor—*Planet of the Apes*, president of the National Rifle Association); Yukio Mishima (Uranus. Sexually morbid writer, paramilitary leader); Curt Jurgens (Mercury. Actor—*Lord Jim*, *The Devil's General*); Lola Albright (Moon. Actress—*The Way West*, *The Treasure of Ruby Hills*); Tina Turner (South Node. Rock singer, actress—*Mad Max Beyond Thunderdome*); Frank Sinatra (Chiron. Idolized singer with ties to the mob); Edith Piaf (Chiron. French torch singer); Alan Cranston (Chiron. California senator, annotated *Mein Kampf* to alert Americans to the dangers of Hitler, anti-nuclear activist); Jeddu Krishnamurti (North Node. Charismatic spiritual teacher, kundalini experiences); Beau Bridges (South Node. Actor—*Norma Rae*); Vance Packard (Chiron. Muckraking author who took on the advertising industry—*The Hidden Persuaders*); Juliette Prowse (Saturn. Charismatic dancer); Johannes Kepler (Jupiter. Reformed astronomy to correspond to the divine and natural order).

20 Pisces

An animated homecoming party with a live orchestra. Outside in the cold drizzle, the guest of honor looks in to see his fiancée dancing with another man.

Descriptive Phrases

Living into a romantic image of oneself and of life and seeing how far one can go with it; promoting one's public image (glamorous, self-created "characters" with a sense of being special); spirited enjoyment of life (big-time partiers); getting caught up in an intoxicating shared illusion and then suffering a sobering moment when one catches a glimpse of a more authentic level of reality; reading unmistakable "signs" (psychic powers); losing oneself in the passionate momentum of life (ill-advised affairs) vs. finding oneself in moments of self-reflection; trying to escape the collective illusions of one's family; social schmoozing; music and dance; raising one's spirits vs. being brought down; enchantment vs. disenchantment.

Examples

Bette Davis (Mercury. Actress—*Jezebel, Dark Victory*); Kate Chase (Uranus. Socialite in Abe Lincoln's circle, adulteress, died friendless); Arthur Miller (Jupiter. Playwright—*Death of a Salesman, The Crucible*, which was aimed at the mass delusion of McCarthyism); Jack Lemmon (Uranus. Actor—*Glengarry Glen Ross, A Long Day's Journey into Night*); Paul Newman (Uranus. Actor—*The Sting*, director—*The Glass Menagerie*); Vanessa Redgrave (Saturn. Actress—*Blow-Up*); Kelley Quinn (Sun. Jet-set psychic); Lauren Bacall (Uranus. Actress—*To Have and Have Not, How to Marry a Millionaire*); Count Basie (South Node. Band leader); Lawrence Welk (Sun. Champagne music for the geriatric set); Diamond Jim Brady (Neptune. Railroad-car entrepreneur, *bon vivant*); Grace Metalious (North Node. Author—*Peyton Place*); Louisa May Alcott (Jupiter. Author—*Little Women*); Cardinal Richelieu (Moon. Hard-nosed chief minister of Louis XIII); Georges Balanchine (Jupiter. Ballet choreographer); Rudolph Valentino (North Node. Actor—*The Sheik*).

21 Pisces

By the light of a lantern, a woman reads
to her wide-eyed child from an illustrated book.
During the scary episodes, she strokes her hair.

Descriptive Phrases

Exploring the inner world of the imagination (literature, art); timeless truths of the spiritual realm; life as an image from a magic lantern (occultism, tarot, Cabala); applying fables and symbols to everyday life; playing the protagonist in one's own myth (trapped in subconscious scripts); protecting the child-self by holding to comforting memories and stories; nurturing a sense of wonder; passing on one's life wisdom to the younger generation; common imaginative threads that run through several generations; trying out different interpretive keys to unconscious symbols; shifting from literal to allegorical readings of experience (bifocal glasses); psychology and occultism (scary vortexes); dramatic readings; gentle guidance.

Examples

Hermann Hesse (Saturn. Writer of novels with occult themes—*Steppenwolf, Damian*); Maya Angelou (Mercury. Poet, writer—*I Know Why the Caged Bird Sings*); Bruno Bettelheim (Jupiter. Psychiatrist who specializes in autism, wrote *The Uses of Enchantment* on the psychological benefits of fairy tales); Edward Gorey (Uranus. Macabre humorist—*Amphigorey*); L. Frank Baum (Neptune. Author of *Oz* books); A. E. Waite (Neptune. Occultist—the Waite tarot); Pamela Smith (Saturn. Illustrator of the Waite tarot); Orson Welles (Jupiter. Filmmaker, actor, radio broadcaster—*War of the Worlds*); Marilyn Monroe (Mars. Childlike actress—*The Prince and the Showgirl*); George Bernard Shaw (Neptune. Playwright—*Pygmalion*); Douglas Adams (Sun. Writer—*A Hitchhiker's Guide to the Galaxy*); Laraine Newman (Mercury. Comedienne—*Saturday Night Live*); H. Rider Haggard (Neptune. Writer—*She*).

22 Pisces

From the top of the courthouse steps, a lawmaker explains a new piece of legislation. Citizens of different backgrounds exhibit varying reactions.

Descriptive Phrases

The creation, interpretation, and enforcement of the law; politicians, judges, lawyers, and law enforcement officers; the two pillars of justice upon which society is based—severity vs. mercy, law enforcement vs. individual liberty; explaining one's final judgment on a matter, once one has looked at all the evidence; teaching and preaching (sincere attempt to communicate in simple, straightforward language vs. pretentious condescension); law based on custom vs. law based on principle; trying to base laws on universal moral principles, rather than giving in to special interest groups; investigating different subcultures and making accommodations vs. dictatorial imposition of ruling class policies; aggressively promoting some reform in policy; humanity and human society as works in progress.

Examples

Otto von Bismarck (Pluto. German politician who united the German people under one government); L. Ron Hubbard (Sun. Founder of Scientology); Evangeline Adams (Venus. Astrologer, defended astrology in court); Clarence Darrow (Neptune. Lawyer, defended a schoolteacher accused of teaching evolution); Lester Maddox (Jupiter. Segregationist who stood outside his restaurant and threatened potential Black patrons with an axe handle; was elected governor of Georgia); Morarji Desai (Midheaven. Arrested five times in the fight for Indian independence, was elected prime minister); Jesse Jackson (South Node. Black reverend, politician, spokesperson); Voltaire (Neptune. Enlightenment leader, cultural relativist, writer—*The Philosophical Letters*); George Bush, Sr. (Uranus. CIA director, U. S. president); Don Knotts (Uranus. Actor—played an ineffectual police officer); Linus Pauling (Mercury. Nobel chemist, vitamin C advocate); Bess Myerson (Uranus. Actress, consumer advocate).

23 Pisces

The wife of a fallen general, springing up from his body, delivers a stirring speech to his comrades, and then leads them into battle.

Descriptive Phrases

Identifying with a cause that will survive the death of the body; stirring up the public and enlisting them in one's cause (rabble-rousers); breathing life into an inert body-politic; demanding that the state serve the people rather than itself; tailoring one's message to an audience vs. getting a rise out of people with blustering pronouncements (muddy rants vs. persuasive spiritual clarity); sharp, critical commentary aimed at demolishing one's opponents' position; political or social humor; spiritual resurrection (Jesus on the cross as an undying presence vs. having a martyr complex); attacking sacred cows (blasphemy); reeducating a misguided public and prodding them to take the next evolutionary step; political or military leadership; populism.

Examples

Ulysses S. Grant (Venus. Civil War general); Margaret Thatcher (Uranus. Militaristic prime minister); Rush Limbaugh (North Node. Right-wing talk-radio host); Bernie Sanders (South Node. Populist congressman); Cesar Chavez (Moon. Organized migrant workers); General George Patton (South Node. Self-willed general in World War II); Francis Ford Coppola (Jupiter. Film producer—*Koyaanisqatsi*, director—*Apocalypse Now*); Norman Mailer (South Node. Writer—*The Naked and the Dead, The Gospel According to the Son*); Gore Vidal (Uranus. Writer, leftist political commentator—*Burr, Live from Golgotha*); Barbara Hershey (Venus. Actress—*The Last Temptation of Christ*); Alice Cooper (Venus. Shock-rock—"Bodies Need Rest"); Tom Robbins (Saturn. Writer—*Another Roadside Attraction*); Anna Louise Strong (South Node. Radical journalist, Communist convert who lived in China); Elizabeth Clare Prophet (Jupiter. Apocalyptic Christian cult leader); Andrew Young (Sun. Civil-rights leader, pastor).

24 Pisces

A European scientist living on a South Seas island among the natives.

Descriptive Phrases

Isolated pursuit of truth; having to figure things out for oneself (perplexity, confusion); establishing a beachhead in some field of human knowledge; intellectual resourcefulness; building on the solid foundation of what one knows from personal experience and experiment, apart from common belief (alienated); intellectual isolation vs. creating common ground for communication; bringing civility to some cultural backwater (anthropological perspectives); trying to forge a link between one's private world and the larger universe (macrocosm-microcosm issues); reevaluating one's place in the world; scientific thought, especially in the fields of physics and astronomy; reexamining basic assumptions and basic terms; disillusioning clarifications.

Examples

Albert Einstein (Sun. Physicist—theory of relativity); Robert Millikan (Jupiter. Physicist who determined the charge of the electron); Bob Denver (Moon. Actor—*Gilligan's Island, Dobie Gillis*); Laura Dern (Chiron. Actress—*Jurassic Park*); McLean Stevenson (Jupiter. Actor—*M*A*S*H*); Ringo Starr (Ascendant. Drummer—"Octopus's Garden," actor—*The Magic Christian*); Havelock Ellis (Neptune. Sex researcher); N. O. Brown (North Node. Studied sexual culture in *Love's Body*); Camille Paglia (Mars. Cultural gadfly who takes aim at the beloved myths of deconstructionism and feminism); Betty Friedan (Mars. Feminist pioneer); Coretta King (Jupiter. Civil-rights activist); Karl Pribram (Mars. Holographic model of brain function); Napoleon Bonaparte (Chiron. Conqueror, civilizer, exiled to the islands of Elba and St. Helena); Colette (Venus. Risqué writer); Camille Flammarion (Uranus. 19th-century astronomer and psychic researcher).

25 Pisces

A giant bear, after ravaging the countryside, is harried by a barking dog. Other dogs arrive and join the fray, as well as a farmer who exhorts the dogs to greater efforts.

Descriptive Phrases

Tracking down major abusers of power and attempting to end their influence; underdogs who take on a much more powerful opponent; using cunning and defensive measures while soliciting aid from others; feints and evasions to protect oneself from attack (run circles around their opponents); postponing a head-on assault until one has enough strength to win, and then going in for the kill (brutality, misuse of power); having the courage of one's convictions; drawing inevitable conclusions from the available facts (paint themselves into a corner, feel compelled to act upon their conclusions); translating what one knows into what one does; acting upon one's religious, political, or philosophical beliefs; consolidating a belief and working out its finer ramifications; inspiring others by one's actions vs. expecting to change the world with mere words.

Examples

Malcolm X (Uranus. Revolutionary Black leader); Emmeline Pankhurst (Neptune. Fought for women's suffrage); Fay Wray (Saturn. Actress—*King Kong*); Yogi Berra (Uranus. Baseball slugger); "Bear" Bryant (North Node. Football coach); Karl Marx (Chiron. Bearish Communist revolutionary theorist); Gabriele Amorth (Uranus. Priest, exorcist); Ida Tarbell (North Node. Muckraking writer—*The History of the Standard Oil Company*); Joni Mitchell (Moon. Folk-rock singer—social protest); Joan Armatrading (North Node. Folk singer); Herman Wouk (Jupiter. Writer—*The Caine Mutiny*); Alan Greenspan (Uranus. Director of the Federal Reserve); John Mitchell (North Node. Nixon attorney general); Meadowlark Lemon (North Node. Basketball player in the Harlem Globetrotters); Cybill Shepherd (Moon. Actress—*Mad About You, Silver Bears*, spokeswoman for Voters for Choice).

26 Pisces

A king contemplates the battlefield by the light of the new moon, while ministers of differing temperaments give him conflicting advice.

Descriptive Phrases

Using both reason and intuition in decision-making; weighing the consequences of possible courses of action, particularly the making or breaking of alliances; knowing who one's friends and enemies are (fear retaliation for split-offs, but also fear that their enemies will subvert their position if appeased); clarifying issues through discussion (don't really listen); holding to one's principles inwardly, but publicly playing a close hand; looking for a way out of a bad situation (environmentalists); vacillation vs. ruthless decisiveness if a window of opportunity opens up (unpopular decisions); the sickle moon as a double-edged axe that ends one cycle and begins another; diplomatic maneuvering; directing society's overall course through policy decisions.

Examples

Indira Gandhi (Chiron. Prime minister of India who suspended civil rights and attempted to destroy her political enemies; assassinated by a Sikh avenging his people); Eugene V. Rostow (North Node. Law professor, expert on international arms control); Edward Koch (Mars. Feisty Republican mayor of New York); Jeanne Kirkpatrick (Uranus. Ambassador to the United Nations, right-wing ideologue); Nat Hentoff (Uranus. Uncompromising civil libertarian); Rachel Carson (Saturn. Pioneering environmentalist—*Silent Spring*); Gertrude Stein (Mars. Author who presided over a literary salon); Lawrence Olivier (Saturn. Played Hamlet); Robespierre (Uranus. Presided over the Reign of Terror in the French Revolution); Bruno Pontecorvo (North Node. Nuclear physicist who defected to Russia); Ingrid Bergman (Jupiter. Actress—*Casablanca, Suspicion*); George C. Scott (Jupiter. Actor—*Patton*); President James Monroe (Uranus. The Monroe Doctrine made the Western hemisphere off limits to European imperialism).

27 Pisces

A melon patch under a full moon. A farmer picks up a melon and finds a snake coiled under it and the bottom of the melon eaten.

Descriptive Phrases

Introducing a delightful and refreshing cultural form that feeds a spiritual appetite in the public and thus takes off (unexpected reversals, must occasionally patch up major snags in their plans); self-cultivation vs. allowing decay to creep in through neglect; entering a new phase of the evolutionary spiral vs. being mired in a cycle of bad habits; seeing both the light and dark sides of life (uncovering ugly truths and denouncing them, alerting others to hidden dangers, sharing inside information); working with dangerous energies or issues vs. cultivating some pleasant field of interest; being cultivated vs. being crude and nasty; serene reflection on what has been accomplished vs. troubled recognition of what is still missing; exposing a hidden truth.

Examples

Billy Carter (Saturn. Peanut farmer, Jimmy Carter's brother); Roger Corman (Uranus. Filmmaker—*Little Shop of Horrors*); Olivia de Havilland (Chiron. Actress—*The Snake Pit, Robin Hood*); Kurt Russell (Sun. Actor—*Stargate, Silkwood*); Kathy Bates (Moon. Actress—*Dolores Claiborne*); H. R. Haldeman (Uranus. Nixon aide, felon); John Wayne Gacy (Sun. Serial killer with a pile of bodies buried in his basement); Emily Brontë (Pluto. Writer—*Wuthering Heights*); Charles Schulz (South Node. Cartoonist—*Peanuts*); Chuck Berry (Uranus. Rock musician); Hugh Hefner (Uranus. Publisher of erotica, muckraker, many exposés); R. D. Laing (Jupiter. Psychologist—family-induced schizophrenia); Papa Doc Duvalier (Mercury. Scary Haitian dictator); Arthur Conan Doyle (Neptune. Author of Sherlock Holmes mysteries).

28 Pisces

Somber queen stands at the prow of a boat as it floats quietly down a river toward the rising moon. In her hands, she holds a coffer containing a sacred book.

Descriptive Phrases

Keeping one's personal goals clearly before the mind's eye; staying on course, undistracted by society's enticements and threats; navigating foreign or hostile territory; guiding others on a journey of the imagination (literature and art, ranging from profound revelations to entertaining romps); drawing others into a compelling vision of reality; getting at the universals of human thought and emotion by working with symbols and archetypes; penetrating insight into the human heart (psychic); discernment of human weaknesses and foibles (holding others' secrets in trust); probing to see how much another person is willing to acknowledge; knowing when the public is ready for the next evolutionary step; magnetic personal presence; bearing a gift for the world.

Examples

Herman Melville (Pluto. Author—*Moby Dick*); Jean Auel (Mars. Writer—*Clan of the Cave Bear*); Luc Besson (Sun. Filmmaker—*The Fifth Element*); Robert Heinlein (Saturn. Science fiction writer—*Stranger in a Strange Land*); E. M. Forster (Saturn. Writer—*A Passage to India*); Merle Haggard (Saturn. "Outlaw" country singer); Vanessa Redgrave (Venus. Actress—Queen Guinevere in *Camelot, Mary Queen of Scots, Isadora*); Frida Kahlo (Saturn. Painter); Liz Taylor (North Node. Actress—*Cleopatra*); Leontyne Price (Uranus. Black opera star); John Sayles (North Node. Filmmaker—*Brother from Another Planet, Matewan*); Joseph Campbell (South Node. Mythologist—*Hero with a Thousand Faces*); Manley Palmer Hall (Sun. Oriental scholar, Freemason, occultist, wrote a book on the chakras, had a library of over 50,000 books); Charles Baudelaire (Mercury. Decadent poet); Fred Hoyle (Jupiter. Astronomer, sci-fi author).

29 Pisces

Trowel in hand, a woman stands in the midst of a brilliantly colored flower garden and surveys her work. Over her shoulder, a rainbow is shining.

Descriptive Phrases

Confidently manifesting a luminous vision of life and the world; living into one's vision by bringing it down into the smallest details of one's life (staginess—as if one were acting in front of a painted backdrop); supplying missing information that brings the picture into sharper focus (puncturing counterfeit images vs. dreamy romanticism); bringing emotional sparkle and color to everyday life; viewing nature's transcendent beauty and poetry as life's primary reality; seeing a higher harmony behind life's varied expressions; nurturing people's spiritual life with affection, attention, and knowledge; awakening people to spiritual potentials within themselves; disseminating vital new cultural impulses; poised unity of behavior and belief.

Examples

Vincent Van Gogh (Venus. Artist); Mary Cassatt (Jupiter. Artist); Rex Harrison (Saturn. Actor—*My Fair Lady, Anna and the King of Siam*); Queen Victoria (Saturn. Presided over the Victorian Age); First showing of *Snow White* (Saturn. 12/21/1937); Judy Collins (Jupiter. Folk singer—"Both Sides Now"); Marilyn Monroe (Uranus. Movie star); Padre Pio (Mercury. Received the stigmata through meditation on the inner Christ); Edgar Cayce (Sun. Clairvoyant, spiritual teacher); Dorothy Kilgallen (North Node. Panelist on *What's My Line?*); Rudolf Steiner (Neptune. Clairvoyant, spiritual teacher); Victoria Sackville-West (Jupiter. Poet with a scandalous love life and a famous garden); Grandma Moses (Neptune. Primitive painter); Maurice de Vlaminck (North Node. Artist who portrayed nature in wild, intense colors, leader of the *fauves*); Henri Rousseau (Jupiter. Primitive painter); Wassily Kandinsky (South Node. Abstract artist who used wild color combinations).

30 Pisces

A prisoner in a chain gang is driven down a cliff-side road by a guard with a gun. Realizing that his shackles are too loose to hold him, he escapes up a gully toward a little settlement on the mountainside.

Descriptive Phrases

Realizing that how high (or how low) one goes depends on limitations in inner consciousness—that heaven and hell are within; doing what one wants, but living with the karmic consequences (don't respect social limits); using one's free will wisely; knowing which desires to follow in life vs. being pushed to the edge of a moral abyss by negative passions; following one's childlike innocence of heart toward a more peaceful state of being (may have to work their way out of a state of bondage); giving oneself the go-ahead to enjoy life and pursue one's dreams vs. trying to police others into accepting one's own limits (slave-drivers, sadists); getting trapped in a rigid self-image vs. breaking the mold and trying out a bold new persona; dead ends vs. new beginnings.

Examples

Sigmund Freud (Jupiter. Founder of psychoanalysis); Elisabeth Kubler-Ross (Uranus. Author—*On Death and Dying*); Robert Stack (Uranus. Actor—*The Untouchables, Unsolved Mysteries*); B. F. Skinner (Sun. Behaviorist psychologist, materialist ideologue); Thalmus Rasulala (Jupiter. Actor—slave in *Roots*); Cicely Tyson (Jupiter. Actress—*The Autobiography of Miss Jane Pittman*); Allen Ginsberg (Uranus. Beat poet who ended up at the Naropa Institute, in the foothills of the Rockies); Jack Nicholson (Saturn. Actor—*As Good as It Gets, The Shining*); Cathy Guisewite (North Node. Cartoonist obsessed with dieting); Maria La Laurie (Moon. Killer with an S & M dungeon in her basement); Herschell Lewis (Uranus. Director of gore films); Al Capp (Mars. Cartoonist—*L'il Abner*); Debbie Reynolds (Uranus. Actress—*The Unsinkable Molly Brown*).

Afterword

Secondary Degree Symbols

While studying the degrees, I made a rather unusual discovery: there is a secondary degree symbol behind every primary symbol. Perhaps I should begin by explaining how you arrive at these symbols. If you had the Moon on 7 Cancer in the sixth house, you would look not only at the symbol for 7 Cancer, but also at the symbol for 7 Virgo, since the sixth house has a natural relation to the sign Virgo. As another example, if you had Mercury on 15 Taurus in the seventh house, you would look at the symbol not only for 15 Taurus, but also the symbol for 15 Libra, since the seventh house is a Libran house. This may seem peculiar, and even arbitrary, yet for some reason, it works. In fact, as you get older, the underlying symbol seems to become increasingly powerful. The houses are the most incarnated aspect of the chart, and people seem to dig into this deeper layer of symbolism as they mature. To test this method, take out the charts of around five relatives or friends and look at the symbols for their Suns and Moons, and then look at the symbols that underlie them.

Notes

1 Frances Yates, *Giordano Bruno and the Hermetic Tradition* (Chicago: University of Chicago Press, 1964), 191.

2 Luciano Canfora, *The Vanished Library* (Berkeley: University of California Press, 1989), 10–11.

3 Pietro d'Abano's symbols are included in Johannes Angelus' *Astrolabium* (Augsburg, 1488). It is available on microfilm.

4 Marc Edmund Jones, *The Sabian Symbols in Astrology* (Santa Fe, NM: Aurora Press, 1993,reprint). Dane Rudhyar, *An Astrological Mandala* (New York: Vintage Books, 1974).

5 That is, direct spiritual knowledge.

6 AstroDatabank can be reached at *www.astrodatabank.com*, or at 1-877-275-0987.

7 Julius Weinberg, *A Short History of Medieval Philosophy* (Princeton NJ: Princeton University Press, 1964), 164–170.

8 The Sabian symbol is "A triangle with wings," which suggests flight into abstract headspaces.

9 Rudhyar has a flock of geese on the wing; Charubel has a labyrinth.

10 The Sabian is "Nature spirits dancing in the setting sun." I have followed Charubel, who has a man with a sickle and a sheaf of corn.

11 Rudhyar has a swan being fed in a park.

12 Jones has "An open window and a net curtain blowing into a cornucopia." Carelli has a naked woman.

13 The Sabian symbol has "Shellfish grope while children play"; this emphasizes different levels of evolution. Volasfera provides a more Masonic bent with "A table upon which a right angle and a plane are lying."

14 The Sabian symbol is a dove flying over stormy waters, also stressing the passage between two worlds. The bees are found in Volasfera.

15 The Sabian symbol has a glass-bottomed boat. The *Degrees of Life* have a magic mirror.

16 The Sabian symbol shows the Garden of Tuileries (presumably before the revolution); Charubel has a huge Corinthian column with a castle on top of it.

17 The Sabian symbol is "Three fledglings in a nest." If this symbol is used, one should see the birds as young eagles squabbling among themselves.

18 The Sabian symbol is "A man trimming palm trees." This emphasizes mental clarification through the elimination of irrelevant opinions or facts.

19 Rudhyar has "A bankruptcy court." The beam in the scales of justice suggests a yoke.

20 The Sabian symbol has "Birds feathering their nest," which has a lot of merit.

21 The Sabian symbol has a diamond being cut to shape.

22 This part of the symbol is taken literally from Rudhyar's *The Astrology of Personality*.

23 The Sabian symbol is a Daughter of the American Revolution, which may relate to the degree's elitism. The *Degrees of Life* give a man standing on the edge of a whirlpool.

24 This is taken almost literally from Rudhyar's symbol in *The Astrology of Personality*.

25 Jones' Sabian symbol has "An untidy, unkempt man." Rudhyar took this in the wrong direction by making the man a yogi. Actually he is a Bohemian artist.

26 Rudhyar has "A canoe leaving narrow rapids."

27 Charubel has a shepherd with his sheep; Jones has a professor peering over his glasses; Volasfera has a centaur. My symbol is closest to Rudyar's, in *The Astrology of Personality*—"A kindly old professor is teaching a class of youngsters."

28 Rudhyar has a stack of circular machinery parts. The concept of meshing gears is preserved in the hurdy-gurdy.

29 The Sabian symbol is "A gold rush," which should be seen as a "shot" which sets off a scuffle of greedy people. A better symbol is found in the *The Degrees of Life*, which has a woman alone in the house, defending herself against robbers.

30 The Sabian is "A child playing with five mounds of sand," implying the full engagement of the senses.

31 The Sabian symbol is a parrot repeating something it has overheard, an apt symbol if it is interpreted as scornful parody. Charubel has a hydra, and Carelli has Cerberus.

32 The Sabian is "A soldier derelict in duty," but there are almost no soldiers in the lists. On the other hand, the Sabian does stress independence of action.

33 My symbol takes off from the *The Degrees of Life*. The Sabian symbol is X-ray analysis. It is a particularly difficult degree to interpret.

34 The Sabian symbol is a cricket match. *The Degrees of Life* has "A crippled man instructs an athletic team." The degree clearly has a strong relationship to Chiron.

35 The wording of this symbol is taken directly from Rudhyar's *The Astrology of Personality*.

36 Rudhyar's version of the Sabian has "Pelicans menaced by the behavior and refuse of men seek safer areas for bringing up their young." This is a good alternate symbol, but does not communicate the dire nature of the threat.

37 I follow Janduz, who has "A Vestal virgin guarding a lamp." The Sabian is "Merrymakers in a canoe." If we keep the river, it should be seen as the river Styx, which, as the boundary to the Underworld, was the river upon which people would swear the most binding of oaths. *The Secret Language of Birthdays* speaks of problems with drugs, and Kozminsky mentions Persephone. To complete the picture one might put burning opium censers on either side of the chest (the poppy is sacred to Persephone). Drugs have often been used ritually to loosen or alter one's reality-set.

38 The Sabians have a Mayan bas-relief, but many examples point instead to Egypt. Janduz has a man with the head of a hawk, pointing to Horus. On an esoteric level, the degree may relate to the mutilation of Osiris by Set into fourteen pieces.

39 The Sabian is a relay race. Though the degree is not particularly athletic, there is at least the idea of cooperation. One can also see the runner as Mercury, planetary ruler of labor and wages.

40 The Sabian symbol is "The performer of a mystery play."

41 The Sabian is the Cosmic Egg. This would work better if one pictured the egg hatching, and the fledgling flying off under the watchful eyes of its parents.

42 Rudhyar in *The Astrology of Personality* has "Watch dog on guard as goldminer sleeps near his strike." My version stresses the sexual nature of the degree. Charubel has a naked man with a snake wrapped around his body.

43 My version is based fairly closely on that of Rudhyar, in *The Astrology of Personality*.

44 This follows closely upon Rudhyar's version in *The Astrology of Personality*.

45 A beautiful female animal trainer and a circus emcee can be seen as additional components of the image.

46 The Sabian symbol is an ancient pottery bowl full of violets.

47 The Sabian symbol is "A butterfly emerging from the chrysalis." It has much to recommend it, but the image of the hare came to me forcefully when I examined the examples. Both symbols refer to emergence into another level or being.

48 Rudhyar has "Moonlit fields, once Babylon, are blooming white." This is a good alternate symbol.

Sources

There are quite a number of books that provide symbols for the degrees of the zodiac. However I really only used the following ten, choosing these according to how accurately they describe the collected examples. A couple of systems got extra points because they come from radically different cultural milieus than the Western lineage. In studying any given degree, I looked at all ten sources every time I went over it.

The most valuable and accurate works I found—in this order—are:

1. Gary Goldschneider and Joost Elffers' *The Secret Language of Birthdays* (New York: Penguin/Viking, 1994). Although this is a mass-market coffee-table book, it is based on empirical research. The main problem in using this book is that it is not always clear which degree the authors are describing, since the book is based on birthdays rather than degrees. However, in most cases, this is fairly easy to figure out—testimony to the book's accuracy. It was heartening to know that the only other empirically derived system besides my own tended to come up with similar findings.

2. Ra Uru Hu's *The Human Design System* (Munich, Germany: New Sun Services, Ibiza, 1992). This is a little-known channeled system that relates the hexagrams and lines of the *I Ching* to the degrees of the zodiac. It is often remarkably accurate. Since there are 384 lines in the *I Ching* and only 360 degrees in the zodiac, you usually have to look at two lines. I generally looked at the hexagram as a whole, as well as the specified lines.

3. Rick Klimczak's *The Degrees of the Zodiac: The Sabian Symbols* (Silver Springs, MD: Arachne Press, 1989). An unusually talented astrologer, Klimczak has the best Sabian interpretations that I have found. Lynda Hill's book *The Sabian Symbols as an Oracle* (Sydney: Hill and Hill, 2002) is also very good, but I received it very late in my research.

4. Rick Klimczak's *The 30 Degree-Cycles: The Numbers of the Zodiac and Their Meaning* (Silver Springs, MD: Arachne Press, 1991). The degree symbols have strong numerological relationships to each other. The 11th degree of every sign, for instance, always has a mystical element. This very useful pamphlet outlines the numerological character of the thirty degree cycles.

5. Marc Edmund Jones's *The Sabian Symbols in Astrology* (Santa Fe, NM: Aurora, 1993). Jones's interpretations are practically Cabalistic, but show depth if you can bring something of your own to them. He bases his interpretations, to some extent, on examples, for he has a collection of five hundred charts in the appendix of the book. Many of these people are entirely unknown to me. I hope that my own examples weather a little better.

6. Chanda Dhi Manthri's *The Degrees of Life* (Van Nuys, CA: Astro-Analytics Publications, 1974). The claim is made that this is from an ancient Sanskrit source. Whether or not this is true, the symbols are entirely independent of both the Sabian symbols and the Western lineage of d'Abano etc. The symbols in *The Degrees of Life* have a lot to offer and, even when inaccurate, they are at least spiritually edifying rather than negative and fatalistic.

7. Adriano Carelli's *The 360 Degrees of the Zodiac* (Washington, D.C.: American Federation of Astrologers, 1951). This borrows very heavily from Volasfera and Charubel, and is therefore solidly in the Western lineage. Carelli generally has better interpretations than either Charubel or Volasfera, but when perplexed often combines the two in an artificial way. His symbols are vastly inferior to the Sabian symbols, but have enough "hits" to make them worth studying.

8. Charubel's *The Degrees of the Zodiac Symbolised* (London: Fowler, 1898). This is medieval in tone, fatalistic and negative to the point of laughability. However, many of his symbols have more than a grain of truth to them. This is something that both Jones and Rudhyar acknowledged, much as they preferred the Sabian symbols.

9. Johannes Angelus' *The Faces and Degrees of the Zodiac* also known as Volasfera. (The Volasfera symbols are also found in *The Degrees of the Zodiac Symbolised.*) This is a 16th-century system that is based fairly directly on Pietro d'Abano. It is medieval in tone, fairly negative, but by no means useless. I did not use d'Abano, even after spending hours translating his symbols from Latin. Despite my high hopes, d'Abano's symbols proved to be the most primitive and simplistic that I came across—testimony to the fact that older is not always better.

10. Willem Koppejan's presentation of Janduz's *The Zodiac Image Handbook* (Longmead, England: Element Books, 1990). This also includes interpretations of the Sabian symbols. I did not find Janduz much of an improvement on Charubel, Volasfera, or Carelli. Koppejan's interpretations of the Sabians are very high-toned, but I prefer the interpretations of Rick Klimczak and Lynda Hill.

I looked at the systems of Isidore Kozminsky in *Zodiacal Symbology and Its Planetary Power* (Tempe, AZ: American Federation of Astrologers, 1993), and Ellias Lonsdale in *Inside Degrees* (Berkeley: North Atlantic Books, 1997) but did not find them particularly valuable. I did not use Dane Rudhyar's *An Astrological Mandala* (New York: Vintage Books, 1974) very often because I found his interpretations of the Sabians highly inaccurate. On the other hand, the Sabian images found in Rudhyar's *The Astrology of Personality* (Santa Fe, NM: Aurora, 1991) are more evocative and interesting than those found in Jones, and I have relied upon them for many degrees.